The Social Life of Spirits

The Social Life of Spirits

EDITED BY RUY BLANES AND
DIANA ESPÍRITO SANTO

THE UNIVERSITY OF CHICAGO PRESS   CHICAGO AND LONDON

RUY BLANES is a postdoctoral research fellow at the University of Bergen and associate researcher at the Institute of Social Sciences in Lisbon. He is coeditor of *Encounters of Body and Soul in Contemporary Religious Practices: Anthropological Reflections.*
DIANA ESPÍRITO SANTO is a postdoctoral research fellow at the Research Center in Anthropology at the New University of Lisbon.

The University of Chicago Press, Chicago 60637
The University of Chicago Press, Ltd., London
© 2014 by The University of Chicago
All rights reserved. Published 2014.
Printed in the United States of America

23 22 21 20 19 18 17 16 15 14   1 2 3 4 5

ISBN-13: 978-0-226-08163-2 (cloth)
ISBN-13: 978-0-226-08177-9 (paper)
ISBN-13: 978-0-226-08180-9 (e-book)
DOI: 10.7208/chicago/9780226081809.001.0001

Library of Congress Cataloging-in-Publication Data

The social life of spirits / edited by Ruy Blanes and Diana Espírito Santo.
  pages cm
Includes bibliographical references and index.
  ISBN-13: 978-0-226-08163-2 (cloth : alk. paper)—ISBN-10: 978-0-226-08177-9 (pbk. : alk. paper)—ISBN-10: 978-0-226-08180-9 (e-book) 1. Spirits—Social aspects. 2. Carribean Area—Religion. 3. Afro-Brazilian cults. I. Blanes, Ruy Llera, 1976–
II. Espírito Santo, Diana.
  BL477.S65 2014
  202'.109729—dc23

                                                      2013015003

♾ This paper meets the requirements of ANSI/NISO Z39.48-1992 (Permanence of Paper).

Contents

CHAPTER ONE

Introduction

On the Agency of Intangibles

Diana Espírito Santo and Ruy Blanes

Just 'cause you feel it doesn't mean it's there—"There There," Radiohead, 2003

W e cannot be too sure what Thom Yorke, the singer and lyricist behind Radiohead, the alternative musical act from Oxford, was thinking when he wrote the song "There There."[1] The line from the epigraph, which is a verse from the song "There There," could be a reversion of a radically empiricist stance ("I only believe what I see"), but it could also be an expression of self-doubt regarding the reliability of our own senses and perceptions ("Should I believe in what I feel?"). Or both. In any case, it brings to mind the notion of "perceptive faiths" (Merleau-Ponty 1968, 17) and of how to understand and integrate perceptive and sensorial alterity in the practice of anthropology and other humanities disciplines. The reliability of the senses, as we know, is a notoriously tricky issue. But we don't have to rely on them to be able to conjure up an assortment of entities whose existence we routinely take for granted—"culture" being one familiar to the anthropologist—but that are as empirically invisible as ghosts.

This book, which explores different conceptualizations of an "agency of intangibles," sets out to unravel the contingency of various "entities" on their effects. This exploration rests upon a philosophical and epistemological assumption, which is also a challenge: the recognition of the anthropological relevance of the mechanics and effects of so-called invisible or intangible domains, whether these are constituted by spirits, quarks, the law, or money value.

This, in many ways, has been part of anthropological inquiry since its inception. Below we explore stories of nineteenth-century concerns with the invisible, which we are heirs to. We could also understand the long-standing interest in spirit possession as one such interrogation. Moving beyond psychological, neurophysiological, metaphysical, and representational accounts of possession, anthropologists have long sought to understand and explain, both emically and etically, contacts, manifestations, and mediations (or mediumships) with the otherworldly, and the regimes of proof and evidence that underlie them (Lambek 1981; Lewis [1971] 2003). In this line of thought, one frequent materialization of spirit possession effects has been located in bodily or embodied practices. Through the body, as Janice Boddy (1989) suggests, we uncover meaning and context, idiom and ideology. This volume inherits these classic attempts to unveil cultural context, while seeking to explore the "alien" dimension of phenomena such as spirit possession: the categories of sovereignty and foreignness (Voss 2011) involved and the spiritual, ontological, and political consequences of such frontier making.

On the other hand, there is no anthropological exclusivity in charting the conditions of possibility of the invisible and its effects. Ioan Lewis describes, in his classic *Ecstatic Religion*, how a body of literature on the occult predicted trance becoming as "easily accessible as electricity" ([1971] 2003, 16). Ever since, scientists have studied and speculated over the invisible and intangible through their effects, conjuring up several assumptions regarding empirical evidence along the way (see Latour 1993b). From this perspective, astronomy, as the study and prediction of "effects" in the interface of empirical observation and theoretical speculation, has long been a discipline of "limits"—one that determines the frontier of the universe, our world, our knowledge, our understanding. Probably for that same reason, it has also been a discipline of systematization and organization, at least since Pierre-Simon Laplace's *Exposition for a System of the World* (1808), in which the renowned astronomer and mathematician sought to explain celestial mechanics through the "apparent movement of celestial bodies," and identified the existence of black holes as phenomena so dense in gravity that they become "un-observable."

If astronomy has its own "black holes," in terms of explanatory theories and refutations that address limits, perceptions, quandaries, and so on, so does anthropology. By tracing the conditions by which such entities have effects, and by exploring crucial dimensions of definition and narrativization involved in processes of recognition and legitimation—and thus, the sanctioning of their social life—we aim, firstly, to sideline concerns with conceptual bounding and instead attend to the production of the "indexicalities" (Keane 2007) that allow them to "come into being" as objects, scientific (Daston 2000) or otherwise. Secondly, our aim is based on a critical reflection on the kinds of problems generated by an epistemology of the senses, both in terms of how we generally think through and about empiria, materiality, and evidence in our practices as anthropologists and persons and in terms of the scope of the senses as producers of knowledge. The assumption here is that entities can reside outside as well as inside this sensorial scope by virtue of the traces, symptoms, and effects they socially and materially engender.

This book's proposal is both old and new. On the one hand, it follows from the commonsense notion that most of the things that affect us as human beings are invisible, disperse; we cannot touch them as we would objects or confine them to a particular essence, space, or time. It also drinks from the discipline's historical openness toward epistemologically challenging objects (Vasconcelos 2008). On the other hand, it follows from anthropology's urge to engage with extramaterial forms of sociality and practice—both by coming to terms with the notion that people develop and live in worlds that are often radically different to each other, where they perceive and interact with different entities, and by engaging in the extension and revision of some anthropological concepts and methods to deal with these ontological differences, particularly those that see "entities" in a purely mental or conceptual sense. The aim of this introduction is to identify some of the problems and dividends associated with assuming (invisible, intangible) entities as objects of research.

One problem has to do with the processes of tracing and defining entities and their effects (marks, manifestations, consequences) in informants' lives. This tracing traditionally relies either on the idea of the unquestionability of the senses—something we intend to bracket in this volume—or on the notion of representations, which we aim to move beyond. A second, subsequent problem concerns how those effects intersect with the realm of the social, becoming part of personal and collective histories and biographies, and identifiable through processes of narrativization. Historian Marc Bloch (1953) would argue that those traces are precisely what makes history "history." By taking Bloch's point to an extreme, and as we discuss below, by treating those traces as objects and processes, it becomes possible to make things "become evident"; however, that should not be taken as an excuse for intellectual laxity but rather as an opportunity to

think about "evidentiary regimes" and how they come about within specific regimes of rationality (Palmié, this volume). Finally, a more general,
methodological question becomes inescapable: How do we work (around,
with, as) an "anthropology of intangibles"?

The chapters in this book coincide by exploring some of these debates
ethnographically within specific religious and spiritual contexts—or, as
in many of the cases presented, by invoking and analyzing some of the
pervasive social consequences of those extrahuman forms of agency: for
instance, their location in specific landscapes and sceneries (the river, the
forest, the streets and crossroads, the room), the tracing of their effects in
particular contexts of experience (dreams, visions, sensations, memories)
and/or interrelatedness (ritualization, conflict, healing), and their materialization in certain orders of discourse and definition (biographies, songs,
drawings). However, as the discussion below on mesmerism, spiritualism,
and nineteenth-century science points out, it should be made clear that
the "agency of intangibles" is not—at least in the way we conceive it—an
exclusively religious problem, or rather a problem exclusively of the anthropology of religion. Our argument on agency and intangibility aims
to transcend the particularities of religiosity or spirituality (regardless of
its configurations) and thus speak to broader debates on invisibilities—
namely, by calling for a similar epistemological leverage to be accorded to
both the domain of spirits, deities, gods and, say for example, that of "the
economy," "the market," "race," or "value" (Palmié, pers. comm.).

But it would be misleading to deny the existence of strong antecedents
in what we could call a "pragmatics of effects" approach to the invisible,
upon which we certainly build, beginning perhaps most obviously with
the work of William James. For instance, in a lecture-turned-essay called
"What Pragmatism Means" (1907), James says the following: "Is the world
one or many?—fated or free?—material or spiritual?—here are notions
either of which may or may not hold good of the world; and disputes over
such notions are unending. The pragmatic method in such cases is to try
to interpret each notion by tracing its respective practical consequences.
What difference would it practically make to any one if this notion were
true?" (2000, 25). As we know, James's *Varieties of Religious Experience*
([1902] 1982), which takes as its axis the intrinsic value of religious feelings and phenomenology—which he sees as analytically primary and
separate to theorizations or historicizations of religion—was crucial to
the subsequent development of body-, psychology-, and emotion-centered
approaches to religious experience. For James, belief is true or realized
inasmuch as it engenders actions, effects, and affects. Irving Hallowell's

pioneering concept of a "behavioral environment" can arguably be seen in its continuity, or at least resonance, with some of James's precepts. Taking self-awareness as one of the conditions for the functioning of any social group, Hallowell proposes that we see "environment" not only in terms of its visible properties or objects but also in terms of a total behavioral field that may include spiritual beings of all kinds, to which man responds and in the midst of which he lives. "Such objects," he says, "in some way experienced, clearly conceptualized and reified, may occupy a high rank in the behavioral environment although from a sophisticated Western point of view they are sharply distinguishable from the natural objects of the physical environment. However, the nature of such objects is no more fictitious, in a psychological sense, than the concept of the self" ([1955] 1988, 87). Hallowell's observations have only recently been recovered in anthropology—for example, in the work of Tim Ingold (2000, 2001), whose ecological approach to dwelling, skill, cognition, and cultural transmission arguably takes root in just the assumptions wielded by Hallowell on the inextricability of lived environment and conceptual experience. For Ingold, human beings "do not construct the world in a certain way by virtue of what they are, but by virtue of their own conceptions of the possibilities of being. And these possibilities are limited only by the power of the imagination" (Ingold 2000, 177). Experience, as an encompassing phenomenon, emerges as inseparable in these approaches from the ontological possibilities it both is intertwined with and brings forth. This is clear in Godfrey Lienhardt's refusal to posit a distinction between "natural" or "supernatural" events or beings in his ethnography of the Dinka (1961). So embroiled were the Dinka's spiritual beings, which he calls Powers or divinities, with the Dinka's experience of events—physical, social, and environmental—that Lienhardt analytically pits them as representations or images of a range of particular "configurations of experience" (1987, 147). For the Dinka, he argues, the Powers are not spiritual beings in the sense that they exist above or separate from man; instead, they are of the world and its events, at once beings and activities or behaviors: "To refer to the activity of a Power is to offer an interpretation, and not merely a description, of experience" (ibid., 148). While to the Dinka—whereas clearly not for Lienhardt—divinities do exist "out there," Lienhardt's analytical collapse of the experience and entities categories (true to the Dinka themselves) meant he never had to make that judgment.

These early theorists of religious, spiritual, and animistic phenomena arguably advocated what we might call an ontology-oriented approach, one that has partly (and regrettably) faded in the postmodern vogue and has at the same time seen a partial niche comeback in the last four or five years. The spirit possession literature in particular still seems trapped with what to do anthropologically with the possession event itself, and this has arguably constrained its analytical frameworks. While possession is conceived of as key in making spirits real or natural (Levy, Mageo, and Howard 1996, 17), and its mechanics are an object of enduring fascination, significantly less attention is accorded to the "work" spirits do in any given society, which is a far more central concern for those who experience it than is their ability to manifest spirits through dissociation or extension of themselves. As Douglas Hollan says, referring to the Indonesian Toraja understanding of self and spirits, "For most villagers the question is not, Which of these spiritual beings actually exist and which do not?, but rather, Which of these beings—at any given moment in one's life—has the power to influence the course of one's fate and fortune, and so should be acknowledged and perhaps propitiated?" (1996, 233). The questions this volume seeks to address run along lines similar to those invoked by the early pragmatists of the anthropology of religion: What entities, spirits, beings become true and evident in any given community? How does this come be, and with what effect or value? For this, we may have to ask not just how concepts give birth to worlds (Henare, Holbraad, and Wastell, 2007) but also how entities can come to be through their myriad traces, whether or not visible, culturally sanctioned, specifiable, or predictable.

The chapters in this book ethnographically and theoretically explore spiritual entities of various kinds, not (just or primarily) as concepts or components of given, shared cosmologies but as effects-in-the-world, with a potential for constant unpredictability and transgressiveness. In this way, our general proposal here is to work *backward*, from effects to form, from tangible to invisible, from motion to substance, from manifestation to agency, and so on—that is, to understand and define spiritual (and other nonphysical) forms of existence as manifest (and ultimately knowable) through their extensions, if you will, on a social and even historical plane, where extensions leave markings, traces, paths, and, ultimately, "evidence." In our view, this is an aim that capitulates less to anthropology's visualist (Clifford and Marcus 1986) or materialist biases, than it speaks to the need to radically disentangle itself from some of anthropology's most counterproductive premises, among which is the assumption that "we are all living in the same world—one best described and apprehended by science," leaving to social scientists the task "to elucidate the various systemic formulations of knowledge (epistemologies) that offer different accounts of that *one* world" (Henare, Holbraad, and Wastell 2007, 9). By working from a general pragmatic perspective, not dissimilar to what James had in mind with his "pragmatic method" (which he defined as "primarily a method of settling metaphysical disputes that otherwise might be interminable" [2000, 25]), in which the truth of notions is interpreted by tracing its practical consequences, we explicitly sideline a formulation of "entities"—spirits, gods, deities—that implies a necessary supernature or transcendent, with corresponding opposites, and likewise we repudiate a gap between what the "native" thinks is there and what we "really" know isn't. While we do not share James's concern with gauging the usefulness of religious notions (if they generate positive effects they are true), and thus a kind of gradation of "truthfulness," we are inclined to agree in some sense with the curious idea that "truth *happens* to an idea. It *becomes* true, is *made* true by events. Its verity *is* in fact an event, a process: the process namely of its verifying itself, its veri-*fication*. Its validity is the process of its valid-*ation*" (2000, 88). Truth being alternatively read here as effect; idea, as entity. Thus, what we are suggesting also is that effects themselves may have further ontological effects; that entities may recursively create multiple versions of themselves as effects, where it becomes less important to locate the original "version" than to analyze its sequels. In our view, it is more valid and productive as anthropologists of "intangible" phenomena to begin from the premises of their influence, extension, or multiplication in the world than from substantive ontological predefinitions.

In order to do this, we must move away from naturalizing, explanatory frameworks characteristic of the anthropology of spirit (and trance) possession and mediation, for example, whose theoretical spectrum ranges from reductive functionalist and medical analyses to the more recent (but still arguably reductive) propositions of a cognitive anthropology of religious phenomena (Barrett 2004; Boyer 1994; Cohen 2007). We wish to consider, on the one hand, the usefulness of phenomenological approaches, which privilege the body as the site of culture (Csordas 1990), and which articulate the ontological effects of entities through a focus on the creation of certain kinds of orientations and subjectivities, and on the other, the acknowledged, taken-for-granted, social dimensions of this experience, in particular, the manner in which it betrays an intertwining of registers—living and dead, visible and invisible, corporeal and ethereal, and so on—that cannot always be conceptually or experientially distinguished. Thus, we seek to understand the existence of particular ontological beings or entities as defined and refracted through the pragmatics of their effects in and on the world, many of which through such forms of intertwining, which are biographical, physical, and social. This also means exploring the processes by which this "otherness" assumes shape and efficacy in different contexts and discourses, reconfiguring expectations and constituting webs of practical and visible effects, effects that are confined neither spatiotemporally nor to bodies themselves. The unseen, unheard, or intangible, may be by all pragmatic definitions *present*, whether or not it is explicitly felt or represented, challenging materialist ontologies intrinsic to social science disciplines whose overarching project has assumed that reality (world, nature) is one, and that difference (and the effects of difference) is thus a matter for belief and representation (see Argyrou 2002).

This core assumption, as Asad (1993) shows, has shaped the concept itself of religion in anthropology in terms that have, among other things, obfuscated important aspects of spiritual experience, including technical, material and sensorial ones. As Fennella Cannell argues in her analysis of the influences of Christianity on the discipline, "Religious phenomena in anthropology may be described in detail, but must be explained on the basis that they have no foundation in reality, but are epiphenomena of 'real' underlying sociological, political, economic, or other material causes" (2006, 4). Indeed, according to her, Christianity "haunts" anthropology, functioning as its "repressed" (ibid.). What we may need is an approach to "entities" that does not expect them to reside either in the minds of believers or in Geertz-like "webs of significance" (1973), masking other more measurable elements of sociality, and more importantly, that does not "neutralize" them, as Eduardo Viveiros de Castro (1998) argues in relation to alterity in general, but that draws out their theoretical and methodological implications instead.

Spirits and Science

Certainly both science and séances had and still have their spirits. The nineteenth century, for instance, generated entities whose ontological status was as (un)verifiable in scientific practice as it was in religious-spiritual communities. Electricity, evolution (social and natural), and the mind's unconscious arguably saw parallels in notions of ether, spiritual fluid, and animal magnetism. In both domains, entities were inferred from their markings or effects: hypnotism, neurosis, light. Indeed, the conflation of scientific and invisible realms was so pronounced that one question we could rudimentarily, even naively, ask is, how did spiritual phenomena and other metaphysical entities come to be excluded from the realm of the scientifically possible, or "real," or measurable? For instance, in a book called *On Miracles and Modern Spiritualism*, published in 1875, Alfred Russell Wallace stated the following: "That intelligent beings may exist around and among us, unperceived during our whole lives, and yet capable under certain conditions of making their presence known by acting on matter, will be inconceivable to some, and will be doubted by many more, but we venture to say, that no man acquainted with the latest discoveries and the highest speculations of modern science, will deny its *possibility*" ([1875] 2009, 41; original emphasis).

Like Wallace, who was eventually ostracized from the scientific community on account of his beliefs in the "inexistent," a number of prominent public figures of the eighteenth and nineteenth centuries, including scientists, experimented and dabbled in the "possibilities" described by Wallace. In fact, most spiritualist movements of the nineteenth century firmly believed that science could be rallied to demonstrate the rational existence of their objects of belief, including spirits of the dead and invisible phenomena such as magnetic fluid, which French and Anglo-Saxon Spiritists thought connected the various dimensions of existence (e.g., the material and the invisible). But as Lynn Sharp argues, Spiritists did not invent the concept of an indivisible, universal "ether": they generally followed in the wake of post-Newtonian scientific thought (and its popular and enduring spin-offs), which had posited a fluid (and invisible) substance that somehow acted on matter (2006, 127), thus allowing spirits to communicate. According to Peter Pels, Wallace "compared the force exerted by these intelligences with light, heat, electricity, and magnetism (all 'modes of motion' of a space-filling 'ether') to show how these diffuse and subtle forms of matter can act upon 'ponderable bodies' and become known to us only by their effects" (Pels 2003, 262). Indeed, nineteenth-century technology itself engendered such imaginaries of discorporation, yielding marvels such as the spiritualists' celestial, or spiritual, telegraph, designed to broach the gaps of life and death through mysterious electromagnectic forces. As Jeffrey Sconce notes, "The Spiritualists' initial conceptualization of 'celestial telegraphy' was not so much a misapplication of technological discourse as a logical elaboration of the technology's already 'supernatural' characteristics" (2000, 28). But Wallace's efforts, like those of spiritualists on both sides of the English Channel, had mixed results.

As João Vasconcelos argues, "The homelessness of the spirits in the world of science is a correlate of the homelessness of the scientists who are committed to the research on 'spiritual' and 'paranormal' phenomena"

(2008, 22), even now; "the spirits conquered a place among the objects of the sciences" (ibid., 25) but were never naturalized. Other entities took their place. The development in the nineteenth century of the discipline of psychology, and later psychoanalysis, began to produce its own ghosts, as did Durkheim's sociology, which brought into existence notions of collective representations and of a symbolic universe divorced from the world "out there." Spirits became intrapsychic or sociological facts rather than "gross errors in reasoning" as Edward Burnett Tylor had proposed (Vasconcelos 2008, 25). They would be safely confined to the subjective "realities" of their believers without posing a threat to the "psychic unity of mankind." This shift from matters of spirit to the spirits of the mind became one of the cornerstones of modern social science. But there was no neat, homogenous transition; instead, the nineteenth century saw the coexistence of a panoply of competing, yet often mutually constituting, forms of truth-making, which rose and fell in the public imaginary, as did the entities that they correspondingly created, made visible, or banished altogether. What is interesting about the nineteenth century as an example of the social life of invisible things is that most machineries for making entities relied on the "evidence" provided by the visible world—photos (spirits), the restlessness of crowds (the power of collectives), parapsychological experiments (ESP, etc.).

Victorian regimes of evidence (or sensibilities) depended greatly on their recourse to the senses, especially vision, and particularly to their potential extension through "things," including new technologies. As Pamela Thurschwell argues, spirit photography, which became a business in the 1860s, brought spiritualism "out of the aural and into the visual realm both as evidence and as entertainment" (2009, 224). The photograph promised a scientific irrefutability that spoke directly to the Victorian struggle to understand the implications of new scientific theories that dislocated received Christian doctrines (ibid.). Visual and communicational technology were not just vessels but provided tropes for new conceptualizations of the mind's capacities, such as telepathy, one of the raisons d'etre for the creation of the Society for Psychical Research in London in 1882: "New phenomena in psychology such as hypnotism, hysteria, aphasias and multiple personalities, which suggested that the mind had unexplored regions, were of intense interest to psychical researchers" (ibid., 184). As the previous century had shown, discerning and defining entities by the senses alone was not just epistemologically problematic but perhaps also politically, for imagination could become pathological, as Le Bon's sociology of crowds had demonstrated (Riskin 2009, 121). Spiritualists thus sought to support their claims by appealing to established regimes of evidence, and in this way, inevitably creating new hybrids, such as parapsychology. But they were also implicated indirectly in the legitimization of entirely new entities, unconfined to the realms spiritualists sanctioned themselves. Such was the case with the famous Mesmerism fraud investigation in France, which led not just to the birth of a new psychology of the unconscious but of the notion of placebo effect (ibid., 119). Nineteenth-century European sentimental empiricism was shaken considerably by the "discovery" of the working of this mysterious unconscious, an imagination capable of generating its own forms of phantasmagoria, and the power of suggestion as demonstrated in the practices of hypnotism. The senses suddenly became notoriously unreliable.

Disagreements on what exactly counts as a "sense" (e.g., is the "sixth" sense a common sense, an extrasensory perception, or a sense of humor, pain, balance, color [Howes 2009]?) have been rife among philosophers throughout history, and still the sensorial spectrum continues to be enriched by cross-cultural ethnographic work on diverse experiential and bodily taxonomies, making any a priori definition redundant. As David Howes (2009, 32) argues in his introduction to *The Sixth Sense Reader*, there can be no natural history of the senses, only cultural ones, and as such, no monopoly on legitimate perceptive or sensorial routes.

But, if the histories of nineteenth- and early twentieth-century spiritualist movements are anything to go by, and as Radiohead's lyrics also allude to, the "sense of presence," to use a term by William James, or the uncanny, by Freud, is not just a question for the senses—it is often linked to what is missing, or unknown, even if familiar. It is uncanny precisely because it is unsensed, or at least, uncertain (see Delaplace, this volume). Thom Yorke could also have sung "just 'cause you don't feel (or see) it doesn't mean it's not there." As Avery Gordon argues in her treatise on haunting and the sociological imagination, "To write stories concerning exclusions and invisibilities is to write ghost stories" (1997, 17). Absence, as well as presence, engenders effects, tracing the contours of bodies, spaces, and histories through its peculiar power for evoking anxieties, nostalgia, and curiosity. In a recent volume on the presence of absence, Mikkel Bille, Frida Hastrup, and Tim Flohr Sørensen (2010, 4) show that spaces or markers of absence paradoxically serve to draw and direct attention to presence, or a longing for it. Absence and presence are mutually implicated and constituted. A missing person in a photograph, vestiges in a historical document of a life lived, an unidentified shadow in a dream or apparition, a whisper on the other end of a ghost box—where is the ghost, then? What marks does it leave in the world, and how can we follow them? If for Gordon the ghost or apparition is a social figure, "one form by which something lost, or barely visible, makes itself known or apparent to you, in its own way, of course" (1997, 8), where haunting reveals itself as a transformative recognition, not through cold apprehension but almost at the margins of experience, anthropology has similarly shown us that it is not just belief that has effects but effects that produce beliefs, rationalizations, sensations, and their corollary—relations—thus, entities of all kinds. For Stephan Palmié (2002, 3), beliefs in ghosts, spirits, and witchcraft cannot come down to faulty reasoning or forms of ideological misrecognition any more than they can to projections of mental states. Ghost stories are, for him, intrinsic to every form of historical knowledge, for "no less than religion, history is, ultimately, an assemblage of collective representations positing realities that are—logically—beyond empirical proof," where "their consequences, of course, are hardly beyond direct experience" (ibid., 4). Is the ghost a mere historical entity, then, a broken record of a repressed past somehow animated by memory or other forms of haunting, or indeed, archival research? Or is it accessible to our senses and minds also, immanent somehow to our activities, skills, thoughts, and dreams, not just in a fleeting or furtive way—or as images and symbols held in the mind that stand for something else—but in a social, integrated, and even productive manner? In what ways can we qualify the aliveness of such entities through us? And what are the consequences of their existence and of encounters both extended and brief? How do they effect changes and induce possibilities for being, knowing, healing?

Defining Entities

The above are general questions that anthropologists of religious phenomena are familiar with. But in posing them here we intend to shift the emphasis slightly but significantly. As we have explained, the idea here is to temporarily suspend any epistemological inquiry that is underwritten by the assumption of a division between inner and outer orders of human experience (natural and cultural, mental and material, real and imaginal, etc.) in favor of a focus on the felt, seen, and narrated consequences of aspects of invisible orders and their specifics, in whichever shape they may come. But in all of this, several other questions are begged. First, what are we dealing with when we speak of entities, even spiritual entities? Secondly, what exactly do we mean by effects? How are they measured, or ascertained? Where do they happen? Common sense would tell us that in order to understand these questions we must ask what the relationship is between the two; that is, how does experience, action, event, environment, or personhood (among other possibilities) reveal itself as a "domain of entanglement" (Ingold 2006, 14) between tangible and intangible "worlds," yielding in turn knowledge of certain types of existences (some of which are more visible, audible, tangible than others)? These are profoundly ethnographic questions, and for this, we have the various explorations of the chapters ahead, whose implicit concern is also to address the particular methodological difficulties associated with these questions. But at stake is also the resurgence of certain key debates in anthropology, such as that over agency, and their purchase with respect to studying what we have called the "pragmatics" of entities, their "social lives."

Dictionary definitions of the word *entity* commonly cite it as a thing with distinct, independent, or self-contained existence and with objective and conceptual reality, even though it need not be material. "Anything real in itself" is another decidedly vague formulation. It is also described as an organization or unit. From the Latin *entitas*, an entity is essentially an existing thing, which at the same time is set apart from other things in some way. In it is also implicit some capacity to act, or exert influence, thus, some agency.

No less heterogeneous definitions can be forwarded of the concept of spirit, which inherits from Greek, Hebrew, and Christian historical formulations, and which has arguably led to much conceptual and theoretical confusion in the anthropology of religion. But even within the former traditions there is little consensus. For instance, theologian Nancey Murphy argues that for Greek philosophers the question was, what are the essential parts that make up a human being? For biblical authors each "part" "stands for the whole person thought of from a certain angle. For example, 'spirit' stands for the whole person in relation to God" (2006, 21). Neither did Hebrew notions of the soul square with Christian ones. Concepts of the spirit or the soul were also influenced by what was thought to happen to it after death. Thus, the Protestant Reformation begot an understanding of the soul that "sleeps" after death, or that lies in a wake, which yields a different version to the New Testament's more psychophysical rendition of the person defined not as a substance but as a relation (ibid., 22). American Protestantism and its derivatives complicated this picture. For instance, charismatic Protestants' emphasis on the Holy Spirit foreshadows a new understanding of self, as well as spirit. Thomas Csordas says, for example, that the "Charismatic deity is really three persons, each with a character corresponding to one of the three parts of the tripartite human person. Thus Father, Son, and Holy Spirit correspond with mind, body, and spirit, and implicitly each divine person is most congenial with its matched subfield within the human person" (1994, 23). With their focus on healing as an alignment of the spirit to the Kingdom of God, charismatics make of the self a potentially holy substance, some aspects of which may be given, communicated, extended (cf. Coleman 2004).

Western popular concepts of spirit seem to draw a great deal from those of philosophers throughout the ages who held dualistic visions of soul and body, such as Plato, Augustine, and, later, Descartes: "The combination of the Neoplatonic emphasis on the case of the soul with Augustine's metaphor of entering into one's own self or soul in order to find God constituted a complex of ideas that has shaped the whole of Western spirituality from that point onward" (Murphy 2006, 31). With Descartes there was a shift from matters of soul to matters of mind, which was an anomaly in an otherwise materialist universe (ibid., 45). The question was how one would move the other. Nineteenth-century Spiritists reenchanted this materialism, albeit in ways that essentially reified this Cartesian individualism to the extreme: the spirit transmigrates, perfecting itself in successive reincarnation cycles, which is at once part of a larger process of collective social and moral evolution. Today's "New Age" channelers and adepts arguably inherit from these concepts of the spirit or soul. Michael F. Brown (1997, 90, 22) describes how American channels work with spirits, which are often referred to as "entities," "energies," "guides," or "beings of light"—terms that Brown says are aptly all-encompassing and ambiguous—conceived to have passed through many incarnations and received wisdom and knowledge. However, as Brown argues, "While nineteenth-century spiritualism saw science as the potential savior of spirituality, the New Age now sees spirituality as the savior of science" (ibid., 51).

In anthropology the word *spirit* or the term *spiritual entity* has tended to be associated with a transcendent, nonmaterial sphere of existence, even if we know from ethnography that this is far from universal (Levy, Mageo, and Howard 1996, 12). We have chosen the term *entity* partly as an attempt to disentangle ourselves from this association, but we are also critical of allying it too closely with the notion of "intangible." When dealing with spirit ontologies, or other religious phenomena, with which this volume concerns itself, we consider it more important to ask, Under what conditions can we understand the "capacity to act" attributed to the definition of *entity*, or its characteristic of being "real in itself," and how does this distinguishes it from other entities, say, of the nonspirit kind? Anthropology's employment of a notion of agency that goes beyond that which is empirically verifiable, or which requires an intentional agent, is by now commonplace. For example, objects and "things" have recently acquired social lives of varying sorts, even "magic," in the recent literature, as in the technology and enchantment of art (Gell 1998), the fetish (Sansi-Roca 2007), and "things" in general (see Miller 2005). This literature has revealed the "imaginative capacities" (Sneath, Holbraad, and Pedersen 2009) behind the concept or idea of "agency," as much from the perspective of the theorist as of his informant, where it is no longer exclusive to physical bodies and human beings but imputed also to other kinds of entities, or collectives of entities. More relevant here is that witchcraft, shamanism, possession, and animism have all been the object of intense study and theorizations, the dividends of which include the recognition that the attribution of agency to the nontangible and even nonhuman dimensions of life is more than mere philosophical speculation: it is quite natural for most people. So much so that we should perhaps ask what the usefulness of the concept of "agency" is in the first place, at least in the anthropology of religion. There is a fundamental conceptual self-evidentiality, to borrow a phrase from Christina Toren, to such forms of sociality, one that needs no justification by way of the projection of agency as thus cognized by anthropologists in their texts. Agency is simply not the exclusive domain of the intellect that represents and distributes it. As Ingold (2006, 16) argues in relation to meteorological phenomena, or entities, "We are not required to believe that the wind is a being that blows, or that thunder is a being that claps. Rather the wind *is* blowing, and the thunder *is* clapping," making a figure-ground conceptualization of agency and materiality redundant. Spirits, ghosts, animas, gods, or any of the other entities that are perceived, transacted with, and worshipped constantly reveal themselves in manners that preclude not just the use of scientific rationalism as an exclusive heuristic device of study, as the one and unique method to describe and understand "reality," but the idea of "a reality" as best understood by science, as we mentioned above. As Ingold's citation alludes to, to talk of "agency" as anthropologists is to already make critical, yet perhaps analytically unwarranted, distinctions that risk reproducing an "us" and "them" dichotomy, since they assume the material world as a canvas upon which meanings (or attributions of agency) are thrust. In animic ontology, he says, "Beings do not simply occupy the world, they *inhabit* it, and in so doing—in threading their own paths through the meshwork—they contribute to its ever-evolving weave" (ibid., 14). This rather vague statement is at the same time highly evocative of one of our main aims here: to understand entities in their incipient and imminent dimensions, as movements and events (and persons), as well as separate, autonomous existences.

As we know, the concept of agency has also been taken up by sociologists and anthropologists of science and technology, with particular vehemence (Latour and Woolgar [1979] 1986; Latour 1987, 1993b, 1996; Stengers 2000), some of whom have, as a corollary to their analyses, produced an equally powerful critique of what "the social" is. For Bruno Latour, it is not simply the case that action is distributed among actors or agents—it "is dislocal, it does not pertain to any specific site; it is distributed, variegated, multiple, dislocated, and remains a puzzle for the analysts as well as the for the actors" (2005, 60)—but that an "actor" is what is made to act by many "others," in potentially infinite sets of associations ("the moving target of a vast array of entities swarming toward it" [ibid., 46]). This complication of the notion of agency has useful implications for a definition of sociality, or the social: thus, the social, for Latour, "is the name of a type of momentary association which is characterized by the way it gathers together into new shapes" (ibid., 65). He is not too far from Viveiros de Castro when the latter says that he believes that "anthropology must escape self-imposed doom and keep firmly focused on its proper object of study: social relations in all their variations. Not social relations taken as a distinct ontological domain (there is no such thing), but all phenomena as potentially comprising or implying social relations. This means taking all relations as social. Not though from a viewpoint completely dominated by the western doctrine of social relations, but from one ready and willing to admit that treating all relations as social may entail a radical reconceptualization of what 'the social' may be" (2003, 4–5). For both these theorists, albeit in different ways, there are no analytical or categorical givens; each ethnographic scenario poses its own set of theoretical problems, where one of the tasks of the researcher is to relate his or her conceptual language to the ontological configurations (problems) he or she encounters. Notwithstanding the fascinating implications of discussions of agency, then, such as those in the anthropology of art and material culture, in this volume we similarly propose a view of agency and action as dislocated and distributed and of the social as a "rugged, mountainous terrain" replete with asymmetries (Latour 2005, 63). This means that there is no easy answer to what an "entity" is, or at least one that bases itself upon a straightforward or preconceived idea of agency. We have only that which is formulated by specific ethnographic observations pertaining to different places and people, although we have suggested as a starting point a pragmatics of effects.

But it also means that we may have only marginal, or vague, parameters to understand what may count as an "effect" in the first place. This does not mean, however, that we cannot identify a series of broad concerns, to which we may be attentive. These are, for example, the centrality of bodily experience (such as possession) in the identification of the effects of entities, as well as of peripheral forms of encounter, such as dreams; the importance of materiality and objects in legitimating the mediation of knowledge and of entities; differing regimes of evidence and validity in the determination of what "is acting"; the relevance of individual biographies and their narratives in understanding the flows and borders of invisible agents; performance and the creative potential of language in the evocation of intersections of life; the role of uncertainty and ambiguity in the generation of presence; and so on. Through their attentiveness to these concerns, in their unique ways, the contributors to this book aim to unwind by way of the ethnographic specifics of their cases answers to the questions posed above: What is an entity? And what are its effects? In a very general sense, this points to the work of a semiotics of knowing: What are the conditions under which entities manifest, are interpreted, become objects and subjects in the world? What kinds of events or experiences are valid indexes of a prior cause? What sort of reasoning, or inference system, is necessary for an entity to come to be? As Charles Peirce notes, everything is a sign, but a sign only in relation to others. Entities need audiences, languages of deduction by which to be discerned, means by which they can arise through the linking of causes to effects, relations of all kinds.

As we have suggested briefly above, this leads us to think through *more* than spirits, deities, or otherwise personable entities with quasi-human biographies and characteristics, perhaps also into the domain of science, and certainly, history. Where are the boundaries of "entities," taken as a heuristic term? What are the consequences of observation or measurement in their production, both from the perspective of the analyst and of those he or she studies? And what do their "effects" reveal about the assumptions of empiricism itself? Thus, as a final aim, we wish to question the limits of an anthropology that understands itself predominantly within the terms of a materialist project.

Biographies, Intersections, and Social Lives

Anthropology has convincingly shown that everything has a life history, a biography, even commodities (Kopytoff 1986). In *The Social Life of Things*, Arjun Appadurai alerts us to the powerful contemporary tendency "to regard the world of things as inert and mute, set in motion and animated, indeed, knowable, only by persons and their words" (1986, 4). The fact is, he says, that although we hold a view of things in which their meaning cannot be readily divorced from our own actions or transactions, this is of little use to the study of the historical circulation of things: "For that we have to follow things themselves, for their meanings are inscribed in their forms, their uses, their trajectories" (ibid., 5). We began this reflection on the "agency of intangibles" in 2010, when we organized a panel at the American Anthropological Association's annual meeting, in New Orleans, called "Researching Spirit Biographies," on the relevance of those biographies in the understanding of social life. It was a proposal with a double objective, which still stands here: On the one hand, to share knowledge about and discuss social contexts where different senses of temporality would not necessarily correspond to Western, academic historiographical systematizations but rather to revealed forms of mediation and agency that transcended the traditional "objectivity"—or objective pretense—of scientific empiria (see Baca, Khan, and Palmié 2010). On the other hand, the point was to reflect upon the epistemological weight of these biographies within the anthropological project, understood generically as a "science of the human."

Our contention here, which we shared with the presenters of our panel, is that spiritual or religious "entities," once projections of collective representations, imaginaries of resistance, and reflections and negotiations of histories and political economies, can and must also be seen through the lens of the social trajectories they trace in the world (see, in this particular perspective, Giumbelli, this volume). Trajectories which are consequential to anthropology inasmuch as they are underpinned and underpin *relations* of all sorts—material, economic, political, logical, cosmological—all of which we take to be imminently "social," following Viveiros de Castro ([1977] 2002).

To assume this position also implies a necessary critique of current conceptualizations of biography as a subjective narrative project that, at least in what concerns the practice of ethnography, projects a bourgeois state of mind into the social (Bourdieu 1986; Comaroff and Comaroff 1992),[2] inasmuch as it accepts that anthropologists and their interlocutors both encounter, react to, and produce alter-biographies. From this perspective, ethics and politics notwithstanding, what makes biographies socially present is the mere fact of their existence, and it is then up to the anthropologist to understand their place and particularities—as well as the rationalizations and productions of coherence/certainty (James 1995) involved (e.g., see Tola, this volume). This is the case of many of the chapters in this volume, in which the memorial narrativization of ghost or spirit encounters is performed through acts of dreaming and consequent dream telling (Delaplace, Cunha, Tola) or envisioning and consequent counseling (Cardoso). As Stephan Palmié has argued, historical knowledge incorporates, in its "spaces of experience," its own "ghost stories" (2002, 3). Therefore, bringing "spirit biographies" into the fore forces us to question Pierre Bourdieu and Jean and John Comaroff: What kind of subjectivity is involved? When we read, in the biographical narratives presented here, about the relocation of agency into a dragon (Greenwood), other animal species (Tola), or the Holy Ghost (Kirsch) are we still obliged to engage, in our anthropologies, with a categorization of a unified, discrete sort of individuality and personhood? What kind of de-essentialization of the self (Battaglia 1995) must we resort to? At stake is a fundamental *de-* and *re*centering of subjectivity and personhood, as we can see in the work of anthropologists such as the abovementioned Viveiros de Castro (1998) and Philippe Descola (1992), who argues for a "'naturalist' conception" of society that need not be centered on human will and thus dispenses with the classic hegemonic dualism of culture over nature (see also [1986] 1996; Tola, this volume).

Biographies are also necessarily unstable, the objects of continuous reformulation, and thus subject to ambiguity (Blanes 2011). This ambiguity and instability is part of what makes history itself (and memory—see Antze and Lambek 1996) unsettled and, ultimately, conceptual (Koselleck [1979] 2002). But, if we challenge once again the Bourdieu/Comaroff critique and take it to an extreme, we could ask: Is biography *just* human? What are the directions and effects (or mobilities—see Kirsch, this volume) that can be explored and understood if we challenge this human exclusivity? Several ethnographies have shown us how biographies and personal histories also occur betwixt and between the "invisible realm"

(West 2005). We find such biographies and effects in bones (Krmpotich, Fontein, and Harries 2010; Ferrándiz, 2006, 2010), elk (Willerslev 2007), war casualties (Kwon 2008), myths (Gow 2001), man-gods (Román 2007), and so forth. These objects, animals, or persons (or personalities) become (dislocated, distributed) *agents* in ways that not only affect social life but also become mutually affected and affective in directionalities that offer up novel understandings of personhood, relationship, sociality, and history. That is, they produce a "certain knowledge" (Lambek 1990), both socially (locally) relevant and historically informed. This is perhaps similar to conventional historiography, with the significant exception that it implies a radical shift in subject and subjectivity (see Palmié 2002). It also allows us to reconsider and analytically reembed the possibility of "temporal incongruities" (Miyazaki 2003), the multiple qualities (James and Mills 2005) and punctuations (Guyer 2007) of time. In any case, alter-biographies, in whatever form they may take, invite other ways of producing historical depth, ones that cannot necessarily be trajectorialized into linear, progressive narratives where the ego is one, centered, protagonist, and convergent. So, when the ego remains intangible or nonhuman, the question must be asked, Who or what is the object/subject of biography? What are the contexts and conditions that facilitate its perception, as well as study? What are the "logistics" invoked in understanding its movement and presence (see Kirsch, this volume)? What are the convergences that make it become socially relevant, salient? What, finally, is the temporal trajectory involved?

To accept this line of reasoning or questioning is necessarily to reclaim a certain anthropological heuristics that returns us to the catch phrase "the social life of . . . "—things (Appadurai 1986), information (Brown and Duguid 2002), even guinea pigs if need be.[3] Where does the social start or end? Should anthropology, as the "science of man," be read literally, restrictively, or open-mindedly? After all, why does the life story of, say, a mandible or an elk skin interest us, as anthropologists and as humans? The chapters in this book, although not responding directly to such questions, do reveal that material boundaries between "the social" and that "something else" become to an extent redundant; the focus then becomes the encounter between what we recognize in our sensuous universe and what we deem as "alter" (the "otherworldly," the "nonhuman," the "supernatural," etc.), different to us, the nonself, if you will, even if constitutive of the self. Or, in other words, relationships (acts of mediation, possession, dreaming, etc.) that accumulate and become meaningful through time, entering our own historical records and senses of self and otherness. And by becoming meaningful, they become intimate, immediate (Kwon 2008; Eisenlohr 2009), taking on form, and even autonomy. Like Latour has shown, even microbes have historicity, albeit a relational one: "The more Pasteur works in his laboratory, the more autonomous his ferment becomes" (1993a, 147), gaining stability as an entity.

Implicitly or explicitly, the chapters ahead show us one pervasion: time, or rather temporalization (Palmié, this volume). Processes of biographization reflect senses of time but also "produce" time, as they presuppose and build upon particular stances and conform social trajectories that are publicly recognized. They also demonstrate how different temporalities can combine and coexist according to evolving (and revolving) combinations of memory, consciousness, expectation and projections, producing shifting temporal frames in the experiences and discourses of those who resort to them. This form of "punctuation" has been explored recently by Jane Guyer (2007), who sought to understand the shifts between different regimes of temporal appreciation and configuration of the future in 1950s and 1960s Britain and 1990s Nigeria.

But this heuristic revision also implies a distancing from the traditional characterization of anthropology as "occularcentric," relying on the methodological cornerstone of "participant observation" (see Engelke 2009; Willerslev 2009; Mittermaier 2011, 84–111). This has been the object of critique by authors such as Johannes Fabian (1983) and Paul Stoller (1989), who sought other paths of ethnographic understanding; later, Michael Taussig (2009) furthered this proposition, by exploring the chromatic dimensions of the world, opening new pathways for researching perceptive regimes. The main challenge thus becomes to "anthropologize" the invisible and intangible while moving beyond academic categories of "proof" and "evidence" toward notions—invented, created, or reappropriated—that are able both to convey diverse ways of seeing and sensing, thus a phenomenological sense of otherness, and to analytically parse them into anthropological understanding. In many of the contexts described here, physicality becomes a "place of evidence," and it is through materialization (including the body) that "evidentiary protocols" are ultimately questioned (Engelke 2009, 1). Biographies and life histories are often presented, both by anthropologists and their interlocutors (although in different ways) as "evidence," testimony of a particular regime of truth and outcome of a production of a certain coherence—or, as Matthew Engelke places it, of convincing others of "being right" (2009, 2); Martin Holbraad (2009) also refers to this as a production of "indubitability." We agree with Engelke (2009, 3) that there hasn't been (at least until the volume he coordinated) a well-developed language for, as well as a significant critique of, the concept of evidence in anthropology; thus, in this volume, we explore, often recurring to mutuality as an epistemological and methodological concern (see Cabral 2013), the shifts between different theories and praxes of evidentiary production without defining clear conceptual boundaries. Rather, we allow for their multiplicity, welcome their spontaneity and unexpectedness, and detect the different acts of mediation involved.

Mediation and the Real

The problem of "mediation" is a central concern of Christianity, as Cannell (2006) convincingly argues. But it is perhaps even more immediate to religious practices whose primary device for knowledge production *is* mediation, and further, mediation through *bodies*. Possession cults are prime examples of how entities manifest more or less directly through the articulations of mediums' bodies and voices, either through moments described by those who experience them as sheer substitution or through more gradated forms of "incorporation," where selves can temporarily coexist without the annihilation of the medium's consciousness. Whereas older studies were guided by medical, therapeutic, even pathology concerns (Bourguignon 1976; Koss 1977; Krippner 1989; Rogler and Hollingshead 1961; Ward 1989), most contemporary studies of spirit mediation tend to usefully emphasize its contextual and phenomenological dimensions (see Boddy 1994 for a review). However, the answers to the question of what exactly is being mediated have continued to resonate in the form of a certain sociologization of the phenomena, which while not as openly reductive as Lewis's classic study ([1971] 2003), reify the underlying functions of possession in terms that are always *other* to it—namely, as an "idiom" for expressing individual, gendered, social, economic, political, or other ailments (e.g., see Boddy 1989; Ong 1987; Stoller 1989). The "effects" of entities here would thus include, following Vincent Crapanzano and Vivian Garrison (1977, 19–20), "self-aggrandizement and self-assertion," "the realignment of marital relations," "an escape from an unpleasant situation," "the attainment of intimacy through fleeting interpersonal relationships desired by the carrier but prohibited socially in the non-possessed state," "the desire for a specific object," and "the assertion of rights among the socially marginal" among other possibilities.

We bring this implicit critique of possession studies to bear here on the question of mediation because it essentially points to a double-edged sword: if, on the one hand, for the persons studied by the anthropologist, "the notion that bodily sensations are 'not made by the human hand,' grants them their role in the cultural production of the real" (Van de Port 2011, 78), then, on the other, for the anthropologist, "when spirit possession is at issue, the need to demystify analytical terms and resist being seduced into thinking that they dispassionately reflect reality is especially keen," as Boddy (1994, 408) notes. The "spirit" in question is, then, for the anthropologist a category of experience (oppressive social relations, economic hardship, illness, boredom, the need for attention and answers, etc.) that must remain opaque to the experiencer in order for the symbolic properties of the same experience to have effects. This disjuncture between the "realities" (and even consciousnesses) of analyst and informant is a disquieting reminder that even studies that have as their primary axis of investigation the socially informed body (or embodiment), such as Csordas's (1994) formidable account of charismatic Christians in the United States, "risk denying the whole of the possession experience, which our informants insist is embodied and disembodied at one and the same time" (Boddy 1994, 426). This does not mean that phenomenological approaches cannot engender languages ingenious enough to render a description of experience both thick and theoretically innovative. One example of this is Todd Ramon Ochoa's (2007, 2010b) recent work on Cuban Palo Monte, a Congo-inspired ritual tradition "too unexpected in its basic assumptions about the status of matter, the dead, and the living, to be seamlessly assimilated into the prevailing ethnographic modes of analysis as these are defined, above all, by their adherence to regimes of knowing organized under the signs of negation, identity, and being" (2007, 479). Ochoa draws from Hegel, Marx, Nietzsche, and Deleuze to devise a language by which he describes Palo's infinite turns of the dead, its materializations in bodies and things, the "morphogenic dynamisms" (ibid., 481) inherent to the immanence and materiality of the spirits worked and embodied by ritual specialists.

Some of the more successful attempts at theorizing the "effects" of spirit mediation (i.e., their social lives) are those that focus on their tangible, discursive effects—words, communication, the repositioning and transmission of knowledge, for example—which allow for spirits to "exist" at levels irreducible to others. Michael Lambek's (1980, 1989) ethnography of Mayotte possession as a system of communication is a case in point; he suggests a method of "looking for levels of constraints, grammars of production and interpretation, modes of representation, avenues of creativity" (1989, 53), a challenge taken up also by some of this book's contributors. Among the Mayotte of Madagascar, as among many other societies, possession is seen as a type of affliction whose cure involves, among other things, a socialization of the spirit and the establishment of an exchange relationship with it. What is interesting is that the spirit generally appears in a host in order to make itself known to a third party and to pass on messages; it must interact with the host's proxies, developing a relationship with these individuals as the cure progresses. Thus, while Lambek suggests that spousal discord may benefit from "spiritual" intervention through possession episodes, the central unit of analysis is increased communication, via both living and dead. Like Jeanne Favret-Saada (1980) argues in her account of witchcraft in the Bocage, the point here is not to "explain away" spirit phenomena but to unwind and understand the processes in which it can exist and have effects.

Another powerful ethnography along these lines is Piers Vitebsky's *Dialogues with the Dead* (1993), which explores how the spirit, physical, and social worlds are intimately linked in the context of the Sora people's relationship with their dead, with whom they have elaborate conversations through mediums. For the Sora, an aboriginal tribe on the eastern coast of India, a healthy detachment from the dead is impossible precisely because the dead themselves are not detached; unlike for Freud, they are not a fictional object of love but are indeed autonomous and active. If the Sora dead are a fiction at all, Vitebsky claims, they are a joint fiction negotiated by many authors: "All persons are both self-authoring and authors of each other's lives" (1993, 254). Vitebsky alerts us to the importance of intersubjectivity in an understanding of how entities come into being, in environments as well as persons. In her account of how Fijians come to embody their history, Christina Toren (1999) suggests that these concerns invite a radical shift of theoretical stance: from one in which the world is seen as a given to the mind, which internalizes and represents it, to one in which the body is the primary means of acquiring a world and its givens. Persons, for Toren, are self-regulating, transformational systems who bring forth their realities through the act of living, which is by definition a historical, cognitively embodied process. This observation squares with what Hallowell has in mind when he acknowledges that people may not be totally constrained by or socialized through their "material" environment, as we mentioned above, but may be guided into existence and action by other important invisible dimensions. Thus, the total "content" of an individual's "behavioral environment" is a function of these orientations rather than some prespecified ontology, as his work on the Ojibwa shows. But questions of "realness" and relativity continue to intrigue anthropologists working on religious phenomena.

Mattjis Van de Port, for instance, argues that "in cultural analysis we can only subscribe to the proposition that there is no such thing as an unmediated knowing of reality. The dream of escaping media is unattainable"; it is a fantasy of immediacy (2011, 76). Van de Port is essentially interested in finding out how people go about this "paradoxical attempt to mediate immediacy" (ibid.). For instance, in an article on the search for and perception of authenticity in Candomblé, an Afro-Brazilian tradition practiced in Bahia in particular, Van de Port proposes a perspective on possession that interprets it "first and foremost as the production of the ineffable in a symbolic universe in which meanings are adrift and truth regimes are in disarray" (2005, 153). It is precisely because possession suggests that certain "realities" are beyond conventional knowledge, he says, that they are able to create a locus for the "really real" (ibid.), augmenting discourses of authenticity.

Van de Port is right in suggesting that "something about possession remains enigmatic, unapproachable, resisting the word, displaying the failure of representation" (ibid., 151). But his approach raises several problems, including the question of what conventional knowledge is, which for Candomblé mediums may encompass those "ineffable" domains he excludes from ordinary knowledge (by siding them with a "symbolic universe" of obfuscated meanings). While it may be the case that possession experiences generate their own forms of ambiguity and thus interpretations of the "real," it is quite another thing to infer from informants' descriptions of inexplicable bodily events that the phenomena is beyond the comprehension of the practitioners themselves, as well as of the anthropologist (Van de Port 2005, 167; see also Greenwood, this volume). That is, it is unwarranted to suggest that belief in the real is grounded in the making opaque of this very "realness." While Van de Port's separation of "medium" and "real" may work for many forms of social and mediational life, as he himself asks, "If one maintains that there is a key dividing line between manifestations of reality that can be attributed to a 'human hand' and those considered beyond the range of such agency, the question presents itself how one should proceed one's analysis in situations where boundaries between human and non-human agency are contested and shifting?" (2011, 86).

In religious and spiritual contexts this is often the case. Indeed, a central concern of the contributors of this volume is that there rarely are such dividing lines or boundaries. The really "real" is neither produced nor found but often *equivalent* to or fathomable *through* the tangible, audible, and seeable, where "evidence" of it lies not in the illusion of the "real" but in ways of being, perceiving, and knowing that are just "commonsense" to those who practice them. Furthermore, the two domains (human and nonhuman agency) may be mutually constitutive, with dividends for a concept of person among others. As Marcio Goldman (1985, 2005, 2007) has convincingly shown, both spirit medium *and* oricha (the Yoruba-Brazilian gods mediums are consecrated to) are "made" in the lengthy process of initiation. A full "person" simply does not preexist his or her making during the course of his or her formal and informal ritual commitments and the relations these forge, and indeed, a person is conceived as multiple—multiple, "not necessarily opposed to 'one,' but as a substantive and an index of a pluralism in opposition to all forms of binarism and its variations" (2007, 113). Neither are the gods simply atomic beings willed onto a human plane. According to Goldman, they too are a modulation of the sacred force—*ashe*—that is constitutive of all beings and things in the world through processes of concretization, diversification, and individualization (ibid., 110). "In a sense," he argues, "each being is a kind of crystallization or molarization resulting from the modulating flow of *ashe*, which starting out as a general and homogeneous force continuously gets more diversified and more concrete" (ibid.). Goldman's Deleuzian approach is arguably taken to the extreme in Martin Holbraad's (2007) analysis of Ifá diviners in Cuba. Holbraad takes the concept of *aché*, which is similar to the Brazilian notion but in Cuba also refers to the powder spread on the Ifá priest's divining board on which he makes markings, and collapses the distinction between divinity and motion, concept and thing. Like the Polynesian notion of mana, *aché* is excessive; it is both power and powder (ibid., 204), but this relationship is internal, one defining the other. "Divinatory power," Holbraad says, "most crucially involves the capacity to engender what we might call 'ontological leaps' on the part of the deity, from transcendence to immanance, or more simply, from radical absence (the 'beyond') to presence" (ibid., 207). Ifá diviners are able to consummate these leaps precisely because of the nature of powder itself: it is pure motile multiplicity. In this sense, Ifá's deities are "motions through and through" (ibid., 209).

We are no longer modern, nor indeed, have we ever been, says Bruno Latour. The modern explanation manages to specify and cancel out the work of mediation at once "by conceiving every hybrid as a mixture of two pure forms" (1993b, 78), which is why we must now focus on exactly those mixtures, he says, the "Middle Kingdom," or "mediators." Latour's understanding of mediation resonates here. Cultures do not exist any more than Natures do; there are only nature-cultures. And, "as soon as we grant historicity to all actors so that we can accommodate the proliferation of quasi-objects, Nature and Society have no more existence than West and East. They become convenient and relative reference points that moderns use to differentiate intermediaries, some of which are called 'natural' and others 'social,' while still others are termed 'purely natural' and others 'purely social,' and yet others are considered 'not only' natural 'but also' a little bit social" (ibid., 85). Relativists have never been convincing precisely because they limit their consideration to cultural difference, says Latour; nature for them was always a given, since universal sciences describe it. According to him, from "cultural relativism" perhaps we should move toward a "relativist relativism" or "relationism" (ibid., 113), which points out "what instruments and what chains serve to create asymmetries and equalities, hierarchies and differences" (ibid., 113). The error of the moderns was confusing the products with the process, believing that the production of a universal science presupposed universalist scientists, or that bureaucratic rationalization presupposed rational bureaucrats: "Science does not produce itself scientifically any more than technology produces itself technologically or economy economically" (ibid., 116). However, this does not mean that these are not respectable beliefs. As E. E. Evans-Pritchard said, in 1934, "It is a mistake to say that savages perceive mystically, or that their perception is mystical. On the other hand we may say that savages pay attention to phenomena on account of the mystical properties with which their society has endowed them, and that often their interest in phenomena is mainly, even exclusively, due to these mystic properties" (quoted in Douglas 1980, 29). Evans-Pritchard's argument can be extended to all entities, visible or not, as he himself noted when he compared British notions of the weather with Zande concepts of witchcraft.

Toward an Anthropological Pragmatics of the "Intangible"

Hallowell tells us that in environments with certain "cosmic dimensions and implicit metaphysical principles," the social may be a great deal more inclusive than is obvious for the ethnographer, and the "self in its relations with other selves may transcend the boundaries of social life as objectively defined" (2010, 35). The question is how to account for, and theoretically locate, these extensive relations that selves may have with others. In particular, what an anthropology of *extrasocial* or *extraphysical* forms of sociality and interaction would look like if it were not guided by the concerns of culture and personality (and to an extent cultural model) paradigms, which are underpinned, arguably, by the basic assumption that "culture" overdetermines belief, action, and perception (even if with relevant margins for personal agency in, through, or despite these models). This remits us to certain methodological and linguistic quandaries: What analytical space or value to we accord nonhuman entities in our ethnographies? What conceptual and formal language do we use to describe their existence and effects? In what ways can we appeal to historiography and sociopolitical contextualization without reducing entities to epiphenomena of more "real" ground facts?

In the title of this volume we allude to Appadurai's "social life of things," and in this introduction we explain that while Appadurai and his colleagues' concern is objects and commodities, and, importantly, following things in themselves, our purpose is to suggest that what we may ordinarily think of as "nonthings," because they may lack physical substance or immediate visibility, may carve their own social destinies, much like Appadurai's things, thus becoming objects of inquiry, not vis-à-vis the minds that sustain them but also in themselves. The essays collected here suggest several peculiar and distinguishable aspects of this "social life," although the stories they tell are by no means encompassed by them.

Perhaps the most significant of these aspects is indeterminacy, or rather irreducibility, which, in turn, has as its corollary, noninstrumentality. Contra prevalent spirit possession study trends, the authors of the chapters ahead forfeit a preoccupation with what beliefs in entities are good for, or what they represent, in favor of a more careful scrutiny of their unplanned and even unexpected character. The recognition that the effects of invisible entities cannot always be accounted for by established cosmological explanations is thus central to a conceptualization of their social and individual potency.

In their revisitation and revision of the concept of "imagination," David Sneath, Martin Holbraad, and Morten Pedersen (2009) argue for an approach that understands it not as a cultural template for action and thought (such as is implicit in the term *social imaginaries*, particularly in globalization studies), nor as something purposeful and instrumental that describes it in terms of how individuals make sense of their world, and even less in the romanticist/symbolic light it is cast in by recent hermeneutic anthropologies. Rather, these authors pursue a concept of the imagination beyond its purely mental definitions by attending "to the processes by which imaginary effects may come about"—namely, through what they call "technologies of the imagination" (2009, 19). In their view, technologies "are 'of the imagination' precisely in as much as the imaginative effects that these technologies being about are *indeterminate*" (ibid.), thus reversing the commonplace notion of imagination as a condition of effect rather than as an outcome of particular generative "technologies." For Sneath and his colleagues, what makes imagination "imaginative" is "precisely that the imagination is not an *effect* as this is ordinarily understood, inasmuch as its relationship to the conditions that engender it is neither deterministic nor teleological. To explore 'technologies of the imagination,' then, is to explore the conditions under which unconditioned outcomes come about" (ibid.). Notwithstanding these authors' concern, which is not ours explicitly, with "technologies" and with the *imaginative effects* they produce, it is this sense of *effect*, and, moreover, of *sociality*, that we wish to recover here. We could similarly say that the definition of an entity as *social* hinges upon the unimagined or unforeseen dimensions of its effects from the native point of view; that is, it is social inasmuch as it escapes the straightjacket of "belief" to which it has been typically relegated by anthropologists, and is considered within the frame of the entirely generative capacities afforded to such things as "technologies" or objects more broadly. By this we refer not just to crude distinctions between conscious/unconscious possession events, for example, in which latter forms are culturally expected to generate culturally "unexpected" knowledge, but to the complex physical and social markers that metaphysical interventions of all kinds crystallize into relations, extensions, existences, and even historical and political changes. There is an advantage, as Nils Bubandt (2009) puts it, in treating spirits as "methodologically real," or even as informants proper, inasmuch as they are often both instruments and actors. Indeed, as he says, "Treating these spirits as informants is only counterintuitive because the category of 'informant' remains linked to conventional, philosophical idea(l)s about the bounded self" (2009, 296). In treating the social life of invisible, intangible, inaudible, or otherwise sensorially alter phenomena through a pragmatic lens, our intention is to also review the possibility that personhood or selfhood does not always end at the limits of body, mind, or conventional space-time.

The Social Life of Entities

The essays in this volume invoke several possibilities within a prospective "anthropology of intangibility"—namely, in the tracing of its effects within the texture of social life. The contributors have explored several paths that reveal different ontologies, notions of personhood and agency, narrative and historicity, place and intersection, and thus blur or rebuild notions of frontier and incommensurability.

The first three chapters deal in one way or another with problems of "presence." Thomas G. Kirsch, for instance, is concerned with an ontology of the Holy Spirit but also in the ways the Holy Spirit becomes "informed" and "located" through its own mobility and portability. Taking as an example Pentecostal-charismatic churches in southern Zambia, he explores the "intangible motion" of the Holy Spirit, or how it emerges within different sizes and shapes (morphologies) within the Zambian Christian landscape. This exercise reveals a connection that exposes the Holy Spirit (*muya usalala*) as something more, other than just abstract power—an "artifact of semiosis," but also and especially a "spiritual agency" that inserts itself in the matter-of-fact dimension of everyday life. Grégory Delaplace reveals a similar conception concerning the habitat of ghosts in rural Mongolia; here, the difficulty defining what a ghost *is* does not remove the stances and regimes of communication, as well as the perceptual faiths that epistemologically bind them. The key moment for Delaplace is the manifestation and encounter, which become in fact the connectors of perception and knowledge. Through his work with Dörvöd nomadic herders, he attempts to pin down and discuss the sensations involved and recognized in those moments, placing them in the core of local configurations of the invisible and its effects. Florencia C. Tola, in turn, correlates notions of personhood with ideologies of spiritual presence among the Toba people of the northern Argentinean region of the Chaco. Here, we find complementary categories of selfhood, in which the human/nonhuman distinction becomes complexified and multiplied into several subcategories: one can be nonhuman and corporealized, and vice versa. However, invoking the thriving literature on Amerindian notions of personhood and nature, Tola nevertheless avoids the appeal of taxonomization and produces an account of humanization and dehumanization through traces and interactions between such entities and specialist (shaman) or nonspecialist Toba. In many cases, as she also shares, those interactions become crystallized in paintings and drawings, which make such manifestations collectivized, public.

Vânia Zikàn Cardoso's contribution picks up on the previous ones to highlight one of the central aspects of the contexts explored: namely, the role of narrative and "story"—a "name-calling quality" or a "dis-ordering sign," as she suggests concerning the case of *macumba* in Rio de Janeiro. Cardoso describes the ambiguities and divergences that seem to be compulsory to the effect of *macumba*, a spiritual activity performed by possession, in the lives of the *cariocas* (inhabitants of Rio de Janeiro). She then weaves an ethnography that follows the stories in the streets, where relationships between people, places, and spirits emerge and develop. Mark Harris, working from the Brazilian Amazonia, is interested in the historical journeys that are devised in the recognition of certain *ribeirinho* (river-dwelling) entities within local rural communities. Here, the river is a locus in which the transitions between the invisible and the visible occur. The river then becomes historicized, as the stories concerning the *encantados* (spiritual beings) accumulate, forming a social history and an intermediate ontological category that surfaces in between the human and the nonhuman. A similar exercise of location in the land, although quite different in terms of heuristic configuration, can be found in Susan Greenwood's contribution, which dwells on the epistemological limits of the anthropological discipline by suggesting an "epistemology of imaginal alterity" built around an autobiographical account of "nature religion" in Britain. In her account, her relationship with a spiritual entity described as a dragon unfolds through landscapes, sensations, and connections, revealing the individuality of processes that are often anthropologically accounted for as collective processes.

Concerning the problem of narrativization, Kristina Wirtz, Ana Stela de Almeida Cunha, and Emerson Giumbelli follow similar paths—namely, in the conjunction of the categories of invisibility, manifestation, and materialization in biographical and autobiographical accounts. In a compelling analysis of the multiplicity of biographies and their mutual entanglements, or what she describes as "realms of imaginative possibility," Wirtz explores narratives of perspicacity and recognition that emerge within the unfolding of Cuban Spiritism and Santería practitioners' careers and those of the spirits they work with. Cunha, in turn, focuses on dreams as instances of manifestation and mediation in the rural Brazilian region of Maranhão, where the *encantados* also dwell. As she describes, the Pajé (an African-based religious manifestation) practitioners have learned to

use dreams in the process of ritualization and socialization of spiritual mediation, in which the intersection of social and spiritual lineages is established. Finally Giumbelli takes a similar yet critically different approach
to the historicization of spiritual presence by elaborating a social biography of a *caboclo*, an Amerindian entity of the Umbanda terrain, and
describes its mutations and the intellectual approximations to understand
(and "materialize") it, producing its "multiple lives." In dialogue with major theories of Afro-Brazilian religion (Bastide, Matory), he builds upon
a spiritual economy of manifestation intersected by multiple (indigenous,
racial, institutional) appropriations. Giumbelli's chapter speaks in many
ways to that of Stephan Palmié, which also critically addresses, through
his study of spiritual work and ritual practice in Afro-Cuban religion, the
problem of historical knowledge. Describing how *los muertos* (the dead)
incorporate postmortem biographies that defy the linearity of historical
materialism, and how the living engage in these multiple temporalities, he
argues for the need for a new anthropology of knowledge that is able to
address such contingencies.

CHAPTER TWO

Intangible Motion

Notes on the Morphology and Mobility of the Holy Spirit

Thomas G. Kirsch

Introduction

Recent anthropological studies on pneumatic churches oscillate between a fascination with the emphasis in these churches on the located (embodied) immanence of the Divine and the observation that pneumatic forms of Christianity have massively grown in popularity and turned into a religious movement of global proportions. The latter is most pronounced in work on the globalization of Pentecostalism (e.g., Anderson 2004; Cox 1996; Martin 2002; Meyer 2004; Robbins 2004), which not only foregrounds the role of modern mass communication and mass organization in creating (imagined) Pentecostal communities but also emphasizes the circulation of Pentecostal messages across continents, more particularly, the spatial diffusion of "ideas, media products, preachers, and believers" (Meyer 2010, 120).

However, astonishingly, neither André Drooger's (2001) reminder that Pentecostalism's expansion should be explained not solely with reference to external circumstances but also with regard to its *internal* religious characteristics nor the emergent interest by anthropologists in Christian pneumatology (cf. Maxwell 2012) has led to a detailed empirical assessment and thorough theoretical reflection of the ways in which the "global portability of pneumatic Christianities . . . depends . . . on the portability of the Holy Spirit and the spirits it battles, on their fluidity and capacity to circulate through flexible transnational church and immigrant networks" (Vasquez 2009, 280; see also Kirsch 2008a; Hüwelmeier and Krause 2010).

This chapter is an attempt to fill this gap in research in relation to Pentecostal-charismatic Christianity in sub-Saharan Africa by, firstly, pursuing an ethnographic analysis of the ontology of the Holy Spirit in African Christian churches, secondly, paying specific attention to the multifarious and wondrous ways in which the Holy Spirit is here experienced to locate itself in and move through space, and thirdly, in this way, exploring the formation of what I call "socio-spiritual communities"—that is, religious communities constituted by human beings and their interactions with spiritual entities.[1]

Take, for example, a paradigmatic scene in Christianity that is reenacted by millions of religious practitioners every year and is familiar to anthropologists conducting research among Christians in all parts of the world: baptism in the Holy Spirit by immersion in a river. For members of Pentecostal-charismatic churches in southern Zambia, the site of my fieldwork (e.g., see Kirsch 1998, 2008b), preparations for this rite include, among other things, prayers spoken over the river by a church leader, hymns sung to summon the Holy Spirit's presence, and submission of the candidates for baptism to a preparatory purification in the form of an exorcism of demons.[2] In some churches, the latter means that the baptism candidates have to register their names with the church secretary and line up on the river bank perpendicular to the waterline. Then, one after another, candidates are splashed with what, as a result of the prayers and hymns, is considered to have turned into "holy water." If the first person in the line shows signs of demon possession such as whimpering, shaking, and falling to the ground, the assistants to the church elders move him or her aside for treatment, thus making room for the next person in the line to step forward and undergo the prebaptismal exorcism. If a baptisand shows no signs of demonic possession, he or she is assisted into the middle of the river to be baptized by triple immersion.

There are several notable aspects about this rite that are relevant to the present chapter. For one thing, in the course of the prebaptismal exorcism, the power of the Holy Spirit is transmitted by vigorously splashing "holy water" from the stream over the body of the baptism candidate. Yet, since splashing water over a distance tends to be a messy affair, it is usually not only the first person in the line who is sprayed with water but also bystanders and some of the other baptism candidates. All the same, in every prebaptismal ritual of this type I have attended over the years, the power of the Holy Spirit had an exorcistic effect exclusively on the first person in the line of baptisands. Even if it turned out later that certain others who coincidentally came into bodily contact with "holy water" in this process were possessed by evil spirits, it did *not* automatically make them fall to the ground or go into demonic convulsions. In other words, though the "holy water" is used in this context as a generalized medium for transmitting the power of the Holy Spirit, its spiritualizing effects are selective in a systematic manner. In dealing with the baptism candidates, the Holy Spirit handles one candidate at a time. Moreover, while the socio-spatial radius of those splashed (and as a consequence affected) by the "holy water" is not clear, the Holy Spirit is unambiguous regarding who its addressee is: the first person in the line. In sum, the Holy Spirit in effect follows the procedural and socio-spatial order as determined by the church secretary in preparation for the baptismal rite, processing the people to be exorcised according to the logic of individualized sequencing in the spatial form of a line.

On the other hand, what is noteworthy about this type of baptismal rite is that the Holy Spirit is here assumed (in principle) to remain immobile in a specific section of constantly running water. It is true that, in southern Africa, most of these rituals are performed on the banks of small rivers rather than broad streams. Nonetheless, the church elders prayed over *flowing* waters, and none of the religious practitioners I talked to thought such prayers had a spiritualizing effect for the entirety of the stream from its head to its mouth. Instead, while access to the ritual site was restricted to church elders, their assistants, and baptism candidates, the religious significance attributed to these areas of spiritualized water did not pertain to the sections of the river further up- or downstream, where local residents continued performing their daily routines of drawing water, having a wash, or doing the laundry. Thus, by remaining immobile in a sphere of mobility, the Holy Spirit metamorphosed secular space into sacred place. In this way, baptism by immersion in a river conveys powerful ideas about spiritual continuity in a changing world and serves as a counterintuitive reminder to practitioners of Christianity that divine transcendence miraculously makes it possible for believers to step into the same river twice, and not in a purely metaphorical manner of speaking.

The ethnographic case above establishes the topic of this chapter. Taking baptism in the Holy Spirit by immersion in a river as the example, the case speaks to the fact that Christians around the world conceptualize and experience this spiritual entity not only as being endowed with extraordinary powers but also as being characterized by superhuman ways of making use of and moving through space. In pursuing this line of inquiry further, the present chapter explores different types of mobility of the Holy Spirit in southern Zambia. Broadly speaking, this topic stands in the tradition of anthropology that stresses not spatial fixity, stability, bounded definitude, and sedentariness but instead fluidity, flux, movement, and mobility. Irrespective of whether this represents a reaction to changes in the contemporary world or is part of academia's thematic autopoiesis, current understandings of the world as a world in motion are already having profound influences on ethnographic methodologies (Falzon 2009; Gille and Ó Riain 2002; Gupta and Ferguson 1997; Hannerz 2003; Marcus 1995), the question of what are considered legitimate objects of anthropological research (e.g., see Appadurai 1998; Carter 2010; Clifford 1994, 1997; Hannerz 1996; Kearney 1995; Vertovec 1999, 2009; Wimmer and Glick Schiller 2002) and theoretical perspectives on key notions of anthropology such as "society," "identity" and "culture." For instance, when probing into the global movement of people, objects, representations, models, ideas and imaginaries, anthropologists have reconceptualized space, reexamined the role of technology and materiality in the constitution of socio-cultural life, and discussed whether different types of material and nonmaterial entities are characterized by different types of mobility. However, Peter Wynn Kirby (2009, 2) has critically reminded anthropologists that "while anthropology and other social sciences have long acknowledged the importance of addressing flux in socio-cultural inquiry . . . attention to the ramifications of movement remains relatively lopsided. Extensive work on migration and diaspora cultures and on social 'movements' provides important insights into the fluidity of people, culture, and ideas. . . . Nevertheless, a focus on certain emblematically transnational or 'global' movements exposes lacunae in, or neglect of, other elements of mobility and flux worthy of anthropological purview." It is in the spirit of this reminder, and against the backdrop of the observation that there is, with few exceptions (e.g., Ingold and Vergunst 2008; for a discussion of "motility" as a general premise of Ifá cosmology, see Holbraad 2007, 2012), a notable lack of attempts to take seriously the cultural variability of emic understandings of "movement," that this chapter seeks to initiate a debate on how anthropology might benefit from rethinking mobility. This means starting by correlating the morphology of an entity with the properties of its movements.

As I will demonstrate, the entity examined in this chapter, the Holy Spirit (in Chitonga, *muya usalala*), comes in various "sizes" and "shapes," sometimes concentrating its beingness on the most minuscule location, at other times expanding its perimeters over large spatial areas. I argue that if we adhere to the common definition of *movement* as "a perceptible change of an entity's position in space," then *muya usalala*'s self-expansion and self-contraction should be considered a specific type of movement. More precisely, it is not a "conventional" movement from A to B, with the morphology of the moving entity remaining unaltered, but instead a pulsation from the micro- to macroscale, which is effected by an alteration in the gestalt of *muya usalala*. Taken together, my exploration of ideas of spirit mobility in Zambia must take account of the morphology of the Holy Spirit, which allows for certain types of mobility and forestalls others, thus shaping the geography of Pentecostal-charismatic Christianity by connecting and empowering religious practitioners through its miraculous ways of moving.[3]

Before coming to a general description of *muya usalala* and an examination of its various types of mobility, two remarks are in order. First, while the scope and relevance of the topic outlined above would certainly lend itself to a comprehensive comparative project on the mobility of spirits in global Pentecostalism (e.g., see Anderson 2004; Corten and Marshall-Fratani 2001; Dempster, Klaus, and Peterson 1999; Martin 2002; Meyer 2010; Robbins 2004), in Christianity at large, or in other religious traditions, the purpose of the present chapter is more modest and mainly consists in demonstrating what can be achieved analytically when we relate the gestalt of a spiritual entity to the ways in which it moves. The ethnographic example I have chosen to show this is present-day southern Zambia, most particularly the Gwembe Valley.[4]

The second remark concerns research methodology. During my fieldwork, I encountered *muya usalala* on many occasions, in various settings, and in different ways. On the one hand, *muya usalala* is the Chitonga expression for what in English-language versions of the Bible is termed the "Holy Spirit." As such, *muya usalala* was and continues to be part of everyday conversations between members of Pentecostal-charismatic churches in the area of my research, as well as, in the course my fieldwork, between myself and my interlocutors in these churches. On the other hand, since for most people in this area *muya usalala* is not merely an artifact of semiosis but a spiritual agency of divine provenience that has an existence as a matter of fact, this entity is not only talked about but also assumed to make itself present in the world in at least two different ways. First, as I discussed in detail in an essay entitled "From the Spirit's Point of View" (Kirsch 2010), members of Pentecostal-charismatic churches presume that *muya usalala* sometimes speaks through human media such as prophets, diviners, and spiritual healers. Secondly, members of these churches agree that under specific circumstances *muya usalala* can enter the bodies of selected individuals in order to either fight demonic spirits occupying this space or empower these individuals to accomplish extraordinary, superhuman tasks such as divination or witch finding (see Kirsch, 2013). When in the remainder of this chapter I look at the types of mobility of *muya usalala*, I will be combining my research data from these different sources. In other words, the following analysis is based on my interlocutors' statements about *muya usalala*, as well as on my observations about how *muya usalala* became a visibly embodied part of their religious practice.[5] As regards the latter aspect, I take up the invitation in recent anthropology to shift the analytical "focus from questions of knowledge and epistemology toward those of ontology" (Henare, Holbraad, and Wastell 2007, 8) in order to explore what we can learn about the Holy Spirit if we take its motile agency as given.

Spirits on the Move

The expression introduced to the Batonga in southern Zambia by representatives of the Primitive Methodist Missionary Society around the turn of the nineteenth century for translating the English term "Holy Spirit" is *muya usalala*. Other spiritual entities—that is, from the missionaries' perspective, the satanic adversaries of *muya usalala*—were called *madaimona* (reminiscent of the English word "demon") or, synonymously, *muya mubi* (with the word *mubi* denoting "bad").

Nowadays, *muya usalala* is of particular relevance in what Harold Turner (1967) has called "prophet-healing churches"—that is, African-initiated Pentecostal-charismatic churches where the divination and healing of afflictions plays a "pivotal role with regard to doctrine, pastoral praxis and the recruitment of members" (Schoffeleers 1991, 2). In these churches, an attempt is made to employ the "life-transforming power of the Holy Spirit" (Hammond-Tooke 1986, 157). Using a "polyvalent metaphor of healing" (Comaroff 1985, 197), the leaders of these churches engage in the treatment of bodily afflictions, socially or mentally odd behavior, and cases of sterility. Witchcraft is considered the main cause of human afflictions; some of these churches accordingly offer protective measures against the activities of witches. The search for the cause of misfortune or an affliction is pursued by means of mediumistic divinations (see also Devisch 1985), which require the prophet concerned to be inspired by *muya usalala*. The treatment, on the other hand, generally involves spiritualized praying with the laying on of hands and the singing of spiritual hymns. Some churches provide herbalist treatment that resembles the practices of "traditional" healers (*bang'anga*). In both cases, however, success in healing presupposes that the healer is associated with the Holy Spirit, which is conceptualized as the main antagonistic force against witchcraft and demons.

As a consequence, religious authority in these Pentecostal-charismatic churches is intricately linked to the idea that certain human beings have a privileged association with *muya usalala*, which assists them in acquiring divine knowledge and curing. At the same time, however, in my area of research, the Holy Spirit is not part of a unanimously shared and timeless system of classification. Besides the common view that the Holy Spirit is a basically benevolent being, its concrete characteristics and powers, and the loci and foci of its manifestations (cf. Kirsch, 2013), are constantly being negotiated and renegotiated in different social constellations.

While much of my previous work on Pentecostal-charismatic Christianity has dealt with religious practitioners' uncertainties in authoritatively identifying the "true" Holy Spirit (e.g., see Kirsch 2002), the discussion below refers to ethnographic situations in which a certain (implicit) agreement had been reached among participants that a given spiritual manifestation represents the Holy Spirit. In what follows I will therefore first present some essential attributes of *muya usalala* in contradistinction to those of non-Christian spirits, most notably its quintessential unboundedness and evanescence. Then, I will discuss three types of mobility that Pentecostal-charismatic Christians in Zambia perceive to be characteristic of the Holy Spirit.

Unbounded, Evanescent, and Beyond Control

When seeking to discern the basic parameters of how *muya usalala* makes itself present in the world, a comparison between this specific spirit and non-Christian spirits in the area of my research is useful. This is because there is a crucial difference between these spiritual entities as regards the question of "storage": whereas it is claimed that the "physical" keeping of non-Christian spirits is possible, this possibility is rejected as far as the Holy Spirit is concerned.

For example, in contrast to the discourse on *muya usalala*, the view that non-Christian spirits dwell in an object is prevalent. Thus, some types of magic items used in witchcraft—especially the *insengo*, *chifunda*, and *chinaile*—are said to contain malevolent spirits.[6] The witches are assumed to posit spirits in the objects, which would then—when, for example, located at the homestead of the victim—lead to illness or death. Moreover, many "traditional" herbalists (*bang'anga*; sing., *mung'anga*) possess paraphernalia, which they present as "containers" for their spiritual assistants. For example, during his treatments in 1999, a *mung'anga* in Sinazeze, a small rural township in the Gwembe Valley, made use of two calabashes that he had stored in his house. The pear-shaped gourds had openings in the top, one of them decorated with beads, the other with a small piece of fur. In the course of a divinatory session, the *mung'anga* conversed with the spirits of two dead people whom he described as living in the calabashes, and whom he occasionally made leave in order to travel to the homestead of the afflicted person to discover the cause of the disease. Such "storing" of spirits is common among *bang'anga* and is also presumed to be essential to the practices of witches. In the latter case, keeping malevolent spirits is thought to be of particular importance because "free-ranging" spirits might turn against their own master.

The relationship between non-Christian spirits, objects, and space is described in two other ways. Some of my interlocutors stated that spirits could serve a witch by conveying destructive magic items (like *insengo*) to their destination. Others felt that most magic items used in witchcraft should be understood as landmarks for the orientation of spirits: an *insengo* would thus represent a point of return for spiritual beings.

As regards the Holy Spirit, on the other hand, the idea of spiritual transportation is completely absent. Distributing the Bible and other Christian paraphernalia is considered to require human carriers, although the Holy Spirit is understood to be a prerequisite *movens*. Likewise, there is no notion of Christian objects being "landmarks" for the orientation of the Holy Spirit. *Muya usalala* is generally assumed to approach people, not objects. I encountered only one case in which the objects of a Christian denomination were interpreted as landmarks for spirits. The leader of a Pentecostal-charismatic church near Sinazeze compared the publications of the Jehovah's Witnesses (see also Kirsch 2007) with the witches' *insengo*, claiming that their publications are distributed in order to provide demons with points of orientation concerning whom to approach with their malevolent activities. It is very obvious, however, that this view denied the Jehovah's Witnesses the status of a *Christian* church; my interlocutor interpreted their dissemination of material objects, in the form of publications, as behavior reflecting non-Christian practices.

Thus, it was unthinkable to my interlocutors that anyone could succeed in keeping *muya usalala* in some type of material vessel. Instead, the Holy Spirit is conceived as an inevitably unbound and evanescent entity, which human beings cannot control in its movements. Against this background, *muya usalala* is presumed never to reside permanently at any particular material location, whether in the Bible or in any other object of Christian practice. And although the buildings of Pentecostal-charismatic churches are often said to be infused with divine powers, this does not mean that the Holy Spirit lives there permanently. For example, when a new shelter for one of the congregations of the Spirit Apostolic Church was constructed in 1999, it was not anticipated that the Holy Spirit might occupy the site itself, not even after a Christian altar had been installed. Prayers and sermons were needed to introduce the new building to *muya usalala*, which would then periodically take on a protective role toward it.

However, there is no guarantee for a Christian congregation that its site of worship is protected permanently. It is thus religious practice that is required in order to come into contact with the Holy Spirit. By themselves Christian symbols and objects cannot secure the presence of divine powers. This can only be obtained through the proper use of objects by actors who are already endowed with the power of *muya usalala*.

The unbounded nature of the Holy Spirit also relates to its association with human beings. *Muya usalala* selects its human mediums itself; it approaches appropriate persons, remains attached to them, and occasionally enters their bodies, and it can leave them at any time. In general, interpretations differ concerning the actual relationship between the Holy Spirit and human bodies. Many maintain that the body of an ordinary human person in its normal state resembles a tabula rasa. If one leads a proper Christian life, however, the Holy Spirit starts to be close to one's body and to surround it. And by means of communal efforts, like the singing of spiritual hymns, *muya usalala* can be induced to enter the body of the person concerned. Then, spiritual activities like witch finding, prophesy, or the exorcism of demons are to be expected. Others oppose the claim that the normal state of a human body can be compared to a tabula rasa. The bishop of the Spirit Apostolic Church in the mid-1990s, for example, insisted that everyone is endowed already at birth with some minor divine spirit and that this basic spirituality is essential to exist. The Holy Spirit in a stronger form could all the same enter the body and would then increase spiritual empowerment. The bishop asserted that having an interior tabula rasa would mean death and explained that invasion of the body by demons would also result in the person concerned dying. According to him, demons generally never enter humans but instead surround their bodies: the interior of a human being is reserved for divine beings. This view was admittedly rare, however, and was not even unanimously shared by the other elders of the same church.

Logistics of the Spirit

In many African-initiated churches in southern Africa, the Holy Spirit is thought to be associated with the "wilderness"—that is, with more or less remote, nonsocial realms. Short periods of meditative seclusion in the wilderness are thus an important element of religious practice. Senior church elders and prospective church leaders are expected to spend some time regularly in spatially and socially remote areas in order to strengthen or, if they are said to have become spiritually weak, reestablish a privileged relationship with the Holy Spirit.

In southern Zambia, when the elders of Pentecostal-charismatic churches return from the wilderness—usually hilltops in the relatively sparsely populated escarpment between the Gwembe Valley and the Central African Plateau—they are said to have become exceedingly powerful in spirituality. Some of my interlocutors metaphorically compared the newly spiritualized state of the returnees with a "battery" that had been "charged" during seclusion and was subsequently "discharged" through engagement in the spiritual activities of the community. Such activities, in turn, serve for the spiritual empowerment of others: through healing, preaching, laying on of hands, and praying, the religious experts bring the laity into close association with the Holy Spirit. In combination, these two processes—importing spiritual power from the "outside" to the social "inside" and then interpersonally transmitting it to members of the laity—constitute what I have called the "logistics of the spirit" (Kirsch 2008a).

Despite the imagery of a "battery," however, instances of the bodily incorporation of *muya usalala* are rare. Spiritually, therefore, capability does not imply that the person concerned "possesses" the Holy Spirit, in the sense of "having it incorporated permanently." Rather, it represents the likelihood that *muya usalala* will use the particular individual as a channel for contacting others. The logistics of the spirit pertaining to the importation of spiritual power from the "outside" to the social "inside" thus does not mean transporting the Holy Spirit as an entity but rather transporting the human channel for it.

At the same time, the interpersonal transmission of spiritual power to others is not only enacted during Sunday services and other Pentecostal-charismatic practices, such as the baptismal rites discussed above, but also constitutes a significant component of intercongregational visits by senior church elders. Broadly speaking, religious authority in the majority of the Pentecostal-charismatic churches in the area of my research evolves in the form of an extended dispersal of charisma (Shils 1958). Most church elders I have come to know over the years had brought about their association with *muya usalala* through an act of mediation involving someone who had previously achieved a reputation for spiritual capacity. In this way, authorization by the church elders is related to previous instances of spiritualization—that is, to centers of origination where the particular dispersal of charisma is supposed to have started.

I have argued elsewhere (Kirsch 2008b), with regard to the Spirit Apostolic Church (SAC), that the attempts by senior leaders of this church to restore their authority in 1999 brought about a complex combination of bureaucratic and Pentecostal-charismatic practices, which, in turn, were intricately connected with the dispersal of religious charisma as described above. On the one hand, the local branches expected the visitations of senior leaders to provide a spiritualizing input. Repeated acts of mediation were deemed necessary for the junior church leaders to achieve a close association with the Holy Spirit. When a branch leader visited headquarters, however, he was not expected to be capable of providing such an input of spirituality. The organizational structure of the SAC thus embedded a unidirectional, top-to-bottom flow of spirituality.

On the other hand, this was paralleled by a bureaucratic institutionalization at the branch level and a subsequent bottom-to-top flow of bureaucratic products. By granting certificates to the officeholders, the top echelons of the church endeavored to institutionalize their relationship with subordinate levels of the hierarchy in a form that resembled legal contracts. This particular form of authority, officially allocated to the junior church leaders, influenced how relationships and communication subsequently evolved. When approaching the senior church leaders, the branch leaders could either address them as mediums of the Holy Spirit—for example, as prophets or healers—or in terms of their function as incumbents. The senior leaders, by contrast, addressed the junior leaders solely as officeholders. Although several of branch leaders acted as prophets and healers in their respective branches, the senior leaders never officially acknowledged these roles. In contrast to the senior church elders, therefore, the branch leaders were not assumed to be speaking from the position of prophets or healers but only from their prescribed position as officeholders.

As incumbents, the branch leaders were consequently obliged to communicate with headquarters mainly by means of formalized bureaucratic procedures: the secretaries of the branches had to record the proceedings of church services. In these service reports, the general course of the worship, attendance numbers, and the amount of money collected were documented. Each year, these reports had to be handed over to the general secretary at the headquarters in Siamujulu village, who would then examine the activities of the respective congregations. Furthermore, membership registers were sometimes demanded from the branches, which would also subsequently be checked by one of the senior church elders. Using such procedures, the branch leaders were made to account for their efforts in evangelizing and their supervision of their respective congregations' religious practices. The Sunday reports and the membership registers thus constituted examples of a bottom-to-top flow of bureaucratic products. Whereas headquarters—apart from occasionally sending letters, distributing membership identity cards in individual instances, and sporadically issuing agendas for church meetings—was very reluctant to deliver documents to the branches, the local congregations were expected to report regularly to the main board in writing.

Thus, in 1999, the Spirit Apostolic Church was characterized by two prevailing flows in opposite directions of the institutional hierarchy: spirit from above and paper from below. This configuration shows, first, that the logistics of the spirit is a sociopolitically charged matter, and secondly, that the attempts of religious practitioners to control and channel the movement and worldly presence of the Holy Spirit form part of power struggles that are enacted not solely in spiritual but also in bureaucratic realms of life, or in a combination of both.

In sum, the type of spirit mobility discussed in this section fundamentally depends on physical movements by human beings in the form of either *journeys* (from the "outside" to the social "inside" and between the spatially distant congregations of a church) or *ritual interactions involving interpersonal contact* between religious practitioners (such as the laying on of hands or sprinkling "holy water" on baptism candidates). In other words, in this type of spirit mobility, the spatial radius of the Holy Spirit's mobility is relative to the readiness of religious practitioners to seek spiritual power by setting themselves in motion or by allowing themselves to be affected by others who have moved previously. People's movement thus precedes and premises spiritual movement; wherever humans have failed to go, the Spirit does not go.

Self-Multiplication

To probe into the second type of spirit mobility, let me briefly come back to the introductory section of this chapter. When describing the exorcisms performed in preparation of baptismal rites, I remarked that the power of the Holy Spirit is transmitted through prayed-upon "holy water," which, as I pointed out, does not automatically affect everybody who comes into bodily contact with it but always only the first person among those lined up on the river bank. I suggested that, in these ritual interactions, *muya usalala* performs exorcisms according to the bureaucratic logic of individualized sequencing in the spatial form of a line, which in effect means that the Holy Spirit addresses baptism candidates one by one, always moving from the first to the next in the row.

During Sunday services, a different type of spirit mobility can be observed whose logic is captured in the term *self-multiplication*. In Pentecostal-charismatic churches in the area of my research, church services continue for about two to four hours, usually involving different types of prayers, singing and dancing, a series of sermons, divination and healing sessions, a collection, notifications by the church secretary, and sometimes short speeches by the laity, in which they thank God.[7] For churchgoers, attending the services promises to enhance their religious knowledge and to enable them to fulfill their duties as Christians, as well as to provide a certain degree of entertainment. An additional and all-important motivation, however, lies in the striving to achieve direct experience of God in the form of *muya usalala*. Most activities during communal religious practice can thus be described as attempts to prepare oneself for personal contact with the Holy Spirit, or as actually enabling such contact.

With a view to the "emergent quality" (Bauman 1977) of church services, it is interesting to analyze how contact between the Holy Spirit and churchgoers sets in and develops in the course of ritual interactions. In all the Pentecostal-charismatic church services I attended, *muya usalala* made its initial appearance by inspiring one of the church elders while he or she was praying, singing, or dancing. What are commonly seen to be signs of a possession by *muya usalala* are a combination of different visible and audible symptoms of varying intensity such as swaying, absentmindedness with half-closed eyes or flickering eyelids, speaking in tongues, sighing and abruptly gasping out the names of biblical figures, and searching hand gestures.

In most cases, following this initial appearance of *muya usalala*, other church elders also exhibit such symptoms, occasionally giving rise to an atmosphere of collective effervescence with impassioned dancing and a blaring cacophony of glossolalic voices filling the church building. It is at this point of the ritual interaction that *muya usalala* starts manifesting itself among members of the laity, a process that can be inferred only *ex negativo* when witnessing what are considered to be symptoms of a demonic possession that is triggered by the presence of the Holy Spirit.

All in all, if the rituals are realized in felicitous ways, the Holy Spirit can thus be said to *self-multiply* in the course of church services, starting out from one of the church elders, then bringing its influence to bear on some of the other copresent elders and eventually on selected members of the laity attending the service. In this process, *muya usalala* manifests itself not in a contiguous spatial area but in distributed form—that is, here and there throughout the ritual space, with the interstitial spaces remaining unaffected by its spiritual powers.

This logic of self-multiplication is not only typical of ritual interactions during Sunday services but at times also of how the different, spatially distant congregations of a church interact with each other. It is common practice among Pentecostal-charismatic churches that a congregation recites prayers for other congregations of the same church in order to strengthen their religious commitment and powers. In most cases I witnessed, prayers of this kind involved appeals to God to empower the other congregations spiritually—that is, literally to inspire them with the power of the Holy Spirit, and as a result to enable them to resist sins, to prophesy, and to conduct healings. At the same time, members of these churches told me that it is possible for them to sense internally if some other churchgoer had been praying for them because, as an instantaneous effect of such prayers, they would feel physically and religiously invigorated by the Holy Spirit and called upon to continue with their Christian work. Thus, comparable to what I noted in relation to Sunday services, praying for other congregations can lead to a self-multiplication of *muya usalala*, in this case covering great spatial distances.

In contrast to what I discussed in the previous section, self-multiplication refers to a type of spirit mobility in which the starting point and the end point(s) of the Holy Spirit's trajectory are *not* interconnected through spatial movements on the ground. In other words, while the logistics of the spirit examined above require the physical and unintermitted transport of the human channel for the Holy Spirit from, say, point A to B, the type of spirit mobility discussed here means, in a manner of speaking, that *muya usalala* perceptibly changes its position in space by making itself present at different locations at the same time. This is surely a miraculous way of moving but also a familiar phenomenon in Pentecostal-charismatic churches, whose members do not inhabit a demarcated and contiguous area but are spatially dispersed throughout different regions, with people of other religious faiths inhabiting the areas in between. It is also a type of spirit mobility that helps us understand why and in what ways Pentecostal-charismatic churches often have and have had subversive effects on the geographies of other religious traditions, non-Pentecostal Christianity included.

Spiritual Scaling

Coming now to the third type of spirit mobility, which I call "spiritual scaling," we need to first explore some aspects of the gestalt of the Holy Spirit as enacted in the area of my research. A comparison with the other two types of spirit mobility discussed in the present chapter makes it clear that each of them is associated with a spirit morphology that differs from that of the others.

In the first type, where the spirit's movements are dependent on and relative to human movements, the "size" and "shape" of the Holy Spirit principally corresponds to the spatial dimensions of the human beings it uses as its physical channels. In other words, when being imported from the "outside" to the social "inside," the spiritual entity called *muya usalala* is actually small and bounded enough to join a church elder on the back of a lorry when the latter returns to his home village from a meditative seclusion in the wilderness (see also Kirsch 2008a), and it is also "handy" enough to be transmitted by the laying on of hands or by sprinkling "holy water" on baptism candidates.

Compare this to the morphology of the Holy Spirit that is characteristic of the second type of spirit mobility, "self-multiplication." In this type of mobility, *muya usalala* also has a bounded shape but differs from each of its human channels in that it is not one but many—or rather, in that its beingness is one and many at the same time, and in that it would occasionally multiply itself from being one to being many or, vice versa, reduce itself from being many to being one. I have suggested above that this self-multiplication is a form of mobility because it involves perceptible changes in the Holy Spirit's position in space. However, changing its position in this way does not mean that *muya usalala* "moves through" or "fills" the space in between the locations of where it makes itself present. Instead, it travels by coming out of transcendence's nowhere and it does so at different places at the same time. Moreover, while synchronous manifestations of the Holy Spirit at different places are believed to be essentially self-identical—that is, to pertain to one and the same spiritual entity—the process of self-multiplication involves a change in the spirit's morphology from a single manifestation of a bounded entity to a spatially dispersed set of self-identical, bounded manifestations of this same spiritual entity.

The existence of these different morphologies of *muya usalala* points to what might be called "the problem of methodological individualism in the anthropological study of spiritual entities." With this I am not saying that anthropologists have unduly concentrated on single ("individual") spirits, nor that I would want to persuade them to pursue analyses with a view to "collectivities" of spirits. I have the impression, however, that not enough attention has been paid to the fact that spirits and human beings differ not only in their respective forms of agency but also in their morphology and—most importantly for my argument in the present section—in their "scale."

As has hopefully become clear in the preceding pages, *muya usalala* as conceived of and experienced by members of Pentecostal-charismatic churches in the area of my research is a peculiar entity that is associated with several conceptual paradoxes. Concerning its essence of being, *muya usalala* is assumed to be identical with and yet also different from God (*leza*). As regards its "size," *muya usalala* is considered to be both a local and a supralocal force. At the same time, while manifestations of *muya usalala* are said to be unique and singular events, it is also considered a truism that it can simultaneously manifest itself at different places at once. In addition, as discussed above, *muya usalala* is conceptualized both as a spatially extensive entity—that is, bound to place and filling space—and on other occasions as an unbounded entity that has the capacity to self-multiply and manifest itself at different places without occupying or traveling through the space between them. Awareness of this paradoxical nature of *muya usalala* can help us avoid the traps of methodological individualism in the study of spiritual entities, where the idea of "ghosts"—that is, humanlike spiritual "individuals" endowed with extraordinary skills and faculties—often serves as a blueprint for the analysis of all different types and classes of spiritual entities.

The third type of spirit mobility examined in the present chapter, "spiritual scaling," is a good example of why such blueprints are problematic when we try to grasp what characterizes the mobility of the Holy Spirit. I have shown above that *muya usalala* has the capacity for self-multiplication, which mostly takes place during church services and during prayers for others. However, collective efforts by churchgoers can also lead to a situation in which the Holy Spirit is felt to be present in such an extraordinary intensity that everyone entering the ritual scene is automatically affected by its power. On such occasions, similar to what I described above, *muya usalala* makes its initial appearance by inspiring one of the church elders while he or she is praying, singing, or dancing. However, in contrast to spirit mobility by self-multiplication, this initial inspiration does not affect only selected individuals positioned at a spatial distance from each other but leads to a *self-expansion* of the Holy Spirit, so that its beingness pervades the entirety of the ritual space and sometimes even stretches beyond it. On the other hand, in case the churchgoers' collective efforts to appease the Holy Spirit lose strength, *muya usalala* decreases its "size" by *self-contraction* and sometimes even retracts in its entirety from the ritual space.

Taken together, while undoubtedly involving a perceptible change of position in space, this type of spirit mobility does not take the form of a movement from A to B. Instead, it represents a spatial pulsation between microscale and macroscale that is accomplished by a self-induced "upscaling" and "downscaling" of the gestalt of the Holy Spirit and results in a spiritual permeation of space on different (local, regional, transregional) scales.

Some Words in Conclusion

In terms of the concepts used, the most radical step undertaken in this chapter probably consists in taking seriously and literally the conventional definition of *movement* as a "perceivable change of an entity's position in space." As I have shown, if applied to the Holy Spirit as conceived of and experienced by members of Pentecostal-charismatic churches in present-day southern Zambia, this concept can bring about surprising and captivating insights into different types of spirit mobility.

I have identified three different types of spirit mobility—"logistics of the spirit," "self-multiplication," and "spiritual scaling"—each of which is implicit in specific aspects of Pentecostal-charismatic practice and associated with distinct spatialized morphologies of the Holy Spirit. One does not have to be intellectually worried about the fact that these different morphologies and mobilities of *muya usalala* are—at least in part— incompatible with each other in terms of their formal logic. From the perspective of members of Pentecostal-charismatic churches in the area of my research, worries of this kind would normally be considered as yet another proof of the fallibility of human intellection and the impossibility of understanding divinity.

The considerations developed in this chapter can be seen as an initial step in what might lead to a rewriting of geographies of Pentecostal-charismatic Christianity. This initial step entails, first, conceptualizing the Holy Spirit not just as an object of knowledge or representation but as an agency of divine ontology in its own right; secondly, carefully avoiding the problem of methodological individualism in the anthropological study of spiritual entities by taking account of the idea that spiritual entities come in different "sizes" and "shapes"; and thirdly, taking seriously the fieldwork observation that, for the Holy Spirit, mobility can be enacted not only by journeying but also through purposely changing morphology. Rewriting Pentecostal-charismatic geographies along these lines promises to shed new light on the Spiritistic dialectics of agency and patiency, identity formation in Christian religions of the spirit, the dynamics of socio-spiritual inclusion and exclusion, and attempts by Pentecostal-charismatic actors hegemonically to legitimize certain types of spirit mobility and delegitimize (subversive) others.

As regards the latter point, the types of spirit mobility discussed above differ in their spatial form: the "logistics of the spirit" takes the form of a *network*, the Holy Spirit's "self-multiplication" produces a *scattering*, and "spiritual scaling" is enacted in the form of an *oscillating permeation of space*. In this way, these types of spirit mobility stand for different strategies in constituting and realizing socio-spiritual communities, with "logistics of the spirit" presupposing the interpersonal transmission of the Holy Spirit, "self-multiplication" allowing for the emergence of semi-autonomous centers of spiritualization, and "spiritual scaling" incorporating virtually everything within its bounds. Against this backdrop, laying emphasis on one of them at the exclusion of the others often serves as a means to establish Pentecostal-charismatic authority or to delegitimize the claims to spiritual authority by coreligionists.

At the same time, however, we always need to bear in mind that ambitions by human beings to keep the Holy Spirit in check have their natural limits in the quintessential evanescence of this spiritual entity, which, as practitioners of Pentecostal-charismatic Christianity never tire of emphasizing, would never allow its own agency to be entirely contained by human agency. Given this unboundedness of the Holy Spirit, should we really wonder about the extraordinary forms of mobility it exhibits? After all, the social life of spirits is but a life of miracles.

CHAPTER THREE

What the Invisible Looks Like

Ghosts, Perceptual Faith, and Mongolian Regimes of Communication

Grégory Delaplace

If you ask a Mongolian herder what a "ghost" (*süns, chötgör*) is, his first answer might well be that he has no idea, because he has never encountered one. He might also add that you should stop believing everything you are told, and that most of the things you might have heard on this topic are mere "lies" (*hudal*). The ruthless repression of the Buddhist clergy in the 1930s, and the promotion of Marxist-Leninist ideology throughout the country during the nearly seventy-year period after Mongolia became a popular republic under the aegis of the USSR in 1924, could account for some of the general skepticism expressed by the population today toward these phenomena, at least in rural areas.[1]

If you insist for long enough, however, you might end up being told that "ghosts" are supposed to originate from the "souls" (*süns*) of people who "could not find a proper rebirth" (*jinhene töröl ooogüi*). The reason for this could be either that they remained attached to persons or things in this world or that funerary rituals were not performed properly—which eventually amounts to the same, as funerary rituals are meant to break any attachment the deceased may keep to their former environments (Delaplace 2009b). Alternatively, ghosts might be described as frustrated beings who died before they could fulfill their "desires" (*taachal*). At any rate, they are imagined to be extremely lonely creatures, craving sociability and trying to lure the ones they loved during life into joining them in death.

According to these ideas, ghosts are mere glitches in the cycle of reincarnations guaranteed by the Buddhist clergy, whereby people are to

be reborn as their own direct descendants, provided they—or their families—performed enough "good deeds" (*buyan*) to be spared a stay in one
of the sixteen scorching or freezing hells (Sazykin 1979), or a vile rebirth
as a flightless insect (Even 1999). Ritual specialists, Buddhist lamas or lay
practitioners known as "skilled persons" (*mergen hün*), are expected to be
able to subdue these ghosts by satisfying their frustrations, or by breaking
the last bonds that tie them to this world.

This ontological definition of what a ghost is, however, fails to account
for the various forms under which ghosts may be reported to manifest
themselves, by people who claimed to have encountered them. Moreover,
it overlooks the crucial clue contained in the doubt expressed by herders on this issue, mentioned at the outset. Saying that we cannot know
anything for sure about ghosts unless we have encountered one ourselves
suggests that ghosts are first and foremost a matter of perception.

It is not only Mongolians who draw this close connection between knowledge and perception of ghosts; this has already been picked up by Pierre
Déléage (2007; see also Taylor 1993) concerning the Amazonian Sharanahua, and it appears clearly too in many ethnographies concerned with
ghosts and/or spirits, from Iceland (Pons 2002, 109) to Nepal (Schlemmer
2004, 115–22). One could argue that the intrinsic link between perception
and knowledge also forms the plot of several Victorian literary ghost stories—ghosts are typically things about which a character's opinion changes
dramatically once he encounters one (e.g., see Conan Doyle's famous novel
The Land of Mist). It emerges even more strongly from the early spiritualist literature, where a "scientific" examination of phenomena related to
the manifestation of ghosts relies almost entirely on the close inspection of
what supposedly reliable witnesses experienced (Flammarion 1924).

In this chapter, I single out and analyze what specific sensation is recognized as an encounter with a ghost in Mongolia. I base this on a corpus
of narratives collected from Dörvöd nomadic herders in northwestern
Mongolia.[2] In these narratives, the beings that appear to people are not
always identified as the spirits of particular persons (what are called
"revenants" in French, as opposed to "fantômes"). Sometimes they are
indeed "souls" (*süns*) of young people, or of old ladies, coming back to
haunt their relatives, but they are actually most often unidentified specters
(called alternatively *chötgör, güidel, oroolon*) encountered in the open,
without any indication of, or concern for, the "soul" they might originate
from. Sometimes, it is even unclear in witnesses' accounts whether the
encountered entity is the soul of a human person, or of a nonhuman "land
master" (*gazryn ezen*)—a spirit that dwells in a specific area and is held

responsible for such phenomena as weather, livestock health, or fortune in hunting. As we will also see, witnesses are not always eager to subdue the ghost by appealing to a ritual specialist: most often the apparition is carefully avoided and left to haunt the place where it was unwittingly encountered. Finally, the corporeal quality attributed to such entities varies greatly from one story to another, as well as across Mongolia. Whereas some "ghosts" (*güidel*) are likened to currents flowing through places (Delaplace 2011), "little humans" (Delaplace & Empson 2007) or "imps" (Swancutt 2008) with apparently full-fledged corporeality might also be reported to haunt houses.

Mongolian people use the broad category "invisible things" (*üzegdehgüi yum*) to refer collectively to all these entities. This expression echoes a point made, once again, by Pierre Déléage (2007): characterizing these things as "invisible" does not mean that *nobody* can ever see them—otherwise they would cause little trouble—but that their encounter is subject to a specific perceptual modality. In other words, they cannot be experienced in the same way as, for example, living people and cattle: rather than absolutely "invisible," these "things" are perceivable only by some people, in certain contexts, and in a particular way.

Meanwhile, the anthropological literature on ghosts, especially the Anglophone literature, has tended to analyze them in relation to the sociohistorical context they arose in. Thus, ghosts have been famously studied as local responses to global capitalism (MacLellan 1991), or as mirrors of the changes occurring with the advent of consumer society (Kwon 2007, Kendall 2008). On the other hand, recent works have shown the importance of ghosts in the way people deal with their recent history (e.g., Mueggler 2001; Bear 2007; Kwon 2008). In contemporary Vietnam, for example, some households find themselves haunted by young soldiers who died far from home and without an appropriate burial. People's experiences, in this context, are organized around the discovery of the ghost's identity and life story, always tightly linked to the country's traumatic history (Kwon 2008, 109–13). In contrast, Dörvöd herders do not seem to encounter ghosts related to their historical past. The history of Manchu colonization, the revolution, and the repressed uprisings that occurred precisely in this region in the 1920s (e.g., Bawden 1968, 266) have not been fodder for such experiences. Yet, the stories told by Dörvöd herders, as opposed to those I could collect in the capital city, Ulaanbaatar, for instance (Delaplace 2010), are primarily concerned with the way people dwell in places.

As mentioned at the outset of this paper, doubt is absolutely central in these narratives. Not only is any story of an encounter with "invisible things" suspected to be a "lie," but the perception through which the ghost appears to the senses of a witness is also ambiguous to himself or herself. As already shown elsewhere (Delaplace 2009a, 249–55), the dimmer and more transient (i.e., the more uncertain) the perception, the more it will become credible to the audience as the manifestation of an "invisible thing." The uncertain and ambiguous nature of these sensations is at the center of what makes them uncanny to witnesses. Furthermore, and on another level, I want to show that the uncertain perception recognized as a ghost casts doubts on human perception itself, shaking what Maurice Merleau-Ponty has called "perceptual faith" (Merleau-Ponty 1968, 3). Mongolian ghost stories—and this probably applies outside of Mongolia too—seem to describe a swift disruption in the witness's bodily engagement in the world by furtively disclosing an invisible dimension to it. Experiences of encounters with "invisible things" seem to give an uncanny hint that the world might not always be "what we see" (ibid.). On this basis, I will outline the specific *regime of communication* that corresponds to interactions with ghosts in Mongolia: that is, the peculiar perceptual modality according to which these entities are encountered.

Encountering the Invisible

In the course of my work with the Dörvöd of northwestern Mongolia, I have collected several stories of people who thought that they had encountered a "ghost" (*süns*, *chötgör*, *güidel*, *oroolon*, etc.).[3] I recorded these narratives not only from people who were famous as storytellers in the region but also from anybody who would recount an experience. Most of the time, these narratives are presented as mere anecdotes and told in a matter-of-fact way; some are highly elaborate and detailed, others quite allusive, but all of them relate an experience interpreted as the manifestation of an "invisible thing."

One of the most talented storytellers I have met is certainly Tselei. In 2004, she was a forty-year-old mother of three, and she was leading a seemingly quiet life herding sheep, goats, and yaks with her husband. However, she had had over the past three or four years quite a lot of experiences related to ghosts. My friend Gansüh, her brother, knew this and took me to her place to ask her to retell these experiences. Here is one of the first stories she chose to tell:

One night I was sleeping, and something like brushed and pulled on my leg. So I woke up with a start and thought that I must have changed my leg's position or something like that. And I went back to sleep. The following evening, a friend of mine was marrying his daughter. I went there and came back after midnight. My daughter was a baby at that time, and I was breast-feeding her. I put her to sleep. At our encampment there was Tsegmed, the ritual specialist, and his family, but Tsegmed had gone to the village. And then while I was sleeping, something, like that, right under the blanket, something like pulled my leg. So I woke up suddenly and I got really frightened, with all these weird things. I was lying on my bed thinking of an explanation for all this, and the baby who was on my belly—*tschiss!*—she burst out crying all of a sudden, in the middle of the night. So I rocked her in my arms, I tried to breast-feed her, but she refused. And my husband, he was sleeping! I was calling him but he wouldn't wake up!

"Wake up, wake up!" I called him.

"What happened?" he said, getting up

"Something pulled my leg!"

"What kind of bloody ghost could pull your leg?"

And here we go *hat hatlag*, arguing in the middle of the night. So I told my husband, "Go and find someone who knows and can!" He went out, and he came back with Tsegmed. Tsegmed took his rosary out. He examined it and said, "One of your very close friends died in the spring. This person's soul came back to you." And indeed, when we were in Ulaangom [the administrative center of the province], it is true that we were with another family. One of them had died in the spring and this person's soul had come to us. So Tsegmed told me to take a notebook on which he put meat, fat, butter, flour, fritters, dry cheese, and sugar. He gave these things to me and read prayers. He put water in a bowl, added milk, and then he prayed again and again. Then he told me, "Walk twenty-one steps from your house. Put this on the ground and come back walking backward. Wash your hands and come back in." I was very afraid so he told me, "If you hear a noise, don't be afraid!" I don't quite remember what happened. I took this thing out in the dark, I walked twenty-one steps, I put it on the ground, I went back walking backward, washed my hands, and then the paper sounded—*sart!* In the morning I woke up and went to see it. On the paper, the meat, the cheese, everything had disappeared. It is as if this man's soul had come, had fed on all this, and then had been expelled by the power of prayers.

Coming back a bit later to this same experience, Tselei commented that "souls come back to those whom they loved," visibly moved by the touching attention, however desperate and gruesome, showed by this young neighbor of hers. This narrative recounts the progressive uncovering of *a Solidifies*

the ghost's identity—from a doubted sensation to an invisible presence, eventually recognized as a named person. Interestingly, this is achieved through a strong dissociation between the *perception* of the ghost and its *identification*: whereas Tselei is indeed the main witness to the ghost's manifestation, she appears to take no part in its designation as such, which is presented as the other characters' doing.

To Mongol ears, the first assessment of the ghost's presence is certainly the baby's behavior. It is indeed generally believed in Mongolia that infants can feel the presence of invisible things, mostly ghosts, while grown-up persons cannot, and the presence of ghosts is a usual explanation for sudden and irrepressible cries from a newborn (Aubin 1975). Here, Tselei does not even draw any such conclusion herself but tries to wake up her sleepy and rather unconcerned husband. Now, even if the husband is being ironic, he is actually the first person to pronounce the word "ghost" (*süns*), articulating what the baby had expressed through her behavior. The husband's ironic comment is later confirmed by the diagnosis of Tsegmed, the ritual specialist, who not only identifies the manifestation as a ghost but also recognizes it as the spirit of a specific person. In this account, clearly, Tselei overlooks her own part in the ghost's identification as her young neighbor. In fact, the ritual specialist only gives a clue—"one of your very close friends died in the spring"—on the basis of which Tselei infers that it must concern the young neighbor they had in Ulaangom. This last step, by which an actual event (the death of a person) is matched up with the specialist's diagnosis (a dead person came back to you), is presented by Tselei as a logical conclusion rather than a personal opinion.

Solidifies

In contrast to the distance she takes toward the ghost's identification, Tselei renders with great care and narrative skill the perceptual dimension of her experience. Her story, on the one hand, brings forth an evocative soundscape punctuated with powerful, or even loud, noises: the baby cries out in the night's silence, with a sudden intensity rendered by the onomatopoeia *tchiss*; then the argument between the spouses rolls in with a thunder-like succession of roaring noises, *hat hattag*. On the other hand, Tselei superimposes on this auditory background two sensory feelings, which stand out as uncommon. If they seem so, it is not that they are in any way stronger than the other perceptions described; on the contrary, they seem dimmer and swifter. They are described as feelings that are gone before they can be fully sensed: discreet sensations felt on the brink of sleep, and yet unmistakably real.

indirect perception of spirit

Tselei renders the particularity of this feeling using, beside the rather common verbs "to brush" (*samna-*) and "to pull" (*tata-*), the preposition "like" (*shig*). It is to be noted that each time she evokes the manifestation of the ghost, she uses the same preposition: she does not say "something pulled my leg," but "something *shig* pulled my leg." This word is rather common in Mongolian (Kullman and Tserenpil 1996, 287, 296, 311): added directly to a noun or a pronoun, it expresses a relation of similitude (*cham shig neg hün*, "a person like you"), and added to a verb, in the expression *yum shig*, it means "as if" (*chi medeegüi yum shig*, "as if you didn't know"). Here, added directly after the verb compound, it seems to qualify the sensation as an uncertain one—it felt *as if* something had brushed and pulled her leg. But even more than this, by likening the sensation to what it could have been, Tselei makes the indirect statement that this is precisely *not* what the sensation was: it was similar to a feeling of brushing and pulling, but it was not quite that. It was something else.

Comparing the Incomparable

As a matter of fact, comparative devices are often found in Dörvöd ghost stories to describe the ghost's manifestation. Here is an example, taken from another story told by Tselei:

> At that time, I was only a child, [. . .][4] I was working in Tarialan's hospital. One winter, one of our doctors was called for a patient [who was about to give birth] in Harhiraa mountains. She took me along me with her, because I knew the way in Harhiraa. I was working at the nursery. So she took me along and we drove to the patient's. I was showing her the way, and right below Türgen's Har Üzüür, the car broke in the snow. So Jumdlaa the doctor and I were together and the night was falling. [. . .] We went uphill together. We were walking and suddenly a metallic *jinger jinger* starts following us closely. I was scared: "What's happening? Something is following us!" I was very scared, and I walked in front of the doctor, I was scared. Then the doctor said, "Come on, my child, these are yaks with their bells passing by, these are fettered horses." But I was really scared, I was a child. [. . .] We arrived at Batsüh's [. . .] and [his wife] had already given birth. The doctor came in to examine the mother, and we were about to leave but it was pitch-dark outside. Going back to the car in the middle of the night scared me, and I said to Batsüh, "I won't be able to walk there! We walked together before. I won't be able to walk, please saddle up a horse!"
>
> "I'll saddle up a horse," said Batsüh, and then he added jokingly, "All my yaks have bells. It's their bells you've heard!"

So the doctor and I rode back to the car. And on our way back, Jumdlaa the doctor said [to the driver of the car], "How dark it is! And we've just encountered a ghost! I was scared, but the girl was scared too, so I pretended these were just fettered horses, cattle with their bells passing by."

This is just . . . I was only a child, and when I came home I tried to strike a piece of metal. But it was not the same sound coming out of this piece of metal. Very strange. *Jinger jinger*, a very soft metallic sound following us closely. Nothing visible. Nothing to be seen with the eyes.

[handwritten margin note: Invisible]

The story features the same strict separation between identification and perception, although in this case it is another kind of specialist who is responsible for identifying the apparition. Jumdlaa, the elder woman with whom Tselei walks in the mountains at dusk, is not only a doctor but presumably also someone who is able to see ghosts plainly and fully. Contrary to Tsegmed, the ritual specialist of the previous narrative, she does not undertake to exorcise the ghost from the place it seems to haunt, neither does she even intend to "recognize" whose spirit it originates from. This does not even seem to be at stake here: the phenomenon is identified generically as "a ghost" (*güits*) by the doctor, who makes sure Tselei does not suffer the sudden "shock" (*cochirol*) that is supposed to be felt by people who come in direct contact with an apparition. The doctor thus lies, with the cunning complicity of the patient's husband, in order to spare Tselei any kind of fright while they remain in this potentially dangerous situation.

[handwritten margin note: in-solidified]

While the composition—the plot, one might say—of the narrative is completely different from the first one, the way its sensory dimension is described seems quite comparable. In this story, a very distinctive sound (rendered by the onomatopoeia *jinger jinger*) stands out from a mostly visual background (the snowy mountains progressively immersed in darkness). The metallic sound interpreted as a ghost here is not as swift and uncertain as the sensation of the first narrative (it is "following" the witness), and yet, it is also rendered using an implicit analogy. In this case, the comparison is made *without* any comparative term. Still, the final sequence in which Tselei tries, and fails, to reproduce the metallic sound she heard using actual metal conveys the idea that what she heard sounded *like* metal, but not quite. In other words, it was a metallic sound that sounded like *no existing* metallic object. This is the way the straightforward comparison used to describe her first experience should also be interpreted: using the preposition "like" (*shig*), Tselei describes a feeling of brushing and pulling that resembled no brushing and pulling experience she had ever had. The

[handwritten margin note: terru-u!]

manifestation of invisible things is described in these stories as something absolutely *singular*, which can only be described in similitude to existing things.

Interestingly, Mongolian herders are not the only ones who resort to similes to describe the apparition of a ghost. The Kulung Rai of Nepal, as documented by Grégoire Schlemmer (2004), when recounting an alleged apparition, insist that it sounded "*like* a bell ringing," "*like* the bell-belts worn by diviners," or "*like* a drumming sound" (2004, 115, emphasis added). Even further in space and time, among the Cluniac monks of medieval Europe, Jean-Claude Schmitt (1994, 40) has reported the use of the adverb "quasi" in descriptions of apparitions. The same phenomenon has been noted by Emmanuel de Vienne (2010, 178) among the Amazonian Trumai, who use the word *nawan*, translated in French by the author as "comme," to describe the way "spirits" (*denetsak*) appear to people. Sensations likely to be interpreted as manifestations of the invisible are described as absolutely singular perceptions, which can only be likened to something else, while remaining distinct from it. The comparisons drawn in ghost stories in Mongolia or elsewhere point to an open-ended sensory space, an object of perception that cannot be fully apprehended, a breach in the perceived world that witnesses can grasp only partially yet cannot circumscribe.

Of course, comparative devices, in the various forms presented above, are not the only ways to describe apparitions of the invisible, not even in Mongolia. A third story resorts to an even more peculiar narrative technique used to render the way a ghost appeared. It was told to me by Bümbeejav, who is Tselei's sister-in-law's husband (HZH). The scene recounted here dates back to a time when Bümbeejav was a little boy traveling with his grandfather.

This happened at the entrance of Yol valley. One of my grandparents had come to fetch me in the village. He was called Aragshaa, and he was a great lama. So we were following a narrow path through the entrance of the valley, when the night suddenly fell. Everything became very dark. And then, right at the moment when we were ascending toward the valley, a smell of fritters came to my nostrils. My grandfather told me, "You go first my boy," so I went forward with my horse, my grandfather behind me. And while we were going I smelt an intense odor of fritter.

"Oh grandfather, are they making fritters up there?"

"Oh yes, I guess so my boy."

And we kept going. Finally we arrived and I went to sleep. At that moment, I had forgotten this odor of fritters. So I was going to sleep and then my grandfather started to talk. He said that I had seen nothing but that there was a smell. He said I had heard the smell, and that just behind the rock of Yerööl, he had seen an old lady. She was taking out large square fritters to drain them. Himself, he was someone who could see things with his eyes. Then he read a prayer and blew on me, in case something had taken refuge in me.

This narrative is built according to the same model as the second one by Tselei. Both narrators are young at the time of the story; they are accompanied by someone who is much older and who seems to see plainly what the witnesses can only feel dimly—I shall come back to this point. In both stories, also, this elder figure lies to the young witness so as to not frighten him or her and to avoid the ghost safely. Then both stories end with the truth being revealed and the true origin of the strange perception being uncovered. Like in the first excerpt, in both these stories the perception of the ghost and its identification are absolutely separate.

Considering now the way Bümbeejav describes his perception, we clearly observe that no comparative device is used. The narrator simply relates that a smell of fritters came to his nostrils. However, toward the end of his story he uses the strangest expression: he says that he "*heard the smell.*" It is not very likely that it could be a mere slip of the tongue, as Bümbeejav repeats again afterward, "I didn't see her but I *heard* her smell." This figure of speech is called in poetry "synesthesia," and it is defined as "the poetic description of a sense impression in terms of another sense" (*New Oxford American Dictionary*). This expression might not be a conscious rhetorical technique used by the narrator to convey the specific quality of what he smelt. Rather, this astonishing synesthesia might be the spontaneous, and perhaps unconscious, rendering of the perfectly singular character of Bümbeejav's experience. The smell was so singular that it almost did not qualify as a smell. The smell was so singular, and uncanny, that it felt almost like a sound. This synesthesia would then constitute a radical version of Tselei's comparative expressions, the evocation of an absolutely unique, nonreproducible, sensory feeling—for what could be more uncannily singular than a smell you *hear*?

What the Invisible Looks Like

On the basis of the material presented so far it seems possible to characterize the particular kind of experience that might be recognized as a ghost in Mongolia. A few comparative examples taken from other parts of the world show that, to a certain extent, this might also apply to other cases. One can stress at least three features to people's encounters with invisible things in Mongolia. First, I already pointed out that there is something to do with the *singularity* of the sensation interpreted as a ghost. Ghosts appear through perceptions that are at the same time similar to past experiences yet absolutely distinct and unique: they look familiar and are yet definitely strange to the witnesses' experience. The eerie feeling produced by the encounter of something familiar yet radically foreign—which has been famously exposed by Freud, although with a very different analytical agenda—seems to be at the center of all the ghost stories considered so far; it is really the crux of all the comparative devices found not only in Mongolia but also in Nepal and Europe.[5]

There is a second feature in these stories that makes the encounters they depict uncanny, and it has to do with *agency*. It is quite notable that ghosts, in these stories, almost never appear as such to witnesses: rather, they occur to them through the actions they perform. You could argue that in Bümbeejav's story, the ghost appears fully to his grandfather, in the form of an old lady, but this is precisely because he is *not* an ordinary witness; he is "someone who sees with his eyes" (*nüdeer yum üzdeg hün*), as Bümbeejav himself specifies. To all others, to ordinary people, ghosts become manifest through the sensations produced by an action they are performing, and witnesses feel compelled to impute a necessary cause to an observed effect. Thus, in the first story, Tselei experiences the feeling of being touched and pulled, which supposes *someone* to perform this action. In the second, she hears a ringing sound, which implies the presence of *someone* activating a bell—or in this case something; the possibility that cattle might also produce a ringing sound being cunningly exploited by the doctor and her patient's husband. In the third account, Bümbeejav smells an odor of fritters, which supposes *someone* in the process of cooking them. In other words, these sensations are strongly indexical of an agency, yet *in the absence of any perceivable agent*—something narrators sometimes insist on ("there was no one in sight").

In some instances, the necessary presence of agency behind the phenomenon perceived by narrators emerges logically from its repetition. The sensations experienced by Tselei, for example, are distinctly persistent, in a way that definitely rules out the possibility of a random and spontaneous phenomenon. A single sensation of pulling on her leg could have been the effect of her own unconscious movement during the night, whereas repeated brushing and pulling could only be caused by someone. The same with the staccato *jinger jinger* following her: a single metallic sound could be mistaken for something else—for example, a stone she unwittingly kicked and which hit on a metallic bit sticking out from the snow. As for the fritters smell, it is obviously linked with a human presence, as they do not grow naturally. The plot of Dörvöd ghost stories is built around the contradicted expectations of witnesses who encounter phenomena that suppose agency while there is no agent possibly present.[6]

Western folklore, on the other hand, is full of ghosts that witnesses actually see, and that they mistake for people; even in Mongolia, as mentioned at the beginning of the chapter, "ghosts" might take a more solid corporeal form than they do in the stories presented. These situations, however, seem to correspond to a parallel and symmetrical situation in which the agents who appear do not act in any expectable, or even understandable, manner. In a way, they are agents with a dysfunctional agency, with whom it is impossible to communicate. This is a recurrent trait in encounters with the invisible across societies: one could evoke, for example, the returning souls among Siberian Nganassan, who appear to people under the guise of persons repeating systematically the words of greetings said to them by unfortunate passersby, who will eventually get upset and enter in deadly fights with the apparitions (Lambert 2002–2003, 313). Open any good collection of literary ghost stories (e.g., Dalby 1988): the plot is often built around the description of the ghost's uncanny mode of action. Conversely, this is what is so funny in Oscar Wilde's short story *The Canterville Ghost* (1887): not only are the witnesses not at all impressed by the ghost but they can talk to him, scold him, comfort him, or convince him to use oil for his old, squeaky armor. What is unusual with the Canterville ghost is precisely that he is an agent with a transparent agency, with whom communication is not a problem.

Finally, a third feature of the sensations described in the stories presented above is that they are somehow *lacking* in their nature. Not only are they often very fugitive, and disappear as soon as they have appeared, but these sensations are also typically fragmentary. Indeed, contrary to ordinary perceptions which stimulate simultaneously several senses, the perceptions described in these narratives only occur to witnesses through *one* of their senses. Whereas in an ordinary situation I would see *and* hear someone talking to me, and I would see, hear, *and* smell someone frying fritters, ghosts in these accounts are heard, *or* smelt, *or* touched, but not seen. Alternatively, when they are seen, they cannot be heard, or they cannot be touched. In other words, the sensations described in these narratives are characteristically *incomplete*.[7] This certainly adds to the uncanny character of the encounter, inasmuch as it shakes what Merleau-Ponty

(1968, 3) has called the "perceptual faith"—the certainty that "the world is what we see."

NoPE

Haunting as Disrupted Dwelling: Shaking the Perceptual Faith

In the *Phenomenology of Perception*, published in 1945, Merleau-Ponty convincingly challenges the view of humans as subjects contained within the limits of their bodies. According to his view, we do not find our way into the world by deciphering the information brought by our senses from the outside into the prison of our body. Perception, moreover, does not consist in the intellectual combination of information provided by all the senses: on the contrary, as we move into the world, our senses merge into a single perception. Thus, in his last and posthumously published work, *The Visible and the Invisible*, Merleau-Ponty stresses that "in perception we witness the miracle of a totality that surpasses what one thinks to be its conditions or its parts, that from afar holds them under its power, as if they existed only on its threshold and were destined to lose themselves in it" (1968, 8).

Merleau-Ponty takes the example of binocular vision to illustrate this "miracle" of perception: binocular vision is not obtained by combining two monocular views, it is a continuous synthesis in which monocular views disappear as such. In the same way, vision, smell, and touch are brought together by the whole body in movement, in a continuous perception of the world. Furthermore, Merleau-Ponty argues that our involvement in the world is prior to our objectification of the world, or that existence in the world is a necessary precondition to perceiving it—we are always *in* the world while we conceive of it. Perception is not the world coming into us; it is "being out there" in the world. We experience perception in action, and we engage in the world by perceiving it with our whole body.

Now, looking back at the witnesses' accounts of their encounters with "ghosts," one could argue that it is precisely this perceptual engagement in the world through the whole body that is challenged by the sensations described—indeed by *one single sensation* (one sound, one smell) that stands out from the others and disrupts the "miracle" of continuous perception. Ghosts seem to be experienced as parts of the world that fail to be grasped in a single perception by all the senses, as ordinary experience does. It could almost be suggested that Merleau-Ponty himself makes this point, when he drops this fantastic comment as a side remark in the *Phenomenology of Perception*: "If a phenomenon—for example, a reflection or a light gust of wind—strikes only one of my senses, it is a mere phan-

tom, and it will come near to real existence only if, by some chance, it becomes capable of speaking to my other senses, as does the wind when, for
example, it blows strongly and can be seen in the tumult it causes in the
surrounding countryside" ([1945] 2002, 137). Here of course, Merleau-
Ponty uses the term *phantom* ("fantôme" in French) as a metaphor, but
his word choice is quite telling, as perceptions that are felt as the presence
of ghosts, in Mongolia and elsewhere, are precisely characterized by their
incomplete character. Any incomplete perception is not felt as a ghost of
course (the one described by Merleau-Ponty is not), but it might become
so, and shake the witness's "perceptual faith," if the other conditions mentioned above happen to be combined in her experience. In the same way
as an incomplete perception "will come near to real existence only if . . . it
becomes capable of speaking to my other senses," it "will come near to" a
ghost experience if, "by some chance," it appears as familiar and singular at
the same time and/or conveys a counterintuitive configuration of agency.

The term *perceptual faith* is introduced by Merleau-Ponty right at the
beginning of *The Visible and the Invisible*. It is defined as the implicit assumption, "shared by the natural man and the philosopher—the moment
he opens his eyes," that "the world is what we see" (1968, 3). Nevertheless,
perception is like time for Augustine: it is familiar to anybody, yet as soon
as we try to explain what it is, many problems arise. It is thus the task of
the philosopher, and therefore of Merleau-Ponty's book, to rethink perception in depth by challenging this intuitive "faith."

Compared to this philosophical, reasoned questioning of perception,
ghosts appear as an immediate, sudden, and irreflexive shaking of perceptual faith. Ghosts, as sensations that challenge abruptly the implicit
certainty that "the world is what we see," give us in a flash the uncanny
suspicion that what we perceive might actually *not* be the entire world.
Ghosts give us an uncertain glimpse of a dimension that usually remains
invisible to us but that might nevertheless be part of the world. These sensations thus challenge our very dwelling in the world by hinting at things
which might well be out there all the time, although they usually escape
our senses. Ghosts, in other words, hint at the uncanny feeling that the
world is not graspable through a single regime of perception.

Invisible Things and Regimes of Communication

Indeed, there is more to Dörvöd ghost stories than the characterization
of people's exceptional and transient glimpses at an unseen aspect of their

environment. The stories reproduced above also feature exceptional individuals who appear to be endowed with special abilities to "see" or to act on the invisible. The narratives crucially point out that ghosts, spirits, and all these things that are called "invisible" in Mongolian are not perceivable by everybody in the same way. Indeed, whereas most people can only have fragmentary glimpses of them, some others seem to be able to see them fully and continually. These persons are said to be able to "see things" (*yum üze-*) or even to "see things with their eyes" (*nüdeer yum üze-*). No reason is really given to account for this special ability: it is simply known that "they have seen things since they were young."

Of course, it is quite frequent across human societies for specific people to be recognized as having special knowledge of, or privileged access to, the invisible world. In many regions of Mongolia, in the North, in the East, and in the capital city, Ulaanbaatar, there are shamans (*böö*) who are credited with the ability to *see* and *act on* invisible things. Yet "people who see with their eyes" in the stories presented above are not shamans (as mentioned earlier in this chapter, there are no shamans left in the region where the narratives were collected). Crucially, and contrary to shamans, "those who see with their eyes" cannot act on what they see: they are powerless to exorcise or satisfy ghosts. All they can do is avoid cautiously the encountered apparition, so as to prevent the dangers of a direct interaction with it. They protect the witnesses by lying to them, so as to spare them a potentially harmful fright. Interestingly, these seers who see but cannot act on invisible things are in symmetrical opposition to ritual specialists who can act on ghosts, by feeding them or expelling them, but are unable to see them. In other words, these narratives describe a distribution of communicative abilities between different kinds of people, a regime of communication featuring three possible relationships with invisible things.

Firstly, there is the relationship that ordinary people have with them: as they can perceive ghosts only occasionally, and in a fragmentary way, ordinary people can suffer their manifestation only passively. Ghosts' manifestations shake their "perceptual faith" by prompting the uncanny feeling that the world is not, or not only, what they see. This fear is unsettling, and indeed is said to be harmful, for it may cause the soul to escape, which will lead to certain death unless a specialist is able to call it back. Secondly, there is the relationship that "those who see with their eyes" are thought to have. For them, arguably, encountering a ghost is not really an uncanny experience, because they can perceive it fully: "invisible things" are not invisible to seers; they are part of the perceived world, so there is nothing disruptive about haunting phenomena for seers. One could almost wonder how they know which are ghosts and which are living people if seers do not differentiate them through their mode of manifestation. However, these seers are powerless; they can neither take actions toward ghosts nor interact with them. Finally, there is the relationship that ritual specialists are credited to have with the invisible: although they cannot see ghosts, they can perform rituals to relieve other people from ghosts' disruptive presence.

This distribution would be completely different if there were still shamans among the Dörvöd, as can be seen from the example of their Tuvan neighbors (Stépanoff 2007). Besides "simple people," who are just blind and passive, Tuvans operate the same opposition between helpless seers and visionless ritual specialists; they however recognize shamans' ability to both "perceive and interact" (ibid., 486) with the invisible. An even broader comparative perspective would show that different societies suppose very different patterns of communicational possibility between living people and the spirit world. Among many other examples, one could evoke here the Achuar, who not only distinguish between different kinds of people but also—as is so frequent throughout the Amazon and elsewhere—between different states (dreaming or wakefulness, among others), in which possibilities of communication follow another pattern (Taylor 1993). Whatever the variables in each case, the possibility that the world might not be perceived by everybody in the same way—and no human society seems to ignore such a possibility—prompts the charting of a specific *regime of communication*, a distribution of possible and impossible sensations and actions.

Conclusion

Ghosts might be highly suspicious in their manifestation, and first of all to witnesses themselves, they might even be "lies" most of the time, yet they are impossible to rule out completely as pure products of human imagination, as objects of *either* belief *or* disbelief. Indeed, the most skeptical among Dörvöd herders might agree with the most passionate nineteenth-century spiritualist, in that some specific sensations effectively shake our intuitive faith that the world is always "what we see" and disrupt our dwelling in it, whatever our cosmological conceptions might be. The notion of a regime of communication has been proposed in this chapter as a methodological framework for the comparison of patterns of experienced relationships with the invisible across different societies. Running counter to a recent trend in social anthropology, this concept argues for the "primacy of perception" (Merleau-Ponty 1974) over "cosmologies" in the analysis of people's relationship with the invisible. This chapter, in other words, advocates for the study of how invisible things are perceived, rather than conceived of, and for the comparative analysis of specific regimes of communication across human societies.

The Materiality of "Spiritual Presences" and the Notion of Person in an Amerindian Society

Florencia C. Tola

Presentation

One afternoon, while working on the oral history of the Toba people (*Qom*) of the Argentinean Chaco,[1] an old man narrated to me the story of a place called *Huoqauo' lae'* (lit. "where the *guaicurú* bird abounds"[2]). The story of this site was collected as part of a study of the places that constitute the old hunting territory of some Toba tribes (*huaguilot*, *ŷolo*, and *no'olgaxanaq*).[3] The inquiry showed that in the names of these places was stamped the history of each tribe, including the military campaign carried out by the Argentinean army against the indigenous people of the Argentinean Chaco, during the last decade of nineteenth century into the early twentieth century.

If some young Toba men considered *Huoqauo' lae'* the place where a slaughter had taken place during that campaign, the version told by an elder named Ernesto of what happened in *Huoqauo' lae'* contained protagonists who were neither the soldiers nor other indigenous groups. Part of his story includes the following:

ERNESTO: *Huo'o ye la'amqa' na huoqauo'. Ŷataqta la'amqa' na huoqauo' qataq da nguitac naxalomm.*

CHILD: *Tesoqo'olec, nache huaña co'ollaxa, yi Huoqauo' lae'? Negue't qo'ollaxa na ilem?*

FIGURE 4.1. *Qasoxonaxa*, the owner of thunder, lightning, and rain, drawn at the author's request in 2010 by Fernando Sosa, a young Toba of the community *Namqom*.

ERNESTO: *Na qom sa namaañi cha'aye huo'o aye huaña alo', cha'aye iyi ye huaña. Ilem asa'aso ỹo'ottac na e'etaxat.*

ERNESTO: There is a place where *guaicurú* birds appear. In that place, the *guaicurúes* really appear and they sing all day.

CHILD: Uncle, is that place where [our ancestors died], *Huoqauo' lae'*? What was the cause of their death so long ago?

ERNESTO: People did not remain [in that place] because there was [the spirit of] a woman, because that [is] the place [where she died]. The cause of her death [was] she who makes the water fall.

The explanation that some Toba men gave was that in *Huoqauo' lae'*, contrary to what the Toba men thought, there had not been any massacre, but a woman had been struck by lightning. Nevertheless, when I transcribed and carefully translated the recorded story, I perceived that the cause of the woman's death (whose spirit still lives there) had been the action of "she who makes the water fall." By means of this periphrasis, Ernesto refers to *qasoxonaxa*, the nonhuman "owner" of thunder, lightning, and rain (fig. 4.1).[4]

This anecdote, told during my fieldwork with the Toba people, will be the starting point to explore the kinds of relations that they establish with entities that, although not human, possess an intentionality capable of directing and exerting actions on the world and on human beings. Far from being considered spirits, characters, or gods who live in the nontemporal dimension of myth, suspended in time, or pertaining to remote scopes of the universe, these entities or "nonhumans" coexist with past and present human beings. Not all of the Toba people have the capacity to see and to interact with these entities of their own will. Nevertheless, and despite the fact that these nonhuman beings are invisible to the majority of humans, their existence and their corporality are not doubted by those who cannot perceive them. This coexistence is perceived through the effects that they produce in space, in human bodies, and in human subjectivity.

Philippe Descola asserted that in Amerindian societies—as in others— "les caractéristiques attribuées aux entités peuplant le cosmos dépendent moins d'une définition préalable de leur essence que des positions relatives qu'elles occupant les unes par rapport aux autres" (2005, 29). My intention in the chapter is not to frame the analysis of nonhuman entities among the Toba people within a taxonomy of different living beings, since as Descola indicated, the identity of humans, animals, plants, and spirits is completely relational and, thus, submitted to metamorphoses that vary according to the adopted point of view (ibid.). Even if perspectivism (Viveiros de Castro 1996) among the Toba people is not as developed as it is in a wide extent of Amazonian societies, it is possible to affirm that "le référent commun aux entités qui habitent le monde" is not, returning to Descola's formula, "l'homme en tant qu'espèce, mais l'humanité en tant que condition" (Descola 2005, 30). In previous publications (Tola 2007, 2009), I showed that the *nqui'i*—generally translated as "soul" or "spirit"—is a corporal property that makes possible agency, cognition, emotion, and communication between different beings and that it is shared by humans, animals, and nonhumans alike.

The Amerindian ethnography of recent decades has demonstrated that the humanization of other entities is not a simple rhetorical figure that only exists in origin myths. Among the Toba, as well as among other groups, entities such as animals, plants, owners of honey, dead people, atmospheric phenomena, and owners of animals are characterized as governing their lives and relationships according to mental, emotional, and social principles, as human beings do. The respect that even modern Toba people have for hunting rules (although the majority of them do not hunt), the use of some parts of animals' bodies for scarifications, and the use of bird organs in the elaboration of amulets designed to obtain benefits (anger, force, agility, luck in sport or in the sale of crafts, etc.) are a few

examples of the attribution of intentionality to nonhuman entities outside
of myth or shamanic practices. We can observe this attribution in concrete
daily activities. Through practices like these, humans try either to enter in
communication with animals and with their nonhuman owners or to acquire the faculties and capacities attributed to animals or plants, by means
of a corporal incorporation.

In order to approach some characteristics of the coexistence and interaction between human and nonhuman beings, in this chapter I analyze
the way in which nonhumans leave traces in space, traces that determine
their name and memory. For that purpose, I particularly focus on the story
of *Huoqauo' lae'* and analyze in it the terms that the Toba people use to
define diverse types of beings. Then, examining individual experiences, I
focus on the influences that nonhuman entities exert on the human body.
I explore the Toba conception of body and person that underlies the possibility that nonhuman beings affect the human person. Finally, through
the graphical material created by a young shaman of *Namqom* between
1999 and 2003, I examine how the shaman's subjectivity is permeated by
the intentionality of nonhuman entities that live outside and within him.

The Toba people, or *Qom*, belong to the Guaycurú linguistic family
and live in the Gran Chaco of South America. The Gran Chaco constitutes
a plain of alluvial accumulation that extends along the territories of Argentina, Bolivia, and Paraguay. In the west, the Gran Chaco is delimited
by the sub-Andean mountains; in the east, by the Paraguay and Paraná
Rivers; in north, by the plate of Mato Grosso; and in the south, by the
basin of the Salado River. During the pre-Colombian period, most indigenous people of the Gran Chaco practiced a seminomadic economy based
on hunting, fishing, and gathering (Braunstein 1983).

Nonhumans in Named and Inhabited Territory

In their ethnographies in the Gran Chaco and in other latitudes, several
authors (Descola 1986; Braunstein 1993; Palmer 1995, 1997; Fernández
and Braunstein 2001; Surrallés 2003; García Hierro and Surrallés 2004;
Salamanca 2006; Censabella 2009) have demonstrated that in hunter-
gatherer societies territory is named for topographic characteristics and
abundances of animals and plants. Also, in these societies places are
named in reference to historical events of particular significance to the
groups that create and transmit the names. In fact, the names of these

places and their corresponding histories are transmitted from generation to generation, giving rise to continuities between events lived by ancestors and the identity and the practices of modern-day groups.

In her study of the names of human groups and places among the Toba people, the linguist Marisa Censabella affirmed that the place-names are formed by "un nombre derivado, un nombre compuesto o un sintagma nominal" (2009, 224). From a lexical and morphological analysis, the author organized the place-names she obtained from written sources dating from the eighteenth century until the end of the twentieth and from her informants in the northeast of the province of Chaco in the following way: (a) traditional campsites, (b) new enclaves where Toba people lived at the end of the nineteenth century and in the first decades of the twentieth century, (c) places with a topographic characteristic, (d) hunting sites, and (e) crossing sites in which historical events or "events of supernatural character" occurred (ibid., 228). According to Censabella, the last category requires special contextualization from the narrators, illustrating how these names usually are not transparent. Her systematization is similar to that proposed by the anthropologists Analía Fernández and José Braunstein (2001) for the Toba people of Pampa del Indio (province of Chaco).[5]

In the compilation of place-names that I have made in the central zone of Formosa (in 2001 in San Carlos and in 2008–2009 in Riacho de Oro and Santo Domingo),[6] I observed that the Toba of this zone name the places in relation to diverse elements. Some of the places receive names according to the abundance of an animal or a plant: *huoiem lae'* ("where monkeys abound"), *qarol lae'* ("where fishes abound"), *relliquic lapel* ("palo santo lagoon"), and so on. Other places have names that refer to topographic characteristics: *euaxai lamo* ("where the river begins"), *no'onaxa logoraic* ("long field"), and *co'oichaxaqui* ("nest"). Also, some names refer to particular events that happened to some member of the group: *Chingolo lche'* ("the leg of Chingolo"), a lagoon where a fisherman (Chingolo) was bit on the leg by a fish, and *Araxanaxaqui* ("mortars"), a place where Toba women macerate fruit with mortars.

I also found numerous names that refer to significant events that took place during the conquest of the Argentinean Chaco. If some of these places allude only to the encounter with the army, others refer to nonhuman interventions or manifestations at the time of the conquest. *Roqshe nalleuo* ("where the white people saw"), for example, refers to the arrival of the army to the estuary where the Toba people were. *Eraxai* ("firefly") designates a dense forest that the Toba used as an escape route that they

FIGURE 4.2. Birds-persons of *huoqauo' lae'* painted by Fernando Sosa in 2010 after he heard Laureano's story.

illuminated with this insect. *Qo'oxoi* is the name of another site whose story is that during the conquest a shaman was asked by his nonhuman companion to dig a ditch to hide those with him; nevertheless, the army found them and shot them all.

Other places have names based on some type of encounter between humans and nonhumans outside the context of the conquest. This is the case of *lashe n'naxaganaxaqui* "lagoon where a beast of the water lives") in which a catastrophe occurred. A menstruating woman approached the lagoon and invoked the anger of the nonhuman people there, who felt repulsion for the menstrual blood. The story of *Huoqauo' lae'* that I transcribe below was told in 2009 by an old man named Laureano from Riacho de Oro and is part of this last type of story. In this one, the nonhuman owner of thunder is not the protagonist—as stated in Ernesto's version—instead the protagonists are bird-persons who, feeling compassion for humans due to the lack of food, warned the shaman of the group, whose powers allow him to communicate with animals, especially birds, that in that lagoon they could find an abundance of fishes (fig. 4.2). As indicated by Amado, another elderly man from San Carlos, "The birds warn. Sometimes they bring bad news. The Toba people did not stay in because the bird warned them to move, because the white people were coming soon. And when the Toba people went away, the army arrived and did not find anybody. The *pi'oxonaq* [shaman] speaks with birds."

I transcribe here part of Laureano's story to show the ways in which he refers to the nonhuman protagonists:

1. *Huaña aye Huoqauo' lae'. So qolloxochiyi ŷape', iyi Candelario Vega,*
2. *ŷa'axattac co'ollaxa yi'iyi se'eso huoqauo'.*
3. *Nache na laqtac yi ŷape' 'eeta' yi'iyi Huoqauo' lae':*
4. *netrañalo qo'ollaxa soua 2 shiŷaxa'u ie'enaxattrac ne'ena huoqauo', huoqauo', huoqauo'.*
5. *Nache qanaxaŷaxata'alo, 2 se'esoua shiŷaxa'u ŷa'axatta'ape ico', ico'.*
6. *Nache qanqo'onalo, qanqo'onalo qo'ollaxa.*
7. *Nache qaipittaxatego' da shiŷaxa'u, qache qoŷo se'esoua,*
8. *qoŷo se'esoua nache da tatrangui yi qauo' lae'.*
9. *Nacheno' na ŷaxa'attac ñi huoqauo'.*
10. *Porque se'eso shiŷaxaua deetaxaŷapegue' so huoqauo'.*
11. *Qache ŷaxatta'ape soua huoqauo' dos,*
12. *Qaŷoqta, nache, se'eso shiŷaxaua hua'aqtega so huoqauo'*
13. *nache ŷaxa'attac soomaxa' qache nŷaq ne'ena huetangui yi'iyi qaim. [. . .]*[7]
14. *Huo'o se'eso shiŷaxaua maye deetaxaŷapegue'.*
15. *Da qache nshetaique, da ego' iquiaxan se'eso shiŷaxauapi da iŷaxa'atega,*
16. *cha'aye se'eso shiŷaxauapi qaica ca chec.*
17. *Qache nŷaq yemaxa dalaxa'ateguec se'eso shiŷaxaua.*

1. There, in *Huoqauo' lae'*, time ago, my grandfather Candelario Vega
2. was talking about the *guaycurú* bird, time ago.
3. And my grandfather's word on *Huoqauo' lae'* was this:
4. Two persons were formerly imitating the *guaicurú, guaicurú, guaicurú* bird.
5. And, as they were listening to the bird, they approached it. It seemed that two persons were heralding something.
6. Then [the two persons] went over there, they went over there, later on.
7. And they thought that [those that sang] were persons, but [they were] birds,
8. two birds in front of the lagoon *Huoqauo' lae'*.
9. This is what the *guaicurú* bird is herald.
10. Because that person speaks with the *guaicurú* bird.
11. It seems that those two *guaicurúes* birds were heralding.
12. From afar, then, that person listened the *guaicurú* bird
13. and he said that within the lagoon there were fishes. [. . .]

14. There was a person with whom [the bird] spoke.
15. It seems that [the bird-person] wanted—it seems—to feed the people it her-
    alded,
16. because those people had no food.
17. It seems those fishes are what that person offered.

In this fragment of the story of *Huoqauo' lae'*, we read that two men listened to the song of *guaicurúes* birds from afar and imitated them. At first,
they thought that those singing were persons, but as they approached the
lagoon, they realized that it was the song of birds, not the song of persons.
One of the men talked with the bird, who advised him that fishes were in
that lagoon, since this bird wished to feed the Toba people. Nevertheless,
what is interesting in this story is that, although the speaker expresses that
the men realized that those who sang were animals and not human beings,
he refers to them with the term *shiẏaxaua* (5, 17). According to other Toba
men that were present during the narration, if one of the men of the story
talked with birds (10), and if birds felt compassion toward men that had
no food (15), the birds were not only birds (*qoẏo*). "When the elders speak
of some animals, often they refer to them as *shiẏaxaua*—that is, people,
person," a Toba man told me.

Diverse nonhuman entities receive the name *shiẏaxaua*,[8] which I chose
to translate as "person." The human people (*Qom* or whites), the dead
people, the nonhuman owners of animals, the companions of shamans, the
personages of the mythical stories, the inhabitants of the night and of the
forest are, from the Toba point of view, *shiẏaxaua*. That is to say, they have
their own point of view on the world, attributes of social life, agency, and
corporal aptitudes that allow cognition and emotions. *Shiẏaxaua* is not
used, then, to designate human persons exclusively. It includes a diversity
of entities that we usually designate as spirits, divinities, or monsters, but
that—for the Toba people—constitute a particular type of person. This is
the case of the bird-person that advised human people that in the lagoon
of *Huoqauo' lae'* there was much fish to be had.

In the Toba language, often when one wishes to clarify that one is talking about an entity that, although still a person, differs from a human, one
usually adds some adjective or adverb to the word *shiẏaxaua* that indicates
that that person is of a particular type. *Shiẏaxaua lẏa* is used, in fact, to
mark a difference with human *shiẏaxaua*. *Lẏa* is translated generally as
"other," and it is used in diverse speech contexts. But when it accompanies
shiẏaxaua and when the subject of the conversation is nonhuman beings,

"person other" becomes a way to talk about the nonhuman condition of a person. *Ŷoqta shiŷaxaua*—whose translation could be "true person"—is used also when people are talking about nonhuman beings. To emphasize that, referring to nonhuman entities, one is not talking about the elders' fantasies, one says that these persons are "true people"—that is to say, as "real" as humans. In this sense, the condition of *true person* is related to the same characteristics that define the human person.

Several studies among indigenous people of the Gran Chaco and Amazonia have shown that names that these groups gave to themselves indicate their human condition, in opposition to other human groups whose condition of humanity is not clear or not naturally given (Cordeu and de los Ríos 1982; Gow 1991; Viveiros de Castro 1992; Turner 1993; McCallum 2001; Hugh Jones 2002; Palmer 2005; Lepri 2005). In fact, A.-C. Taylor (2006) expressed that in conceptualizing personhood and humanity, the Amerindian traditions are more restrictive than the Occidental tradition. She argued that usually the terms that designate the human person correspond to ethnic names. What is interesting is that the restriction on the condition of humanity that is evident in ethnic names coexists with the attribution of personhood to a large diversity of entities that we usually consider nonhuman.

In the case of the Toba people, the most widely used name—which is also an ethnic name—is *Qom*. This term derives from the personal pronoun of the first-person plural (*qomi, qom*: people; *-i*: plural suffix) and designates, thus, a relational position. In a restricted sense, *Qom* defines those who speak the same language (*qom laqtac*, lit. "the word *qom*") and share the same practices and representations about the world. Although the Toba people distinguish their neighboring indigenous groups and those of other regions, in a broad sense *Qom* is used to designate all the indigenous people. In fact, *Qom* works as a category which contrasts with *roqshe* or "nonindigenous people." This last term defines, in a general sense, those who are neither *Qom* nor Toba.[9] The limits between *Qom* and *roqshe* are determined by the different ways of appropriation and categorization of the territory; by the oral transmission, throughout successive generations, of knowledge, practices, and representations; and by a shared language, an important marker of identity.

We state thus that *shiŷaxaua* is not what the Toba call themselves. It does not work, in fact, as an ethnic name. In this sense, this term does not function as some ethnic names that indicate also the notion of person or humanity, as several authors have attested for other Amerindian societies (Lepri 2005; Taylor 2006). This category includes the Toba people but also other human beings, such as *roqshe* (whites) and nonhumans. This category does not refer to the ethnic condition (as in the case of *Qom*) and includes entities that have certain common elements: the agency of the subject and the social life.

Also, the conjunction of these faculties differentiates persons (*Qom*, *roqshe*, human, nonhuman) from animals (*shiguiÿac*). However, as we have seen, even if all the *Qom* people are *shiÿaxaua* ("person," although it is not possible to affirm the contrary) because they have a *nqui'i*—the corporal aptitude that allows agency, thoughts, feelings, and the capacity to communicate—all the beings who own a *nqui'i* are not persons. This means that even if a given animal has a *nqui'i*, it is not necessarily a person. The nonhuman owners of animals—among others—besides owning a *nqui'i*, have a social life, maintain kinship relations, live in towns, hunt and fish, and own a body with metamorphic capacities (Tola 2010); these being the attributes that altogether define the condition of person.

Traces on the Body

The cosmovision has to do with blood, the senses and intellect. — Timoteo

In this section I analyze some of the nonhuman entities' manifestations on the body of human beings. For this purpose, I set out the conception of body and person that underlies the possibility that nonhuman entities affect human entities. More than considering the body as something natural subject to external causes, or as a cultural product that contains the implicit idea of a natural ground, the Toba people perceive the body as a manifestation of the person who crosses regimes of corporality based on situations that involve human and nonhuman beings. The body goes through diverse regimes or states (birth, affection, disease, death, etc.) that constitute the person in constant transformation.

The notion of agency is central in the corporal manifestations that a person adopts, not only in human beings but also in nonhuman people. The person-body is indeed susceptible to transformation as a result of the action—and of the intention—of nonhuman entities. A person-body can combine elements and aptitudes of human and nonhuman beings alike. This combination is possible because the body does not always contain the elements that form the person. In fact, the person is not confined to corporality, due to the fact that some components can exist outside the body, allowing the fusion of different person-bodies.

As I have previously mentioned, among the Toba people certain components of the person-body are susceptible to exist outside the corporal package, without ceasing to form part of the person. To think of the person as composed of elements that are the self but at the same time are not necessarily close to each other, nor share a fixed location, allows us to avoid a dualistic reading that opposes a body to a mind, an *I* to a *we*. Several authors have reconceptualized the body/soul dualism in Amazonian societies (Taylor 1996; Surrallés 2003; Descola 2005; Vilaça 2005; Fausto 2007) and have shown the more complex ways in which the body and the soul are related to each other.

In her study on gender and person in Melanesia, Marilyn Strathern critiqued the hegemonic vision of gender studies and the standard notion of person. Her point of view is that this vision focuses on masculine domination and antagonism between the sexes.[10] Her critique consists of questioning the Western "root metaphor" (i.e., commodity; Strathern 1988, 134). According to this metaphor, things exist by themselves and are defined through intrinsic properties and attributes. This metaphor entails a conception of persons as differentiated entities that establish "external relations" with other differentiated entities. For Strathern, persons are "constructed as the plural and composite site of the relationships that produced them. The singular person can be imagined as a social microcosm" (ibid., 13). Opposing *dividual* persons to *individual* ones, the author tries to account for the relational and divisible character of the person in Melanesian societies. Aparecida Vilaça proposed to adapt the concepts used by Strathern (1988) for Melanesian societies to Amazonian ones. She expressed that "while Melanesia reveals dividuals conceived as male and female, in Amazonia we are faced with dividuals conceived as human and non-human" (Vilaça 2005, 453). Among the Toba, the person is not conceived as a natural product, created only by parents, and closed inside the limits of the individual body. The Toba person exists neither alone inside a body nor only in the body. Moreover, some fluids, parts, attributes, capacities, and names are thought of as the *extensions* of the person-body, because they can be located outside the body and they can come from other person-bodies. The description of these *extensions* will allow us to show that the Toba person is defined through relations with other persons (humans and nonhumans), relations that are bodily mediated.

First of all, certain bodily fluids (blood, semen) are conceived as corporal extensions because they come from other person-bodies.[11] In a constant process of transformation, masculine blood is transformed in semen and, later on, in maternal milk. Feminine blood becomes maternal milk and the blood of the nursing baby (Tola 1999, 2002). In this sense, fluids are visualized by the Toba people as components of other bodies in their own bodies or as their own extensions that, once passed to the bodies of their kin, become elements of other people. As bodily fluids transport intentions, capacities, emotions, and thoughts from a body to another (Tola 2009), their circulation and transformation between those who share fluid-food-affection create a consubstantiality.[12]

Secondly, there are parts or prolongations of the body (hair, odor) and other nonsexual fluids (spittle and sweat) that express the extensive condition of a person when they are manipulated by others. An action exerted on these prolongations can directly affect the person to whom these extensions or fluids pertain. Here I refer specifically to sorcery practices in which a sorcerer takes a personal object that has been in contact with the victim's body, and as a result of which, the victim begins to suffer some disease related to the captured object.[13]

Finally, another type of extension exists that is a person's unfixed components: the shadow, the *nqui'i*, the nonhuman companions of shamans, and so on. Like certain bodily fluids, these components can come from other persons and are susceptible to capture by sorcerers and to have repercussions on the will, intentionality, emotions, and thoughts the same as corporal extensions or body parts. For example, even if the idea of God's participation in the attribution of the *nqui'i* to a baby during gestation is widely accepted, it coexists with the idea that parents are those who, during gestation, give the baby his or her own *nqui'i*, understood as "corporal appearance." During gestation, persons receive their distinguishing sign—their appearance, *nqui'iyaxac*—from their parents.

However, during transitional moments such gestation, birth, the first menstruation, and death, the body is more permeable to nonhuman actions and the reception of extensions from not only humans but also nonhuman entities. During gestation, ancestors and nonhuman beings play a central role in the appearance and personality of the baby. Because the influence of nonhuman beings on the body is risky during gestation and the first years of life, men and women respect nutritional and action prohibitions.[14] The risk is not necessarily related to the problem of capture. Carlos Fausto expresses that in Amazonia there exists the common conception that the "baby's vital principle is not securely attached to the body and can be captured" (2007, 504). Even if for the Toba people the newborn is not entirely fabricated (as in Amazonian societies), the most important risk during the process of the baby's corporal transformation is the fusion—

and not the capture—with an animal or a nonhuman being. Despite the fact that among the Toba and other indigenous groups of Amazonia the consequences vary (fusion or capture), the "couvade and other abstinence rituals clearly show that human bodies, subject to a continual process of fabrication, can be attracted by other subjectivities, such as animals, and transformed into them" (Vilaça 2005, 450). *Nauoxa* is the Toba term that synthesizes the consequences that the human person-body suffers if one does not respect the rules which govern the relations with nonhumans during moments of "corporal formation and transformation."[15]

Some *Qom* translate *nauoxa* (-*uoxa*: root of the verb "to heart") as "contagion" in the attempt to define the process of transmission of the formal characteristics or behaviors between human and nonhuman entities. A Toba man translated it as "imitation," expressing the similarities between human and nonhuman entities after a moment of excessive proximity between them. Another young man, trying to transmit the amplitude of the *nauoxa* phenomenon, used the term "influence." I think that the idea of influence gives more account of the implied process. According to his reflection, "influence" refers to the process carried out between two beings that "crossed paths," which left a trace on their corporal-vital constitution. This trace is lived as an influence susceptible to transform the corporal regime, the behaviors, and the personality of the implied person. As Vilaça has expressed, the body of the newborn "runs the risk of being made like the body of other types of people (or simply as an animal)" (2002, 359). In this sense, among the Toba, the newborn can become a person of another kind (*shiỹaxaua lỹa*).

The following story is of a young shaman, Juan Carlos, who told me how he cured a boy of the influence (*nauoxa*) exerted by a little mouse. The boy suffered insomnia and (like the mouse) he lived at night. When the shaman acted on the mouse affecting the little boy, he was cured.

All the animals have their [nonhuman] owner. When you kill [some animal], his spirit [*nqui'i*] enters the baby. The son of Zunildo was ill and he could not recover. He brought him to me. The third night I saw [the cause]. It was the mouse, *choxonaxa* [. . .]. One day, when Zunildo arrived at his house, he saw a lot of mice and he threw them out to the rain. He killed them all. The [nonhuman] father of those [mice] got angry. Sometimes, the [nonhuman] father acts. And he attacks the baby; he wants to kill him. When I stopped curing the boy, I asked Zunildo, "Have you ever killed a mouse? You have not to kill any animal when your son is small or when your wife is pregnant. Some [nonhuman owners of animals] ask me to give a name to the baby so that they never return. But, in this case, I killed the mouse because it wanted to kill the baby. I had to kill the mouse in dreams. I spend several days killing it, because it is very quick. I had to persecute it and to put it a trap, just to be able to take it. It went away and I had to follow it under the earth. The doctors [shamans] can enter the earth. There is water below, and I pass to the other side. In the last earth, there is pure earth. When I arrived at the last one, I had to return. Down below, I saw people who walk. It seems that they are dead people, because they walk. I do not believe that they are natural persons, they are *shiŷaxaua lŷa* [person of another kind], but our ancestors, who live down below."

I will focus on diverse elements of this testimony that have to do with the relation between human and nonhuman beings. On one hand, the importance of the respect of animal life is crucial, as crucial as the consequences brought by its indiscriminate slaughter. The owners of animals—widespread in hunter-gatherer Amerindian societies (Tomasini 1969–1970; Bonilla 2005; Fausto 2008, Tola 2010)—have a central role in the regulation of relations with animals. In this case, the slaughter of several mice invoked the anger and the desire for revenge of the mouse's nonhuman master. Also, the shaman—who has the capacity to talk to nonhumans— transmitted the cause to the family and began the treatment. This consisted in catching the mouse *nqui'i* that was affecting the boy. This hunting was alongside diverse levels of the earth, shedding light on the existence of several worlds inhabited by nonhuman persons (Métraux 1946; Miller 1979; Wright 2008; Tola 2010).

As I have previously stated, during the first and the successive menstruations, women must respect some prohibitions (not approaching rivers, not touching prey, not cooking, not sharing kitchen instruments, not touching men's arms, etc.) that, if not respected, could give rise to dangers, diseases, and catastrophes that would affect her, her family, or her local community. Within the possible consequences, the Toba people mention the actions of *qomonaxalo*. This nonhuman being can be a rainbow or a water snake, and when a young woman does not respect the prohibition on going to the river, *qomonaxalo* is able to cause diverse misfortunes. The most habitual is to trigger a strong storm and invert the world: the terrestrial world of humans is buried under the earth, and those who live under the earth rise to the surface.

The fragment of the story that I transcribe here is part of the stories of place-names that the Toba people told me in San Carlos and Riacho de Oro during 2008 and 2009. An old woman, Julia, told me the story related to her by her grandmother about the lagoon near her community in which numerous families died because of the infraction of a young woman.

> In those times, my grandmother was thinking and talking about *Mala'* lagoon. Her group passed through the border of the lagoon. People were escaping during the war. The Toba people fought with the whites. For Toba people, this lagoon was really the place where they lived. And there was a river called "where the tiny water-beast always appears." And our people were buried there. There was an old man who said, "Grandsons, it would be good if we left this camp, because our companion with the menstruation was very thirsty and descended upon the lagoon." They were waiting for what would happen that night. And the rain and the wind arrived and everybody was buried. It seems a thunderclap, but the thunderclap is not simple. The next day some people went to see and they saw that all was already buried. The Toba people were buried with their animals, their donkeys, and their children.

When Julia says that the thunderclap was not "simple," she is saying that it was not a natural phenomenon. This thunderclap was the consequence of the anger of *qomonaxalo*. Besides *qomonaxalo*, other nonhumans usually take part in the social life of humans when women do not respect the mentioned prohibitions. *Veraic*, for example, are the nonhuman inhabitants of the water that take people under when a woman does not notice that she is menstruating. *Veraic*, who combines human and animal bodies, kidnap humans and usually take them to live under the water. When the Toba people hear human voices laughing near the river, they know that these voices are from humans who, now, live with *veraic* people.

"I know that I had my body, I know that I am a person, but I do not know why I am like this: without a body"

As I have analyzed thus far, among the Toba people, nonhuman beings are not present exclusively in mythology. Places whose names refer to nonhuman actions, the human violation of strict rules of behavior, and some actions that denote violence toward animals are some of the elements of daily life in which we can observe how nonhuman entities interact with human beings. As we have seen, the existence and the intentionality of nonhuman entities are visible for humans in the effects that these entities leave on the space and on the body.

On the other hand, shamans are the ones who administrate the relations between humans and nonhuman entities. They are able "assumir o ponto de vista destes seres e principalmente de voltar para contar a historia" (Viveiros de Castro [1996] 2002, 358). *Pi'oxonaq* (shaman) maintains the communication between species since "sendo capazes de ver os não-humanos como estes se vêem (como humanos) . . . podem ocupar o papel de interlocutores ativos no diálogo inter-específico" (ibid.). The Toba shamans are able to travel among the different levels of the universe and to perceive the human nature of nonhuman beings. After their journies, they transmit the information acquired from nonhumans. During therapies, shamans tell people about the appearance of nonhuman beings, their habits, and the magnitude of their powers. This capacity allows shamans to hold their position of healer since nonhumans teach them the therapeutic songs, the medicinal plants to use, and the causes of diseases that afflict their patients.

The capacity of corporal metamorphosis is one of the main characteristics of nonhuman singularities. Although human beings can be witnesses of the metamorphoses of nonhumans into humans, humans habitually perceive these entities to have an appearance not entirely human. But, when these nonhumans entities appear to shamans, they show their human corporal appearance.

The majority of nonhumans can pass from one corporal regime to another, as if they are changing clothes or ornamentation. If in Amazonian societies it is frequent to speak of "clothes" (Viveiros de Castro [1977] 2002; Chaumeil 1983; Århem 1993; Hugh-Jones 1996) when evoking the metamorphic capacity of nonhumans, among the Toba people we find also the notion of "cloth." A Toba shaman told me that "under the Earth there is another earth where *qomonaxalo* lives. When *qomonaxalo* is entering the water, he leaves his clothes outside. The colors of the rainbow are his clothes." Without clothes—in this case, the colors of the rainbow—nonhuman persons are perceived by shamans to have the appearance of human persons. At those moments, the *interiority* and the *physicality* coexist (Descola 2005).

Between 1998 and 1999, I lived at *Namqom*, a Toba district located eleven kilometers from Formosa city, with the family of a recognized shaman. When he passed away, he left his shamanic powers to one of his children, Seferino, with whom I used to work. Seferino was not only an excellent narrator of stories. In our first encounters, his reflective and critical capacity quickly became apparent, as much as his ability to talk about his own culture and his tendency to attribute the condition of person to an

extensive range of entities that lived inside and outside him. These entities, which Seferino called "my spiritual presences," accompanied him in
dreams, while hunting, in the memories of his birth and his childhood, in
the re-creation of his family story, in the evangelical cult (cf. Miller 1979,
Wright 2002), in his trip to Buenos Aires, and in his short sojourn in the
army.

The *spiritual presences* of Seferino are, perhaps, the paradigmatic expression of the notion of flexible extensions that constitute the human
person in continual relation with humans and nonhumans. Among the
Toba people, shamans are thought of as composed of nonhuman entities
that enter and leave their bodies. During the years in which Seferino felt
like an insane person due to the spiritual presences that bother him in
dreams, he drew some of them for me and described to me the interactions
he had with them.

Regarding figure 4.3, Seferino stated:

> This is me, sleeping. When I am alone, some nights, he appears. He is *qasorot*.
> He is a good person because he takes care of me when I sleep. He put away
> those who take my blankets. This happened to me when I was a little boy. Some-
> times, he who has one vertical eye and one horizontal eye appears to me. He
> wants to frighten me. I leave my body, and I see that my body is there, intact in
> my bed. I leave my body because I am afraid. Then, I remain seated behind my
> bed. [. . .] Later on, other people appear to me; they are fighting. The snake, the
> iguana, the spider, and a black bird appear to me. They are used by shamans
> to kill people. [. . .] The *pi'oxonaq* [shaman] knows the spider, in dreams he
> talks to her. [. . .] *Pi'oxonaq* has a poisonous spider inside him. And I am above,
> watching these people fighting. I know that they are *pi'oxonaq*. And I have a
> cat's perspective. At night, I am a cat. And I have my cat in my back. These are
> the signs of *pi'oxonaq*. We have differences between us. Animals protect us.
> *Qasorot* gave me a cat to protect me. He had the cat inside him, and he gave it
> to me. I was a baby and I didn't know anything; I was therefore always fright-
> ened. When he gave me the cat, he opened his chest and he had inside a brilliant
> sword, and when he takes it, it was not a sword, but a cat.

In this description of the drawing we can observe that the body of the
shaman is inhabited by nonhuman entities (*nattac*) that acquire different
corporal forms (spider, snake, bird, cat, etc.). These entities are the shaman or the extensions of his person-body. Furthermore, the possibility of
leaving the body; the existence of people who fight at night and that are,

FIGURE 4.3. Fighting with other shamans. By Seferino Flores (1999).

simultaneously, animals and extensions of shamans; the reality of being at the same time man and cat, sword and cat; and the fact of being able to kill enemies in dreams suggest multiple possible readings. We could think that these elaborations are the product of the cultural imagination or elements of the shamanic ideologies of power. Nevertheless, I suggest the idea that the conception of a body inhabited by other beings, a body that possesses elements coming from other persond-bodies, permits us to escape binary approaches that separate the inner from the outer, the individual from the collective, the singular from the multiple. The conception of a body in permanent connection with other bodies (humans and nonhumans), which are also conceived as multiplicities and possessing other's exten-sions, is coherent with an ontology that puts more emphasis on transfor-mations and multiplicity than on stability and on individual entities, more

FIGURE 4.4 (a and b).
Fingers that scare. By
Seferino Flores (1999).

on processes and on relations than on substances and on given or natural things or beings.

"At night, when I sleep," Seferino expressed, "two fingers appear to me. I feel that they have beautiful hair, and that they are the hands of a human person who touches me and calms me. When these fingers touched me, I felt that there was a person behind them." Seferino explained, showing me figure 4.4, "When he appears to me, a little thread appears also with an ear. It makes this noise: *qui qui qui.*". Seferino described the subject of figure 4.5, "He observes me. First of all the ear appears and later on the face. But this face has no body. At that time, I had no house but I thought I had one. I felt a great swelling in my head, and I felt that my body was my head, that my veins were swollen. And I was scared, I shouted. I wanted to commit suicide because I had a tremendous pain that bothered me."

The ideas expressed by Seferino in the description of his drawings make more sense if we consider them in relation to the Toba way of conceiving the body, relations, and continuities between humans and nonhumans. If, beyond perceiving the body as something individual, the Toba people live it as a manifestation of the person who traverses corporal regimes that depend on interactions with other beings, Seferino's suffering does not surprise us. His perceptions and corporal distortions were the manifestation of nonhuman persons, whose corporal extensions and parts entered his body, confusing him with respect to his limits and his identity. On this matter, Seferino said, "I did not know how it was the human body. These drawings show the signals that I received [from the nonhuman persons who initiated me]. First, I saw the head of a goat, with a little horn. He had not eyes, but I knew that I was a goat [. . .]. This small goat always ap-

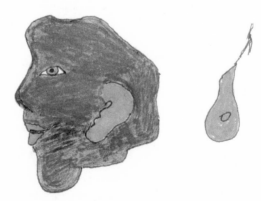

FIGURE 4.5. The ear and the face without a body. By Seferino Flores (1999).

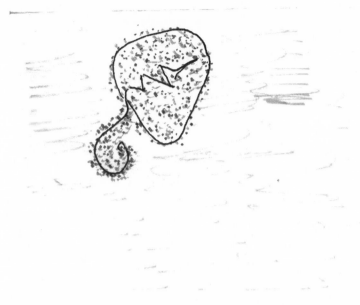

FIGURE 4.6. The goat that scares. By Seferino Flores (1999).

peared to me. I know that I had my body, I know that I am person, but I do not know why I am like this: without a body" (fig. 4.6).

The Body: Site of Differentiation or Expression of Continuity with Nonhumans?

I have intended to show in this chapter that the Toba define the relationship between the person and other human and nonhuman entities as one of continuity. This continuity is possible because humans and nonhumans possess a *nqui'i*, which is not a soul or a spirit but rather the corporal aptitude that enables feelings, thoughts, and agency. This assertion explains how the process of individuation comes about—that is, the process of singularization of persons apparently determined by identical ways. In fact, for the Toba, the person exists as a manifestation of a relational framework. Depending on interactions with nonhumans and on circulation of fluids, attributes, and capacities, the person adopts different corporal regimes.

That is why, when we study the notion of person and body in a society that does not limit the human condition to the human person, we should not circumscribe the analysis to the human person and his or her corporal limits—conceived implicitly as the border of an individuality. If the Toba do not have a reduced concept of person, if this notion includes both humans and nonhumans alike, and if the body is in a constant process of transformation as a result of the relations with other beings' bodies, a person's constitution depends on the transformations of other person-bodies and the circulation of their corporal extensions. As the vessel in which the "formation and the transformation" of the person takes place, the body may be understood as the vector of production of the social life that integrates humans and nonhumans.

This approach to the body and the different entities gives rise to certain questions regarding the individuation process. How can the idea that the body is what differentiates individuals from other beings coexist with the idea that what creates it are the relations established with other "multiplicities"? Subjectivity is a given, shared by all entities, and the difference between them is the body that makes them singular. This formula of Amazonian perspectivism (Viveiros de Castro 1996), which is also the foundation of animism (Descola 2005), is valid, too, among the Toba if we consider the times described in myth. Several myths describe an original condition in which personages share a human subjectivity despite having an animal body (Tola 2005). Differences arise with the creation of human and animal bodies. If, in those times, animals and humans could transform their corporal appearance and alternate between animal and human bodies, after the described corporal transformations, beings begin to differentiate in the way in which subjectivity is shaped in their bodies. The body is the site of differentiation between the descendants of mythological beings, potentially differentiating a human existence from a nonhuman one.

Nevertheless, even if the body plays a central role in the process of differentiation, it is possible to affirm that the possession of a body is neither a necessary nor sufficient condition for the existence of a person (the human person exists as a potential before existing in a human body and persists even after death). Also, even if nonhumans are persons, they may exist without a body. However, when the human person becomes a body, he or she requires other human and nonhuman persons to exist as a multiplicity formed by corporal extensions. In sum, if the body is the center of the combination of other entities, it expresses the continuity with the different beings more than the difference between them. That is, if the body is the vessel in which other people's corporal extensions are combined, more than differentiating these entities, it enables their existence.

Multiplicities and Identities

In short, the question here is, how to reconcile the existence of dependent persons with independent singularities that differentiate them from other singularities by their bodies? If the persons are in interdependence to exist and to constitute themselves through corporal relations, is it possible to conceive them as individuals? Considering the existence of multiplicities in a constant process of transformation and reconfiguration, what sense does it make to speak of "identity" and "individual"? Moreover, how does the process of individuation take place in an ontology in which persons are conceived as multiples and made out of others? Is it possible to think that individuation might take place through multiplicity? In sum, what defines the individuality of a person in an ontology in which bodies are conceived as extended, metamorphic, and collectively transformed by humans and nonhumans alike?

To answer these questions it will be necessary to consider the way in which the Toba conceive the *nqui'i*. The *nqui'i* is unique and exists as a singularity before becoming a person. The Toba usually refer to the existence of "spirits of babies" (*o'o nqui'i*) who live in the sky before descending to the womb. The *nqui'i* also exists as a singularity when the person dies and it continues to exist in an individual way, as a spirit without a body (Tola 2006). Death does not represent, in fact, the end of a person's existence. It is possible then to affirm that even if there have been human and nonhuman actions involved in that person's acquisition of a body (the reiteration of the sexual relations, the arrival of the spirit of a baby from the sky, etc.), the person exists as an individuality before and after life on earth. What's more, once this singularity acquires a body it is then through this body that it becomes a multiplicity.

Throughout this chapter I have also developed the idea that it is because of the actions that the "spiritual presences" evoked by shamans—but not only by them—exert on the human body, that humans apprehend the material dimension of these entities. The nonhuman's actions exerted in the human body determine different corporal regimes (deformities in newborns, diseases, animal's characteristics or behaviors, affection, etc.) and allow human beings to know the corporal manifestation of nonhuman entities that only shamans can see during treatments and dreams.

Following the general arguments of this volume, in this chapter I have explored the "agency of intangibles" in an Amerindian society in which the notion of person in not limited to human beings. I recognize the importance of reviewing anthropological concepts and methods with which the ontological differences are approached. I have tried to show different instances in which indigenous interlocutors face a diversity of entities, especially through the effects of their actions. These effects are the traces that they leave in a space covered with names, in the manifestations in the human body, and in the subjectivity of shamans.

CHAPTER FIVE

Spirits and Stories in the Crossroads

Vânia Zikàn Cardoso

It is in the nature of the spirits that populate the rituals of *macumba* to intervene in the lives of the people who seek their help in consultation sessions that take place in religious houses dispersed throughout the suburbs of Rio de Janeiro, Brazil.[1] Spirits of the *povo da rua* ("people of the streets") respond to the call of ritual songs and the sound of drums to come dance, eat, and drink, to give counsel, and to commingle with those who seek their help in solving the mundane and the extraordinary problems of everyday life. Spirits of prostitutes, known as *pomba-giras*, and of *malandros*, trickster-like social characters who occupied the streets of Rio in the early decades of the twentieth century, these are spirits of folks who inhabited the socially marginal spaces of the city. Known for their power to appear where they desire, for their capacity to interfere in the everyday in unexpected, and often feared, ways, the *povo da rua* are the subjects of a large part of the rituals of *macumba* aimed at either taming them or claiming their intervention to open one's path toward the solution of difficult problems.

The *povo da rua* are central to the very constitution of *macumba*, not only because they attract a large number of the participants of the rituals, but also because their presence is directly linked to *macumba*'s popular association with black magic, malefic witchcraft, and even criminality (Contins 1983; Contins and Goldman 1985; Maggie 1992). *Macumba* is a term often used as an accusatory attribution to practices that are objects of fear or derision, an ascription attributed to practices deemed to be linked to witchcraft of one sort or another. At the same time, however, *macumba* can also be used as a generic term that refers to all Afro-Brazilian religions, from the *candomblé* houses more closely associated with African practices to the *umbanda* centers, where the influences of indigenous practices and European Spiritism commingle with African deities.

It is partially this lack of a precise referent and its accusatory connotation that has led to the disappearance of this term as an analytic concept in the anthropological literature.[2] If other terms used to refer to Afro-Brazilian religious practices, such as *umbanda* and *candomblé*, are also umbrella terms that in practice congregate a variety of practices and beliefs, their use still evokes ideas of religious tradition and uniformity. They work as proper names, even if they are unable to properly contain that which they refer to. *Macumba*, on the other hand, is always already a reference to the ambiguous sources of one's religious practices.

While the term has been exiled from academic writing, it has, nonetheless, retained great social currency, taking part in a semantic play that refers to the myriad of rituals of consultation that take place around the city, in religious centers as well as in small rooms temporarily transformed into ritual spaces, without actually naming or providing these rituals with a positive or objective identity. *Macumba* is at once this ambiguity and the practices that fall under this dis-ordering sign. This is an ambiguity unequivocally saturated with racialized meanings, an in betweenness that feeds the mixture of desire and rejection toward *macumba* that one finds in Brazilian society.

If *macumba* has acquired a name-calling quality, it also appears in people's references to their own practices. In the public imaginary *macumba* obtains its meanings precisely by being the antithesis of the discursive construction of a fixed referent, in its historical constitution as an index of dis-order, of a lack of precise identity. Thus, to name oneself a *macumbeiro* is inevitably to signify upon these known connotations of the name. Unable to fit under the propriety of a name, *macumba* eludes the fiction of bounded identities. To call oneself a *macumbeiro* is not a moment of categorization but a process of naming through a subtle discursive play on the divergent meanings that converge under that sign.

My own insistence on referring to these practices as *macumba* in the ethnographic text emanates from the fact that such practices do not skirt the (religious, social, cultural, racial) tension between such competing (in)definitions, being, instead, continuously and inescapably haunted by them. Instead of evoking a particular religious identity or affiliation, *macumba* here denotes a sociality inextricably marked by the presence of spirits that move beyond the boundaries of "ritual" and "everyday," "sacred" and "mundane," "past" and "present," "personal" and "public," "real" and "imaginary." *Macumba* is then taken to be a way of perceiving, imagining, and engendering the everyday as imbued with the presence of spirits.

The presence of these spirits is not commonly glossed under the name of *possession* among the practitioners of *macumba*. When one of these spiritual entities manifests its presence on the body of a *filho de santo*, an initiate in the religious practices, that person is deemed to be *virado no santo* ("turned with the spirit")[3] and to be *trabalhando com o santo* ("working with a spirit"). These ways of referring to the embodied presence of the spirits express a relation of transformation in the presence of an other, and *to work* with spirits is taken as a process, not simply a moment, in which persons and spirits are both transformed and transforming. As a trope that indicates a "taking over," "possession" arrives as a closure—not only in the cultural othering signified through it but also in the possible implications of control, subjection, or appropriation of a person. On the other hand, to work with spirits arises in the midst of what that signification of the verb *to possess* negates—ambiguity, contradiction, an interruption or disorientation through the presence of difference.

To work with spirits is to be entangled in a sociality that exceeds the enclosure of the boundaries of ritual. Beyond the framed space and time of rituals honoring the spirits and the musical evocation of their presences in the bodies of the *filhos de santo*, other moments, other places, and other people are also infused with the presence of the *povo da rua* through a continuous narration of their presences. Partially told, partially heard stories narrate the workings of the spirits, tell about their lives and their deaths, tell about their doings and undoings, and evoke their present and their past, inevitably imbricating in a continuous relation the lives of the spirits and those of their followers.

The *povo da rua* are brought into the heart of religious rituals at the same time that their presence in the "everyday" of this world disrupts their confinement to either of those realms. The movement of the spirits between these realms at once extends the boundaries of ritual outward and brings the outside world into the frame of ritual. To follow the movement of the *povo da rua* is to take the reader through different realms of the presence of the spirits, and through the lives of the people who share their memories and experiences with those of the *povo da rua*. It is to weave the ethnographic narrative through the meandering multitude of stories that, akin to verses of incantation, continuously bring the spirits into existence here and over there. It is to take the reader to the profane streets where the traces of the spirits are present, to the sacred rituals in and out of the streets where the spirits are incorporated in bodies and stories. It is to try to evoke the shared sociality of this acquired sensibility to the at once hidden and markedly present existence of the *povo da rua*.

To take the sociality in which the *povo da rua* are implicated as our ethnographic object it is necessary to engage with the making and unmaking of meaning as it unfolds in the midst of this tension-filled process of social enunciation. It is thus necessary to track the very "disseminatory act" (Bhabha 1990, 300) of these stories, their insinuation of difference in the interstice of generic representations of the social. The cultural poetics of the object itself demands that we replace the epistemological distance of representation by an attention to the very performativity of signification. It also requires that we situate ethnography within an analytical space that seeks to articulate something akin to a provisional constellation, which, as Kathleen Stewart (1996) puts it, gives notice to the dizzying effects of cultural imagination and to the dense entanglement of cultural practices.

It is necessary, then, that we pause to reflect upon the very role of ethnographic narration in the articulation of the stories about the *povo da rua* as an ethnographic object. Rather than being caught by what Se$rematakis (1991) identifies as the anthropological desire to capture events in a linear narrative, which produces a sequence of discrete events that progressively illuminate one another until arriving at an explanatory closure, we might allow the ethnography to be "contaminated" (Stewart 1991) by the poetics of the object itself. Akin to the stories about the *povo da rua*, the ethnographic narrative produces certain relations between places, people, and spirits. These relations could be thought of in a similar way to what Tim Ingold (2007, 90) argues in regard to storytelling, where, instead of providing "a connection between pre-located entities," or connecting points in a network, every relation is "a path traced through the terrain of lived experience," or "one line in a meshwork of interwoven trails."

Ingold's argument about storytelling also points to a different concept of knowledge. Instead of a building up or an assemblage of "fragments into structures of progressively greater inclusiveness" (ibid., 88), knowledge is forged in the movement between places, themes, stories, and histories (ibid., 84–92). I am, in turn, suggesting that to be "contaminated" by the poetics of storytelling is also to insist on ethnography as a similar kind of movement. Besides highlighting its necessary incompleteness, such ethnography might allow for the restoration of the perception of other presences, to borrow Marylin Strathern's coinage (2004, 25–27). I think this is what Strathern means when she refers to ethnography as a personification of ethnographic experience, without centering it on an individual fieldwork, and as an evocation of partial connections to other presences (ibid.).

Let me then return to that sociality of *macumba* where the sharing of stories at once performatively brings the spirits into existence as subjects and materializes the very sociality in which their "lives" are lived.

*   *   *

If you want me to kill, I will kill
If you want me to give, I will give
If you want me to defend you
I will be your defender

Se quiser que eu mato, eu mato
Se quiser que eu dê, eu dô
Se quiser que lhe defenda
Eu serei seu defensor

Ritual song for the *povo da rua*

Many of the deeds of the spirits are done within the confines of the spiritual world where they dwell, even if the effects of such acts present themselves in the world of the living. The *povo da rua* often perform their "work" that way. But not always. Stories abound about their actual presence in the everyday life of those who believe in them—and even in that of those who are foolish enough not to.

Sometimes there are just traces of them, like an overheard whisper in one's ear, or a faint smell of alcohol or strong perfume in the air. Tony, a young man who used to work with—that is, incorporate—a *malandro* spirit called Zé Pilintra, told me that the spirit was always with him as he went around town taking care of his daily business. "Sometimes, when I'm in doubt about what to do, I hear this voice in my ear. . . . He just points me in a direction, or turns me away from something," Tony once explained to me, as we waited for the beginning of one of the weekly consultation sessions at the *macumba* house he belonged to as a *filho de santo*.[4] Sometimes, however, there is much more than just this faintly felt presence.

Stories about such encounters with the *povo da rua*, about their vivid presence in the everyday life of this world, are told by those who happen

upon them and by the very spirits who erupt amid our daily affairs. Alongside the laying out of offerings for the spirits in crossroads, railroads, cem-
eteries—liminal places between the here and there, the space where the
povo da rua dwell—the multitude of stories mark the deep connection
between the spirits and the everyday, between their lives and the lives lived
in this world.

The presence of the *povo da rua* in people's lives is one charged with
the sense of the unexpected, the sheer power of the spirits to appear at
their will in the midst of one's daily affairs. Everyone knows that the spirits
will go anywhere they have to in order to carry out whatever task someone
might have appealed to them to do. They will also just show up if their
presence is needed and they feel generous enough to actually grant their
help. One such story about the fortuitous help of the *povo da rua* was told
me by Elza. A middle-aged woman, she had belonged to several different
religious houses during her life. Of late, however, she was simply staying
away from commitment to any place in particular, only attending public
ceremonies at different places.

Despite these comings and goings in and out of religious houses, Elza
claimed to have kept her own connections to the spirits. So much so that
they had come to her aid one unfortunate day. She had been riding on a
public bus, on her way to work, when a man walked up to the bus driver,
and pulling out a gun, he announced a robbery and ordered the frightened driver to keep on driving. The man turned to the passengers and
demanded that they hand over their valuables. Elza had started shaking
uncontrollably as she watched wallets, watches, wedding rings, gold and
silver crucifixes find their way into the sack the robber was menacingly
shaking in people's faces. All the while Elza had been silently calling on
the people of the streets to protect her. Her calling must have been so
strong that all of a sudden her *pomba-gira*, a spirit called Dona Maria,
took over her body. Dona Maria jumped up from the seat, landing in the
middle of the bus aisle, bent knees on the floor, her shoulders swinging
with the unmistakable lascivious laughter of the *pomba-giras*.

Elza herself could not have been a witness to the actions of Dona Maria, and it was the other passengers who had told her the story she was in
turn telling me some years ago. The robber took one look at the laughing woman, knees spread on the floor, defiantly telling him to come and
get the money from in between her breasts, and that was enough for him
to turn around on his heels and demand to be let off the bus. Dona Maria also departed, leaving Elza disoriented and surprised by her dirtied

clothes. A young woman who had been sitting next to Elza explained to her that she had fallen ill, frightening away the robber. Elza laughed hard when she told me this part of the story, very much enjoying the euphemism[5] used by the woman to refer to her *pomba-gira*'s presence. She was obviously amused by Dona Maria's intrusion in the botched robbery. At the time, however, she had felt so embarrassed that, like the robber and Dona Maria herself, she too was quick to leave the bus.

The robber, and probably many of the passengers, including the young woman who spoke of the presence of the spirit through the commonly used euphemism of "health affliction," had recognized the woman on the floor as one of the people of the streets. The robber, at least, must have recognized her as a *pomba-gira*, a spirit who, like him, occupies the marginal spaces of the streets. The robber's reaction to the presence of the *pomba-gira* was most likely the result of other encounters he himself had had with *pomba-giras*, or of stories he had been told about the spirits and their powers.

Elza's was not the first story I had heard of the *povo da rua* coming to the rescue of someone in danger, even though the spirits most often offer their help without showing their presence. In the stories that circulate about their sudden appearance in crucial moments in one's life, sometimes their presence is not seen through their incorporation in someone's body but simply as a materialization of the spirit. One such occasion was when Cacurucaia, a well-known *pomba-gira*, rescued a man from certain death. Having been called to carry out some spiritual deed or other, Cacurucaia had kept some of the *filhos de santo* helping her well into the night at the *macumba* house where she gave weekly consultations to a great number of "clients." It was very late when the man was able to leave. The story of what happened afterward was told to me and other *filhos de santo* by Cacurucaia herself on an evening not that different from the one she described in her story.

Cacurucaia, sitting at the foot of the door to the room where she provided consultations, shared her ever-present *cachaça*, sugar cane liquor, and her boastful memories of a past feat with those of us who stayed to help her. Once upon a time, then, on his way home, this man had run into a couple of armed men giving chase to two other men. The *filho de santo* had frozen in his path, as one of the escaping men fell to the ground with a shot to the back. The other one kept running, chased by the sound of flying bullets.

The *filho de santo* had nowhere to hide and was certain of his impending death for witnessing the killing. Cacurucaia, who reassured us that she would never let any harm happen to someone who had just helped her out, told us that she used her own body to shield the *filho de santo* from being spotted by the gunmen. "He didn't see me coming. All he saw was my big black arm pushing him still against the wall. I just stood there, in front of him, like we were a couple making out against the wall," she told us with obvious joy at the surprise of the *filho de santo* and the deceit to the armed men. "The gunmen finished off the other guy, and looked around. They saw no one!" Cacurucaia proudly told us. She ordered the *filho de santo* quickly into his house and commanded him not to say a thing about what he had seen. She probably did not really have to give him the last advice, as he would have been a fool to volunteer any information to the police or anyone else. He lived in the neighborhood and would certainly have been found by the gunmen well before the police could find them. In any case, as one of the *filhos de santo* listening to Cacurucaia commented, one could never be certain that the gunmen were not policemen themselves.

The unexpected character of the presence of the *povo da rua*, the unbounded quality of their movement, and the transgressive nature of their identity narrated in these stories are at the heart of the qualities that constitute the *povo da rua* as spirits who open (and close) pathways and who generate (and foreclose) possibilities. This association with willful disruption is at the center of their power. It is at once the source of their identification with trickery and mischief and of their association in Brazilian popular culture with the evil doings of the Christian devil.

The stories about the *povo da rua* exist in a space of narrative tension between excessive narration and obscurity, in which their lives are caught between the generic tales of *pomba-giras* and *malandros* and the tantalizing mystery of their individual histories.[6] The stories about this or that spirit, like the Zé Pilintra who accompanies Tony through the city, or Elza's Dona Maria who comes to her aid in a time of dire need, stand in tense relation to the general category of *malandro* or *pomba-gira*, their individuation related to an ongoing composition. However, if in their individuation, the spirits are linked to a particular person, they are by no means framed by that singular relation.

Here the spirits are not only given a central role as subjects of stories told about them but, most importantly, also as narrators of their own storying, and this storying is in turn always already in relation to multiple other stories, enmeshed in a sociality partially engendered by the threads of narration. Furthermore, at the same time that the stories reveal details about their lives, the spirits re-veil themselves in a continuous production of uncertainty about who they are. On the one hand, stories about their lives abound in a rich mythology fed by folktales and conveyed in inexpensive publications available in the newsstands. The stories about the *povo da rua* are the focus of intense elaboration by the authors of popular books on *umbanda*, *candomblé*, and so forth. This repertoire of possible stories also include the many available books elaborating on the divisions and relations of spirits along categories of classification pertaining to the attributes and affinities—or lack thereof—of their powers, modes of work, relations to nature and to morally ordained cosmos, and so on.

On the other hand, the stories about the lives of the spirits you happen upon in rituals or who you might encounter in the everyday are as elusive as the *povo da rua* themselves can be. In the spirits' ongoing individuation through the process of narration, their uniqueness stands in tense dialogue with categories that would contain them within a given identity.[7] The endless stories you hear about the people of the street never quite tell where they lived, never quite tell when their lives took place, never quite tell who they are.

It is not the case that these details are unimportant, as snippets always surface in conversations. The references, however, are always ambiguous, with details piling up here and there, weaving an impermanent collage of memories that gives fragmented images of who the spirits once were. One can end up with a story of sorts to tell but never with the certainty that one knows it all or that what one has been told is the total truth. Cacurucaia herself kept promising me that, one day, she would sit down and tell me the story of her life. "You won't really like it, though. . . . It's too sad," she would insist on warning me every time I probed her.

Cacurucaia's endless deferral of telling was not a simple silence, as she would tell me (and whoever happened to be around to hear) a little of this, a little of that, here and there. Bits and pieces of a story not entirely her own, as she would always include details about things she had done for, or to, people who had been her clients, details that intertwined her story with the lives of her clients—like Tony entangled his life with that of Zé Pilintra. The telling of the stories of the people of the streets keeps reveiling their lives in mystery at the same time that it reveals enough to lure the listener into that narrative space—the lacunae in the tale even more seductive than the clarity of knowledge.

Details of a spirit's life become part of the ongoing narrative as they happen to be relevant to the moment. Events that took place, fates people encountered, advice given, people who came seeking the spirits all become props that elicit fragments of stories that envelope them. Not a story shot through with information, that form of communication that for Walter Benjamin lays claim to prompt verifiability and whose prime requirement is that it appears "understandable in itself" (1968, 89). Rather, it is a story that grows out of the commensality of experience. Benjamin tells us that "experience which is passed from mouth to mouth is the source from which all storytellers have drawn" (ibid., 84). Stories are then not unlike the passing of food from the mouth of a grandmother to a child that Nadia Serematakis (1993) describes in Greek society—an act of exchange that is part of the larger "exchange of sensory memory and emotions, and of substances and objects incarnating remembrance and feelings" (ibid., 14) that constitutes the commensality which Seremetakis finds at the root of social knowledge and historical consciousness. For Benjamin, a storyteller "takes what he tells from experience—his own and that reported by others. And he in turn makes it the experience of those who are listening to his tales" (1968, 87).

In this commensality, the stories, the words in them, acquire a taste, as Bakhtin would have it, as "each word tastes of the context and contexts in which it has its socially charged life" (1981, 293). To partake of these words, of these shared tastes, of these stories, is not to participate in the creation of a coherent story, a verifiable account, or even to engage in a marked, identifiable moment of storytelling. The words in these stories are dispersed in the everyday, in the various moments of ritual, in songs and conversations, crisscrossing time and space in a mimetic play with the movement of the spirits themselves.

Or should we say that it is the multiple arrivals and dislocations of the spirits that are mimetic of this form of narration? Take a night of counseling, when the *pomba-gira* Cacurucaia had been presiding over the presence of several other *povo da rua*—all performing some form of work or another for the people who sought them that evening. A woman had come to Cacurucaia complaining that nothing in her life was turning out as she desired. I never learned much about her—like most of Cacurucaia's clients she was black, like some she was young, like all of them she needed help. No matter how hard she tried to steady her path, things would turn out wrong—the promised job had not come true, her family life was in disarray. "Her paths are closed," decreed Cacurucaia, as she held the hand of the young woman and requested that a particular song be sung in order to call for the presence of another *pomba-gira*, whom Cacurucaia thought had something to do with the woman's troubles:

[. . .] when the coffin lowers to the grave
you will have to look sideways.
A girl with a skirt of scraps,
by her cross she bursts out laughing.
Ô Mulambô [Ragged], mulambá,
your ragged skirt has stories to tell.
What is the use of new clothes if the skirt is ragged?
Small bits, small bits, its all ragged!

Cacurucaia sat back while Maria Mulambo, or Ragged Mary, the other *pomba-gira*, incorporated in one of the *filhos de santo*, carried the young woman off to a corner to talk. "It was because of this one," Cacurucaia pronounced with scorn as she pointed to Maria Mulambo, who had kept an eye on Cacurucaia since the moment of her arrival. The atmosphere in the room grew tense, as a very sarcastic exchange of sharp words unfolded between the two spirits. Cacurucaia spared no swear words, making continued explicit, derogatory references to the other *pomba-gira's* vagina, while praising her own sexual aptitudes. Nobody wants to be around when two *pomba-giras* fight, as one can never predict the outcome. I had watched a couple of heated disputes before this one, and people had talked about feeling the effects of them for weeks to come—body ailments, accidents, and other mishaps had all been attributed to the ire of the *pomba-giras*, who had no qualms with bringing all people present into their dispute. To everyone's relief Maria Mulambo decided to cut her presence short, announcing that she had "to take care of this girl's business somewhere else . . ."

Cacurucaia guffawed at Maria Mulambo's departure, asking anyone within earshot if they had seen the other *pomba-gira's* slashed face. People around me nodded in recognition of the bodily marks and the torn clothes I myself had not seen, being unable to see beyond the body of the woman who had incorporated the spirit. "I did that!" Cacurucaia remarked with a bitter smile. "This is the whore I killed," she announced. Only then did I understand Cacurucaia's anger, as fragments of her story I had previously heard sprang to memory. I, like the other *filhos de santo*, could finally identify Maria Mulambo as the woman who, in life, had betrayed Cacurucaia and had been the cause of their deaths.

That night I had a momentary feeling of knowing Cacurucaia's story, of having a discernable life story that I could easily convey within my own ethnographic story. I could produce a somewhat coherent life history, that narrative genre that, as Barbara Kirshenblatt-Gimblet (1989) points out, is a Western textual convention so commonly deployed by ethnography to reflect upon experience. But, to know the story, to simply add all the parts and convey the story of Cacurucaia or any of the *povo da rua* is to place oneself as a narrator outside of the space of collective retelling, to remove oneself from the very sociality inhabited by the spirits, their clients, and the *filhos de santo*. To focus on the content of the story would be to miss the poetic force of the very process of weaving such a story—a narrative experience that is constitutive of the power of the *povo da rua*.

Take another night of consultations a few weeks before Maria Mulambo showed up. On that evening the clients had even more in common with Cacurucaia's own story—they, like the *pomba-gira* once upon a time, were young black women who worked as prostitutes. Cacurucaia talked to all of them behind the closed red and black door of her room, having taken the women, one by one, into the room. One could only faintly hear the whispering tone of the women's voices, but Cacurucaia's own voice came thundering out of the room, so loud that one had to wonder why she had bothered closing the door at all. She had yelled at them, egged them on about things she thought they could or should do, chastised them for bringing problems upon themselves, and advised them on a number of things. After talking to all the women, Cacurucaia proclaimed exhaustion and demanded drinks and music to improve her mood. She flirted with the man who had come to play the drums for her that evening, as she waited for a *filha de santo* to remove the safety pins Cacurucaia had secured into the skin of her own wrists and stored away the blade she had stashed in her bosom.

Amid all the play, Cacurucaia told the people around her that her clients that night were foolish women: "You all want a *man*! Don't I have better things to do? I'll help with money, job . . . But a *man*? What is their use?" After many drinks she confided that she too had wanted a man once upon a time. She had left her life in the streets for him, tended the fields for him, kept a home for him, only for all to end in betrayal, she had recounted with a self-deprecating laugh, before going on to offer to initiate that night's drummer in the pleasures of sex that only she could offer. It was after Cacurucaia's departure that evening that a *filha de santo* told me that Cacurucaia had caught her lover in bed with a woman she had sheltered in their home. In her anger Cacurucaia had killed her lover, slashed the other woman's beautiful face, and then turned the knife upon herself, slitting her pregnant belly open and dying in despair. It was this woman, now a *pomba-gira* spirit, whom I was to meet several weeks later.

The story of Cacurucaia's death gave me images of murderous rage, of evil betrayal, of suffering and wisdom, all of which resonated with the images of *pomba-giras*, and particularly of Cacurucaia, as passionate women undeterred in their will by moralizing propriety. I would, however, be as much of a fool as the women that evening if I were to be seduced by the power of this narrative closure, by its aura of knowledge, as, like them, I would be searching for the wrong thing. Those details about Cacurucaia's life are important in constituting who she and other *pomba-giras* in general are. But the mode through which this knowledge is conveyed and the way in which the spirits and their audience—clients, *filhos de santo*, believers, the occasional listener and anthropologist—partake in the construction of an ongoing narrative are at the root of the very power of the story and of the people of the street.

Mary Steedly (1993) and Anna Tsing (1993) argue that the narrative power of a storyteller resides in his or her ability to convene an audience. That is, it implies telling "the kind of story that counts for something to those for whom it is intended" (Steedly 1993, 198). In the case of the *povo da rua*, the power to "convene an audience" resides just as much in the ability to tell a "good story" as in their refusal of a finished story, their delaying of an end so as to continue the telling. In other words, the *povo da rua* convene their "audience"—their clients, the *filhos de santo* who work with them, the ones who seek them, and the ones who fear them—by maintaining the telling of a story continuously inhabited by the *povo da rua* and their audience.

The people of the streets insist on exceeding the framing that knowledge might create around them. The stories tell enough to assure the return of the audience (and here audience is far from a passive corpus of listeners, nor does it exclude the spirits themselves), at the same time that they create an aura of secrecy that maintains the seductive power of the *povo da rua*'s ambivalence. It is by remaining mysterious that the people of the streets can keep offering a story, that they can keep offering the counsel people seek. After all, as Benjamin points out, "Counsel is less an answer to a question than a proposal concerning the continuation of a story which is just unfolding" (1968, 86).

In this unfolding story the people of the streets retain a radical otherness. Not simply the otherness of the exotic Other—a place in which such otherness is fixed within what Trinh Minh-Ha (1991, 13–16, 185–192) has called a "regime of visibility," captured into the realm of the known and visible, of the appropriable. It is rather an otherness that rejects a fixed and autonomous subject position. By their very nature, the spirits cannot

be autonomous subjects, their very presence in this present being mediated, even in their most concrete form, as they become embodied by a
filho de santo.

As (co)authors/narrators of their stories, the spirits thrive on the ambivalence of identity, playing off the doubleness of things to reenchant
their own mystery. Rather than take the spirits as subjects positioned in
a given social map, whose location would authorize their enunciation as
spirits, we should think of an ongoing constitution of the *povo da rua* that
takes place through the performative operations of narration.[8] To speak of
the *povo da rua* as emergent in the performance of narration is certainly
not to speak of pure creativity, whatever that might be, as they are always
already implicated in a social recognition. But such recognition does not
identify or locate the spirits, rather it evokes who they might be. It is in
the telling of their stories that the texts, discourses, and contexts that surround the spirits are themselves conjured into a play of signification. That
demands that we think of both their stories and the sociality of their telling as emergent in performance.[9] It is through these mutually formative
relations, in which *filhos de santo*, clients, and spirits are implicated, that
macumba is engendered as a sociality.

We return here, through my own meandering way, to Ingold's (2007)
idea of "relations" as a path, in contrast to a concept of "connection between pre-located entities." Ingold argues that to "tell a story is to *relate*, in narrative, the occurrences of the past, retracing a path through
the world that others, recursively picking up the threads of past lives, can
follow in the process of spinning out their own. But rather as in looping
or knitting, the thread being spun now and the thread picked up from the
past are both of the same yarn. There is no point at which the story ends
and life begins" (2007, 90; emphasis in the original). In a similar fashion,
to seek the *povo da rua* is to be provisionally linked through a narrative
chain to both the spirits and other folks—the clients and *filhos de santo*
who share in the benevolent deeds and the feared wrath of the spirits. The
insertion in this chain provides links that cut across people's individual
experiences, bringing the "marginal" and "individual" into the center
of collective narration. To partake in these stories, to become an active
character of these tales, is not to recognize one's experience as "just like
someone else's." It is, rather, to burst it out of the apparent ordinariness
of the everyday, to free it from the familiarity of the mundane, investing
in one's life the power of the "strangeness" of the spirits. The narrative
performances bring forth a crossroads—the space of dwelling par excel-

lence of the *povo da rua*—where stories, subjects, places, and histories cut across each other, creating temporary connections where multiple narrative strands rub against one another. To resort to the counsel of the spirits, to request the help of the people of the streets is not to transcend the "real" or obfuscate the "truth" of things but to reenchant the social by placing it in another path of relations.

CHAPTER SIX

Enchanted Entities and Disenchanted Lives along the Amazon Rivers, Brazil

Mark Harris

This chapter examines the social and historical lives of some entities that play a role in the world of Amazonian *ribeirinhos* (river dwellers) in the state of Pará, Brazil. The current volume provides an opportunity to consider ribeirinho histories from a different angle. I will focus on how certain visible and invisible forms have acquired, or continue to hold, special significance over time. This perspective allows me to examine these entities' historical journeys as they pass through different periods and societies. The main entities to be analyzed relate to the watery environment: the river, which is a massive physical force in these people's lives, and is also the home of certain spiritual beings, *encantados* (especially the enchanted dolphin), who live there in a kingdom full of luxury and pleasure (the *encante*). Water, and its special nature, offer some important ways of thinking about agency and intangibility.

Following my informants, I will investigate the instability and the transitions between the visible and the invisible. The value of a thing is not dependent on its material form but in its power and ability to transform, affect others, enchant, and offer protection. What is revealed in this new perspective is a distinctly Amazonian peasant nonanthropocentric view of the world. The human is caught in a weblike pattern of relations between forces of potency located in certain visible and invisible forms and the human universe of everyday goings on.

The use of personal experience to convey ribeirinho understanding of the unstable space between the visible and invisible is fundamental here.

Encantados, as a kind of person, enjoy stories to be told about them, their cunning and antagonistic nature, and their enchantment. Through narration, entities are made a part of community history and self-identification, but they don't acquire humanity. My questions are as follows: Have the powerful entities and invisible beings influenced ribeirinho participation in general over time? What do the social lives of entities reveal concerning the history of the lives of ribeirinhos?

Patricia Spyer has written of the "fetish" as a material object, which gains its potency from avoiding a positioning in a fixed time and place (Spyer 1998, 3). Although in this Amazonian case we are not dealing with straightforwardly material objects, we are examining entities that are fetish-like—the river that is given qualities of life or the dolphin that is a living being and whose real nature can never be known. My argument is that these entities speak for the people who try to know them. These entities are complex historical "beings" rich in various influences, and what they "know" exceeds what any one person can tell.

* * *

A brief note is necessary on the historical and ethnographic context before continuing. Ribeirinhos are Brazilian Portuguese-speaking peasants who fish, hunt, and raise crops and animals along the banks of the Amazon and the lower parts of its tributaries. They tend to live near towns and cities and to market their produce on a regular basis. Their economic and social organization is seasonal in that it is linked to the availability of products and the rise and fall of the river. The rural-urban divide in Pará is roughly split equally, but not all rural dwellers are ribeirinhos. They may be large, medium, and small-scale farmers of soya and cattle ranchers. Still about 30 percent of the inhabitants of the municipality Óbidos, where I have been carrying out fieldwork since the early 1990s, live along the river (Harris 2000), which is near Santarém. Most of this chapter concerns this area, which is known locally as the Lower Amazon and lies at the heart of the Brazilian part of riverine Amazonia.[1]

Following the initial period of conquest, peasant societies along the river were made up of the Indians who survived and were forcibly settled in missions and colonial villages. By the beginning of the nineteenth century, the inhabitants of these places had spilled out along the fertile banks and achieved a measure of autonomy in the organization of their labor and social relations. Over time all sorts of ethnic mixtures emerged with Europeans and Africans, not to mention their cultural traditions. From an external perspective, this is history full of ruptures and reconstitutions (Nugent 1993; Cleary 2001; Harris 2010).

Nowadays ribeirinhos are spread out along the riverbanks; their houses are built on stilts to protect them from the annual floods. Their villages are largely composed of kinsfolk. They spend time in cities for education and life experience, though the ones I got to know prefer the life of the floodplain for its access to food and personal independence. They live there in the shadow of their powerful bosses from the city and with threats to their livelihoods in the form of overfishing and low market prices for their products. Yet resilience is embedded in their lives (Smith et al. 1995). Nevertheless the variety of political and economic and religious forces, which have made the modern Brazilian Amazon, has given rise to a complex and unruly set of practices and beliefs. In order to grasp a little of this confusion we will turn to the conquest period.

The Haunting of the Hanging Mummy

The following story took place sometime in the 1680s in Santarém, the main town of the Lower Amazon—the Jesuit chronicler, João Bettendorff, is often vague about what happens when, unless it concerns his order and the activities of its missionaries, especially the famous Antonio Vieira. The Amazon at this time was coming to the end of the early phase of colonial occupation. The Portuguese founded Belém in 1615, amid warring Indian nations and strong European interest in the area. The Lower Amazon, about 800 miles and a two-week journey, by rowing and sailing, upstream from Belém, was similarly subjugated by the Portuguese in the mid-seventeenth century, though fear of warfare was constant for colonists and missionaries. The mission in Santarém (then known as Tapajós) was started in 1661 by Jesuits. At any one time there were no more than one or two missionaries conducting affairs with the support of a handful of soldiers, compared with thousands of Indians—from the Tapajós nation in the case of Santarém.

Bettendorff's chronicle is a fascinating and sprawling narrative offering much of value to ethnohistorians.[2] Yet it has been little used except by Kurt Nimuendaju (2004) on the Tapajós. The Tapajós Indians, according to Bettendorff, had a mummy (*corpo mirrado*) of their great ancestor, called *Monhangarypy* (which means "a first father"[3]). It was kept wrapped in cotton in some sort of case and strung up in the rafters of a special house, located some distance from the mission in a clearing in the forest, as though this was the permanent resting place for the dead person. They had honored this figure for many years with ritual offerings and dances. Bettendorff, the founder of the mission, wrote that he had wanted to exterminate this "intolerable abuse" of the Catholic faith but always feared an uprising if he did. Sometime after 1682 the missionary, Antonio Pereira, however, did not have this fear. After consulting with indigenous leaders, he decided to burn the place down, reducing it to ashes. Apparently, the Indians felt the loss deeply but did not revolt (Bettendorff 1990, 353–54).[4]

From other sources, we learn that there were several mummies in existence in the Santarém area at the end of the seventeenth and beginning of the eighteenth century (e.g., Daniel 2003 and Leite 1943). These were secreted in the forest far from the Portuguese, in places known only to ritual specialists and male village elders. Since the earliest times these bodies were worshipped, each with their own invocation: god of maize, god of manioc, god of rain, and so on (Leite 1943, 305). Even as late as 1742, almost a hundred years after the mission's founding, a missionary discovered sixteen "idols," consisting of mummies (said to be the first ever people on earth) and painted stones. Rituals and festivities took place near these sacred beings. Aside from burning down these secret huts, missionaries were accustomed to throw ritual objects into the river or smash them into pieces (Bettendorff 1990; Daniel 2003, 1:323). Such was the destruction of the religious possessions of the Tapajós people. None of these material objects have survived to the present day—nothing to keep in museums.

When the missionaries first mention these idols they are located in the village. About eighty years later they can be found only in the depths of the forest (see Leite 1943, 304–5). Whether this move was a deliberate attempt to avoid the prying eyes of Europeans and their castigating ways, or just selective reporting on behalf of missionaries, we do not know. Other questions of significance might include: Was there an increase, or a wane, in the numbers of mummies and stones? Were Christian symbols and practices incorporated into these rituals (e.g., compare with the *santidades* of Indians in Bahia; Vainfas 2005). But the fact the practice continued for at least three generations of Tapajós Indians suggests a prolonged attachment to Amerindian loci of symbolic power.

Nowadays saints' icons are present in many houses, adorned with ribbons, cloth, flowers, magazine images, and candles. We could say that the place of the mummy has been appropriated by the Christian icon, while the loci of symbolic power has proliferated and become available to all those who wish to have a representation of the saint.

The most precious items of this ancient world still in existence today are the *muiraquitãs*, small green stone amulets. Also known as the *pedra das Amazonas*, it was made from green stone, was attached to a cotton string about an inch and a half long, was cylindrical and narrow, held much symbolic value, and was very well polished. The stone is a form of jade, very rare, and was probably mined from near the source of the Trombetas River to the north. The amulet was associated with the Lower Amazon and, in particular, the Tapajós Indians at the time of conquest. The *muiraquitã* could also take the shape of a frog, a symbol of fertility and transformation (Daniel 2003; Spix and Martius 1981). As far as I know, the originals are in museums and private collections, far too prized and valuable to be on public display. Until the early twentieth century they could still be found on a person (Nimuendaju 2004). Henry Bates, who traveled extensively in the Amazon in the 1850s, said no one would give him his or her piece even for massive amounts of money.

In addition, ceramic shards (sometimes whole pots) lie scattered on river beaches and forest floors. Ribeirinhos have told me that on fishing trips they occasionally come across a fine example of Indian pottery from a long time ago. Unable to pick it up at the time, they come back at a later point only to find it has vanished. They attribute this to the mysterious nature of such items: "Like the Indians who first lived here the piece just disappeared," they say. This perception of the past is less about it having enduring value for the present than the sense of an ongoing movement between visibility and invisibility, as shall become clearer. In addition, archaeologists dig up intact ceramic items, some with ritual purposes (e.g., burial pots) and others with more mundane uses. All these pieces are carefully put on display in museums and have no popular circulation. Both the archaeological finds and the random fisherman's booty share a restricted field of meanings. Neither party really knows what the items were used for, and they are subject to speculation and debate.

In a similar way, the mummified ancestors and painted stones haunt the contemporary context, though they will never return to view. The textual references are a reminder of the lack of continuity between Tapajós Indians in the early eighteenth century and the peasant riverine societies of today. The historical ruptures may have prevented oral testimonies and histories from being passed down from generation to generation. Instead the memories and meaningful associations have become transformed—

repressed perhaps—by the inheritors and progenitors of the new modern Amazonian societies. Some entities may have been lost as material presence but their cultural absence endures. The old world of benign gods has become "an invisible universe of evil," according to one commentator (Cravalho 1993). Instead of mummies and stones, ribeirinhos are surrounded by *encantados*, enchanted spirits, ghosts, and other ambiguous entities that cause illness and madness. It is as though in that moment of burning the ritual house the "irreducibly material," to use William Pietz's phrase describing the fetish (1985), of some sacred objects became immaterial, while maintaining their power and value. The fire caused a change in state and the Amerindian fetish became invisible.

In other words, the material form of the mummy and stone could not be translated from one culture to another. Whereas the muiraquitã and ceramic pots have been subjected to a limited extent to a new regime of value. In the rest of this chapter I will explore some of the entities to have replaced the idols and stones in a much more vigorous way. My argument is that out of these transformations and new mixtures emerged a particular kind of understanding characterized by lack of self-centeredness and a fatalistic worldview. Something of this must have been shaped by the racism, slavery, unfair economic demands, political marginalization, and religious discipline imposed on these new Amazonians. A curious combination was produced for these riverine peasants at the end of the colonial period in 1822: a natural world that was seen as enchanted (mysterious and unknowable) and a political and social life that was seen as disenchanted (open to the instrumental authority of others). Ribeirinhos conceive of themselves as subject to the control of outsiders, symbolically invisible and marginal. This relates to the physical reality of their lives on the edge of the river, having to cope with the river's constant movements and changes in level. Before coming to the river and its entities, we need to address how the invisible universe can be characterized.

The Visible and Invisible in the Worldview of the Ribeirinhos

Contemporary ribeirinhos often say that the world is divided into two: the invisible and the visible (see Lima 1992; Maués 1998; Cravalho 1993). This double construction is not an impermeable barrier, rather the opposite. It is crossed by all sorts of entities, including people, but most importantly shamans, who travel there to find out the cause of an illness. Interestingly, the invisible in this sense refers to immaterial beings such as encantados, rather than the Christian perception of the spiritual nature of presence and powers of God and the saints.

Deborah Lima-Ayres, who worked with ribeirinhos in the Upper Amazon near Tefé, writes that there is a "blurred division between the material and the metaphysical world." This same vagueness and fluidity characterizes the connection between the divine and the human through the mediation and communication with saints. Both "other worlds," saints and invisible spirits, are conceived as near to and in close contact with human society. "However, while the gap between this world and heaven is bridged by the intimate relationship between humans and saints in the form of their icons, the world of the encantados is an invisible realm of this world, and thus it is even closer" (Lima-Ayres 1992, 128).

Ribeirinho "representations" of the invisible world are best discerned from their ways of talking. According to my informants in the Lower Amazon, the invisible world is present in the here and now. It is understood to have a timeless presence, though no one put it exactly that way, for the beings do not live and die as humans do. One shaman told me that there are all sorts of *espíritos* (lit. spirits) wandering around.[5] These espíritos are of various kinds, most usually *encantados* (enchanted magical forms), *visagens* (ghosts of dead people), *bichos visagentos* (demonic animals), and folkloric animals (e.g., *cobra grande*, *curupira*).

These are the basic categories of invisible beings and, along with the *encante* (the dominion of encantados at the bottom of the river), comprise the invisible for ribeirinhos in the Upper and Lower Amazon (Galvão 1955; Lima-Ayres 1992; Cravalho 1993; Slater 1993; Maués 1995). However, while all are invisible, they have different powers, presences, and effects in visible reality. These broad categories that constitute the invisible realm do not form neat taxonomic classifications that everybody agrees with. Ask different people and sometimes irreconcilable information will be given. Candace Slater (1993), who traveled to many rural communities and urban centers in the Lower Amazon, very nicely brings alive these contradictions. Rather than explain them away, she allows them to develop and become part of her story. Nothing is settled or fixed according to Slater's informants; there is no institutional control or disciplining of these classifications. Like the dolphin itself, as we will see below, stories change and avoid being pinned down or essentialized. Ribeirinhos do not conceive of the invisible world in terms of a stable cosmological order. Instead there are a range of entities around which meanings gather.

In summary, the visible is not the world of commonsense experience. Instead it is only invoked when there is talk of strange and demonic entities. The visible world is not exactly physical reality, as we might understand it in the West. The visible and the invisible exist together, and there can be passage between each state by some beings. So we, as anthropologists, cannot assume that we understand the visible any better than the invisible. Given some of the features of the encante, it would seem that the invisible is sociohistorically shaped with relevant contemporary artifacts.[6]

Does the contemporary ribeirinho understanding of the distinction between the visible and invisible relate to other dyads such as mind and body, mental representation and materiality, spirit and matter? Are these also local categories in the ribeirinho view of the world? These questions are best answered in reference to the following entity—the river. The ever-present and changing waters of the Amazon afford a different view of matter and its representation in the world of ribeirinhos.

The River as a Powerful Working Entity

We have already heard something of the river—how missionaries cast icons and fetishes into the muddy and fast-flowing waters. Similar to burning, nothing could be regained from the river, for it would become lost in the soft, dark riverbed. Apart from swallowing up disdained material objects, the river played a central role in social and economic life. It provided a means for traveling around, a place for washing and cleaning, a plentiful source of food and water, and so on. Indians were much valued by colonial officials for their knowledge of the environment, their ability to access products suitable for export, and their navigational skills (Flynn Roller 2010). Practically the river was, and still is, an enduring presence in the conduct of the life and the imaginative and economic possibilities it affords.

Elsewhere I have sought to capture the historical (Harris 2010) and contemporary features of riverine life and its seasonality (1998). Here I develop this understanding to consider the way in which living next to a river influences the perception of the world in general. Given the absence of historical material to deepen into the past this perspective, my discussion is limited to the present. Nevertheless there may be some general characteristics of life on the Amazon that stretch across time (and perhaps for all people living next to a river; e.g., see Krause 2010).

Different historical riverbank societies have had to contend with the river's seasonal rhythms of ebb and flow associated with rainfall in the huge drainage basin. The river has such overwhelming force to modify the environment that little of the human past survives for long. Wood rots, banks get eroded, new levees are made, and so on. Yet scholars have found that there have been large- and small-scale efforts to transform the riverine landscape (Raffles and WinklerPrins 2003) by building new streams, redirecting watercourses, and encouraging silting.

One of the most comprehensive contemporary studies of the interface between people and the river is by Hilgard O'Reilly Sternberg in his wonderful book *A água e o homen do Careiro*. The original field research was carried out in the early 1950s (though it was updated for the second edition of the book in 1998), during which he witnessed one of the highest floods in the twentieth century. He shows that there are two alternating landscapes on the floodplain (wet and dry) and that people have to learn to work in these two very different kinds of places, each requiring its own set of skills (Sternberg 1998, 245). At the center of his book is the river, the chief protagonist in the drama of floodplain life. The title of the first chapter reveals something of its creative and destructive power, "The Water and the Product of Geomorphic Activity: The Land." Indeed Sternberg was told by one of his informants in reference to land formation, that "the water put it there and the water will take away" (1998, 99). It is not difficult to understand why: each flood can wipe away traces of the previous year's work and renew the soil with nutritious sediments—the "river is the plow" in the memorable words of another commentator (Higbee [1945, 410], who also writes that "Nature herself prepares the farmer's seedbed").

In my own research in the Lower Amazon, in the state of Pará, near the town of Óbidos, the river is understood by peasant riverbank dwellers to create the land and impart power during the flood. The land and water are inseparable in the local perception of the landscape, and their merging is an integral part of land use. The river then is not a domain of water rather than land, nor do the banks of the river mark a boundary between the two. On the contrary, it is a domain of water-becoming-land, or land-becoming-water, as one season follows the next.

Here the notion of *taskscape* is especially helpful in the floodplain context. Tim Ingold (2000) has coined the term to indicate "an array of related activities," stressing their patterning, sequence, and timing. The taskscape is thus composed from a multitude of activities and will change depending on the work that people do. The landscape is the accumulated imprint of the taskscape on the environment; it is the "taskscape made visible" (2000, 204) and is also varied in quality. *Taskscape* is a powerful term in the wetland context because, in stressing temporal patterns, it avoids privileging natural or social elements. Instead, different seasonal rhythms around people's activities—and those of the river, fish, animals, weather, and plants—interweave. Just as people can leave traces of their work, so the river does. The river then is not an object to dominate but an agent and living part of the environment.

Obviously, the river is not a living being since it is not capable of reproduction and growth. Water is nevertheless a fundamental ingredient of all living things. And the river provides a home to various living creatures, as well as the enchanted kingdom, which I will look at below. It is conceived of as a dynamic and mighty force in contemporary people's lives. Moreover it grows and shrinks like a living thing (but not a life cycle since it is reborn each year), it needs to be tamed, and it has its own rhythmic patterns. So it is comparable to a life form. In other words ribeirinhos experience the river as though it were a kind of living thing, with its own peculiar type of life force.

Something of the distinctness of the watery environment of the Amazon is captured by the great Brazilian writer Euclides da Cunha in a series of essays first published in 1909. He writes of the Amazon that "the changeability of the river infects the human being" (2006, 13). He remarks that as a traveler moves along the river it appears monotonous in the extreme, with green walls of forest lining the banks, occasionally broken by houses and cattle pens. But if one remains in one place, there is constant and often unexpected change. This paradox is genuinely important, despite Cunha's negative characterization of the Amazon as a "green hell." The river is identified as having both a temporal and a spatial dimension. The river flows in time and is a place, or environment, in which fish swim and on which birds hunt and people live and travel.

My argument is that the peasants in the Amazon live with the river, rather than next to it and adapting to it. The river is a part of people's lives not as an object to be controlled but as though it were another form of life. Cunha is correct in writing that there is a contamination between person and water: floodplain life is not an interaction between established objects but a continuous interweaving of the activities of the people, river, plants, land, fish, and weather. From this anthropological perspective, the environmental features and social and economic processes are part of the same unfolding movement.

This subject-oriented view of water and its features has been discussed more generally by the French philosopher Gaston Bachelard. Since water is generally an ambivalent object he has argued that it lends itself to an alternative "imagination of matter." He wrote, "Because we fail to de-objectify images and deform forms—a process which allows us to see the matter beneath the object—the world is strewn with unrelated things, immobile and inert solids, objects foreign to our nature. . . . By grouping images and dissolving substances, water helps the imagination in its task of de-objectifying and assimilating. It also contributes to a type of syntax, a continual linking up and gentle movement of images that frees a reverie bound to objects" (quoted in Krause 2010, 7–8). The river and its floodplain border zones caution against objectification and neat classificatory thinking. Each day each person encounters the force of the river and the motion of its mysterious matter, part soil, part water, its blending with the landscape, its mixing of past and present and future.

This continuous and restive mingling of the river and human finds an extremely strong expression in the Amazon. The different parties to have occupied the riverine environment for any length of time—preconquest Arawak traders and Tupi chiefs and their followers, Portuguese soldiers, European missionaries, Africans, peasants, and the odd anthropologist—may have regarded the river in their own ways, but they have been united in their relationship with it. The experience of the river shapes the way people think about the world. The intimacy between river and person makes for a stronger appreciation of the transitions between entities, and their shared characteristics. Therefore great cultural value is placed on the transformative and the ambiguous. It is a world in constant movement where there is continuity between one state and another.

Are these many human pasts somehow involved in the present? Does the riverscape, like a more permanent landscape, hold on to memories? Does the river remember having sacred objects thrown in it? Does it hold on to them in some mysterious way, unknowable to the present but pregnant with the possibility of return—the absence of the painted stones declaring a loss waiting to be paid back, openness in need of closure?[7]

However, there are other living things that dwell in the river and its margins: fish, birds, insects, plants, and so on, and, more pertinent to the present discussion, the enchanted entities of folk stories, such as the boto (the pink dolphin). What about their uncertain priorities in this border zone? It is important to state that the stories people tell of encounters with encantados always arise from personal experience, of their own or someone close to them. And as such the encantados live within those relations and will cease to be recounted as the relevant people pass away.

The Encante—the Kingdom of Invisible Beings

The river is an uncanny realm. Prominent among the stories contemporary ribeirinhos tell of the river is the encante, an underwater dominion of encantados. There, all manner of modern luxuries and gold-plated goods can be found. Houses are large, painted, and spacious. Nothing goes wrong or rusts. Festivals are constantly held and the praying is very clear and resonant. People are dressed in white clothes, signifying their lack of sinfulness; it is easier for children to go there because they have less sin. Sometimes the festival music can be heard by those who fish or travel at night on a river or a lake.

The encante is not located in a particular part of the river, unlike other aspects of the invisible, but in the river generally, and even under the floodplain land as well. This placelessness and timelessness are peculiar features of the encante and grant it a vagueness that allows it to be revised and resignified. It is to this place the *pajé* (shaman) travels when he wants to call on his spirit helpers (encantados but also called *companheiros* or *mestres* in this situation) to cure evil and find answers to questions from patients. God is also there, but the encante is not heaven. The shaman can travel there in spirit form, so long as he remembers to come back and suffer with his fellows. Ordinary visitors can also be taken there by guides, but they should not eat any food or else they will never return. Yet most people who go there are taken against their will by the boto who steals spirits (*sombre*; on the encante, see also Slater 1993, 203–6).

So water-dwelling spirits have a marvellous time! Nobody needs to work for a living and still there is no poverty. This is in complete contrast to the daily lives of ribeirinhos. Sometimes there is speculation about the origin of this excess and wealth. But nobody knows where it all came from. It is simply over there, just out of arm's reach. The encante is not exactly a substitute paradise; in any case, local Catholicism shows little interest in the next life, especially the punishment of sin.

Although we know little about the historical perceptions of the river, there are some references to an encante-type place in one chronicle by the Jesuit missionary João Daniel. Living in the Portuguese-speaking Amazon from 1741 to 1757, he regularly traveled from mission to mission. His two

volumes, which address varied topics from the types of animals to the beliefs of Indians, are among the most evocative writings from the colonial
period (for the purposes of historical reconstruction). In the Tapajós mission (same as the aforementioned) an Indian headman told another Jesuit
the following anecdote: One day he was out with some colleagues attending to business with other Indians. They were walking along a beach when
suddenly out of the water came a line of men, women, and children. They
were laughing and singing and speaking among themselves in an unknown
language. The headman crossed himself and called on the Virgin Mary to
protect him from these demons. Soon enough the apparitions returned
to the water and left no trace behind.[8] On a separate occasion another
missionary was convinced he saw a man get out of the river, come ashore,
and wander around, before slipping back to the water. Daniel had also
been told of the drumming noises that can be heard on a quiet night on
the waters. One person was said to have disappeared for nine years and
then on his return claimed to have lived underwater for that period. There
would appear to be a continuity from these accounts to the more recent
encante.

One of the most significant inhabitants of this realm in current tales is
the enchanted dolphin being. Daniel does not mention the boto, but in a
chapter on fish in the Amazon, he informs the reader of the existence of
a man-fish (*homen marinho*; 2003, 90–91) and proceeds to reinforce the
claim with reference to European antiquity of such figures as mermaids.
So it should not surprise readers, the logic goes, to find them in the Amazon. He also gives us some local stories told to him by various people. This
figure echoes earlier colonial commentaries that wrote of the *ipupiara*,
a water demon spirit, which was known to take people down the river's
depths (see Cunha 1999, 157; and also Spix and Martius 1981, 146).

I have, in fact, found no references to a figure that resembles closely
the contemporary encantado dolphin in the colonial records.[9] Yet according to some the boto was a colonial invention, probably quite late on as
people started to find conceptual bridges across their mentalities and to
create new practices and ideas appropriate to their own experience. For
example, here is the English naturalist Henry Bates, who lived for eleven
years (1848–1859) in the Amazon in the mid-nineteenth century, on the
boto. His empathy with riverine-dwelling Amazonians is unparalleled for
the period, as can be viewed in this quotation:

> We lay awake conversing until past midnight. It was a real pleasure to listen to
> the stories told by one of the older men, they were given with so much spirit.

The tales always related to struggles with some intractable animal-jaguar, manatee, or alligator. . . . Many mysterious tales were recounted about the Bouto, as the large Dolphin of the Amazons is called. One of them was to the effect that a Bouto once had the habit of assuming the shape of a beautiful woman, with hair hanging loose to her heels, and walking ashore at night in the streets of Ega [nowadays Tefé], to entice the young men down to the water. If anyone was so much smitten as to follow her to the waterside, she grasped her victim round the waist and plunged beneath the waves with a triumphant cry. No animal in the Amazons region is the subject of so many fables as the Bouto; but it is probable these did not originate with the Indians, but with the Portuguese colonists. (Bates 1863, 264)

Similar stories endure into the present. And they are invariably connected to a particular person, as Bates implies above. The dolphin seduces women and is the father of many children. At festivals he transforms himself into a handsome young man, tall, white, strong, a great dancer and drinker. He appears at the dances and courts the girls, sometimes disappearing into the forest. Before dawn, he jumps in the water and returns to being a dolphin. These encounters are not told for their sexual adventures rather because they frequently result in near death maladies, with patients suffering from high fevers and listlessness and requiring shamanic intervention to recover the soul (see also Camara Cascudo 2002).

The classificatory challenges the boto poses are central to its contemporary character. The boto stories, as Candace Slater (1993) has so well pointed out, have many facets to them. Above all, the dolphin is a mammal that is a fish living in water. It breathes, has pink skin, gives birth to live young, and has human-like genitals (and is considered inedible). The boto is perceived as an unwelcome impostor to human affairs; when a man he looks like a rich colonial-type, in an elegant white suit and hat. Moreover, the boto is associated with powerful sexual potency, *cagila* in the vernacular. Its eyes, and genitals, are used to attract the opposite sex. It is mischievous and shameless, and sometimes downright evil (it has much *safadeza*), causing death with its enchantments. Yet it also helps shamans discover the origin of an illness when he calls on it. As such it is an ambiguous and a complex character, ready for all sorts of cultural elaborations at the interstices of diverse historical influences.

The American anthropologist Robert Murphy carried out fieldwork with his partner Yolanda Murphy among the Mundurucu Indians on a tributary to the Tapajós River in the early 1950s. Robert Murphy heard stories of "freshwater porpoises that swim by night and at night can be transformed into handsome men or beautiful women who dress in white clothes and travel in land" (1958, 17). He also reports that the boto was not as dangerous as some of the other evil spirits (known generally as *yurupari*) according to the Mundurucu. Unlike other yurupari, the porpoise spirit has a fixed abode at the bottom of the river, recalling the encante. Noting that the boto story is very common among ribeirinhos on the Tapajós River, Murphy reckons that it is not autochthonous but is derived from the non-Amerindian neighbors of the Mundurucu (Murphy 1958, 18). Neither Bates nor Murphy offer any evidence to support their suspicion of the origin of the boto story. Given the richness of the boto legend in Amazonia for the past two hundred years, I suggest, in line with Slater's comprehensive work, they are not appreciating the whole picture. Here we can also return to the idea of the fetish in the cultural border zones.

Slater exhaustively shows that the boto legends "display [their] culturally hybrid nature, but also their more specifically human one" (1993, 100). This human side is the intensive sexual being as well as the capacity for mischief and, in Slater's account, a range of human emotions including sadness and jealousy (1993, 100). In other words, as the boto has been encountered by different generations of Amazonians since the late colonial period, it has gathered diverse meanings and associations. Yet it is not a passive object but an active living being, even if an anomalous one, effectively participating in the course of events of the region. For it can heal, harm, engender children, cause fear, and so on. On a microlevel the boto is involved in and influences daily life in these villages. Thus it is a unique kind of a subject and agent, in the same way the river has a special identity.

Yet the boto has become also a kind of fetish in the way the river has not. In Amerindian cultures the boto had symbolic significance but not the kind of elaborations it has for ribeirinhos now. Its force as a cultural subject in Amazonia is precisely from its ambivalent nature and its occupation of interstitial zones in between different histories. Moreover as a living being it is a material entity but that materiality is life itself. And that means its intentions, as a subject, cannot be known fully by humans. The use of some of its organs as fetishes to attract lovers supports the idea of the continuity between object and subject, dead body part and live body.

My point is not to revisit the argument Slater makes but to consider the boto's historical journey and how it influences the lives of people who encounter it. If we take stories in terms of their content and as expressions of experience, we can see the work of the boto is to keep challenging the riv-

erine human world. To remind the people of the river that they do not own
the environment nor are they the dominant party. And that the river and
its entities are ultimately mysterious, capricious, and uncontrollable. For
Slater, the boto narratives are a mental representation of the resistance ribeirinhos feel toward the outside-induced changes affecting the Amazon.
The dolphin, being impossible to pin down, is emblematic of this empowerment.[10] In the terms of this chapter, I have tried to turn this around and
see the dolphin not as a social construction of human experience but as
a viable subject in its own right. If the boto were a social construction, it
would be a passive object. Since this is not the case, anymore than the river
or other animals and fish are, they are all present and in some way historical beings perhaps "moving in patterns older than history" (Macfarlane
2007, 128). As Spyer says, "Social constructionism explains away the extraordinary power that with fetishism is precisely the problem" (1998, 5).
The boto is a bridge across diverse histories that absorbs all sorts of powers: to heal and harm, to steal and save souls, to attract and repel men and
women, to harness excess and luxury and lose it again.

Stephen Nugent captures this multiplicity well when he writes, 'Rather
than being an amorphous, structureless and in most respects incapable
of humming a simple tune, caboclo [ribeirinho or peasant] culture has
too many structures, traces of several histories which overlap and inter-
penetrate and generally misbehave, making it difficult to get a grip on
guiding principles" (1990, 125). This cultural top-heaviness implies that
the social and economic underpinnings—kinship and other relations and
domestic organization, for example—are not mutually implicated. The
various parts of the contemporary ribeirinho lives do not correspond to
each other as they are all interrelated and functioning together. They are
out of time and place with each other, in the sense that the historical experience and influences are in excess of their contemporary expression.
So, in any one historical situation, the boto narratives, for example, are
underdetermined, and their meanings go beyond a singular expression.
This approach allows for features to be repressed or submerged, only to be
reactivated if the context changes. This is a rich area to explore the legacy
of conquest and colonization.

*   *   *

In this chapter I have offered a schematic view of three kinds of entities
and their movements, or lack thereof, in Amazonian history—the final
one necessarily receiving the most attention. The first was the mummies

and stones belonging to the Tapajós Indians in the seventeenth and early eighteenth centuries. Too "other" for the European missionaries, these items had to be destroyed. The second was muiraquitã and ceramic pots. Over time these gradually moved out of their original sphere in ritual and daily life to having a very limited and policed presence in the contemporary Amazon. Like the Amerindian revered objects, their value has been taken out of the hands of ribeirinhos. They have nevertheless endured as extremely precious articles, albeit within a limited frame of reference, and have not acquired new layers of meanings. They are the traces of a past that cannot be recovered. The third category has, however, flourished since the end of the colonial period. The river and two of its elements, the underwater realm of spirits and the enchanted dolphin, have gained renewed significance drawing on older values and meanings. Colonization and settlement followed the rivers. The river network connected the vast region—the various parties deliberately using it for their interests—and allowed for an intermingling of people, their knowledge of the environment, and their imaginations. In this process these entities were charged in unpredictable ways. They gained in potency as they became a focus for converging traditions.

Yet in phenomenological terms, none of these entities are empty of significance. They either have their own life or are accorded with special animating qualities, and thus affect the activities of daily life. As sources of vitality in the world, ribeirinhos and others have struggled to tap into them and draw on their strength. This can be quite literal in terms of making a livelihood from the river. Equally, it could be something intangible, such as the shaman calling on the enchanted dolphin to help him see the cause of a client's affliction. My argument is that this difference, between the visible and invisible, is not relevant to the ribeirinho worldview, for it separates the origin of the vitality in the first place, namely the watery realm and what emerges from it. The duality of matter and spirit is not the premise from which ribeirinhos start to appreciate their environment.

Instead they are at ease with a world of instability and uncertainty. They don't placate invisible beings with offerings and put little effort in protecting themselves from their malignity (though if detected, they will of course act). All entities are part of a complex of protagonists, mutually implicated in the workings of the riverine environment. The nonhuman forces are known less by their appearance at any one time than their inherent potency and influence on the human history, as evidenced most clearly in the personal narratives.

In conclusion, I hope to have revealed two distinct trajectories, one of animated entities and their histories, and the other of people and their stories. I have adopted a historical phenomenology approach to make this distinction, which does not explain away the invisible power of beings or things with spiritual force and the way people experience them as a source of strange vitality. In this chapter, the social lives of humans and entities are as belligerent participants in a centerless, perhaps even anarchic, taskscape.

CHAPTER SEVEN

Spirit Materialities in Cuban Folk Religion

Realms of Imaginative Possibility

Kristina Wirtz

Introduction

M. told me that her godfather, a babalawo (divining priest), had his protector spirit come in a dream and give him the address where he had lived, in order to verify it. So he actually went to his house and found out that he really had lived there. — Fieldnote entry, Santiago de Cuba, August 18, 2008

When B asked [the spirit] give me proof, the spirit said remember what I told you in a dream, [*handclap*] [KW: Uh-huh] and [B] says, yes, this is my mother. Because it was true that my mother had told B something in a dream.
—Transcribed conversation in which A recounts how his sister, B, recognized the spirit of their mother in a ceremony, translated from Spanish, Santiago de Cuba, July 16, 2006

Evidence of nonmaterial entities—spirits—is everywhere in the practice of Cuban folk religion. Folk religious practices, diverse as they are, all share a common focus on managing relationships with a complex world of nonmaterial entities. As Diana Espírito Santo (unpublished MS) argues, these practices constitute an intersubjective realm of sociality encompassing spirits and the living that is concerned with self-actualization through spiritual discovery. Some of these spiritual entities are benevolent, and some malevolent; some come unbidden, but most must be coaxed into cooperation. Some are fully deified as saints or orichas (deities of Santería), and some are personified with biographical information of their former lives, while others are massed into undifferentiated spiritual potentialities. All are imbued with powers exceeding and saturating the mundane plane of everyday human existence, powers enacted through the immanence of nonmaterial entities in the material world.

This essay concerns spirit immanence as enacted and reported in and through talk of the sort exemplified in the two epigraphs. I approach such discourse as a key form of spirit materialization, in which the scattered details that coalesce into spirit biographies intertwine with the autobiographical trajectories of religious practitioners, who sense and narrate the agency of spirits in their lives. This narrative work of self-fashioning is always incomplete because it is ongoing. It is also important to recognize a commonality with Vânia Zikàn Cardoso's analysis of Brazilian *povo da rua* spirit narratives in her contribution to this volume: that spirit biographies are perhaps necessarily fragmentary, mysterious, and even obfuscating rather than fully revealing or coherent. As she argues, the performative power of such narratives lies in their "strangeness" and capacity to "reenchant the social" by engaging spirit agency.

Each of the major, named modalities of Cuban folk religious practice—Santería, Spiritism, folk Catholicism, the Reglas de Palo—attends to its own particular set of saints, deities, and spirits while recognizing that the other modalities are necessary to attend to other kinds of nonmaterial entities. All emphasize the importance of *muertos*—spirits of the dead.[1] In the eastern Cuban city of Santiago de Cuba, the site of my ethnographic research, most folk religious practitioners also draw upon a substrate of practices for working with muertos that local Cuban researchers refer to as Muertería (Millet 1999). This array of Cuban popular religious modalities is best thought of as a set of complementary practices, because many folk religious practitioners work across multiple ritual modalities in order to tend to different aspects of their material and spiritual needs.

All of the practices of Cuban popular religion share an emphasis on the imaginative possibilities and potentials afforded by attending to spirits and the ways in which their trajectories and interests intersect with those of living people. Although there are important differences, even polarizations, between (and within) Santería, Spiritism, folk Catholicism, and the Reglas de Palo, my emphasis will be on their shared framework of spirit potentialities and materializations. I suggest that understanding spirit agency requires attention to materiality and perspicience, or knowing awareness, in order to address how materializations of spirit presence impact the social trajectories of spirits and people alike.

I will give particular attention to biographical stories about the spirits as a distinctive kind of materialization of spirit presence and a key way of knowing about spirits as immaterial agents. The stories in the epigraph are examples of such materializations of spirit presence, perhaps not in the initial dreams, but in the speech reporting on them and their further circulation each time they are retold. In the first epigraph, the spirit proves its veracity by providing a previously unknown street address that can be checked. In the second epigraph, too, it is the spirit's speech, revealing hidden information, that verifies the spirit's identity. In the course of this brief excerpt reporting on an interaction between a person and a spirit, the spirit shifts from a generic "it" to a very specific "she," the narrator's deceased mother. Such narratives are often intertwined with autobiographical narratives about a practitioner's spiritual development, as apparent in abbreviated form in the first epigraph, where the dream and the subsequent visit to the address mentioned in the dream provide a religious practitioner with confirmation of his spirit protector. I will emphasize the extent to which spirit presence and the character of spirit agency are matters of personal urgency for Cuban religious practitioners by examining how one practitioner has narrated her relationship to the spirits to me over the course of many occasions.

Signs *of* and Signs *about* Spirits

After more than a decade of engagement with Cuban folk religious practitioners in Santiago de Cuba, instances of spirit presence are everywhere in my fieldnotes, as are testimonials to their importance. Spirits manifest their agency through materializations of various sorts that those who have developed their spiritual sensitivities can detect. Consider the following typical note I wrote after a spiritual consultation with the Spiritist and santera I'll call Josefina:

> As we talked, Josefina kept running her hands up and down her forearms, saying that she was feeling energy in her arms, signifying that the spirits were all around us. [At the end of the consultation] she pointed out that of the two candles I'd given her for the altars, the one for Elegguá [an oricha of Santería] was still slowly burning and barely consumed, while the one for the spirits had

been "eaten" by them and had gone out and melted all over the place. She explained: That's because that was where the spirits were working, so they "ate" the candle. Eleggua opens and closes the [ritual] way, and so his candle kept burning to show the way was still open. It was finally a stub, still burning, when I left at 3:50 p.m. (Fieldnotes, July 2006, p. 14)

Josefina sensed the spirits and saw their actions in the world, pointing these things out to me, and I dutifully created a written artifact as the further step of a process by which embodied sensations of spirit presence and perceived signs, like rapidly or slowly burning candles, become transformed into discursive objects through which people talk and write about spirit immanence. Nor do Josefina and other religious practitioners need an ethnographer around to stimulate talk about spirits. Talk about (and with) spirits is constitutive of Cuban popular religious practice precisely because relationships with the spirit world are of primary concern. Many forms of talk among practitioners focus on spirits, in ritual genres and in everyday interactions, whether addressing them directly, pointing out their actions, discussing their messages, or telling stories about them. Notice, for example, that Josefina's observation about the candles conveys information about Eleggua to explain his effect on one candle: he controls the domain of openings and closings, and so his long-burning candle can be taken as a sign of his cooperative presence in "keeping the way open" during our consultation. Josefina expressed confidence in Eleggua's cooperation because she knew she had properly called upon him: soon after I had arrived, she set out his candle in front of his small altar by the door and lit it while shaking a maraca (rattle) and singing several invocations to Eleggua in Santería's esoteric ritual register, Lucumí. Rattles and bells often precede and accompany such invocations because they call for the attention of the deity.

These communications were directed at the small cone of concrete with cowry shell eyes sitting in a ceramic dish next to Eleggua's little house—Eleggua himself, as materially represented by this ritually prepared icon (fig. 7.1). The lumpy little statue receives and witnesses material ministrations intended for Eleggua, the nonmaterial entity, and is even referred to as Eleggua, but always with the understanding that such material representations are no more than conduits to interact with nonmaterial entities not bounded by the edges of the physical world. Statues, shells, and stones can be infused with spiritual energy, much as people's bodies can be possessed by spiritual presence. Such objects and bodies can, in santeros'

FIGURE 7.1. Two Elegguas with cowry shell eyes, one inside and one next to the casita, or little house, next to the front door, with bowls containing implements of the warriors (orichas) behind them and offerings, including water, in front. Photo by Kristina Wirtz, August 15, 2008.

idiom, have the deity permanently "seated" in them, such that the concrete cone will always be referred to and treated as "Eleggua" and the initiated devotee will always be a "child of" the particular saint thereafter said to "own" his or her head. But these are special cases where ritually mediated identification with a spiritual entity redefines the object or body as permanently housing a spirit presence. And spiritual entities, unlike physical substances, are limitless: there is no end to the number of possible "Elegguas" or "children of Eleggua" in the world.

In most other cases, even including plaster saint statues or cloth dolls that durably represent particular entities, the spirit's residence is more temporary. Generally speaking, spirits are understood to be fleeting presences infusing everyday objects and ritually treated substances alike, or causing bodily sensations, even spirit possessions, as temporary changes of state, albeit with the potential to leave traces.[2] Ritual interventions, which necessarily involve bringing together different kinds of material objects (the concrete Eleggua, his little house, the bell, the candle) and manipulations of materials (speaking, singing, lighting candles, ringing bells), are necessary conditions for spirit materializations of all kinds that practitioners, in turn, perceive and comment on.

I am interested here in the relationship between two different orders of spirit materialization: call them sensation and discourse. Both sensation and discourse are necessary to recognize spirits as agents acting in the world. By sensation I mean the perception of spirit presence, and by discourse I mean the circulation of signs about spirits, principally through language. There is a broadly shared understanding in Cuba of spirits as immaterial, incorporeal agencies that nonetheless can infuse things—objects, bodies, places, events, speech, even dreams—without themselves being embodied things or having material form. The agency of spirits and their amenability to the agency of people become evident through material relations, including those of language. Speech itself is a physical thing—sound waves—however ephemeral and ethereal it seems when compared to candles, bodies, and other more durable objects. Speech, as part of social interaction, travels between persons and relies upon sensory engagement with its primarily auditory (and visual) modalities. Speech, then, is material and accordingly can be as infused by spirit presence as any more durable part of the material world. As Cubans understand it, then, spirits act in the world through materializations involving all these kinds of things, and religious practitioners seek to capture the attention and power of spirits through complex manipulations of the material world.

I therefore suggest that a consideration of the "social life of entities" in Cuban popular religion must consider two kinds of circuits: the circulation of signs *of* spirit presence, manifested through materializations of all kinds, and the circulation of signs *about* spirits, such as the spirit biography narratives I will examine here. It is crucial to note that speech can fall into both categories, since inspired speech of the sort Josefina channeled to me during my spiritual consultation is a sign *of* spirit presence in authorship of the message, while our discussion of the spirits' messages afterward, as well as my reports in my fieldnotes, are signs *about* spirit presence. Both aspects of speech, as materialization of spirit presence and as discourse about spirits, are indexes in the Peircean sense of being signs in which the representamen (signifier) points to its object through a relationship of contiguity or co-occurrence, but they differ in what kind of index they are. That is, while signs *about* spirits are taken to have indexical properties established by social conventions and discourse histories, like any other category of speech, signs taken to be *of* spirit presence are interpreted (in the local semiotic regime of practitioners at least) as natural signs, like

smoke indexes fire or blowing leaves index wind. Both kinds of indices are
also metapragmatic, involving judgments about signs *of* the spirits, including their conditions of possibility. For example, in my fieldnote excerpt,
repeating what Josefina had said, I specify indexical connections between
Josefina's shivers and present spirits, and between burning candles and
working spirits—indices *of* spirit presence that come to seem natural because of the metapragmatic work of discourse *about* spirit presence.

Spirit biography narratives, in their retellings, are *about* the spirits, but
it is important to note that practitioners who tell them regard them as
originating in what spirits have said about themselves, either directly or
by inspiring the thoughts and words of their mediums and devotees. Cuban religious practitioners even describe having spirit-inspired visions and
dreams, as in the epigraph examples. Narratives *about* spirits may thus
approach the status of being natural indices, within practitioners' semiotic ideology. Josefina told me she had more than once been approached
by strangers on the street who told her they saw the spirit of a Gypsy
hovering near her. On another occasion she described her Gypsy spirit as
having been born in Andalucía near the Guadalquivir River in 1830 and
as resembling her, perhaps even being an ancestor, details she received
through inspiration. She repeats these same details in the song of *plegaria*
she sings to call her Gypsy spirit to ceremonies, where the song's rendering
of biographical details uniquely identifies which spirit is being called.

Whether coming to a person as visions, sensations, sudden thoughts,
or inspired words, such experiences can be—are meant to be—narrated,
contributing to spirit biographies, whether sung, spoken, or even written. Spirit biography narratives are thus materializations *of* (as well as
about) spirit presence—they tangibly circulate and thus can be tracked,
as can claims about the agency of spirits manifested through them—and
they are also, at the same time, circulating objectifications of spirits in
discourse, serving to stimulate and shape the imagination of the social life
of spirits. This imaginative construction of selfhood extends to the spirits themselves, who can continue to reappear over time when they hear
themselves uniquely identified out of the vast undifferentiated mass of the
dead. Josefina's song to invoke her Gypsy, for example, renders the spirit
recognizable to itself as well as to Josefina and other human participants
in a ceremony.[3] This social life of spirits follows a trajectory defined by
spirits' identities and social positions during life but transcending those to
achieve new and greater kinds of agency in death—agency that might be
understood as a coachievement of spirits and the perspicient living who
call them into being.

Consider another passage from my fieldnotes, in which I record what Josefina told me about the origins of her ritual house, which she refers to as a "cabildo," or religious cofraternity of the sort organized by and for Africans in Cuba during the era of slavery (see Brandon 1993; Howard 1998). The spirit biography narrative she gives is brief, referring as it does to a collectivity of otherwise undifferentiated spirits, but it does important work:

> Josefina welcomed [my colleague] Sarah [Hill] and me, and almost immediately started talking about herself and her cabildo, a turn of phrase that greatly interested Sarah, who wondered afterward whether anyone else besides Josefina knew of her "cabildo." Josefina greatly emphasized that her cabildo originated with *cimarrones* [maroons] who had formed a *palenque* [maroon settlement] located right under where her building currently is located, and that the spirits of these Africans were [the ones] who originated her cabildo. Back then, she explained, this whole area was all vegetation, and *negros cimarrones* founded a palenque here to hide [from recapture into slavery]. They were the founders of her cabildo, these negros cimarrones. (Fieldnotes, May 15, 2008)

This passage reports (with some ironic distancing) on Josefina's self-presentation as the inheritor of a religious cofraternity founded by the spirits of a community of escaped slaves (a palenque). One might then ask, as I did on several occasions, how someone can know this, since no signs of this palenque are apparent on the busy urban street where Josefina's building is located. Indeed, the topic came up in a conversation I had with a santera and researcher in which we established a mutual acquaintance with Josefina, again as recorded in my fieldnotes:

> I asked her if she knew Josefina, and she did—described her as *blanca* [white], having a cabildo below her house. She had been there for ceremonies before, knew right where she lived even without remembering her name. I asked her about what this cabildo thing meant, and she said that Josefina had explained that a group of people had once lived on that site—Africans, it seems—and that she had sensed the energy of the place from their presence. She agreed with me that it was really interesting that someone of Josefina's background would have this connection with an African cabildo in her spiritual work. (Fieldnotes, August 14, 2008)

This reported conversation provides more context for my skepticism in the first excerpt about Josefina's deep connection to Africans, deriving as

it does from my observations that, in all domains except her spiritual practice, she takes pains to emphasize her whiteness and social distance from
Cubans of color (obliquely noted by my interlocutor and me as "someone
of Josefina's background"). Nonetheless, Josefina's story about the maroon spirits she works with, whose energy she sensed and tapped into in
developing her spiritual work, has circulated robustly enough that other
religious practitioners in the area have heard it and may even recognize
who Josefina is from this particular detail. She is the one whose spiritual
sensitivities—shivers and other signs—made her receptive to the energies
of maroon spirits present on the site of her home.

Clearly, nonmaterial entities have a social life through signs *of* and signs
about them, including narratives about them, and these circuits of and
about spirit presence are part of the self-presentation of religious practitioners. This approach of working between signs *of* and signs *about* spirit
entities in spirit biography narratives raises additional questions about
how the circulation of discursive objectifications is related to the ongoing
materializations of spirits in the narrators' lives—loosely speaking, the
relationship between meaningful shivers and stories about the causative
agents of those shivers. I suggest that the way in which shivers become
meaningful as signs of spirit presence is tied to the circulation of signs
about spirits. This connection will be evident in exploring Josefina's interweaving of spirit biography narratives and autobiographical narratives
about her spiritual development, from a child with undiagnosable ailments
to a skilled spiritual medium.

Narratives of Imaginative Possibility

An additional key question I will address is how practitioners mobilize the
biographies of spirits they work with as realms of imaginative possibility
to negotiate their own subject positions, taking Josefina as my case study.
There is tremendous creative potential in how people envision the salience
of spirit biographies to their own lives, and particularly because religious
practitioners emphasize that it is usually the spirit or deity who selects the
person, which can be because of some affinity or some need the spirit can
fill. Affinities can range from the chance of one's birthday on or near a
saint's day to an aspect of a person's personality or their profession, skills,
ethnicity, or even presumed sexual orientation, to an actual or presumed
genealogical connection. Sometimes the guardian spirit or principal saint

is thought to balance out someone's personality. Practitioners I have discussed this with can point out many examples of affinities, but also tend to assume that the basis for some bonds between particular spiritual entities and particular people sometimes remains mysterious.

At a broad level, the relationship between humans and spirits is contrastive: living versus dead, mortal versus immortal, material agent versus immaterial agent, supplicant versus powerful entity. But beyond that, the spirit biographies people narrate are also contrastive in another sense. As religious practitioners elaborate and intertwine fragments of particular spirit biographies with their own more filled-out autobiographical narratives, they create points of intersection, rather than simple parallels, between narratives. Spirits and saints are not always to be emulated, nor is their relationship to a person always justified by obvious similarities or affinities. Rather, it is the divergences and contrasts between people's lived experiences and the biographies of spirits, the personalities of saints, that open a virtual space of imaginative potential for what might otherwise be unspeakable, unacceptable, unattainable, or transgressive possibilities in the practitioner's own life. Cardoso gives examples in her chapter of the transgressive *povo da rua* spirits dramatically intervening in the lives of their devotees at moments of crisis (and then narrating these interventions as signs of potency). I am interested not just in interrupted robberies and heroic rescues but in more mundane and long-term unfolding possibilities explored through contrastive biographies of spirits and the living. To stretch this idea a bit, spirit biography narratives might be considered experiments—disguised, projected, or metaphorical experiments—with possibilities that do not otherwise seem open to the narrator. I suggest approaching such narratives as imaginative, personalized histories that entail gendered, racialized, ontological, and historicized positionalities for all kinds of entities, both living people and spirits.

Having laid out the field of issues and questions to address, I now provide a more thorough introduction to Josefina, pulling together all the bits and pieces of her autobiographical narratives to show the claims she makes through them to spiritual sensitivities and affinities for authoritative African spirituality. I examine how narrated spirit biographies allow Josefina to reimagine her own subject position through her relationships with a host of spirits representing forms of agency she strives for. I then more closely examine the interactional context of one instance in which she mingled information about spirits with autobiographical information and explanations of ritual practice, showing the workings of the logic connecting spirit agency and practitioner perspicience, that knowing awareness through which spirits are sensed and spirit agency is successfully materialized.

I have chosen to focus on Josefina because her religious practices are in most ways typical of many Cuban religious practitioners I have worked with, while her personal story allows me to dramatically illustrate certain points about how the social lives of spirits and practitioners are entwined through signs *of* and stories *about* the spirits. Nonetheless, I do so mindful of dragging various interpersonal complexities into the harsh ethnographic light: Josefina and I are now longtime friends, and in caring about her, I feel protective of her. At the same time, it is fair to say that many of her mannerisms and attitudes—especially regarding religion and race—irritate me. In her intense obsession with matters of the spirits and her repetitive retelling of the same stories, she can be hard to be around. And indeed, aside from her small immediate family, Josefina lives a relatively socially isolated life, especially in comparison with some two dozen other religious practitioners I have also worked with. This relative isolation, coupled with hard times, means that Josefina pins many hopes of material advancement on our relationship, adding a certain tension. Moreover, her mediumship performances strike me as rather overly theatrical and self-interested. That said, irritation can be a source of fascination, and I have found it very productive to try to understand Josefina's perspective and its logic. While I cannot help but convey moments of distaste, I hope that I also convey empathy for Josefina.[4]

One way in which Josefina is, in fact, quite representative of the Cuban folk religious practitioners I know is in her expectation of receiving direct economic and social benefits from her religious practice. Most folk religious practitioners I have worked with openly enlist their spirits in their projects of material advancement, if sometimes more gracefully than Josefina manages. Cuban folk religious practices have a decidedly this-worldly focus: practitioners expect their relationships with spiritual entities to help them solve practical problems and advance materially as a result of advancing spiritually.[5]

As I relate Josefina's stories, my concern is not with their historical verifiability: whether a particular spirit's biography actually matches up to a real historical person is quite beside the point, as is whether Josefina's account of her life is entirely factual or coherent (whose is?). Spirit biographies do indeed violate empirical notions of historicity, requiring those of us who are partial to the academic discipline of history to hold our empiricism in abeyance if we are to understand the significance of spirits (Palmié in this volume). Instead, such narratives can serve as diagrams of semiotic relationships that create histories and life trajectories for people and nonmaterial entities alike.

Abundant scholarship on narrative constructions of the self has shown how the figures and characters that populate the stories people tell do not simply *reflect* the categories of the social world but serve to actively *construct* them (e.g., Basso 1996; Bauman 1986; Hymes 1996; Ochs 1994; Ochs et al. 1992). Stanton Wortham (2001) and Susan Harding (1992, 2000), among others, have traced parallels between portrayals of the self in autobiographical narratives and the interactional work of negotiating one's identity. Wortham has also examined other kinds of narrative projections of the self and others, asking what social consequences emerge from repeatedly narrating oneself—or hearing oneself narrated—in particular kinds of roles and alignments in stories (Wortham 2005; Wortham et al. 2011).

Josefina's Stories

Josefina, now in her midsixties, has lived a life circumscribed by the 1959 Cuban Revolution, which took place when she was a teenager. Her autobiographical stories, repeated to me on almost every visit over ten years, describe a painful loss of class privilege after the revolution that she has dealt with over the past twenty-five years, at least, by turning to spiritual practices that allow her to tap into sources of subaltern power. Through her stories and positioning as head of her own religious family, now including me, Josefina emphasizes her role as a maternal figure, in parallel to the oricha she most identifies with, Yemayá, whose domain is motherhood and the ocean. Her stories authorize her access to esoteric African spiritual knowledge by describing her lifelong spiritual sensitivities and her success in joining the ritual lineage of a prominent black religious authority in the Havana suburb of Guanabacoa, a location recognized throughout Cuba as a center of black Cuban culture and religiosity. Through these narratives, which often interweave autobiographical and spirit biography narratives, Josefina has added a new layer to her own sense of agency under difficult circumstances.

Josefina's religious practice is primarily based in a form of Spiritism crossed with Santería and the Reglas de Palo, or what scholars taxonomize as *espiritismo cruzado* (Argüelles Mederos and Hodge Limonta 1991; Espíritu Santo 2009, 2010; James Figarola 1999; Román 2007). She has also undergone initiation into Palo and Ocha (Santería), joining a Havana-based lineage. The cultural marronage and potential for social critique within Santería and, even more obviously, the Reglas de Palo (which are, after all, also referred to as "witchcraft") are well recognized by practitioners, scholars, and many ordinary Cubans alike (Hansing 2006; James Figarola 2006; Palmié 2002; Routon 2008). Less recognized is that Spiritism too, in its many local forms, "also has a critical bite," as Reinaldo Román (2007, 34) puts it. He goes on to describe how, beginning in the late nineteenth century, "practitioners invaded the terrain of medical science and astronomy, corroded the natural-supernatural divide, multiplied the spheres of life, disaggregated the soul into multiple components, and denied scientific 'materialism'" (2007, 34).

Spiritist practice was, and remains, an often idiosyncratic bricolage of fragments of Catholicism, Western science (as conceived in theories as varied as evolutionism and mesmerism), and various West African and West-Central African influences (as filtered through Santería and the Reglas de Palo). At the same time, Spiritists often take pains to distance themselves from the "Africanisms" of Santería and Palo, stressing a European cultural origin and spiritual practices that emphasize moral purity and enlightenment (Espírito Santo 2010; Wirtz 2007b, 41–43). Spiritists cultivate relationships of reciprocity with individual, personified spirits, as well as call upon the spiritual aid of anonymous collectives of spirits, which they refer to as *comisiones* (commissions), a word evoking military formations as a metaphor of spiritual force (Jalane Schmidt, pers. comm., October 26, 2009). Sometimes spirit commissions share some common characteristic, as in the various commissions of maroons, Gypsies, and doctors that Josefina invokes during ceremonies. She once sensed a commission of German spirits ready to help me, after learning that my mother was born in Germany. This sense of being able to command legions of spirits is in itself a form of empowerment.

In my final week of dissertation fieldwork in 2000, Josefina called me. She had learned about me from a mutual friend and thought my project on Cuban popular religion would benefit from her expertise as a Spiritist and santera. I almost declined to meet her, as I was busy preparing to leave, but she was very insistent, so I paid her a visit, which I have repeated on almost every trip to Cuba since then.

Josefina was a striking figure, an elegant, light-skinned, older woman who kept her long, wavy hair jet-black, dressed as elegantly as her situation permitted, talked a mile a minute, and lived amid the decay of a once well-to-do, upper middle-class life "declassed" under the Cuban Revolution, in one rundown, subdivided apartment of a large building her family had built in the 1940s around the time she was born. Every room had displays of plaster saint statues, and the large living room was given over to her spiritual *bóveda*, or altar. By the end of our first conversation, she had announced that she was now my spiritual godmother, my madrina. Indeed, her personal stories were, rather pointedly, full of loving godchildren, often foreigners like me, who enjoyed the benefits of her nurturing care and gratefully brought her gifts from abroad. Clearly, I had no say in the matter, and her conviction that she is my godmother has only grown since then.[6]

Godmother and Universal Mother

The relationship of godparent to godchild, one in which the godparent assumes responsibility for the godchild's religious development, is formalized through initiation in Santería and the Reglas de Palo. In Santería's initiation ceremony, the godchild also formalizes a relationship with one particular oricha identified as the person's principal oricha, who protects, commands, and shapes the person's destiny. When Josefina was initiated into Santería, she was confirmed as a "daughter" of the oricha Yemayá, female deity of motherhood and the littoral ocean, whose image as the Catholic Virgin of Regla hangs in a large oil painting on Josefina's wall (fig. 7.2). Josefina often describes Yemayá as the one commanding her cabildo and emphasizes the parallels between Yemayá, the universal Mother, alternately nurturing and fierce, and herself as a mother and a maternal head of her own religious family.

In addition to celebrating the annual Catholic saints day of the Virgin of Regla, which she dedicates to Yemayá, she also dedicates annual ceremonies to the twin orichas known as the Ibeyi and often pictured as children (fig. 7.3). While she typically mentions the characteristic of motherhood she shares with Yemayá, she instead emphasizes taking care of the Ibeyí, as a mother cares for her children. It has often struck me that she describes these three orichas as an idealized version of her own family (as it happens, she has two children of opposite genders, just like the Ibeyi) and of the relationships she desires to create as head of her own religious house: as a mother to her children.

FIGURE 7.2. Oil painting of the Virgin of Regla, associated with the oricha Yemayá, above a Spiritist altar with photos and memorial card of deceased relatives to the left, various plaster saint statues, and a doll representing the muerto El Doctor Negrito Fino y Precioso, dressed in white and holding a cigar, to the right. On the chair to the right sit dolls representing the Gypsy and Petronilla. The flowers, candles, and glasses of water are offerings. Photo by Kristina Wirtz, May 30, 2007.

Intrigued by her practice and her story, and despite often feeling caught in her web of "maternalistic" fantasies and naive schemes, I have returned over the years to chat with her and sponsor ceremonies, including personal spiritual consultations and spiritual masses. And she was always eager to repeat what she felt were the key points of her religious and personal autobiography. Her stories, in her repeated tellings over the years, always center on her unusual spiritual sensitivities, her religious devotion, and the host of spirits with whom she works. One cannot say that she directly *identifies with* her principal spirits in the way she identifies with her principal oricha, Yemayá, and yet the alignments and intersections she creates between her story and theirs advance her claims to special spiritual sensitivities and to spiritual authority as a healer.

Born with Muertos

Josefina narrates her own life in terms of the many hardships she has overcome, beginning with her family's fears about her early spiritual sensitivities. Josefina told me she was born "in a golden cradle": her father was a doctor who owned several businesses, and her mother came from a prominent family esteemed for its musical talent. As a child, she lived in luxury,

FIGURE 7.3. Cloth dolls representing the twin orichas called the Ibeyi (Lucumí, "twins") on an altar, surrounded by offerings of children's party favors, sweets, and glasses of water. Photo by Kristina Wirtz, May 14, 2007.

attending a Catholic convent school as was deemed proper for a girl of her social class. When she started having the spirits talk to her at age three, her worried family took her to every doctor in town: to neurologists, to psychiatrists, to everyone, but no one could find anything wrong, medically or psychologically. Indeed, nothing was wrong: she had simply been "born with muertos" (spirits of the dead), who told her to "go to the monte, collect certain plants and sticks" in order to do spiritual healing work (quoted material from my fieldnotes of our conversation). One suspects that this spiritual explanation might not have been entirely acceptable to a family with the professional and class standing of hers, and reading into Josefina's silences and elisions, I suspect that she did not begin to develop her spiritual sensitivities into a Spiritist practice until she was already an adult.

Around age fifteen, in short succession, Josefina lost her mother, got married, and had her privileged world upturned by the Cuban Revolution. Although her husband was an educated professional who came to hold a respected job in the Revolution, they lost many of the class privileges she had taken for granted as a child. Most galling, by her account, was the loss of all the extra, rentable apartments in her family's building, which were nationalized and given out to many different families, with her family retaining only their own residence. She frequently comments on her neighbors' lack of education and refinement, an unsubtle way of declaring that the families who received the apartments under revolutionary housing reforms are from lower class backgrounds. In Cuba's officially classless society, socioeconomic distinctions are often expressed through such euphemisms.[7] The ups and downs of life under the Revolution are evident in the decayed elegance of Josefina's apartment, where she, her husband, and their adult children daily struggle with the nearly impossible household economics of ordinary Cubans, despite holding prestigious professional jobs (for views bracketing the time since 1989, see Rosendahl 1997; Weinreb 2009).

Josefina's Godfather in Guanabacoa

At some point during the mid to late 1980s, long since a married adult, and coincident with the time when official hostility toward religiosity diminished (Ayorinde 2004; Clark 1986; Orozco and Bolívar 1998), Josefina found her way to a well-known santero and palero in Guanabacoa, just outside Havana, who became her godfather and initiated her into Palo and Santería. As she told me the story on one occasion (and I reported it in my fieldnotes), one day the spirits simply brought her to her godfather's house, even though she didn't know him at all. From that moment, he became her godfather. Whenever she mentions him, she always emphasizes that she is part of his cabildo, or that he is the "chief" (*jefe*) of hers. This story of the spirits simply leading someone to the proper doorstep is meant to be taken as a proof of spiritual sensitivities, a report about a sign *of* spirit presence, since indeed the man living at that unknown house did become her godfather. The story also warrants her claims to religious expertise.

In her narration, this prominent santero, palero, Ifá divination priest, member of an Abakuá lodge, and grandson of a slave confers a certain authenticity on her claims to expert religious knowledge that she clearly sees as a racial inheritance she otherwise would not share. In Josefina's telling, his grandmother was an African-born "Conga Luanda," captured at age fifteen and liberated with abolition in 1886 at age twenty, who shared all her African secrets with her daughter, who passed them on to him. Josefina also once told me that he was descended from maroons from an eastern Cuban palenque (although perhaps not the very maroons whose spirits inhabit the site of her building). The implication of these details is that Josefina has a direct connection to authentic African religious wisdom through her black godfather in Guanabacoa.

The Fine Congolese Doctor

Josefina also speaks of her work with African spirits as giving her a direct claim to African religious authority. Just as she describes maroon spirits as the founders of her religious house (a cabildo, no less, making a claim on a specifically black Cuban form of association), and her godfather as the "head" (*jefe*), the spirit she describes as her cabildo's president (by which she means its presiding spirit and her spirit protector) is *el Doctor Negrito Fino y Precioso*, the Fine and Precious Little Black Doctor. She has elaborated his biography, based on years of channeling him as a medium during ceremonies, and has even created a relationship with the spirit of his mother. As his title, part diminuitive and part praise-name, suggests, the Doctor Negrito carries complicated associations for Josefina.

Josefina has told me that the Doctor Negrito was born in Luanda, in the Congo, in 1815 and studied medicine in France. Fluent in five languages, he lived out his life in Africa, and his refined tastes and cosmopolitanism in life have stayed with him as a spirit. He came to Cuba only as a spirit, when

Josefina's Virgin of Regla appointed him to be the president of Josefina's cabildo. There remains a mystery at the heart of why particular spirits decide to help particular people, and Josefina's invocation of the intercession of the Virgin of Regla, or Yemayá, expresses this limit on knowledge. He is clearly a spirit with expert knowledge and an aspirational figure for Josefina, who has never traveled abroad and who desperately wishes to learn English and travel in the United States and Europe. His expertise parallels that of Josefina's own family, which includes several generations of doctors, particularly her father and her son. And Josefina often emphasized to me her own calling as a spiritual healer, manifest in the health advice she freely gave to all.

The Doctor Negrito Fino y Precioso is, in the Cuban imagination, an unlikely African for 1815, and indeed, most of the ubiquitous African spirits Josefina and other Cuban religious practitioners work with are thought to have been slaves or former slaves (such as maroons, escaped slaves, and mambí, independence fighters who were often ex-slaves): two other muertos who serve as Josefina's "masters of ceremonies," the spirits who reliably appear at the onset of her trance of mediumship and who channel other spirits, are the "African" muertos Pa Alberto and Pa Roberto. Similarly, African, black Cuban, and even Haitian muertos abound in ritual practices around Santiago, often bearing what Cubans understand as names once given to elder and respected African slaves (e.g., Ma Rufina, Pa Francisco). In contrast to these more typical muertos, Josefina emphasizes the refinement of the Doctor Negrito Fino y Precioso: she describes him as having "fine" features (meaning a face conforming to white Cuban notions of attractiveness with a thin nose and lips), and his doll is elegantly clad in a white suit and holds a cigar (see fig. 7.2).

The Doctor Negrito Fino y Precioso is also unusual in being part of a spirit family (fig. 7.4). Josefina also speaks of an African woman spirit named Gaífa who was the Doctor Negrito's mother in life, and who closes out each ceremony when she possesses Josefina, grabbing a broom and sweeping the bad influences out of the house. The parallels are clear enough: Gaífa and Josefina are both mothers of doctors who are themselves spiritual healers, but Gaífa the African spirit is but a shadow of Josefina, who strongly identifies as white and Spanish descended (on both sides, as she emphasizes). The powerful Gaífa and her talented son, the doctor, are muertos, spirits who come to Josefina's aid, and while they have qualities that Josefina finds admirable and sees in herself and her family, they are, in the end, Others in their Africanness and immaterial agency.

FIGURE 7.4. A group of cloth dolls representing muertos whom Josefina calls "the Africans" and "the African family," with Gaífa in a white dress (second from left), with assorted offerings. (Her son, the Doctor Negrito, sits on a more central altar.) Photo by Kristina Wirtz, May 14, 2007.

Muerto Subalterns

It will not have escaped the reader's notice that the spirits mentioned so far all represent marked and marginalized social types: Africans, Gypsies, slaves, and maroons. Indeed, the muertos who serve as spirit guides and protectors for spiritual work in Cuba are almost always from subaltern or exotic social categories, not just Africans and Gypsies but Haitians (Cuba's most exoticized internal Other, thanks to a wave of immigration from San Domingue after the 1791 Haitian Revolution and another wave of labor migration in the early twentieth century), Arabs (popularly conceived as medical healers), Chinese (another labor migrant group, often depicted

FIGURE 7.5. A plaster statue representing a muerto called El Árabe, head of a commission of Arabs that works on issues of health and medicine, on a Spiritist altar surrounded by statues and images of other saints and spirits and offerings to them. Photo by Kristina Wirtz, August 18, 2008.

with plaster or porcelain buddhas), and even Indians (often pictured as iconic American Plains Indians) (fig. 7.5).[8] One Spiritist of my acquaintance has an otherwise unidentified "white man" as his rather anonymous spirit protector, but he and others describe both the anonymity and whiteness as unusual.

Many times, religious practitioners will place dolls of cloth, plastic, or porcelain and statues (usually plaster but sometimes wood or porcelain) on their altars to receive offerings of fine clothing, flowers, food, rum, or cigars, in accordance with their preferences (see figs. 7.1–7.7 for many examples). When they manifest by possessing someone or speaking through a medium, sometimes their voices take on distinctive qualities, like speaking gruffly or in a higher pitch, or accents, like the "broken Spanish" of the Bozal sociolect associated with African slaves (Castellanos 1990; Wirtz 2007a).

Over my decade of recording Josefina as a medium, I have heard her shift into more and more marked ways of voicing African spirits she channels. Whereas in 2002 the spirits merely had a gruff voice, they now speak in Josefina's version of Bozal, marked by phonological shifts toward the most colloquial pronunciations (e.g., aspirating or dropping /s/) and by disfluencies (e.g., lack of agreement in gender and number). I probably deserve some responsibility for inadvertently suggesting this shift by asking her about how African spirits speak (and drawing her attention to the matter). But larger processes of social transformation in Cuba are also at work, in the movement of Afro-Cuban religion toward the center of Cuba's self-representation, particularly for attracting foreign tourists (Ayorinde 2004; Routon 2008; Wirtz 2011). In this sense, the ever-increasing African presence in Josefina's spiritual work is perhaps a disguised recognition of how the dice have fallen in revolutionary Cuba, at least from her perspective of having lost considerable power, privilege, and wealth and having to now follow fashion in seeking Afro-Cuban authenticity for her religious practice. (That is, after all, what attracts foreigners with money.)

Family Spirits

Quite different from the muertos representing subaltern groups, another very important but much more intimately felt group of spirits are those of one's deceased relatives, all of whom require the surviving family's spiritual interventions to smooth their transition into the afterlife, and some of whom may decide to offer spiritual protection or occasional advice to a living descendent. Josefina ministers to her deceased parents, uncle, and grandfather with regular spiritual masses, and she encouraged me to do so for my father after his passing. During spiritual masses, the spirit of her deceased father in particular often manifests itself in the succession of muertos also including Pa Alberto and Pa Roberto, the Doctor Negrito, the Gypsy, Gaífa, and, to my politely restrained incredulity on a few recent occasions, my own father's spirit. While spirits of nonfamilial muertos, those who are often less personified and more representative of types, can demonstrate their veracity by revealing hidden information or making diagnoses or prognostications that come to pass, family spirits

FIGURE 7.6. Photographs of deceased relatives on a Spiritist altar with offerings of cool water, accompanied by plaster statues of Catholic saints, a doll representing a muerto, and other images of saints and spirits. Photo by Kristina Wirtz, August 18, 2008.

must convince their relatives of their veracity by acting with the knowledge and mannerisms of their living selves. Those recently deceased may manifest themselves by crying or speaking only in weak voices, because they have not yet accepted their death and begun to gain spiritual force. Often, their photographs will be placed on spiritual altars and offered the same refreshing glasses of cool water and vases of flowers as other spirits, but expressly to help them on their afterlife journeys (fig. 7.6). But family spirits do not ever seem to be reduced to social types and represented as dolls or statues.

Petronila, Black Servant in Life and Death

Given the clear distinctions between muertos who represent social types and family spirits, it is telling to examine how Josefina works with the spirit of a deceased domestic employee, a black woman named Petronila who cared for Josefina as a child in her parents' household and moved with Josefina into her new household when she married. Petronila was an actual person in Josefina's life, although since death she has been assimilated to the "African spirit" type on Josefina's altar and in her practice. When I arrived at Josefina's house in May 2007, she immediately pointed out two dolls (representing spirits) on a chair to the right of her altar, the first a gift from another foreign goddaughter: the plastic Gypsy doll who is her spirit guide, and next to it a small black cloth doll (fig. 7.7). This doll, she told me, was for the spirit of Petronila, the woman her family hired to clean Josefina's house and help care for Josefina's children after she married. Petronila had already worked in Josefina's parents' household and was elderly, having long since raised eighteen children of her own, nine boys and nine girls. Josefina described Petronila as petite but spry. Petronila's

FIGURE 7.7. Dolls representing two muertos on a Spiritist altar: a plastic Gypsy standing on the left and a cloth Petronila seated on the right, with an offering of water before them. Photo by Kristina Wirtz, May 14, 2007.

poverty-stricken situation was clear: she had borne her children "in the bush" and had come to the city seeking better-paying work in domestic service than she could earn in rural agriculture.

Telling me about Petronila got Josefina talking about her own life again, and she recounted how her mother had died when she was fifteen, and how she had married the next year and had two children by the time she was twenty-one. Petronila was a surrogate mother to Josefina as well as to her children, and by Josefina's account worked for her family for the next twenty years until her passing, most of which would have been after the revolution. As my notes of Josefina's story recount:

> So she had promised Petro that even after her death she would have a doll for her to "always keep her in the house." She said that Petro laughed (I bet: last thing she wanted was to be trapped for eternity as a servant in someone's house). Later Josefina repeated that Petro was like a mother to her and that she liked her best of all her many children and called her her white child on Z. Street. And Petronila was close to the children, who called her abuela Petro. She was illiterate but smart, and Josefina's son taught her to read at eighty years old by working with her every day after school. She died at ninety "y su espiritu se queda aquí" [and her spirit remains here]. (Fieldnotes, May 14, 2007)

Josefina attributed agency to Petronila's spirit in having chosen to remain in Josefina's house, explaining that they had already agreed that Josefina would care for Petronila's spirit, as one should do for family members. But Petronila was clearly hired help, however long term and intimate her relationship with her employer. She worked for Josefina because that was her best option to make a living, and she remains a servant, however beloved she is, as a spirit helper on Josefina's altar, a black cloth doll next to the Gypsy doll, in contrast to the loving photos of deceased family. One sees either disingenousness or willful self-delusion in Josefina's claim that Petronila thought of her as her "true, white daughter" and loved Josefina more than her own children. Alas, the Revolution came too late for poor Petronila.

For Josefina, the story of Petronila is told with nostalgia for easier times, as her family no longer has resources to afford domestic help, and this at a time when the market for clandestine domestic help is booming among Cubans who, through remittances from abroad or entrepeneurship at home, have access to the cash to afford it, even as many other Cubans are in desperate enough financial straits to willingly take on such work for their one-time "comrades." And the interracial intimacy suggested by Josefina's story of Petronila's motherly role in her family is shallow: on many occasions, Josefina has made overtly racist comments about black Cubans—for example, in claiming that they are driven by petty jealousy of her white skin and refinement, or that black religious practitioners generally envy the superior religious knowledge achieved by white Cubans like (scholars) Fernando Ortiz, Lydia Cabrera, and Natalia Bolívar. The reader must forgive my lack of ethnographic neutrality here: the place of Petronila among Josefina's spirit biographies exemplifies how Josefina distances herself from black people as she simultaneously claims spiritual authority by detailing her intimate connections and sensitivities to African and black Cuban spirits like Petronila.

Josefina's attitudes are hardly rare among white Cubans I know, even some of those who are active in Santería and other practices marked as "African" or "black." Similar narrative dynamics are evident in Cuban literature, where the tropes of Afro-Cuban mysticism are romanticized to the point of cliché.[9] At the same time, Cubans of color experience what Mark Sawyer has perceptively called "inclusionary discrimination" (de la Fuente 1998; de la Fuente 2001; Sawyer 2006).

Through the biographies Josefina narrates about her African and black Cuban spirits—the fine and precious Doctor Negrito and his mother Gaifa, the African spirits, the rebellious cabildo of marooned slave spirits under the house, the legions of spiritual commissions, the almost-but-not-quite-familial spirit of her deceased servant Petronila—Josefina, the perfect Mother, the refined homemaker amid the ruins of her elite life, has created a realm of imaginative possibility where she can maintain her class distance but align herself with the subaltern spiritual knowledge, healing powers, and even covert rebelliousness and will to survive that she associates with black Cuban culture, an alignment that also has allowed her to function, however imperfectly, in the Cuban revolutionary society of the late twentieth century and early twenty-first century. Josefina and other members of her small immediate family are the most socially isolated people I know in Cuba, and Josefina in particular spends a great deal of time in her home alone. She has few material resources or social connections, beyond her spiritual practice, to meet her family's needs, in a society where such informal networks and opportunities are vital for everyday survival. Her spiritual cabildo, built upon her sensitivities to spirits all around her, gives her a supportive religious community, even if most of its members are muertos.

Perspicience: Knowing Awareness of the Spirits

I have suggested that the agency of spirits (of all sorts) requires materialization to become manifest, and thereby to impact the possibilities for human agency. I have further suggested that spirit biography narratives constitute an important kind of materialization of spirit presence. They circulate understandings *about* spirits at the same time that they point back to spirit presence as their ultimate source—spirits as authors or spirits as principals in the interactions recounted. Josefina's stories about the spirits minimize their spatial and temporal distancing from her lived experience and are instead entangled with autobiographical details and ritual practices, as I will illustrate by examining an audio-recorded excerpt of one of our interactions in detail.

Cuban religious practitioners like Josefina understand the material world to be permeable to—indeed, animated by—spirits. To recognize the immaterial agency of spirits in the material world requires a special kind of sensory orientation, one I seek to describe with the archaic term *perspicience*. A near synonym of *discernment* and a cognate of the more familiar *perspicacity*, *perspicience* expresses knowledge and knowingness, especially through the role of the intellect and the senses. *Perspicience*, like *perspicacity*, carries a metaphor for vision in its etymology: it is indeed about seeing, and by extension about sensing more generally.[10] But *perspicience* also conveys the role of knowledge in sensory awareness: to discern spirits requires being inculcated into a culturally specific phenomenology in which the material effects of immaterial agencies become sensible experiences.

Perspicience as sensory awareness is inseparable from perspicience as discursive imagination. Consider the bodily orientations required to perceive signs of spirit presence: shivers can signal spiritual energy, just as do fast- or slow-burning candles. Consider too the participation frameworks practitioners develop in rituals so as to enter into interactions with spirit presences, much as Josefina does when she consults the spirits, calling upon them and receiving their messages in the form of inspired words issued from her mouth but in the voice of the spirits she channeled as a medium. The shivers and the messages, both, are interpretable as materializations of spirit agency because of and through Josefina's perspicience—her ontological orientation toward experience.[11]

The analytical framework I propose helps make sense of a characteristic of Josefina's speech, which is her tendency to move between topics without making their connections explicit. In fact, Josefina is following a logic of topic coherence based on how agency, materiality, and perspicience work together, so that spirit biography narratives are intertwined with autobiographical details that show their material effects in the world, effects that are possible because of ritual practices developing and manifesting one's knowing awareness.

On one occasion I recorded, as Josefina and I planned our preparations for a spiritual mass she was to hold for my deceased father, we had a meandering two-hour conversation. After recounting a spiritual consultation she had given me the previous year and telling me how many people seek her out for spiritual consultations, she began talking about all the necessary preparations for the ceremonies she holds every September for the saints days of Yemayá and her fellow female oricha Ochún (September 7 and 8). Pointing out the dilapidated state of her home, she said, "And I have to close up and seal off half, half of the entire house. You saw how this house is. And I pray to God and the saints for the conditions, that the spirits of the cabildo will help me, so I can manage what I have to do later. And then I will be able to paint my house, set up the cabildo as, as I want to maintain our cabildo."[12]

Her plans required cooperation from the spirits, who would have to intercede in order for her to be able to find and afford paint for the walls and otherwise improve her home. When Cubans talk of "conditions" they specifically mean material conditions of housing and food that represent adequate financial resources to live decently well. She then discussed her preparations for the ceremonies, implying that the spirits and saints intercede because she knows how to care for them. She described the extensive purchases and detailed preparations necessary to hold a festive ceremony for the saints and spirits, from mixing up cold salad with ham, pasta, and mayonnaise to setting out offerings for the saints and for her family's "fundamentals," or ritual power objects in Palo Monte (usually called "prendas" or "ngangas" in the Reglas de Palo). She paused to tell me that her family were all "rayados como paleros," or initiated into Palo Monte, and knew how to prepare their prendas, a tidbit of autobiographical information. She then returned to detailing her ritual practice, telling me that she always prepares *omiero*, or water infused with herbs, like the one she pointed to that she had prepared already for our upcoming spiritual mass. Speaking of the importance of omiero, she then described the commission of maroons who founded her cabildo:

JOSEFINA: When the time arrives to put . out everything,[13] to have everything in order to be able to say, okay, that people can start coming in, it has to already be here from, from the tub that you saw . that is, the omiero, with everything it has to contain to charge the hands [KRISTINA. Yes] to the other tub that I have to put in that corner of the altar over there, down below, which is for the commission of the healer of the founders of this cabildo, who are buried underneath there. Because you know the history of this cabildo, that those who founded it were slaves, in the time of slavery, like a settlement of maroons, and that's a commission that works here. That you have to give them their, their receptacle, a basin or a tub, and that with its candle, and within that have to go the things that they contain there, for them, with all [unclear]—

KRISTINA: Like the herbs.

JOSEFINA: The herbs associated with them, and in addition to the herbs the ground eggshell, and other things they like, alcohol . . .

KRISTINA: And so you make the omiero?

JOSEFINA: The, the omiero I also make.

KRISTINA: And this is omiero in the jar there? [*pointing toward jar in front of Eleg-guá's little house by the door*]

JOSEFINA: That there? Yes. And I have a, a tall white tub to [unclear].

KRISTINA: Yes, I've seen it, yes.

JOSEFINA: What do I want to say with this? This . is a combination of the two things. Of the spiritual with the saint, because the muerto . gave birth to the saint. There are no saints without muertos, there being here a deity and a spirit.

KRISTINA: Ikú lobí ocha. [*laughs*]

JOSEFINA: That's it, yes, yes.[14]

In this brief exchange explaining ritual procedures, Josefina evokes biographical narratives of spirits and autobiographical information, making them relevant to the here and now of her ritual practice. Josefina's explanation of how to prepare for a spiritual mass and why particular substances and steps are necessary is grounded in her religious expertise, including as an initiated palera, and her relationship with a particular set of spirits she regards as founders of her ritual house. This connection, in turn, proceeds from a recollection of her material circumstances, living in one, rundown apartment of a house her family once owned, a house located on the site of a long-gone maroon settlement.

To explain the purpose of the omiero, Josefina repeated a common proverb describing the nature of the connection between muertos and santos: the dead give birth to the saint. I repeated this proverb in its Lucumí form as I frequently heard it among santeros in the city. Then, perhaps recalling that Josefina does not have much knowledge of Lucumí ritual speech, I went on (rather pedantically) to explain what each Lucumí word meant. When I had finished, Josefina responded as follows:

> Just now, when you said that, when you were saying that, and I begin to feel in my feet, in my legs, in all of my body, my arms and everywhere. And my head, I am prickling with this, with the current, with the practice you achieved, that only in saying these words. [*Kristina laughs*] And that is true, and it is true, yes [*Kristina laughs*] ¡Aaaaa! [*marked rising then falling intonation like a siren*] It is the proof! [Kristina: Yes.] The first of us to state the proof is me, with what you were saying, with nothing more than saying these words. And I, to answer them, tò whom? And I am, not right now, but I did feel a current that just now seized me, and that's the truth [*Kristina laughs*] throughout my entire body.[15]

Josefina, dramatically reporting to me her strong sensation of spiritual energies coursing across her body, speaks of proof and truth. Our appeal to nomic truth in reciting a proverb triggered the sensible presence of spirits, charging the very air with spiritual currents that Josefina perceived and described. Her description of prickling currents across her body, culminating in her siren-like cry, "¡Aaaaa!" (construed as a natural index of feeling spirit presence), mark a confirmation of her spiritual sensitivities and religious expertise. Indeed, Cuban religious practitioners frequently calibrate the veracity and potency of spirit presence according to the evidence of their senses, and especially the senses of seeing and feeling.

If *perspicience* translates any particular emic term of Cuban religious practitioners, it would be *conocimiento*, knowledge, or better yet, knowing that comes from familiarity. Cuban religious practitioners use this word to refer to religious experience and understanding of the sort that comes from long practice but that can also be informed by (but emphatically not replaced by) academic study. Other emic candidates might be the cognates *claridad* and *clarividencia*, clarity and clairvoyance, as related to the sensible qualities of clear water offered to the spirits and used by some mediums for divination. Both terms describe spiritually developed minds attuned to the vibrations of the spirits. Perspicience partially captures the experiential and therefore sensory aspect of conocimiento and claridad, and it resonates with a Cuban folk religious emphasis on tests, proofs, and confirmations as necessary aspects of religiosity and in particular of identifying and *discerning* the role of spirits in events of the material world. As a personal characteristic than can be developed, perspicience also points to the self-making work of developing one's spiritual knowledge (see Espírito Santo, unpublished MS).

Perspicience, as an orientation to sensory experience and ritual practice, is evident as well in the entwining of autobiographical and spirit biography narratives. Such narrative entanglements demonstrate the knowing awareness that practitioners like Josefina cultivate of how spirits move in and through their lives, shaping events and possibilities. The narrative imagination is itself a site of spirit presence, with all the potentialities and hidden desires that therein find expression.

Conclusion

My case study of Josefina illustrates how Cuban folk religious practitioners mobilize signs *about* the spirits, such as spirit biography narratives and descriptions of spirit actions, to develop sensitivities toward signs *of* the spirits. Such nonmaterial entities as spirits, saints, and deities can only manifest agency in the world through their materializations, and materializations in and as discourse turn out to be key to the very interpretability of materializations in a range of more durable material objects, including statues, dolls, other effigies, and even human bodies. Josefina weaves together autobiographical narrative and biographical details about her host of helping spirits to demonstrate her spiritual perspicience and the spirits' past efficacy, and these narrative entanglements create the conditions of possibility for future efficacious ritual practice. Her mobilization of narratives about the social life of spirits, as once-living people and as nonmaterial agencies in her own life is itself a materialization of the spirits that demonstrates and therefore entails the perspicience necessary to detect further materializations. Signs *about* spirits can thus become signs *of* spirit presence, mobilizing realms of imaginative possibility that have consequences for the social trajectories of spirits and religious practitioners alike.

CHAPTER EIGHT

João da Mata Family

Pajé Dreams, Chants, and Social Life

Ana Stela de Almeida Cunha

Introduction

It was João Guará's birthday party, there were drums, drinks, and conversation. At a given moment, Princess Iracema entered, followed shortly after by her three brothers, Itaci, Espadinha, and Pirinã. Their father, João da Mata, arrived at the *terreiro*[1] slightly late, for he had come from the forest, and as soon as he arrived he proposed a *presentation doctrine*:[2]

> *Eu sou o Caboclo da Bandeira*
> *João da Mata falado*
> *E no abrir da minha mesa,*
> *o caçador de São José!*

> I am the Flag Caboclo
> João da Mata when spoken
> And by opening my table,
> Saint Joseph's hunter!

At that point, the drums *viraram* (turned) to the *linha da mata* (forest line)[3] and other families appeared, such as the Tapindaré family and Dona Mariana's family. The *assistência* (audience) knew that the drum rhythm had changed and that other *Caboclos*[4] would begin to enter. Later, the rhythm would turn again and other families and *encantados*[5] would appear.

The visit by João da Mata and his family occurred during one of the many *festas*[6] (parties) and *curas* (healings) that take place in *Pajé barracões*.[7] The members of the João da Mata family are the encantados: the entities that appear in Pajé—an African-based religion that is extensively practiced on the western border of Maranhão state, in northeastern Brazil—who sing upon arrival, talk to people, and provide remedies for those with spiritual or physical problems. This chapter looks at the encantados' families and social networks; through the conversations, dreams, and chants sung by and for them; it will attempt to present the diverse relations between *os de cá* and *os de lá*,[8] as well as the cosmology involved in these exchanges and interactions. The analysis is especially concerned with relations between the encantados' different *lines*[9] and their social interaction with *here people*, which takes place primarily through the Pajé's words and dreams.

João da Mata's family will be the primary focus: he is an encantado who ordinarily belongs to the *Caboclo line* (he is the King of Turkey's son); however, as we shall see, these are malleable ascriptions that oscillate according to the *casa* (house)[10] and experience of each practitioner/Pajé. Thus, João da Mata is also identified with the *freshwater line* (as he practices healings) and with his place of residence: as his name suggests, he comes from the *mata* (forest), but he can also come from the sea, as he is enchanted in the *Pedra do Itacolomy*—a rock situated in Maranhão, in the São Marcos basin, between the state capital of São Luís and the Alcântara municipality.

In Afro-Brazilian religions, Caboclos are almost always identified as Amerindians,[11] but in Pajé and *Tambor de Mina*[12] they have various origins—they can be cattle drovers, sailors, or even Turkish royalty (Ferretti 2001; Prandi 2001, 121)—and have quite nationalistic characteristics: João da Mata is also known as the Flag Caboclo and his main celebration takes place on the nineteenth of November, the same date as Brazil's *Dia da Bandeira* (Flag Day), which commemorates the creation of Brazil's republican flag. Other general Caboclo traits include "verbal communication and close public contact. . . . Another marking characteristic is their healing power. The Caboclos are believed to be profoundly knowledgeable about forest secrets, which allow them to efficiently suggest the correct leaves for medicinal remedies and baths" (Prandi 2001, 121; author's translation). In Pajé, Caboclos are ontologically different from the Umbanda Caboclos; while the latter are usually related in some way to the indigenous universe, in the former this is not always the case. In some terreiros, for example, João da Mata is seen as an Amerindian, in others however he is simply a *gentio* (savage), a hunter (who often appears as a black man), as in the following verse:

João da Mata tem a cor morena,[13] ele é caçador
Caçador da Jurema
Ele jurou, e tornou a jurar
A ouvir os conselhos que a Jurema vai lhe dar

João da Mata has black skin, he is a hunter
Jurema's Hunter
He swore, and swore again
To listen to the advice that Jurema provides

Based on ethnographic research carried out with Pajés/healers and mineiros over more than eight years in the *Baixada Ocidental*[14] region of Maranhão, this chapter is an attempt to outline the ways in which paths are created between diverse dimensions by demonstrating the importance of encantado sociability through interactions between there and here worlds. As mentioned above, interaction takes place in two ways: through the Pajés' dreams (in which they enter the *encantaria*[15] world) and through language (when the encantados come to earth *riding their horses*,[16] in trance rituals, to interact with the here people by singing and giving advice). These are symmetric and complementary; they form part of the same unit of interaction, through which reality can be redefined.

For a better understanding of this interaction, this text analytically considers *narrativity* or "the understanding of complex networks of ever-new deeds and changing attitudes by which humans perceive any given action not only as a response to the immediate circumstances or current imputed mental state of an interlocutor or of oneself but also as part of an unfolding story" (Michael Carrithers 1990, 269, quoted in Vitebsky 1993, 8). Through dreams and verbal/sung language, social life constructs itself in a complex mosaic in which relations between Pajés/assistência and encantados become ever closer and complementary. Before exploring the relations between the here and there worlds, a short introduction to the Caboclos and their families is necessary.

The Caboclos' Social Life

The encantados are involved in a complex tangle of kinship relations and lines, which form broad social networks as part of their collective existence. The source of distinct encantado lines and their relationship to natural elements lies in the encantados' characteristics, though it is not possible to say whether these entities possess specific characteristics due to their location in geographic contexts (the forest, freshwater, etc.), or whether these habitats form the encantados' traits—so that, for example, a freshwater source promptly suggests the ability to cure (as with the mata line), whereas saltwater (the *maré* line) encantados are almost always considered to be more experienced with spells. Often the line refers to a mythical space: the mata line, for example, is related to Cambinda and Angola, although more to the ethnic groups of that region than to the geographic locations.

In contrast to the Candomblé *eguns* or the Kardecist spirits, the encantados are not mythical beings or deceased ancestors who communicate through mediums, as Prandi notes (2001, 218; author's translation):

> Encantados[17] are spirits of people that one day lived but did not die; they became "enchanted" and went on to live in the invisible world, from which they return in their initiate's body, in ritual trance. By manifesting thus, in their children's or initiates' heads (their "crown," as it is commonly called in mina), the encantados come to Earth, descend into the guma [terreiro] to dance and cohabit with mortals, establishing ties of affection and patronage with all those who frequent these spaces.

They inhabit specific places in the local geography, such as streams, waterholes, tucum trees, and rocks (such as Itacolomy), as well as bays, inlets, and ponds. They may also be present in certain animals, such as Dorinha (a princess that is a *troirinha*, or lizard), the Menino Lera (who becomes a butterfly), or even Guará (found at the beginning of this chapter, who can be a bird, the Guará-Mirim).

The encantados need the Pajés to carry their messages, cure, or cast spells; known as *aparelho* (apparatus), *cavalo* (horse), or *matéria* (matter), the Pajés are the link between the two contiguous universes of humanity and encantaria. As Ferretti (2001, 20; author's translation) claims, however, this designation (Pajé) can also refer to a notion of "syncretism," "degeneration," or even "rupture"[18]: "In Maranhão the term 'Pajé' (or healer) is used to designate both religious specialists from indigenous cultural traditions and the most syncretic of black cultures, that is, the most distant to the jeje or nagô models, such as those currently found in the peripheries of São Luis or beyond the capital." The encantados are grouped into families in the invisible world, from which they return through their mediums in *festas* and *curas* but also involuntarily when they appear to their horses.

There are numerous families in the encantaria and the most important belong to *nations*. As Ferreti (2001, 123; author's translation) indicates, "the King of Turkey's family is 'tapa,' the Surrupira King's is 'fulupa,' Légua Boji Buá's is 'mata' (Angola or Cambinda)." Other important families are: Lençóis, Gama, and Juncal (the latter is of Austrian origin); the Boto family, who primarily practice cures; the Sailor and Mata families, to which many Umbanda Caboclos also belong (such as Caboclo Pena Branca, Caboclo Zuri, Cabocla Jussara, and Caboclo Guaraciara); and lastly the Bandeira (Flag) family, which is the ethnographic focus of this chapter.

These families are divided into lines: the enchanted forest, or *mata* line, and the freshwater and saltwater lines, which are the healing and witchcraft lines, respectively. But families and/or lines are not fixed categories. Dona Mariana, for example, is the King of Turkey's daughter and she has other sisters from the Mata (Surrupira) line, Chica Baiana and Cabocla Ita, as shown by the following doctrine:

Somos três irmãs, de língua ferina
É a Mariana, é a Cabocla Ita
Inda tem a flor, que é Chica Baiana

We are three sisters, with sharp tongues
Mariana, Cabocla Ita
Inda has the flower, she is Chica Baiana

When she was young, Dona Mariana was adopted by the Codó family, so she is Légua Boji Buá da Trindade's adoptive daughter and sister to many other encantados, such as Bernardino and Maria Teresa. There is one doctrine that shows Dona Mariana no longer as a cabocla but as a princess (and thus from the noble line):

Chegou a mamãe do povo
Por este povo sem fim
Princesa, Princesa do Mearim!

The people's mother has arrived
For this never-ending people
Princess, Princess of Mearim!

The entities' categorization as Turkish, caboclas, nobles, and so forth, is therefore very malleable: each Pajé's personal experience, the terreiro's story, the situation in which the encantado appears are all elements that lead to a broad variety of possible configurations. As Ferretti writes (1992, 8; author's translation):

> Entities classified as peers in one terreiro can be seen by others as voduns Cambinda, Caxeu, Felupe, "Taipa," etc., such as Pedro Angaço, well-known in Codó (Maranhão) and in São Luis, in Caboclo terreiros. Others can be classified as voduns by some and as Caboclo by others. . . . For many adepts of Tambor de Mina (Légua) he is a Caboclo, because he likes to drink and to party, something which does not suit vodun. It can be said that Légua, like Seu Turquia, tends to come as a Caboclo (despite not being one) in a conciliatory manner, because he entered the forest and arrives on the Caboclo current.

Thus, one entity can manifest in several lines and currents, according to the terreiro and the Pajé in which it is presiding.

The encantaria universe has a vast network of parental and social relations that are independent to the here world; however, its relation to this world is necessary, because as one of the Pajés affirms, "It is in these comings and goings that encantados pick up more of our manner and that we also come to understand the encantados better." And, as in the words of another Pajé, "The closer we are to them, the more they understand us, until it reaches the point that spoken communication is no longer required; it is all in thought. And the same is true for them." The concept of person seems to be intimately related, here, to the development of contact with one's encantado: these are not separate beings; they are in continuity with the Pajé.

Luzia, a female Pajé (a *Pajoa*) from Guimarães, tells that "in each place visited by an encantado he modifies himself. In each *crown*,[19] each terreiro, there is a change," which confirms that entities are flexible and acquire traits from the spaces and adepts with whom they come into contact. And vice versa.

Interactions become closer over consecutive encounters and are fundamental for the relation between Pajés and encantados, to the point that they take place without the need for speech. That is, communication between the religious practitioner and his or her entity becomes such that there is no need for articulated language, which is reserved for communication between the encantados and the *assistência* (audience) made up of people that frequently attend the terreiro for vow payments, consultations, or even *simpatias* (basic spells).

I will deal with these experiences in an attempt to demonstrate their importance in the learning process, for both sides—that is, for those from the here world and the there world—and how these relations are formed in the encantados' social life.

The Flag Family

João da Mata, the *Caboclo da Bandeira* (Flag Caboclo), at times presents himself as an old, wise, hunched Amerindian; at others, as a proud and dynamic young man of thirty-five with a plume on his head and an arrow in his hand. As one of his doctrines states, he is a black hunter and the head of a family of hunters, fishermen, and warriors. These are noble, mixed-race encantados. He has many children and siblings, such as Tombacê, Maroto, Caçará, Araúna, Guará, Araçagi, Longuinho, Pindorama, and the princesses Luzia, Linda and Iracema, and Jatiçara and Senhora Dantã, as well as cousins, such as João da Cruz and Mariano. He also has twin daughters, who only appear every three to six months and whom I only came across in a *Vura*[20] terreiro in Guimarães.

> *Seu João da Mata tem a cor morena*
> *Ele é caçador da Jurema de lá*
> *Ele jurou, e tornou jurar*
> *De ouvir os conselhos que a Jurema vai dar*

> João da Mata has a black skin
> He is their Jurema's hunter
> He swore, and swore again
> To listen to the advice that Jurema provides

Although at times identified as (the saint) São João Batista himself, for other Pajés this does not make any sense, because "saint is in the sky, under God" and "encantos are in the astral, in the encantaria." Nevertheless, Christianity has a marking presence in Pajé and Mina terreiros, be it in iconography, prayer beads, censers, or even through the doctrines, such as in the following alternative presentation for João da Mata:

> *Eu sou o Caboclo da Bandeira,*
> *João da Mata falado*

Na presença de Cristo,
por Jesus abençoado!

I am the Flag Caboclo,
João da Mata, when spoken
In the presence of Christ,
Blessed by Jesus!

The presence of nobles and Caboclos in the same family is also evident here, as in the doctrines below, one of which is presented by João da Mata himself, and the other presented by one of his children:

Eu mandei içar bandeira, na folha do ariri
Caboclo é moço nobre, é filho do rei da Turquia

I commanded the flag be raised, on ariri leaf
Caboclo is a noble young man, son of the Turkish King

Por cima daquele morro eu avistei um laço verde
Caboclo é moço nobre, filho do Rei da Bandeira

Over that hill I saw a green ribbon
Caboclo is a noble young man, son of the Flag King

According to one of João da Mata's doctrines, he is the Turkish King's son, but many Pajés have no knowledge of this nor accept this version. Despite being from the Mata line, the Flag Caboclo (João da Mata) is enchanted in the Itacolomy rock and should thus also be from the saltwater line:

Sou Caboclo da Bandeira, da folha do ariri
Sou Caboclo da Bandeira, pedra de Itacolomi
Sou Caboclo da Bandeira, João da Mata falado

I am a Flag Caboclo, of ariri leaf
I am a Flag Caboclo, Itacolomy rock
I am a Flag Caboclo, João da Mata when spoken

The Flag Caboclo is known for having many children and numerous doctrines confirm this, such as those by Camarão, João Guará, Princess Iracema, and others who announce their filiation in doctrines.

Eu sou Camarão Vermelho
da praia do Araçaji
Tem Camarão na trincheira
filho do Rei da Bandeira

Eu sou João Guará
Filho do Rei da Bandeira [bis]
Toma cuidado meu pai
Ô tem Caboclo na eira [bis]

Sou da mata quem me chamou? Sou da mata!
Eu nasci na mata virgem
Ah! Eu sou mulher guerreira
Eu me chamo Iracema
Filha do Caboclo da Bandeira

I am Red Prawn
from the Araçaji beach
Prawn is in the trench
son of the Flag King

I am João Guará
Son of the Flag King [*repeat*]
Be careful my father
Oh there is a Caboclo on the edge [*repeat*]

I am from the forest, who called me? I am from the forest!
Born in the virgin forest
Ah! I am a warrior woman
My name is Iracema
Daughter of the Flag Caboclo

However, some of his children were adopted by other families, such as Princess Dora (Doralice) or Guajajara, who were adopted by the Turkish family.

As they are frequently identified as *Índios*,[21] the Caboclos of this family do not drink much (according to many Pajés, they only drink water from a gourd); they are serious entities and not very playful—in comparison to the Légua Boji Buá's family, for example, who drink a lot and always play

with the audience, telling stories and jokes and actively participating in
the festivities.

Anaíza Virgolino e Silva (1976, 232, quoted in Ferretti 2000, 320; author's translation) also indicates that in terreiros in Belém do Pará (the neighboring state's capital, west of Maranhão, with many migrants from Maranhão), João da Mata (the Flag Caboclo) is also known as Oliveira or João da Mata de Oliveira.

> It is possible that in Maranhão, João da Mata, from the Turkish family, is the same João Oliveira or Prince Oliveira, and he could also be Oliveiros, a character from the well-known "Story of the Emperor Charlemagne and the Twelve French Pairs," a Christian who defeated Ferrabrás in battle and converted him to Christianity. According to the accounts heard in the terreiros of São Luis, Oliveiros became such a good friend of the Turkish King that he came to be thought of, by the latter, as his brother and, having become part of this group, was also considered to be his (adopted) child.

According to Ferretti (1992), one of the possible explanations for the Turkish imaginary (which is very present in Maranhão religious life, where one of the most famous nineteenth-century terreiros was called the *Terreiro da Turquia*, or Turkish Terreiro) is the marked popularity of the medieval stories about Charlemagne, cited above.

In the terreiros that appear in the present ethnography, however, there were no references to the connection between the Flag Caboclo (the same as the Flag King) and the encantado Oliveiros, who was neither mentioned nor heard from in any doctrines from the Baixada Ocidental terreiros. However, the Flag King (João da Mata) is considered to be the King of Turkey's brother or even (more frequently) his son, as suggested by the following doctrine (already quoted):

> *Eu mandei içar bandeira, na folha do ariri*
> *Caboclo é moço nobre, é filho do rei da Turquia*
>
> I commanded the flag be raised, on ariri leaf
> Caboclo is a noble young man, son of the Turkish King

The same occurs with Dantã, an encantada that in some of São Luis's terreiros (especially those from the Egyptian terreiros) is thought of as João da Mata's sister; in the present ethnography's terreiros she is always mentioned and presents herself as his daughter.

Entering the Spirits' Life: The Dreams

With limited iconography, the encantados are materialized in specific ways: through sung or verbalized language (in conversations and consultations) and through dreams. The dual manifestation of these entities' social life is complementary and becomes necessary for a jointly constructed sociability.

Language is a common form of materialization in many religions (especially in those from the African matrix). For this to take place, the adept is thought to lend his body (as a device or horse) so that the entity's materialization can be experienced and shared with many other people, religious or otherwise. Dreams, however, indicate a distinct form of materialization, requiring the Pajé's entrance into the encantaria world: more than the encantados' materialization, the focus is the adept's experience with these entities—it is not just the experience but also the distribution of materiality, while also being a solitary exercise, felt only by the adept.

Both of these forms of sociality with the encantados will be discussed here: they are complementary and symmetric ways in which here and there people experience friendship and kinship relations. We begin with the dreams.

Among the accounts given by Pajés, stories are often told about how they first made contact with their *head*[22] encantados; invariably this takes place through dreams, experienced in moments of great anguish and suffering (physical or spiritual). Sometimes this happens in a more diffuse and gradual manner, other times not so, and the Pajés say that they lucidly experienced the dream, through complete immersion in the encantaria universe.

Fernando, a twenty-eight-year-old Pajé from Guimarães, tells that he had his first *visões* (visions) when he was about nine years old, but his family did not want him to follow this path, which led his maternal grandmother to *amarrar* (tie up) his vision—that is, she made it so that he no longer had these visions, at least until he became a teenager. Thus, when he turned sixteen he began to dream frequently with his guide,[23] an encantado called Beira Mar.

He says that at first he only saw a shadow and heard things that made no sense, but little by little he began to discern his *contra-guia* (counterguide): the encantado that accompanies him most frequently. These visions took place only during his dreams, which were becoming more frequent and clearer. Today, Fernando tells that he knows the encantaria very well:

he has already had three failed (earthly) marriages because of encantaria women, and the guidance he receives for the preparation of remedies and cures is provided through dreams, when he travels to the *fundo*[24] (deep) and receives the necessary instructions and preparation.

It is common to hear the Pajés say that they were born prepared or became prepared in the fundo through dreams. Thus, more than experiences, the dreams are actions, constructions of meaning and reality.

Senhor Carmo, a (deceased) Pajé from the Vura community (Guimarães), with whom I had a lot of contact, told of his marriage to a woman from the fundo (an encantada), and how after the first time they slept together, he woke up to find a spot of blood in his hammock: evidence that the encantada had been a virgin. In a similar account, another Pajé from Guimarães told me that, from time to time, a knotted, yellow ribbon appears in his hammock, indicating that his there wife had spent the night with him, events which seriously affected his earthly marriage. However, some Pajés indicate that their here wives are understanding and tolerant, which facilitates this dual matrimony. Evidently, relations with each wife are distinct, as in the following statement: "I don't even like to be with the wife from the deep, because she is always provoking the wife (the here wife). But I'm lucky that my wife has an understanding, you know how it is, and often she attends to my deep wife's requests; she gives her some perfume, earrings, to the one from there, so that she doesn't become angry or capricious" (Fernando, Guimarães). But this understanding relation and even appeasement of the encantados is not common, and the rupture of marriages due to jealousy or intolerance is more frequent among the Pajés.

Accounts by female Pajés indicate the possibility of assault by encantados rather than marriages; these tend to refer to entities that become enamoured with them, but a union never takes place, suggesting the need for a more careful consideration of gender difference among Pajés.

Unlike many studies written about dreams, in which symbols are treated as ways to interpret hidden meaning, here, dreams are about individual experience (Stewart and Koulack 1993; Csordas 1994) and require no collective guarantee or reconstruction. However, that does not mean that these dreams are purely psychological experiences, as Edgar (2002, 80) states, "Dreams are a cultural, rather than a solely psychological activity, is something few people other than interested anthropologists . . . usually emphasise."

Attention is drawn here only to those experiences that can be categorized as cultural, but not collective, since they lack the social reconstruction and reinterpretation necessary for their legitimation. Here, the dream is an experience of the "I" that transforms and reshapes the "person" (self). As Ewing (1990, 57) indicates, "Through this reflective process, self representations became signs, like the units of language and other cultural representations such as myths and images. The dreams, which we experience through language and imagery, are also made up of signs." Anthropology has constantly been confronted by problems associated with the analysis of dreams: from the tendency to approach dreams as repressed desires, as proposed in psychoanalytic theories, to the search for meaning in experienced signs. Tedlock (1987) inaugurates a new direction for social anthropology by redefining the boundaries between both practices.

In this chapter I argue that among the Pajés dreams are experienced actions, not subjective interpretations or subject to collective interpretation. For a Pajé, dreaming is neither a premonition nor the experience of something that will happen or a space for decoding a specific action/situation. Dreaming is simply the experience of everyday life: visiting the there wife, conversing with friends from the encantaria, exploring the trade that exists there, receiving instructions for cures. In the end, dreaming is socialization and even instruction, because many of the Pajés are *preparados* (prepared or initiated for religious life) during dreams in the encantaria; an encantado prepares and is responsible for a future Pajé, which grants him or her greater credibility before the community in which he or she lives.

The Pajés' dreams operate as the possibility of entering into a restricted universe, the encantaria, where he or she dives into another world and preexisting social networks; there are kingdoms, cities, and families, with their own commerce and administration, as shown in an account given by Senhor Carmo, a Pajé from Vura (a village in Guimarães):

DOC: Are you familiar with their world? Have you ever been there?

INF: I am. . . .[25] I've already been there, in the dream. They [the encantados] say that their city is called the Eastern City, their kingdom, right? It is beautiful.

DOC: And do other encantados live there?

INF: Yes, yes, many. There, all commerce belongs to them, is owned by them. Others cannot open a business like here, right—here one opens a store here, another on over there; not there, it all belongs to them.

By entering into that universe, the Pajés are introduced into the entities' networks and social life; as mentioned above, many marry encantados, provoking jealousy and marital breakups on this side, because women from here don't always understand this double life, and they don't accept the wife from the deep. Jealousy is felt by both sides, because both the here and the there wives can be jealous of this double relation. As one Pajé explains, "Ah, most of the Pajés are separated or live alone. They can't stand it. . . . A woman can't stand this encantaria life, and many times the wife from the deep (the encantada) becomes jealous and does things, some malicious things, to frighten off the here woman. That is what separates us from a family, right?" Relations between encantados and humans are sometimes ambiguous, because by socializing with those from the deep (from the encantaria) the Pajés break with certain relations from here (such as marriages) or become socially marginalized, due to their acquisition of certain encantado characteristics (such as femininity) and vices (such as drinking), through their close relationship with encantados and especially with their guides.

These relationships occur invariably through dreams and language: the Pajés have the sole privilege of being able to enter the encantaria, because (as many have said) if the *despreparados* (unprepared) look at an encantado or go to their land, they would never return—the possibility of transiting between these two universes is reserved for the initiated and those with the *dom* (the gift or vision). Thus, it's not enough to dream with the encantaria to have such experiences; one must first have the capacity to experience it, or there is the risk of becoming trapped in that land. And, having that capacity is almost always connected to a gift, which may require initiation or not; the experience of encantaria dreams is a gift (Boyer 1996).

Unlike with language (songs, consultations), which is the vehicle for negotiating with those that come here—the encantados—in dreams the Pajés are those who travel the inverse path. This journey is symmetric and complementary, because (as the accounts show) this relationship is essential for the strengthening of affinities: it's necessary for the encantados to come here, but it is equally important for the Pajés to enter into these kingdoms. This complementarity is necessary for the learning process on both sides: for Pajés and encantados.

Spirits Entering Our Lives: Language

Verbal language remains one of the most obvious forms in which the dead and spirits are materialized, and in African-based religions—where music and language are given the same definition—songs are the most evident form. It is thus to be expected that materializations take place through doctrines and songs. As one of the Pajés commented during an interview, "The doctrine is a trademark of an encantado. It materializes the spirit, it makes him appear, disappear, become angry or take our side. I don't even like singing that much for no reason, because then they just come."

Words are existence itself; this is not a novel assumption, and even though linguistic distinction between "things" and "concepts" (Saussure 1969) has faced more resistance in anthropology, given its ontological assumptions, it is evident that words are in themselves a form of so-called agency. Following Laura Ahearn's (2001, 111) proposition "that agency refers to the socioculturally mediated capacity to act," while being aware of the temporary and open character of this definition, I use multiple concepts of agency here to observe how the ability to act is synchronized with the Pajés' and encantados' linguistic expressions.

Productive dialogues between linguistics and anthropology have begun to appear in recent years centered on the notion of agency in each discipline.[26] Specific ethnographic studies have redirected understandings of this concept, opening new perspectives for broader description and discussion.

In this section I will try to discuss the language uttered by the encantados through their horses (mediums), especially in its sung form, and how it articulates social networks among the encantados and between them and the here people. I thus intend to take language as a form of "social action" (Duranti 2004) that is constructed through mutual social negotiations and interactions (Gumperz and Levinson 1996). As Ahearn states (2001, 111), "Within these contexts, as meanings are constructed, social reality is also constructed. In the approach advocated here, then, language does not merely reflect an already existing social reality; it also helps to create that reality." On June 23, 2010, there was a party (*toque de tambor*, or drumming) at Dona Luzia's house, the same Pajé mentioned above. It was her birthday and her *farrista* (reveller), Manezinho Boji Buá (from Codó's line) requested the beating of drums on this date, every year. It was a small party, with only her and two additional dancers, but others came to watch. Dona Luzia danced all night in the barracão, talking with the audience and providing consultations to those who needed them. I was one of the many people there who received indications for baths and *defumações* (fumigations)[27] to open pathways and heal certain ailments.

The next day I asked Dona Luzia what Manezinho had prescribed me exactly, because no one was familiar with the ingredients he had suggested for my bath, immediately she replied, "We, those who are with the invisible, we hardly know what they say to you. I understand everything, but my understanding is one and yours is another."

This explanation provided me with the real dimensions of the relationship between the Pajés, the encantados, and language, the latter as mediator and creator of social networks. The assertion of linguistic autonomy, which is not subjectively fixed and can exist without the subject, shows that words have an existential level that lies beyond both listener and speaker—*my understanding is one and yours another*—that is, the same signifier has different meanings according to the interlocutor, something which John Du Bois (2007) calls a "dialogic syntax."

This statement also implies that the speech made by Manezinho, the encantado who possessed her at the time, was understood by his horse in one way and by the audience in another: not that the meanings were different (in the Saussurean sense) but that the constructions of meaning attributed to his statement were. Insofar as the "horse" (Dona Luzia) has a different degree of affinity and relation with this encantado, constructions of meaning are distinct, which is to say that social relations involving Pajés and encantados determine the language used by them. By being acted on (i.e., giving consultations and singing), Dona Luzia was not there to mediate the encantados' statements, but one perceived the close relationship between them, for "languages, like cultures, change over time through drift and contact despite their supposedly self-reproducing structure" (De Graff 1999).

Certain areas of linguistics (such as discourse analysis and sociolinguistics) have worked with the idea of language as a social construct for some time, even prior to current debates taking shape in anthropology (influenced mainly by Anthony Giddens). Thus, the attempt to reconcile concepts of agency, from both an anthropological and linguistic point of view, has led to considerations of grammatical structure, its functions and categories in discourse and semantic constructions (Dixon 1994). In this way, grammatical markers are seen as ballasts for how we think about our own actions, as Bernard Comrie (1981) states (quoted in Ahearn 2001, 125), "Although each language has its own set of linguistic resources that can be used to exercise, attribute or deny agency, some features can also be found in every language."

Thus, the universal grammatical principles that underlie all languages indicate the first person's (ego) discursive salience and significance, though in evident interaction with the second person (with whom he speaks) and the third person (of whom he speaks): these subjects are most marked by agency exactly because they are present and active in the dialogue (in the above order).[28]

The use of these concepts, here, seeks an understanding of how the Pajés' songs and doctrines differ grammatically (observing only the use of grammatical persons) at the different moments in which they are sung: when there is a *chamamento*, or call; when the encantado is already *trabalhando* (working); and during the *despedida*, when the encantado leaves. The intention is to observe how and when Pajés and encantados are synchronized, while considering that "ritual speech also enables its users to lay claim to a social identity that transcends the spatial and temporal limits of the individual, mortal body.' (Keane 1997, 697).

As I affirm that the encantados socialize with the here people through language—that by *baixando* (entering or, literally, lowering) into their horses they interact with the audience by singing, giving consultations, and participating in the social life of certain communities—the aim here will be to try to observe how this form of agency is expressed linguistically: at what moment the Pajés stop appearing so as to allow the encantados to enter.

Although it seems obvious, the relationship between language and agency is linked to broader issues, such as whether it is a purely human category (in this case, whether spirits have agency, how they interact with human agency, how they cohabit), whether it is intentional agency (if the encantados enter alone, or if other elements stimulate the apparition, such as the doctrines themselves), and whether agency is applicable only to the individual or whether it could be categorized as a collective element. The introduction of this discussion on agency and linguistic production thus raises a debate that does not end here, but it encourages us to think about relations of "power" and "interaction" between there and here people, implying their sociability.

The inauguration of a party in a Pajé barracão almost always takes place with a *chamado* called the *Imbarabô*, then songs for the *voduns*—usually songs to *Averequete*—and then to the house *dono* (owner, or the Pajé's guide), the counterguides, the families or *nações* (nations), and finally the Pajé's revellers.

There is no singular way to organize the drumming; each house uses its own order and preferences, according to the hierarchy of the house's and Pajé's lines and families. The only general rule is to begin with one line's doctrines and then call the encantados that belong to the same line and that enter the house or its dancers.

Thus, at Senhor Hildo's house, a *toque de tambor* (drumming session) on September 24, 2007, for a *despacho*, or funerary ceremony (for one of the house dancers who had died three days previously) began with a song to one of the house voduns, with the following doctrines:

> *Mamãe, eu sou doce como o mel e amargo como o fel*
> *Baixou em guma*
> *Ela é feliz*
> *Oh Deus salve a estrela do Oriente*
> *Oh canta, canta canário, eô, oh Badé, foi pro mar . . .*
>
> *Oh, Badé me chama, Orum, Boborema*
> *Imbalaô, eh, meu pai . . .*
> *Oh Badé chorou, chorou, na mina de ouro . . .*
>
> *Badé se tu me dá eu dou, oh, Badé, se tu me dá eu dou.*
>
> *Ê mamãe, ê mamãe, ê mamãe*
> *Ê mamãe cadê Badé, que eu não vejo aqui?*

> Mother, I am as sweet as honey and as bitter as the gall bladder
> Entered Guma
> She is happy
> Oh Lord hail to the Eastern star
> Oh sing, sing mockingbird, eoh, oh Badé, went to the sea . . .
>
> Oh, Badé calls me, Orum, Boborema
> Imbalaô, eh, my father . . .
> Oh Badé cried, cried, in the gold mine . . .
>
> Badé if you give me I will give, oh, Badé, if you give me I will give.
>
> Eh mother, eh mother, eh mother
> Eh mother, where is Badé, I don't see her here?

They are singing to Badé,[29] a vodun that, like the encantados, also has siblings, a father, and a mother; he is Sobo's son and brother of Averequete and Loco. In the encantados' hierarchy they are a level above the Cabo-clos and nobles, because the voduns are more African, according to many informants.

The doctrines always use the third person, when calling the vodun or talking about him or her: the vodun hasn't arrived yet and his or her absence is thus marked. The voduns will only begin to speak directly to the vodun after the last doctrine, although this does not mean that he or she has necessarily arrived; the doctrine is a *provocação* (provocation), an indirect call rather than a proper conversation, even though the dialogue is with the second person.

At this point, the Pajé is still *puro* (pure, i.e., has not gone into a trance) and begins to feel the first *calafrios* (chills), one of the indications that he will go into a trance. He moves restlessly and puts perfume on the back of his head, to delay the encantado/vodun. In this exchange, between calls and attempts to delay the trance, the relationship between linguistic practice and social structure becomes more evident. The Pajés then begin to chant doctrines—messages from the vodun, such as the following:

> *Oia Verequete mandou avisar*
> *Ele é Imperador na terra,*
> *Governador no mar.*
> Oia Verequete said to inform
> He is Emperor on Earth,
> Governor in the sea.

They proceed with the third person, and here agency is assigned at times to the Pajé and at others to the encantado: there is still no dialogue between the encantado and the audience, and hence, introduction into that social network has not occurred. In another doctrine the Pajé calls the vodun, as shown below: addressing the drums, he asks them to call Averequete. It is important to note here that the Pajé does not say this in the first person—by transferring action to the drums[30] he is no longer the agent, which reminds us of earlier discussions on agency, its manifestations and definitions:

> *Chama Averequete, Averê*
> *Chama Averequete, Averê . . .*
>
> Call Averequete, Averê
> Call Averequete, Averê . . .

A ritual follows and the doctrines are sung for Cearencinho (head of the house), then for Zé Raimundo (the counterguide), and then, having carried out all the ceremonies required for the despacho, the Pajés begin to chant:

> *Virou, virou, virou o tambor*
> *Virou, virou, virou o tambor*

> Turned, turned, the drum has turned
> Turned, turned, the drum has turned

Thus, by warning the audience that the drum rhythm has *turned* (or changed) to *mina*, they begin to chant doctrines for different families. I shall focus here on the Flag family, as mentioned above. At this point they sing the most well-known doctrine for the head of the family:

> *Eu sou o Caboclo da Bandeira*
> *João da Mata falado*
> *Nas promessas de Cristo*
> *Por Jesus abençoado*
> I am the Flag Caboclo
> João da Mata when spoken
> For Christ's vows
> Blessed by Jesus

The first person is used and it is (the encantado) João da Mata who speaks; the Pajé is already in a trance and the song brings the Flag King to the house. Although the speaker is both the Pajé and the encantado, all those present know who is speaking at all times. The deictics are pragmatically conditioned and the audience has insight into the actions performed by Pajés and encantados.

The songs follow almost entirely in the first person, with presentations, accounts, and descriptions about personal preferences. When not in the first person, these doctrines are *avisos* (warnings), spoken in the third person (about what or who is being discussed), as follows:

> *A mina não é pra quem quer*
> *É só pra quem sabe baiar*
> *Quem está dentro não queira sair*
> *Quem está fora não queira entrar*

> Mina is not for whom wants it
> It is for whom knows how to fall
> He who is in does not want to get out
> He who is out does not want to get in

The encanatado continues speaking and linguistic agency is semantically marked. The same situation is evident in imperative phrases, as in the following doctrine (quoted above):

Chama Averequete, Averê
Chama Averequete, Averê

Call Averequete, Averê
Call Averquete, Averê

Here, the encantado retains agency; although the first person is not linguistically expressed, his presence is evident through a syntactical (though not semantic) absence. The relationship between agency and linguistic markers is obviously permeated by semantics, through the meanings given to and constructed out of language: these aren't always synchronized, which invites us to critically reflect on what we define as agency and its mobility/ plasticity. The doctrines seem to emphasize the process of "role/agency shifts" so well because they provide the real dimensions of constructions formed during the encantados' visits to earth.

Conclusion

This article sought to portray the social life of spirits (encantados) through extensive ethnographic description, involving material from over eight different Pajé houses (Tambor de Mina healings) in three different municipalities from the Baixada Ocidental region of Maranhão, the western frontier of a northeastern Brazilian state. This region's demographic history is strongly marked by the presence of Portuguese colonists and West African slaves, especially from Bantu-speaking groups (Gomes 2005), as well as local indigenous groups (many of the encantados are Amerindians[31]).

The text attempted to indicate the importance of dreams and doctrines (songs) in a process of mutual learning between Pajés and encantados, who move back and forth between the fundo and the earth. The social

networks between religious adepts and spirits are shaped and strength-
ened primarily through the dreams of the Pajés, who enter the encantaria
universe, and words (mostly sung) when the encantados enter into their
medium's crown to provide consultations, to sing, and to refine their relations with humans. It is thus proposed that these are complementary and
necessary forms of materialization. Through dreams, the Pajés experience
a different type of relationship than that experienced through language;
since dreams are personal and solitary, in them the encantados' materialization takes places without the presence of other humans and from the
external visible world inward.

Through language, however, the spirits' materialization and social life
takes place from inside the encantarias outward and requires Pajé and
audience for the development of social relations. It is thus proposed that
language is autonomous, being neither simply a vehicle of transmission
(Reddy 1979) nor just a conductive vehicle of referential meaning (Goodwin 1990). Such affirmations are evinced in the conjunction of approaches
to notions of agency, through existing (and absent) linguistic markers in
the doctrines and songs proffered during the encantados' visits to the Pajé
houses.

What we can observe is that the doctrines' linguistic markers are not
always sufficient for the creation of a direct relationship to the agent; in
other words, the notion of agency involves semantic and pragmatic relations that are not always visible in the doctrinal texts but are constructed
according to shared collective criteria. Language has a central role in the
encantados' materialization, and both dreams and language are modes of
socialization and relational construction among the encantados and the
here people. This interaction is crucial for a reciprocal learning process.

CHAPTER NINE

Amerindian and Priest

An Entity in Brazilian Umbanda

Emerson Giumbelli

Chegou! Chegou!
Chegou ... com Deus ...
Chegou! Chegou!
O Caboclo das Sete Encruzilhadas![1]

Approach

The protagonist of this text is a *caboclo*, an Amerindian entity that inhabits the spiritual territories of what is known as *Umbanda* (in Brazil) and whose manifestations are combined, in many accounts, with the religion's origins. All attempts to approach this entity are frightening, even when we trust in its proclaimed moral qualities and even when a direct meeting has not yet taken place; here, I refer more to the intellectual search involved in this approximation, for it does not necessarily lead us to fixed referents. Part of this search consists of tracing this entity's spiritual biography, with recourse to the diverse narratives that tell of its material existence and current characteristics, and entails an exploration of the various histories and geographies through which the Caboclo's own identity modulates. This search also obliges us to situate and characterize Umbanda at the confluence of paths laid by Catholicism, Kardecist Spiritism, and Orixá cults. I engage in dialogue with Roger Bastide and J. Lorand Matory, with the intention of characterizing Umbanda's spiritual economy and the place of certain entities within it, a starting point that leads to the attempt to trace the lives of the *Caboclo das Sete Encruzilhadas*—the Caboclo of the Seven Crossroads.[2]

According to official Brazilian statistics about Umbanda, its adepts are sparse and in decline, going from 542,000 in 1991 to 432,000 in 2000 (Prandi 2004) and 407,000 in 2010, which corresponds to 0.21 percent of the total population. Statistics, however, do not communicate the generalized social presence of Umbanda references in Brazilian common knowledge, which can be found on the magazine stands of any major Brazilian city or even in the services of Pentecostal churches (whose adepts are much more numerous) that denounce their enemies. Certain public rituals led by *Umbandistas* on specific dates can also congregate a small multitude (Silva 1995). Many Umbandistas cite 1908 as the year in which the religion emerged, yet the term *Umbanda* only began to designate a specific cult modality after middle-class intellectuals embraced its leadership in the 1930s. As has become common in academic parlance, however, it is possible to insert Umbanda as one variant of so-called Afro-Brazilian religions: another of the Orixá cults' avatars in the African diaspora's post-colonial composition on American soil.[3] In the end, Umbanda's spatiality and temporality is multiple, as is its very definition: stretched between numerous cultural references and challenged by the proliferation of modes of understanding and practice.

In his most important work, written at the end of the 1950s, Roger Bastide affirms about Umbanda that "there is nothing more exciting for a sociologist than observing the birth of a new religion, with his own eyes" (1971, 466). Bastide was one of the intellectuals who sought to understand Umbanda's constitution as part of the Orixá cults' cultural re-elaboration caused by the insertion of Afro-descendants into Brazilian society. If Candomblé corresponded to the pre-twentieth-century result of this process, Umbanda crystallized a solution corresponding to the subsequent period: the moment in which Afro-descendants became socially reintegrated, following the end of slavery (definitively abolished in Brazil in 1888). This process, however, took place in an ambiguous manner, conjugating low social status with access to education. For Bastide, the result for this population was an ambivalence of feelings and attitudes: on the one hand, the valorization and affirmation of autonomy before the white population, on the other, a desire for assimilation and an inferiority complex. In the first half of the twentieth century, this could be detected in the black press as much as in Umbanda, the "new religion." In the latter, African references appear dislocated by identification with white world logic; a world into which Afro-descendants were anxious to become integrated, though not without resentment. According to the French sociologist, this is the key to understanding the articulation of various cultural references in Umbanda's constitution.

Although I believe that Bastide apprehends a fundamental dimension, I would also problematize his argument. In relation to Candomblé, based above all on his research in Bahian *terreiros*, Bastide observes urgency in the African collective memory and states that the slavery period created the conditions for the black population to develop social structures that reproduced African cultural references. Even syncretism with Catholic figures, understood in light of the black population's insertion into colonial society, could not disfigure the Orixás. In the case of Umbanda, however, which corresponds to another period in Brazilian history, Bastide concludes that what takes place is the product of a single direction, from society to culture. Let us look at how Bastide concludes his chapter on Umbanda: "Previously, the images of Catholic saints served as the Orixás' masks; currently, it is the Orixás that serve as masks for the new needs and attitudes of an ascending social group" (1971, 471). Or rather, the new social conditions uncovered by the black population, even if only in a virtual sense, in itself offered the relations that came to define this "new religion." Thus, the same theoretical framework produced distinct results, since Umbanda can be understood as being socially more than culturally determined, creating a situation in which African gods "corrupt themselves": "to 'ascend,' the Orixás are obliged to whiten themselves" (1971, 456).

In Umbanda the Orixás change color; this is easily observable in drawings and sculptures, representations in which Catholic references—Jesus, Mary, and saints—are a strong presence. On the other hand, it is also possible to apprehend Umbanda's characteristics in a manner that confers greater density to its ontological dimensions. In response to Bastide, it is not a matter of rehabilitating culture to the detriment of society. I agree with Matory, from whom I borrow the notion of ontology, when he affirms that "spirit possession by multiple beings is a vivid idiom in the management of social marginality at cultural crossroads" (2009, 243). Or rather, culture and society must be articulated in our efforts to understand, by provoking the search for notions and concepts that achieve such a result. In attempting to seek greater ontological density, while producing the articulation between social and cultural dimensions, I recur to a certain idea of the sacred; if Émile Durkheim (2000) appropriates this category to suggest a correspondence between religion and a society's moral center, others will produce distinct associations. I refer specifically to Roger Caillois (2004), Michel Leiris (2002), and Georges Bataille (1987), who are interested in the sacred as marked by ambivalence, since it conjugates sanctity and crime, righteousness and transgression, purity and impurity. This sacred was sought by them both inside and outside religion. In any case, the inspiration found in Durkheim will yield another topography, one which demonstrates the affinity between the sacred and social and cultural marginality.

Moreover, I hope to demonstrate how Umbanda can be seen as an elaboration of this latter sense of sacred. I insist on a discussion with Bastide to indicate how he came to perceive that ambivalence was a fundamental property of the situation in which Umbanda emerged. This can be explored not only through social structure but also in elements that lead us to a cultural dimension, brought out here with the notion of sacred, which was the object of one of Bastide's (2006) last pieces of writing. In it, the sociologist asks himself what the "savage sacred" could be. He begins with a description of religious and social forms in which the domestication of the sacred takes place, such that new religious and social conditions can generate a de-domestication. It is interesting to note that, to illustrate this position, Bastide recuperates his approach to trance in Candomblé and in "disaggregated" African forms. In contrast to the mythical framework provided by Candomblé, in these other forms possession becomes a channel for the anxieties and frustrations derived from social conditions. But I believe that Bastide himself signals a distinct perspective when he proposes trance as a counterpoint. I place special emphasis on a section in which Bastide refers to the type of entities that interest me directly, when he notes that in a context of social and religious "anomie" possession "usurps the Amerindian's barbarism to express a counterculture in formation or an anti-society, against white culture" (Bastide 2006, 259).

It seems like there are connections between the clues cast by Bastide and the notion of sacred outlined above. Before going on to show how I found inspiration in these elements to consider Umbanda and its entities, it is necessary to indicate another understanding of this new religion's genesis and configuration. If Bastide's argument in *The African Religions of Brazil* illustrates what could be called a "sociologism," what now enters on stage could be called "culturalism." The basic idea is as follows: Umbanda is a "Brazilian religion" not only because it was created on national soil but also (and above all) because it brings together references that allude to the dominant narrative on the formation of nationality. What sustains this proposal is the observation that in Umbanda Catholic saints, *caboclos* (Amerindians), and *pretos* (slaves) constitute the principal cosmological figures, which corresponds to the narrative that conceives of Brazil as the encounter of three "races" or "peoples"—white Europeans, native Amerindians, and black Africans. Thus, the argument goes that, Umbanda is the expression of this narrative on a religious level, constructed during precisely the same period, the 1920s and 1930s. This culturalism—for it is a matter of thinking about Umbanda in terms of the expression of a narrative that synthesizes Brazilian culture—has exponents among Umbandistas as well as among those who study their discourse and practices.[4]

While also indicating fundamental elements of Umbandista cosmology, this approach ignores some central considerations. First, anyone who dedicates himself to analyze the debates about Umbanda's origins will note that Brazil is only one among many possibilities: there are those who consider the new religion to be a type of ancient wisdom, a legacy from civilizations that once occupied Egypt, India, Lemuria, and so on. As we have already seen, the Orixás' presence leads to a strong interpretive line that inserts Umbanda as another manifestation of African-based religiosity.[5] And, as I will demonstrate further on, even when Brazil is established as its place of birth, the existence of an (ethno)geography that passes through other locations is not abolished. Second, there are reasons for refusing the exaggeration of Umbanda's singularity in its claim or attribution as a "Brazilian religion"; other religions from the same period also sought nourishment from nationalist indices. Catholicism and Spiritism are currently going through this process, finding much greater audiences than could be attained by the Umbandistas.[6] Finally, it is necessary to confer greater protagonism to Umbandista intellectuals, by treating their elaborations as something more than an expression of the dominant narrative. The current relevance of these elaborations suggests another approach, which accords the Umbandistas with greater agency. Although a dialogue with broader references must take place, the specificity of the Umbandistas should be considered. If Brazil figures as a theme discussed by Umbanda, perhaps we should treat this as a form of discovery—to use a suggestion by the historian Marlyse Meyer (2001). That is, the question should be: Which Brazil does Umbanda discover?[7]

Caboclos in Umbanda

This text is concerned with an entity known as the *Caboclo das Sete Encruzilhadas* (the Caboclo of the Seven Crossroads), but more generally *caboclos* are a specific genre among the entities who provide advice and guidance in Umbanda, and who can also be found in other religious settings, including Candomblé (Santos 1995; Boyer 1999). In Umbanda, however, their presence is obligatory and structural: it is possible to find mention and descriptions about caboclos throughout its history. Leal de Souza, a journalist who converted to the new religion and published what is probably the first book on Umbanda in 1933, states, "The authentic caboclo, comes from the forest to the *Tenda* through a learning process in the space, has the intolerant enthusiasm of the new Christian, is as uncompromising as a monk" (1933, 47–48). From a classic study by Renato Ortiz, who was supervised by Bastide at the beginning of the 1970s: "The arrival of the Caboclo is always accompanied by a strong cry, denoting this spiritual entity's energy and strength. . . . In the trance, the mediums embody lordliness and walk with heads held high, with a proud and arrogant attitude" (1978, 65). Finally, from Omar Ribeiro Thomaz's more recent work—written specifically about the caboclos—in a section about the statues of various dimensions that can be seen in terreiros or shops that sell religious artefacts: "Dark in colour, usually with an athletic gait indicating physical strength, he has a fixed and authoritative look. Many adopt postures indicating movement, combat. Others, rigid and lordly, have the attitude of a true chief" (1992, 207).

The repetition of indices from the same semantic field is clear, leading to ideas of strength, virility, determination, obstinacy, and rebellion. The caboclos are always identified as Amerindians that lived in the forest, the first inhabitants on Brazilian soil, and their names evoke this origin. This is not the sixteenth-century Amerindian, however, but rather the nineteenth-century native: as many studies have suggested (Ortiz 1978; Thomaz 1992), the referent for this Umbanda figure is the Amerindian portrayed in romanticist literature, whose Brazilian exponents include José de Alencar and Gonçalves Dias. Such authors were important in the sense that they attributed Amerindians with the role of national heroes, placing emphasis on their resistance to assaults by Portuguese colonists. Bastide's (1971, 436–37) observation of the association between the Umbanda caboclos and liberation heroes in nationalist ideology is thus pertinent. The relationship between white society and the indigenous figure is translated in the very designation caboclo, which in Brazil is predominantly applied to the white-Amerindian mix. As Thomaz notes (1992), this also leads the images to portray North American Indians (probably influenced by the cinema) with feather headdresses trailing down their backs. It is also common for these and other caboclo images to use green and yellow props, the colors of the Brazilian national flag.

In Umbanda, the caboclos form a pair with another genre of entities: the *pretos-velhos* (lit. old blacks). Much like the caboclos, these are protagonists in ritual manifestations, who often lend their names to terreiros. The preto-velho's stereotypical characteristics, however, are very different to the caboclos' own: their principal characteristics are piety, humility, and availability. In this case, the basic reference is the slave that lived on Brazilian farms and in Brazilian houses, during or following the colonial period, and not just any slave: above all, he was loyal to his owners and resigned to his position. These manifestations suggest an old person, hunched due to the weight of work and suffering. The images portray black men or women, with grey hair and/or beards, smoking a pipe and carrying a walking stick, normally seated; in fact, it is common to see the female counterpart, *pretas-velhas*, once again in contrast to the caboclos, among whom the female gender rarely appears. Nevertheless, the opposition should not be exaggerated: as Lindsay Hale (1997) shows, some pretos-velhos are presented as rebels and some lived their whole earthly lives in Africa. There is no fixed characteristic for either pretos-velhos or caboclos; what matters most seems to be the relation between two diffuse sets of characteristics.

This also serves as an understanding of the entities' roles and participation, as described by Leal de Souza, my primary source for the Caboclo das Sete Encruzilhadas. His description of a caboclo continues thus: "Upon hearing complaints from those suffering hardships in their lives, he responds angrily that Spiritism does not exist to help anybody in their material life and attributes our suffering to our own mistakes and faults, for which we have to pay. But, after two or three years of contact with the bitter misery of our existence, his intransigence is softened and he eventually materially assists his incarnated brothers, because he pities their destitution and wants to see them content and happy" (1933, 48). I will return to the reference to "Spiritism" and its theodicies in a moment, but for now, I would like to highlight the similarities of caboclos and pretos: both serve the needy. But the caboclo does not completely renounce his intransigence, which remains residually, corresponding to the mark of his own savagery. The force that translates this savagery represents a fundamental element in the Umbanda configuration, since it does not exist only to serve the needy, according to Leal de Souza, but it is also concerned with the spiritual combat against morally opposed forces. Umbanda is configured around "seven white lines," each commanded by an Orixá, whom Leal de Souza describes as a "general." The lines group entities according to their functions and affinities, which are integrated in the combat "against elements from the Black Line, that is, the Exu, to the people of the Cross-roads" (1933, 58). For this, the caboclos' strength is essential and shared among the other White Line entities.

In reality, we have a much more complex picture here, for Leal de Souza explains that the last of the White Lines is distinct from the rest; there is no single commanding Orixá, and with workers spread throughout the other lines, the entities are the "Black Line's egresses" (1933, 62): caboclos and pretos that have already been *exus*. In another sense, the same movement is contemplated in the "baptised exu" figure (Ortiz 1978, 125); these elaborations allow morally inferior entities to be recovered. Differently to the caboclos and pretos-velhos, the exu has no corresponding historical referent: the archetype certainly refers to the Christian figure of the devil (Meyer 1993), but due to his transmutability, he also operates as a vector that incites the multiplication of entities. Some exus are scoundrels, others are prostitutes, still others incarnate as gypsies, sailors, seamen, cowboys, garbage collectors, beggars, and country bumpkins. These figures are con-fused with caboclos, preto-velhos, and various "Oriental" types—on one level, there are clear distinctions between them, but on another, they are all equally involved in the struggles that oppose and compose them, as-sisted by Orixás who maintain a more cosmological than agentive role.[8]

Another common element among the Umbanda entities are marginal figures: there are geographic marginals, but above all, there are social and cultural marginals, including Amerindians and Afro-descendants, who are inserted into the national narrative as subordinate to whites. In Umbanda these marginals are powerful, and their power to do good and their cen-tral position in the cult transforms them into a source of ambivalence. In reference to the empowerment of marginality, Bastide argues, "Can-domblé's 'other' society is one in which humble street sellers and maids from good families represent the role of Gods and Heroes" (2006, 262). Matory (2009, 252) also draws attention to the presence of the *topoi* of nobility and royalty in the Orixá cult. If we remember Bastide's own asso-ciation of Umbanda with social mobility among the black population, and if we note the presence of many white people within the nascent Umban-da's leadership, it is then easy to perceive the inversion: the Umbandistas' *other society* is constituted by the reunion and participation of entities that share indices of marginality. In relation to Candomblé, if Umbanda's origi-nal formulations clearly represent a type of "whitening," Umbanda also provides the entities that it mobilizes with recognition and a privileged agency, through spiritual biographies that provoke alternative visions of history and geography.

In any case, Umbanda's initial phases, principally, cannot be discussed without touching on Spiritism: records indicate that the first collective event organized by the new religion's adepts, in 1941, was called the Congress of Umbanda Spiritism, the same name given to the first Umbanda federation, created two years previously in 1939. In my view, this was not merely a matter of seeking legitimation by appealing to a more socially acceptable reference but the incorporation of certain central concepts into Umbanda's structure. Based on Kardecist formulations in France, Spiritism arrived in Brazil in the nineteenth century, inspiring adherence and organized groups among the social elites. But its practices also reached a broader circle, in social and cultural terms. From the Spiritist cosmology, the fundamental point to retain is its evolutionary conception, which allowed for incorporated and unincorporated spirits to be hierarchized. Superior spirits occupy the source both of doctrinal knowledge and moral behavior. The same spirits can help people to cope with their material conditions and guide unincorporated spirits who act in accordance with their low spiritual evolution. In Spiritist centers, these superior spirits were normally associated with figures who dominate official and erudite knowledge (doctors, priests, historic heroes).[9]

Umbanda not only owes Spiritism its name but also its evolutionist conception;[10] however, Umbandista evolutionism makes use of the virtuality offered by Spiritism to produce a new configuration. Spiritism affords direct communication with historic figures, who return as entities after their deaths: caboclos, pretos-velhos, and other Umbanda entities are understood in this manner (and rarely as ancestors, in the strictest sense). At the same time, Spiritism supposes complementarity between the entity's nature and its actions. Exploring this point and noting that the spirits who guide Kardecists are generally white, the Umbandistas responded, "Now, in our race's tradition and the affinities of our people, these caboclo or preto spirits, and those that present themselves as such, are humble and good, and invariably promote . . . the doctrine summarised by the ten commandments and expanded by Jesus" (Leal de Souza 1933, 103). Therefore, on one level, Umbandista intellectuals sought continuity between the new religion and Spiritism, including the assent of Christian references.

At the same time, however, since the action of its entities does not annul their own nature, Umbanda associates itself to a new spiritual configuration. Or rather, caboclos and pretos-velhos are not merely likened to

the superior spirits, even when presented as such: their spiritual inferiority is positive and necessary. At least two points can be mentioned here,
once again in reference to Leal de Souza's presentation. First, requests
for spiritual combat confer greater force and efficacy to entities that have
an affinity with their enemies; in other words, savagery is useful against
impiety. Second, "these space labourers [caboclos and pretos] want to be
considered backward, so that individuals who are reputed to be superior,
when obliged to turn to these inferior spirits, come to perceive and understand their own inferiority" (1933, 53). In this case, embodied persons are
forced by the entities to lower themselves in order to find their dignity; the
result is that the source of religious authority is displaced to the spiritual
hierarchy's lower ranks. Although the possibility was opened by Spiritism,
only Umbanda consecrates the paradox that by showing traces of inferiority an entity can act with superiority.[11]

In the text on the savage sacred, Bastide mentions Jean Rouch's film
Les Maîtres Fous, a documentary that follows an African sect, as a record
of an example of "trance de-domestication" (2006, 262). In ceremonies,
adepts incorporate the spirits of characters and objects associated with
the (British) colonial powers, culminating in the sacrifice of a dog: a demonstration of the native's power. We can approximate this situation with
that of Umbanda possession, not to indicate a de-domestication but to
acknowledge that an *other society* is being targeted. In Umbanda, marginal figures are incorporated, whose actuation is linked to a Christian
ideal. The attribution of power to marginals, focused on indigenous and
Afro-descendant peoples and elements taken from the dominant nationalist narrative, suggests the primitivization of Brazil. It is in these inferior
but kindly figures that the country should recognize itself. It seems that in
this we identify "Brazil's discovery," above all when combined with other
national narratives in which Amerindians and Afro-descendants were an-
nulled even when they were being recognized. But there are also other
possibilities in the spiritual geography of the Umbanda configuration.

The Indigenous Life of the Caboclo das Sete Encruzilhadas

Accounts about the Caboclo das Sete Encruzilhadas (Caboclo of the Seven
Crossroads) are strongly associated with events that took place in Zélio de
Moraes's life (1891–1975), especially one specific moment in 1908. Many
versions of varying lengths exist about this incident; however, even the

shortest narratives integrate a series of points that are maintained in other longer examples.[12] Zélio, a young man at the time, was stricken down by a series of unexplained disturbances that led him to a Spiritist session. An entity manifested through Zélio calling itself the Caboclo das Sete Encruzilhadas, for whom "there will be no blocked paths." The entity was resisted by those present during the session and thus he invited them all to Zélio's home on the following day, which was in what is now called the municipality of São Gonçalo, in the metropolitan area of Rio de Janeiro. The Caboclo manifested once again during this second session, accompanied by a preto-velho, proclaiming the creation of a new center, called the *Tenda Espírita Nossa Senhora da Piedade* (Spiritist Tent of Our Lady of Mercy), and a new religion, called Umbanda. The Caboclo and the preto-velho produced miraculous cures during the session. According to these accounts, the Caboclo manifested himself again on other subsequent occasions to determine the creation of new Umbanda temples and a federation.

Although the narrated events took place during the first decades of the twentieth century, these accounts do not appear to have been amply divulged prior to the 1970s. Yet, what is important to highlight is the relevance conferred to the Caboclo, who is attributed with the creation of the first Umbanda temples in Brazil, not to mention the religion itself, through the annunciation of his name and a few basic liturgies. The following transcription seeks to indicate the role of certain entities in what was being created. It has been ascribed to Zélio de Moraes, who speaks at times as himself, at others as the Caboclo's intermediary: "From that moment, he [a spiritual envoy] would create the Umbanda Law, where the preto and the caboclo could manifest themselves. Because he did not agree with Kardecist Federation, which did not receive either pretos or caboclos. For, if Brazil—what existed in Brazil were caboclos, natives—if in Brazil, those that came to explore Brazil, brought pretos from the African coast to work and to exalt this country, how could a Spiritist Federation neither receive caboclo nor preto?" (*apud* Cumino 2010, 322). In this extract, caboclos and pretos become associated to challenge Kardecist Spiritism and to produce a religion that speaks to the national formation.

National traits are also inscribed in representations of the Caboclo: the image from Zélio's own center depicts an Amerindian in the foreground, holding an adornment and a bow and arrow, behind him is a crossroads with seven paths cutting into the forest, with the sky and the forest dominating the background. Near the Amerindian, close to the crossroads, there is a mast with the national flag—shaped much like those found in Brazilian army barracks or schools.[13] In another representation, this time a bust, the Caboclo das Sete Encruzilhadas is adorned with blue and white necklaces and bracelets. National traits also appear on another statue, depicting a golden Amerindian with yellow, white, and blue adornments and carrying green foliage, once again referring to the national flag; in the only available photograph of this statue, the Brazilian flag hangs in the background.[14] The date associated with the Caboclo is November 15, which is also the day on which Brazil commemorates the Republican proclamation of 1889.

The accounts that detail the Caboclo's life story also carry references to national mythology, but before turning to these, it is once again worth looking at how Leal de Souza refers to this entity. Before becoming an Umbandista, Leal de Souza visited Zélio de Moraes and found the Caboclo accompanied by Pai Antônio, a preto-velho, practicing what reminded him of Spiritist consultations and cures but with songs invoking and greeting the Catholic pantheon's principle entities and figures. The Caboclo does not gain any further mention in this first account,[15] but this changes in Leal de Souza's book, which he wrote once he had become an adept of the new religion. The Caboclo is then treated as a *chefe* (chief) and is conferred leadership by at least four Umbanda temples, united by common ritual determinations and other activities. Leal de Souza associates the Caboclo with Christian references, presenting him as a "missionary of consolation and redemption." His distinguishing traits are "between extreme humility and geniality, his piety flows over those who seek him" (Leal de Souza 1933, 78). His great knowledge is recognized and miracles, above all cures, are indicated as proof of his great power. He is, in short, a "spirit of light . . . that presents himself with a rough appearance and with the savage name of Caboclo das Sete Encruzilhadas" (ibid., 77).

In Leal de Souza's description the Caboclo has preto-velho characteristics, which can be summarized as humility, geniality, and piety; in many narratives the Caboclo is paired with Pai Antônio, and both are incorporated together by Zélio de Moraes. One could thus say that, despite the Christian incursions, there is an approximation between the Caboclo and Afro references. Leal de Souza inserts the Caboclo in the Ogum line, diverging from other accounts that mention Oxossi. But the journalist also comments on *Orixá Mallet*, which is equally present in other accounts about Zélio de Moraes. According to Leal de Souza, in this case we are not dealing with a line chief but the Caboclo's assistant, whose last incarnation was as a "Malay" on a "beautiful Oriental island" (1933, 74). Aside from the Orixás, the figure of exu also finds resonance: Leal de Souza himself defines exu as a leader of the "people at the Crossroads." Throughout Umbanda's history designations and locations multiply associations between exus and crossroads, and although other justifications for the name Caboclo das Sete Encruzilhadas exist, nothing seems to overcome the tacit connection with exu. In this case, it is a connection that emphasizes the strength of the Caboclo and his opposition to the opposite line. In other words, the Caboclo das Sete Encruzilhadas is a type of everted exu.

It is significant that the account that narrates the Caboclo's terrestrial life begins with a warning against confusing him with the *Exu Rei das Sete Encruzilhadas* (Exu King of the Seven Crossroads). How does it continue?[16] The Caboclo is presented as the offspring of the union between a white Portuguese woman and a Tupi-Guarani chief. Their meeting takes place in the "period of Colonial Brazil," on a coffee and sugarcane farm, whose owners have good relations with the Tupi-Guarani and refuse to adopt slave labor. The farmer's daughter, who is pregnant by the Tupi chief, is the only survivor of an attack by rival Amerindians. Her son, the Caboclo das Sete Encruzilhadas, "received his education from two cultures: the Christian tradition adopted by his mother and the other guided by a Pagé from his father's tribe." His life is driven by his protection of the Afro-descendant population. After graduating in law in the capital, he worked as a defense attorney for slaves that were being accused by their owners, but this did not prevent him, "as chief of his indigenous community," from leading incursions to liberate slaves and take them to a secure location. This account ends where most begin: "Following his disembodiment, he returned through Zélio de Moraes mediumship, in November 1908, as a messenger spirit who placed Umbanda's foundations in Rio de Janeiro."[17]

It might be useful to conclude this section by mentioning another entity, who is linked in this case to the *União do Vegetal*, a religious variant with Christian and Spiritist elements, constituted around the consumption of a tea known as *daime* or *ayahuasca* (Melo 2010). João Gabriel, who founded the União do Vegetal, was an Umbandista who migrated from Bahia to Amazonia in the mid-twentieth century, accompanied (or perhaps guided) by a caboclo called the Forest Sultan. The União do Vegetal's mythic creation is combined with this entity's transfiguration into a master who is illuminated by the tea's power, João Gabriel himself. Or rather, this caboclo's journey to his origins in the forest results in his transfiguration, substituting mediumship with "concentration." In the case of the Caboclo das Sete Encruzilhadas, his terrestrial life describes the inverse voyage:

from the indigenous tribe to the national capital. Biologically and culturally he is the product of the interpenetration of Amerindians and whites.
This is probably what differentiates him from the Amerindians who killed
his father and grandparents. At the same time, his work focuses on helping the Afro-descendant population, to whom he becomes a hero. The
Caboclo leaves the jungle without losing the power that it provides him;
combined with white knowledge, it will serve in the redemption of the
black population. Prior to Umbanda's birth, its founding entity—a chari-
table Amerindian, who returned through Zélio—was already concerned
with building the nation.

The Caboclo's Christian Life

In the above account, the Caboclo das Sete Encruzilhadas becomes integrated into the white world without abandoning his indigeneity. In other
accounts, the same Caboclo converts himself into a white man in another
incarnation. This is already suggested by Leal de Souza, who associates
the Caboclo's profound knowledge of the Bible with a past life as a Christian priest. By speaking of *protetores* (protectors), the book indicates that
"among the caboclos, many were Europeans in previous incarnations"
(1933, 68). This is certainly the case for the Caboclo das Sete Encruzilhadas, whose knowledge of Western medicine is also often emphasized. To
confirm these indices, more information is offered: "The first time that the
medium sees him, at the beginning of his mission, the Caboclo das Sete Encruzilhadas presented himself as a tanned middle aged man wearing a white
tunic and a sash across his body, on which the word *Cáritas* shone, alight.
For a long time after, he would only appear as a caboclo, with a feather loin-
cloth and other such forest *pajé* [witchdoctor] traits" (1933, 80).

Other later narratives are more precise in their identification of the
Caboclo's Christian incarnation. Statements attributed to Zélio de Moraes
himself, at certain points, mention a Jesuit priest, and at others, the name
Gabriel Malagrida or Gabriel de Malagrida (Brown 1986, 39; Oliveira
2008, 96; Cumino 2010, 130). In the Caboclo's words, incorporated in Zélio: "I brought an order, a mission, because for a long time I have foreseen
what will happen, ever since the Lisbon earthquake in 1755 until now, and
everything that I have said would happen has happened" (*apud* Cumino
2010, 326). The author of the book from which I have taken these accounts
explains that "Gabriel de Malagrida . . . was the victim of intrigue, which
led him to the stake during the 'Holy Inquisition,' the primary accusation

against him was his premonition of the earthquake" (*apud* Cumino 2010, 130 and 326).

Umbandistas speak of a historical figure, a man called Gabriel Malagrida who lived between 1689 and 1761, was born in Italy, went to Brazil on two occasions during the eighteenth century, and died in Lisbon, the last person to be burnt at the stake by the Inquisition. Certain sources describe this biography, starting with the work of a French Jesuit, translated to Portuguese ten years after its original publication in 1865. But what interests me the most is Malagrida as described by the Umbandistas. My attention was particularly drawn to this figure when reading Marlyse Meyer's book (1993). Meyer finds clues about a certain Doña Maria de Padilla, a fourteenth-century figure and lover of a Spanish king. Maria Padilha is the name given to certain entities that appear in Umbanda terreiros in Brazil. The book follows clues about the "invisible roads" that connect the two Padilhas, passing through Europe, Africa, and Brazil. Padilha appears in sixteenth-century Portuguese novels, in African-influenced invocations apprehended by the Inquisition in Brazil in the eighteenth century, and in Umbanda books that describe the female exus (or *pomba-giras*) in the twentieth century. Although it is not possible to trace the precise connections between all of these points, Meyer suggests that a certain line brings them together (1993, 124).

The line that joins the Caboclo and Gabriel Malagrida is of a different order: not a single name and its factual connections but a spiritual biography that refers to a historic figure. In Maria Padilha's case, there are indices of the same kind; some mediums differentiate this pomba-gira, who appears as a prostitute, by her European nobility and the whiteness of her skin. These traits accentuate the entity's ambiguity, combining benevolence and malice, Europeans and Africans, whites and blacks. This ambiguity is also produced when dealing with the Caboclo, who is both indigenous and white, European and Brazilian, priest and heretic. Through Malagrida, Umbanda connects itself directly to Christianity. Returning to Leal de Souza's presentation: "The Caboclo das Sete Encruzilhadas belongs to the Ogum family and fulfils a mission commanded by Jesus, under the Virgin Mary's irradiation" (1933, 77). He is "Christ's messenger" (ibid., 78). In the narratives about his mission, the temples that follow the Caboclo's determinations possess Catholic names, like the Tenda Nossa Senhora da Piedade in which Zélio worked before an altar (congá) full of Catholic statues. According to Oliveira (2008, 97), even the seven paths from the Caboclo's image remind us of "the public squares found in front of many churches from the interior" of Brazil.

The identification of the Caboclo das Sete Encruzilhadas as Christ's messenger in Leal de Souza's book also reminds us of one work written by Chico Xavier, Brazil's most well-known medium.[18] The book *Brasil, Coração do Mundo, Pátria do Evangelho* (*Brazil, Heart of the World, the Gospel's Homeland*), published in 1938, had an important role in the legitimation of the Brazilian Spiritist Federation as the heir of the Kardecist legacy (Giumbelli 1997). It is an account about various events in Brazilian history, starting with the colonial period, in light of spiritual enterprise. In this case, Christ's messenger is Ismael, who rallies diverse figures for the fulfillment of a prophecy that combines Spiritism and Christianity and that plans a central place in the world for Brazil. Chico Xavier continued to publish more and more books, many imputed to a spirit identified as Emmanuel, Chico Xavier's guide, who appears as the prefacer in the book. Emmanuel's spiritual biography indicates one of his incarnations as Manoel da Nóbrega, another Jesuit (Lewgoy 2004).

Thus, the links made to Christianity by Umbandistas, as much as by Kardecists, until the mid-twentieth century, pass through the Jesuits; the emphases, however, are distinct. Nóbrega is a central figure in Portuguese colonial history in Brazil in the sixteenth century: he is present at the foundation of the city of São Paulo and the recapture of Rio de Janeiro. Lewgoy (2004, 50) finds a reiteration of the sign of nobility in the assimilation of Emmanuel to Nóbrega. Malagrida, however, is a marginal historical figure, who lived in the North and Northeast of Brazil, and who was condemned as a heretic. Two points are highlighted by the Umbandistas by presenting Malagrida: the virtues and powers he exercised for a specific segment of the national population (including indigenous peoples and prostitutes) and the injustice of his death.[19] These differences correspond to more global configurations depicted by Spiritism and Umbanda. *Brasil, Coração do Mundo, Pátria do Evangelho* describes the formation of a "Brazilian civilization" through the conjunction of three races, situating the spiritual envoys always among whites, including the Jesuits. However, in the book written by José Alvares Pessoa (who was very close to Zélio de Moraes), *Umbanda: Religião do Brasil*, certain passages evaluate the leadership of the Caboclo das Sete Encruzilhadas, suggesting another role for Afro-descendants and Amerindians in the "difficult task of giving [to Brazilians] a genuinely Brazilian religion" (*apud* Cumino 2010, 362).

In its efforts to associate itself with Christianity, Umbanda approximates itself to Catholicism and appropriates Catholic figures, including Christ himself, who is associated to Oxalá, one of the Orixás who commands the Umbanda lines. It is curious how the icon consecrated by Umbanda reminds us of a modern representation of Jesus Christ, harnessed to his majesty as humanity's redeemer. The same icon corresponds to the Catholic Sacred Heart of Jesus, whose traditional representation highlights suffering. At the beginning of the twentieth century, the Catholic church chose a Christ with open arms—his heart exposed, but triumphant—to celebrate Brazilianness (Mainwaring 1986). This is the icon appropriated by Umbanda and associated to Oxalá, still visible today in many terreiros. One reference to the Sacred Heart of Jesus can also be found in accounts about the Caboclo das Sete Encruzilhadas, since from his very first manifestations the drawing used to invoke him (his *ponto riscado*) is "an arrow crossing a heart," which for Leal de Souza means "the upward direction of sentiment, to God" (1933, 77). But the drawing also reminds us of Christ's suffering heart, an emblem of devotion whose first disseminators in Brazil were Jesuits like Gabriel Malagrida.[20] Does this lead us to perceive signs for another "invisible road"?

To answer, we would be obliged to confront dilemmas similar to those raised by Palmié (2002) in his narration about the diverse periods of African-derived cults in Cuba. Palmié attempts to elicit the direct consequences from his own encounter with the theme, as provoked by an entity that had once been a slave. His narrative passes through the historic constitution of Cuban society, in particular through events connected to an Atlantic complex that allows *modernity* and *tradition* to be followed as two sides of the same coin. In a less ambitious vein, I believe that my own encounter with the Caboclo das Sete Encruzilhadas raises similar questions, in terms of what can be defined as history, since it appears that to trace the socially attributed agency of a spiritual entity implicates the discovery of further elements and connections in the historic terrain. To consider its presence is to include more accounts, incorporating various materials and agents, including its temporal localization, and to catch a glimpse of other paths, amplifying the flows that connect elements in distinct spaces and times. The result is not located so much on the plane of what "really happened" but rather from what directions we can take, in time and space, by following the accounts that we encounter.

In Search of the Caboclo das Sete Encruzilhadas

While I collated the material required to write this chapter, I maintained the hope to meet the Caboclo das Sete Encruzilhadas: I imagined that I would see him manifest during a session in an Umbanda terreiro. However, the information to which I had access undid my expectations.[21] Faced with the report that the Caboclo was manifesting himself in a certain medium, Zélio de Moraes's granddaughter reacted thus: "According to information received through other entities with whom he works, at the Tenda Espírita Nossa Senhora da Piedade, after completing his mission with Zélio de Moraes, the Chief passed on to higher spheres of the superior astral and is no longer conducting work on our plane" (*apud* Cumino 2010, 358).[22] According to the same statement, when the Caboclo finds it necessary, he sends messages offering assistance through other caboclos and pretos and, on special occasions, announces his presence silently, in a form already evoked by Leal de Souza (1933, 80): "A blue vibration shines in the air and a light of the same colour hovers in the same ambient."

It appears that Zélio de Moraes's family and those who support it prefer to keep a certain control over the entity: there are few records of the Caboclo das Sete Encruzilhadas' manifestations, some of which have been identified and commented on here. According to one of them (Cumino 2010, 127), even when Zélio was still alive these manifestations only took place on special dates. In these records, narratives of Umbanda's annunciation and the events that culminate in the creation of the first federation in 1939 predominate. The identification of the prophecies' power and humility also recur, as do reiterations of ritual configurations that refer to denominations oscillating between *Christian Umbanda*, *pure Umbanda*, or *white Umbanda*. In some versions of Umbanda's annunciation by the Caboclo, instructions appear prescribing something "very simple, like low harmonious songs, white clothes, the prohibition of animal sacrifice. Dismissing drums and clapping. . . . Herbal baths, the *amacis*, concentrations in natural settings, together with the doctrinarian teachings, based on the Gospel, constituted the main elements of the medium's preparation."[23]

There is no scope here to consider whether such prescriptions are obeyed without variation. As argued on other occasions (Giumbelli 2003), the dissemination of narratives that situate the origins of Umbanda on the outskirts of Rio de Janeiro in 1908, and which impute Zélio de Moraes's protagonism, only occurs at the beginning of the 1970s. At that time, while Umbanda was celebrating its broad diffusion in specific regions of Brazil, it also proliferated in multiple ritual forms that were resistant to attempts at unification. Or rather, it is not possible to disconnect the propagation of accounts associated to the Caboclo das Sete Encruzilhadas from a series of conflicts surrounding the "real Umbanda." It is thus unsurprising that today it is possible to encounter spiritual messages that include other entities in Umbanda's foundation,[24] whose origins (it is worth remembering) are always stretched between Oriental and African roots. In the end, one of the paths in the search for the Caboclo leads us to a type of sociology of Umbanda ritual diversity and its correspondents through the alliance and network of specific social actors.

Clearly, the route that I have taken here is different, as my preoccupation with plurality has remained central: I tried to demonstrated that multiple references come together to constitute the life of the Caboclo das Sete Encruzilhadas. In reality, there are at least three lives: Jesuit priest, Amerindian born to a white woman, and his manifestations through Zélio de Moraes. Each of these lives is the product of articulations between diverse elements. The priest approximates himself to Amerindians and dies at the hands of the church. The Amerindian is a benefactor who dedicates himself to the liberation of the black population. The Caboclo manifests himself, with the preto-velho's humility, to create miracles as part of his Christian mission, or even with the force of an everted exu, with the help of Pai Antônio and Orixá Mallet in the struggle against opposing forces. In a specific sense, and in connection with the efforts of a Christianized Umbanda, the Caboclo das Sete Encruzilhadas stages tensions and oscillations that refer to the themes of ambiguity and marginality. Cultivated by people that lack greater intellectual or social projections, this entity allows the formulation of narratives focused on the imaginary of Brazil's national formation.

On the other hand, Brazil does not determine or circumscribe the limits of the search for the life of the Caboclo das Sete Encruzilhadas; his paths pass through various places and take him to many others. The Umbandistas' "other" society—or in Matory's words "the sacred Other Place" (2009, 244)—is certainly not located in a continuous and closed territory, whatever it may be. The Caboclo of so many crossroads can take us not only to the forests of a slave society but also to a Brazilian interior traversed by a Jesuit to occidental Christianity, from its origins in a benevolent Jesus to its more recent past at the hands of the Inquisition, and still to the Malay Orient, translated into an African Orixá. Of course, these are not places that share the same value, but even so there can be no doubt that this is a translocal religion (Matory 2009) in many senses, including in its temporal dimension. Thus, Umbanda can be seen not exactly as a domain in which these multiple connections become possible, but more that these connections produce Umbanda in its excessive plurality. Anthropology is left with the problem of accepting the challenge to encounter and trace its manifestations.

CHAPTER TEN

Toward an Epistemology of Imaginal Alterity

Fieldwork with the Dragon

Susan Greenwood

During my fieldwork with British practitioners of what are commonly called nature religions—western shamans, witches, and druids—the dragon seemed to come through me as a distinct presence. This was an initial impetus for me to research magical processes of mind (Greenwood 2005), and subsequently I came to understand the dragon as an imaginal entity that was simultaneously of me and not of me. However, it was only by temporarily holding in abeyance my analytical, classifying mind for the duration of the interaction, and developing what I have termed *magical consciousness*, as a holistic intuitive perspective, that I could start to understand this communication and the effects that it had on my thinking. The concept of magical consciousness has assisted in explaining my communication with the entity of the dragon; it overcomes the previous classificatory divide between different aspects of human experience, whether it be shamanic shape-shifting, spirit possession, vision quests, religious mysticism, spirit channeling, trance, meditation, or any other number of different practices found cross-culturally. By opening myself up to the experience of communication with the dragon spirit entity, my objective was to further research on a participatory aspect of human cognition as it melded with the nonhuman and the nonmaterial. Drawing on previous work on magic and altered states of consciousness, such as that by Jeanne Favret-Saada (1980), Paul Stoller and Cheryl Olkes (1987), Jean-Guy Goulet and David Young (1994), Goulet and Granville Miller (2007), and Edith Turner (2006),[1] I started to become immersed in magic as an alternative perception; this was one which many indigenous peoples would recognize in principle, and that may have been familiar before the rise of a scientific worldview (Henry 2002, 2–3). Like Favret-Saada in particular, I realized that to understand what was really going on I would have to involve myself deeply in the experience of magic. I looked back through my life to see the patterns of magical connections that I came to describe in a shorthand manner as "the dragon." In this chapter I will explore my communication with the dragon entity and the effect that it had in material reality through my writing, especially of *Magical Consciousness*, a sequel to my more theoretical *The Anthropology of Magic*. In the process I hope to work toward developing an epistemology of imaginal alterity.

The Dragon and Fieldwork

The dragon is a symbol in all types of societies—from surviving small-scale to complex multicultural societies in a globalized world. The creature is called in China *lung*; Hawaii, *kelekona* or *mo'o*; Croatia and Serbia, *zmaj*; Finland, *lohikaarme*; Poland, *smok*; Turkey, *ejderha*; Hungary, *sarkany*; Japan, *tatsu*; Wales, *draig*; Germany, *lindwurm*; and Holland, *draak*. For the Maori of New Zealand, it is known as *tarakona*; for the Lakota Sioux, *unhcegila*; and for the Cherokee Indians, *unktena* (Jones 2000, 2–3). The word for dragon in Anglo-Saxon or Old English is *wyrm*; in Old High German it is *wurm*, whereas in Old Norse it is *ormr*. Frequently the meaning of the term *dragon* relates to serpents, worms, and snakes, and these creatures appear to be interchangeable one with another. A winged serpent, the dragon generally lives underground in a cave, and it is symbolic of the elements earth, air, fire, and water, as well as spirit. Above all, the dragon is a mutable beast that can transform into many creatures. In many contemporary European cultures, a dragon is a serpentine creature connected to worms and snakes and is generally perceived to be evil, being vanquished by Saint George. However, in Chinese and Japanese cultures the dragon is generally seen as a positive manifestation of life. It is often portrayed with a horse's head and a snake's tail; alternatively, it has a camel's head, stag's horns, eyes of a demon, neck of a snake, belly of a clam, carp scales, eagle claws, soles of a tiger, and the ears of a cow (De Visser [1913] 2008, 70). The dragon is a polymorphous being that means different things to different peoples, cross-culturally and through historical time. It appears that the dragon is both a universal and highly specific symbol, a condensation of varied human experiences. Working with practitioners of British nature religions,[2] many of whom were pagan, my view of the dragon was in accord with the their understanding that it was an elemental creature of earth, fire, wind, water, and spirit, a fearful but positive manifestation of the creative process of life and death. I decided to open myself up to the experience of this dragon to further my research on magical consciousness. In so doing, I discovered that it was methodologically important to pay attention to moments that may be overlooked during more conventional fieldwork and develop a sensitivity to subtleties for working with such entities. Magic, understood as an alternative mode of consciousness, is notoriously difficult to put into words, and even more difficult to explicate within an academic framework that seeks explanations through classification and analysis. I had been striving for some time to find ways of expressing what seemed like the impossibly vague and inexpressible nature of magical thought.[3]

When I first started fieldwork with British practitioners of magic my aim was to create a "bridge of communication" between what seemed to be at the time two very different worlds: of scholarly critical analysis on the one hand, and the magical panorama of my informants on the other. I wanted to make one explicable to the other, and vice versa. Over the years I worked according to this aim with my academic work and also by writing an encyclopedia on magic and witchcraft, a book that attempted to make anthropological ideas more accessible for a more general audience (Greenwood 2001). Now, perhaps, the dragon was using me as a bridge of communication. It was challenging to keep an open mind and explore the possibilities in the spirit of anthropology as a "sustained and disciplined inquiry into the conditions and potentials of human life" (Ingold 2011). And so it came to be that I experienced the dragon.

The dragon came once as the wild elements of an alien nature, cold and totally nonhuman, so much so that any communication—certainly through words—seemed all but impossible. The dragon seemed to take me to an extreme place of alterity difficult to describe. At the time, I did not have a strong sense of a being that I could identify as a dragon, but later I had the feeling that the elements of nature that I had experienced were some of its aspects. Another time the dragon came more definitely as a palpable dragon, a red primordial energy that not only felt as if it took me deeper into my blood and bones, but also into a feeling of the essence of life and death itself through what seemed like cycling rounds of eternity. It was these early encounters with the dragon that prompted me to start recording and thinking about my fieldwork experiences with imaginal "entities of otherness."

As to why the dragon had shown itself to me, I could only guess. Perhaps it was due to my rather solitary childhood whereby I had formed close attachments to nature rather than any organized religious affiliation, or maybe because as an anthropologist I was working with altered states of consciousness and was open to this sort of otherworldly mediation, or even because some people are more sensitive to spiritual communication from nonmaterial realms than others—at this stage I could only speculate. Rather than becoming distracted by such questions, I decided to leave them until later in my fieldwork, trusting that the reasons for my developing relationship with the dragon would eventually become clear. I knew I was going into areas where my academic credibility or even my sanity could be questioned, or considered "new age" and dismissed, but my pursuit for anthropological knowledge of this area was strong and so I continued. In time, my exploration of my "data" on the dragon led me to write an autobiography of my encounter. It was only through coming to understand the pattern that the dragon had made in my life, unbeknown to me at the time, that I could develop the idea of a methodology for magical consciousness.

Over time, I had become increasingly keen to try to explain encounters with a nonmaterial reality that were difficult to articulate using more conventional anthropological methodological and theoretical frameworks. Deciding that for the present I had gone as far as I was able in an academic mode, I thought I would write about my life as an anthropologist studying magic. I chose to use my own experience as a matrix, or so I thought at the time. On reflection, I think that it was not so much my decision as that of the dragon. I decided to explore the possibility that this entity had decided to work through me, for whatever reason, to put across a certain message. As to what that message might be I was unsure, but I decided to trust the process as long as it coincided with my sense of integrity. I entertained the possibility that entities, such as the dragon, could be searching for appropriate "vehicles" to communicate certain information. It had long been my impression that otherworldly entities manifested in a variety of forms to communicate with anyone willing.

Magical Consciousness

In order to fully understand the experience of the entity that I call "the dragon" as an anthropologist, I searched for theories that could help me explain magical consciousness as a "language" for communication with "beings of otherness." I started with Lucien Lévy-Bruhl's notion of *participation*,[4] a social psychological perception of the world based on a mystical mentality, "the emotional association between persons and things in contact with a non-ordinary spirit reality" (quoted in Tambiah 1991, 91). Magical consciousness employs associative thinking and makes connections primarily through feelings and intuition, and then secondarily through symbols and metaphor (Greenwood 2005, 89–118; 2009, 63–73; forthcoming). This orientation to the world is encapsulated in the languages of mythology and poetry. The dragon is a participatory being—it resides in feelings, emotions, relationships between one thing and another. Chameleonlike, the dragon changes from creature to creature transmuting into many things—it is a force of nature running through all.

An early example of the dragon's participatory nature that I recall is an occasion when a friend and I were talking about magic as we walked by a stream that flows into a river close to her cottage in the Brecon Beacons, one of the sources of the river Taff in Wales. As we reached a few trees by the side of the stream, I stopped to look at the beautiful reflection that the tree branches and the sky made in the water—at that moment the depths of the water, with its little rushing eddies over the stones of the river bed, combined with the sun and the white clouds in the blue summer sky. All formed part of a pattern of participation—the sky was mirrored in the water and they intermingled. My friend threw a stick into the stream for her dog to fetch and instantly the pattern broke into a myriad of shimmering fragments. Ripples gradually spread out from the point where the stick hit the water, forming another pattern until the waters regained their own momentum and the reflections of the clouds reappeared in the river. Watching the movement of the ripples on water, I realized that participatory moments like these could take me into magical consciousness. The dragon is this moment: the participation of tree, sky, water, river bed, sun, the ripples, my friend, the dog, the stick, and all the feelings and connections that this myriad of kaleidoscope associations makes in time.

In physiological terms, this participatory awareness can be said to equate with the workings of the right hemisphere of the human brain; this has a wide take on the world, compared to the narrow focus of the left hemisphere. Both hemispheres are involved with all the brain's functions, such as emotion, reasoning, visual imagery, and mathematical thinking, but they have different orientations (McGilChrist 2011, 1068–69; see McGilchrist 2009). Through the right hemisphere, it is possible to understand the fullness of the mutability of the dragon. At one time it may be a worm or snake, at others a horse, wolf, owl, or some feature of the natural world, such as a stone or a river. This orientation is dominant in shape-shifting—for example, when shamanic practitioners "become" their spirit guides in their imagination. In my experience of shape-shifting, I have found it perfectly possible to "be" the creature that I have "become" in imaginal reality and still understand myself to be lying on the floor during a drumming session, or whatever the left hemisphere of my brain understands my physical body to be doing. The two orientations, arising from the two hemispheres, function interchangeably; with experience the move from one to the other becomes fluid. In a sense, all experience is inherently potentially participatory and magical; it is just the orientation that changes according to how it is perceived by the individual and through which brain hemisphere. Perhaps the dragon's very mutability means that it can communicate in a variety of ways, according to the needs of each person through whom it is communicating.

Being concerned with the whole body, not just with the brain, magical consciousness is an awareness that is receptive to bodily feelings as well as sensitive to nonmaterial, spirit dimensions. It participates in alterity. In this wide perception everything has consciousness—the locus of consciousness moves to potentially the entire cosmos, the spirit realm of the dragon.

Toward Epistemology

My relationship with the dragon was a communication with an imaginal spirit entity. This raised the anthropological dilemma of a belief in spirits—they might exist in the imagination, but not in reality. I found that developing the concept of magical consciousness could overcome the difficulty: "When a person is 'in' that part of their awareness [magical consciousness] it makes no difference whatsoever if they believe in spirits, or if spirit communications are labelled as psychological—if they are explained as a part of their own internal thought processes—or whether they think the entities with which they are communicating are independent of them and have a being of their own. Whilst participating in a magical aspect of consciousness the question of belief is irrelevant: 'belief' is not a necessary condition to communicate with an inspirited world" (Greenwood 2009, 140). Questions of belief or the reality or nonreality of spirits, while interesting themselves, are a "straightjacket" for an alternative perception afforded by communication with nonmaterial entities. The issue is one of a different perception.

We tend to see consciousness as a product of the brain, but magical consciousness is concerned with a widening rather than a narrow orientation. Historically since Descartes associated mind with individual human reasoning, mind has been located in the brain. Descartes claimed that the human body (as opposed to the human mind) acted from mechanical instinct like animals. Social scientific views of consciousness tend to be restricted to individual brain activity, but if the concept of "mind" is extended to body-mind, it overcomes the Cartesian division between body and mind. Further, if body-mind is defined as the personal aspects of individual process, and "consciousness" as an intrinsic quality of the wider universe of which individual body-mind is but one part, then body-mind and consciousness are linked. If consciousness is wider than the individual human body-mind, then that body-mind might be shared with other beings. If we understand these other beings as spirits that have a different order of existence to the material dimension of reality, or are invisible but none-the-less real dimensions of material reality, then it is possible to take the view that these beings also have body-mind when they "inhabit" a physical being.

If we entertain the proposition that during an experience of magical consciousness spirits share a degree of corporeal materiality and possess mind, then the minds of entities—in whatever form—and ours can meet in a wider consciousness (Greenwood 2009, 139–41). This was a view common before Descartes, and one that the eighteenth-century poet and artist William Blake tried to reinvoke. The view that all of life is infused with spirit, soul, and consciousness was common in the ancient world prior to the dawning development of the rationalizing scientific worldview of Blake's time. Aristotle (384–322 BCE), for example, thought the soul was equivalent to psyche—it was the "principle of life" that animates. It is only relatively lately that psychology has developed as a discipline to study psyche in the human mind; originally psyche was considered much more widely as inherent in all things. Harking back to the earlier view, Blake envisioned a world in which every creature was an inspirited person living within the total freedom of its Imagination (Raine 1991, 11–12).

The magical imagination needs to work *with* something—it needs such an inspirited imaginal cosmos. The first record of the word *imagination* dates from the fourteenth century as a "faculty of the mind that forms and manipulates images." It comes from the Old French *imaginer*, which in turn comes from the Latin *imaginary* (to form a mental picture) and from *imago* (image), and also from *imaginare* (to form an image of, or represent, something). For Kant the imagination was a basic faculty of consciousness, an ability to bring to mind that which is not entirely present to the senses. Kant saw the imagination as a function of the soul (see Sneath, Holbraad, and Pedersen 2009, 9–13). Imagination could thus be a link to a nonmaterial realm, as well as a key to creativity, and creativity is central to magical consciousness.

Creativity is a faculty of the imagining mind; creativity involves, as neuroscientist António Damásio says, rapidly combining and recombining an assortment of ideas, the most plausible juxtapositions of which are then remembered:

> The first requirement here is the *strong generation of representational diversity*. What I mean by this is the ability to generate—to bring to your conscious mind—a variety of novel combinations of entities and parts of entities as images. These "images" are prompted by a stimulus that comes either from the world outside or from the inside world (one that you generate and recall). . . . Many of these representations have to be discarded because they are not relevant; but the images are there to choose from. . . . The lay term "a very good imagination" really is an effective description of this diversity generating mechanism. (Damásio 2001, 65)

Damásio's "diversity generating mechanism," a combination and recombination of internal *and* external ideas, is reminiscent of Claude Lévi-Strauss's notion of intellectual *bricolage* whereby things are brought together depending on whatever is at hand (1968, 17). But if a wider perspective is taken, we can also investigate what lies beyond the horizon of the here and now by venturing into the imaginary (Vincent Crapanzano in Sneath, Holbraad, and Pedersen 2009, 9–13). It is possible to imagine an interactive space of magical consciousness where communication with imaginal entities might occur, closer to Kant's notion of the imagination as a working of the soul. In terms of the dragon, this space is in and through an inspirited nature.

Gregory Bateson, in his characteristically bold way, saw such an interactive space in nature. He argued that the body, the mind, and the whole ecosystem were linked within a metapattern or a "dance of interacting parts (only secondarily pegged down by physical limits)" (Bateson 2000, 467; see also Greenwood 2005, 97). Bateson, a holistic thinker, saw the mind as being a part of nature. In *Mind and Nature: A Necessary Unity* (1985), he tried to understand an integrated world, and he sought to find a language of relationship with which to communicate. Thinking that logic not suitable for the description of biological patterns, he turned to metaphor as the language of nature. Seeking an "ecological epistemology" in *Angel's Fear* ([1987] 2005, with Mary Catherine Bateson as coauthor) and *A Sacred Unity* (1991), he attempted to build a bridge of communication between all branches of the world of experience—intellectual, emotional, observational, theoretical, verbal, and wordless (Bateson 1991, 231–32; cited in Harries-Jones 2002, 3–9). Bateson was interested in cybernetics, the science of communication in machines and living beings. He looked at the nature of mental processes and the relationship of communication between thought and the material world in terms of interconnection and interdependence of ecosystems. Bateson thought that evolution was *stochastic*, able to achieve novelty by a combination of random and selective processes (Bateson 1985, 29–30).

Bateson's theory of consciousness challenges Enlightenment notions of rationality that separate mind from nature (Harries-Jones 2002, 15), as does Tim Ingold's work, which, taking its cue from Bateson, adopts a worldview envisaged from within a "total field of relations whose unfolding is tantamount to the process of life itself" (Ingold 2001, 13–19). Both Bateson and Ingold see the mind as immanent in the whole system of the organism-environment.[5] Gaining inspiration from this perspective, my aim is to try and understand mind, as body-mind, through a process of interconnection with the inspired imagination of magical consciousness.

The Dragon Working through Me

When the dragon first came to me I decided I would experience what happened as part of my research into a wider conception of consciousness. In essence, the dragon had a physical reality through my body and actions in the world. Of course, I am not arguing that I physically became a dragon—that somehow I manifested into a fire-breathing monster—but nevertheless the dragon had a form of corporeal as well as imaginal reality; it *was* a dance of synchronous interaction. A participatory association between the individual body-mind and an inspirited cosmos can be understood though Carl Jung's notion of synchronicity whereby relationships are based on causally unrelated events of spirit coming together in a meaningful way (Jung 1960, 417–519). The notion of synchronicity does not threaten anthropological analysis or causality but reveals the different *modus operandi* of magical consciousness. It was through synchronicity that I would discover my relationship with the dragon. In the process of shamanic shape-shifting, when boundaries become less discrete during periods of magical consciousness, I was able to feel the dragon.

On one of the initial occasions, I experienced being taken beyond myself in a confrontation with my own fear and terror. And a subsequent time, more reassuringly, I was spiraled into a deeper internal understanding within what appeared like a cosmic process weaving through time.

My fearful encounter with the dragon as the cold, alien elements of nature took place at Cae Mabon, a retreat space of several indigenous dwellings situated in a clearing amid an oak forest in Snowdonia, north Wales. As part of my participant observation for my research I had slept alone in a black *shavan*, an Iranian canvas tent, by the side of a rushing stream coming directly down from Mount Snowdon. That night was like no other I have ever experienced. The sound of the water was deafening: it drove my numbed mind into spiraling eddies of whirlpools and underground currents. I later wrote of the experience in my fieldnotes: "In the all-consuming marauding blackness, I was visited by elemental spirits of the river, the trees, the earth, and beings that were so totally nonhuman that they took me to a place of extreme terror. I experienced myself being engulfed and consumed by what felt like an alien elemental otherness. No words can fully express the feeling, but bare, cold, desolate, exposed and stark come close to the experience of having all security of life removed in a confrontation with the waters of this place as they crashed down the mountainside" (Greenwood forthcoming). My tongue had erupted in mouth ulcers from the trauma when I eventually woke as dawn was breaking. This confrontation with elemental entities on the Snowdonian mountainside brought me in direct contact with the nonhuman realm of elemental otherness. I came to associate this experience with the dragon, the part that was other to me, and with which, for some reason that I had yet to understand, I was communicating.

The second communication with the dragon occurred some time later when I was painting a drum. I was staying in a small fisherman's cottage, in a village on the harbor in North Norfolk, while I was doing fieldwork with a group of shamanic practitioners and witches, many of whom used the rhythm of a drumbeat to send themselves into a trance for visualizations.[6] I had bought the drum previously so that I could participate. One day, I sat on the floor with paints surrounding me, and I had an experience of the dragon. I felt a deep pulsating presence of a blood-red dragon that seemed to be coming from the base of my spine. The presence slowly took over as I started painting the drum. As the first strokes of paint met the drum, the drum seemed to sing in response, and my whole being felt as if it was coming into alignment with something vaster. I felt the dragon's tail twitch deep in my being. The air seemed to go thick and I felt a tingling in my ears. I sensed myself disappearing into each brushstroke, around and around into a spiraling vortex of red. I had a feeling that my body already knew the dragon, deep down, even though I had not previously been consciously aware of it.

After my Snowdonian encounter with the elements, and the dragon experience while painting my drum, I began to see another dimension to my academic work, one that was becoming increasingly hard to write about. I was making all sorts of synchronous connections that seemed to be telling their own story. I had started to write down the beginnings of an experiential book about the dragon, but when my publishers suggested writing a textbook on magic, eventually published as *The Anthropology of Magic*, I reluctantly put the idea to one side. Writing *Magical Consciousness* started in earnest later in 2008 during a period of economic crisis commonly termed the "credit crunch." When it seemed that the whole capitalist world order was being shaken to its roots, I was discussing magic with a friend who was visiting from Australia. This got me thinking about what I had learned from my anthropological research on magical experience. I started to think about magic from an applied perspective. After the conversation with my friend, I stayed awake all that night feeling what was important from what I had learned over the years. I realized that I wanted to show how I had come to understand the dragon as a source of a participatory perspective on life. In the morning I had nine component themes that acted as waymarkers for writing the book.

What I did not realize then was that I was being used by the entity that I had come to recognize as the dragon. It slowly dawned on me that I was not in total control of my writing. I did have some inkling that this was the case—I knew that the book was being written while I was in a participatory state of magical consciousness. I had intuited the chapter themes and had subsequently tried to alter them through a process of analysis, but I found that this did not work. Deciding to trust the process that "something" was writing through me, I eventually saw the reasoning behind it. I was beginning to understand that the entity of the dragon was giving me messages about communication. In the process of planning the writing of *Magical Consciousness* I sought out a special notebook with nine sections of differently colored paper. Each section was devoted to one of the component themes that had come to me on the night of my Australian friend's visit. Over the following weeks I took the notebook everywhere with me, and as a thought came, I would write it down and meditate further on the meanings. In addition, I was running a small shamanic journeying group at my house for my students, most of whom had completed courses or workshops on shamanic consciousness with me at the University of Sussex, and I invited them to journey on the themes, all of whom accepted. Week by week, we worked through each of the themes, and all participants found some deep insights into their own lives through the process.

Over time, I started putting thoughts and meditations in the format of a book. In the physical production of words—on the computer screen and in my body-mind through meditation—these themes became woven into the story of my life. As I wrote, they seemed to take on a life of their own through a stream of consciousness, a type of intimate recording of the everyday minutia of life made popular by Virginia Woolf, especially in her novel *Mrs Dalloway*. This mode of writing, so different to the formal academic style, seemed to reach different parts of my awareness and my memory. I recalled sitting on my grandfather's knee at his desk, when I was about two or three years old, while he told me stories about the horses he used to ride in the Boer War and the First World War, as I recorded:

> The words unlock an experience that allows participation in the moment, to be inside the moment: to participate in the life of the moment. Those moments at Grandpa's desk lay dormant for me, until now, but the magic is always present, it surfaces from time to time and, dragon-like, it now comes through my mind:

> The memories lie dusty in a drawer
> glimpsed through a crystal half darkly.
> Distant time brought to light
> an image recalled
> and passing once again
> into
> obscurity.

> Fond memories of time past,
> of being held

close and warm.
Darkness through the years of living memory
to return once more
on this sunlit, silent schard.

Connecting, weaving as a dream
they come to mind this time
to have voice.

My memories are mute until I can give them voice. The anthropologist in me
asks: Has the dragon come to express that which was previously silent? It feels
so. I need to know another way of knowing. (Greenwood forthcoming)

Deciding to write using poetry and a stream of consciousness style to
"bracket" my analytical thinking, I tried to access the participatory and
synchronous language of magical consciousness by working through the
nine themes the dragon had conveyed to me. The first draft of the book
was largely incomprehensible to anyone but me, and on the recommenda-
tion of two stalwart people who had offered to read it, I added explanation and details that made it more accessible when I had achieved some
distance from the immediate process of writing.

Dragon Communication

When I was working on the theme of "place," Geoffrey Samuel, an anthropologist colleague from the University of Cardiff, invited me to participate in a research project on the River Taff. This invitation was indeed
synchronous. The dragon had taken me back in magical consciousness to
the place of my birth, to reconnect with my early life, and I had just written
about the river near where I was born. Now it presented an opportunity
for me to find out about a very different type of river. The idea of the
Taff research project was to build up feelings and experiences as part of
an ongoing mythological and historical story of the environment around
the river. South Wales was once a land of coal mines, and the Taff was so
polluted that it was said to run black with coal dust: at one point it took
one hundred thousand tons of colliery waste each year. Pitheads and slag
heaps once dominated the landscape, but the coal industry had declined
from 620 working mines in its heyday to none (the last mine closed in

1994), yet the remains of its industrial past can still be seen surrounding the river. I would find out that the dragon would communicate with me further though this project.

It was a freezing cold day in February and the British Army was on manuevers when the small group of people that Geoffrey had invited arrived at Taf Fawr, the "Big Taff," one of the two sources of the Taff arising in the Brecon Beacons. Soldiers carrying rifles were running over the mountain in camouflage gear; there was an air of activity blowing across the snow-covered terrain, and this was echoed in the river, which was rushing down from the mountainside, cold, clear, and bubbling. I stood beside the river and tried to let go of all my thoughts to let the place speak to me. Rivers have hidden depths and labyrinthine, subterranean elements; they also flow along, linking people and places. It was necessary to have just enough information from maps, history, folklore, and so on, to set the scene, but not too much because it can cloud direct experience.

Shifting my perspective, I started to feel the whole course of the river as it flowed southward on its way into Cardiff Bay. A different pattern emerged resulting from its complex history from early prehistoric settlements to the intense industrialization of the coal mining and iron working around Merthyr Tydfil. I let the clear, cold waters wash through my awareness, my internal thought processes started to drift away, and I began to feel the raw pulse of life through the water.

The rapid movement of Taf Fawr was in stark contrast to the second source of the Taff, Taf Fechan, or "Little Taff," a few miles away. All was silent and still at Taf Fechan, which is tamed into the Talybont Reservoir by weirs managed by the Wales Water Company. The river was frozen and looked like a scene from the Arctic. The dark gothic architecture of the Victorian waterworks added to the eerie atmosphere of the place; it could almost be the surface of the moon. Everything felt to be held in abeyance; there was a peace and quietness here, a time for reflection.

The Taff, like all rivers, has accumulated its own memories, but this river has a special history because of its industrial past. The Welsh valleys were rich in coal, and collieries were opened to meet the demands of the iron trade, and coal and iron were carried by canal barge south to ports at Cardiff and Newport. Working conditions were tough for the miners, who included women and small children as young as six years old. The younger children controlled ventilation systems, while older children and women hauled coal from the bottom of the mineshaft to the face. Thousands of miners died due to underground roof falls and explosions. The situation of the miners was made worse by overcrowded housing and unsanitary conditions, both of which led to outbreaks of cholera. There was pain and deprivation; it is said by some that the souls of the dead linger here.

Moving on downstream, we came to the confluence, sometimes called "the dark pool," the swirling part of the river where the Taf Fawr and the Taf Fechan meet at Cefn Coed-y-Cymmer, just below Merthyr Tydfil, home of the eighteenth- and nineteenth-century Industrial Revolution. The first train to run on rails operated here, and it was the place that gave birth to the Labour movement—the Merthyr Rising of 1831 saw between seven thousand and ten thousand workers march under the red flag as a protest at their working conditions. The confluence feels like a very powerful area due to this history, and also the meeting of different aspects of the Taf Fawr and the Taf Fechan. The meeting of the two source rivers of the Taff feels like the coming together of two opposing forces. According to Welsh folklore, "The whirlpool of the River Taff at Cardiff forms a small lake when the bed is almost dry. . . . People said it was fathomless, and that in its depths a monstrous serpent dwelt, and gorged on the unfortunate victims that were drowned in the river and sucked into the pool. When any bodies were not recovered from the whirlpool, people said they had been swallowed by the serpent"(Trevelyan 1909, 9, 14; cited in Simpson 2001, 48). The place has a power, but now it has been neglected—there are lots of slag extraction piles, rubbish, and a feeling of an abandoned river. The industrialization process has taken its toll on human beings and the land.

Rivers have different currents, eddies, and depths, and all are part of the general stream; they form their own ecological habitats, as well as tell many stories and hold feelings, memories, and emotions. The river holds many different ripple patterns. What images, feelings, sounds, and memories come from the water? I want to feel another knowing of the body, through breath and the pulse of blood through the earth.

The Pontycafnau Bridge over the Taff, near the confluence, is the first iron railway bridge ever, built in 1793; it also served as an aqueduct. On this day the shadow of the bridge transmuted the natural habitat of the river as a reminder of the dragon in the swirling waters—I stood on the bridge and looked into the depths, picking up memories of the past.

I reflected on how water is the matrix, a deep and ancient force. According to Chinese mythology, the dragon "is a benevolent horse, the vital spirit of river water. . . . It's neck is long, and its body is covered with scales. It has wings at its shanks, and its hair hangs down its sides. . . . It walks on water without sinking" (De Visser [1913] 2008, 57). The dragon was there

FIGURE 10.1. Pontycafnau Bridge dragon. Photo by Susan Greenwood.

in the water, as was the horse—the dragon was a dragon-horse that can shift consciousness. My grandfather, the horse, the water were all connected. The river held my reflections. A perspective from the other side: What would the river see?

Something trying to communicate
through frosted ice.
Spirit
to
spirit.
The land and the spirit are one.

I cannot speak for the river;
maybe I am a vague flash in its memory.
Through aeons, what do I matter?
Small, insignificant, a whisper then gone.

But then again,
perhaps the river does ken with a kenning within its unfathomable depths.
A sense of yearning to hold space;
to share the second of eternity in the moment.

In the moment we both flow as one.
And that is all that matters.

The dragon was helping me see things from a different perspective. I felt
I had accumulated some of the history and the pollution of the industrialization process of the Welsh valleys from reading about the Taff. I felt that
it was important to clear up the rubbish and litter along the riverbanks,
but there was also a corresponding process within me that told me about
letting go of unnecessary psychological baggage.

After visiting the Taff, back at Geoffrey's house, three of us went on a
shamanic drumming journey—an active meditation guided by the rhythm
of a drumbeat. The dragon came again, this time as a purifying force to
me; it appeared as the rivers of the land and took me deep down into the
underground waterways. These needed spirit purging of human exploit-
ative activity. I was taken into a white spiral and a red dragon emerged
strongly, fiery and angry at not being recognized; it told me that the Taff is
part of a whole process of extraction that has drained its lifeblood without
acknowledgment.

The dragon took me down blue smoke tendrils deep into the mineshafts and caverns of the earth. It felt like the red dragon was the angry
emotion of the earth that had been plundered thoughtlessly. The dragon's
smoke tendrils were messages from the earth, and I could follow them
down into the source of the pain. To feel the anger and to feel the pain was
to experience the roar of the dragon; going snakelike into the mineshafts
and dark caverns was to acknowledge the thoughtless plunder of the earth
that had caused so much suffering:

Fire of red dragon,
burning bright volcanoes,
sending smoke spirals upwards.

To follow them curling downwards snakelike,
is to see and to heal the hurt that is done.

The ivy tendrils grow once more.
Now salmon swim, gone is black coal dust.

Communicating with the water dragon has opened up a process of knowing that everything is connected through ripples of relatedness.

The water holds the place
of my deep knowing
of the past;
it takes me
darkly
through time.
And lingers
in my being
to connect with ripples
Brightly.

The spirits of the waters give life and flow through all beings before returning once more to their source, there to be reborn and renewed. The message was about acknowledgment and renewal as a healing process.

Reflections

My experience of revisiting my life synchronically through the dragon had
given me personal insight, and I felt that the book *Magical Consciousness*
was written to heal a fragmentation of mind that I hoped could help others, but the anthropologist in me required further explication. Perhaps the
dragon wanted communication through analytic thought as well as magical
consciousness. Consequently, I turned to Bateson's exploration of Jung's
Seven Sermons to the Dead, the result of Jung's three evenings of psychic
exploration of dreams, visions, and reflections in 1916 (in Bateson 1986),
with the aim of further examination of magical consciousness. Bateson
viewed Jung's *Seven Sermons* as a much healthier first step than Descartes's
dualism of mind and matter. Above all, Bateson was concerned with communication, so perhaps here was a line of investigation through Jung that
I could follow to explain the dragon's communication with me.

In *Seven Sermons* Jung outlined differences between *pleroma*, an eternal
unstructured realm containing all opposites and all qualities, and *creatura*,
the individual ego, a part of pleroma that creates difference and distinctiveness in space and time. The word *pleroma* comes from the Greek; it is
used in various form of Gnosticism and means a totality of divine powers.
Jung came from a family of pastors, theologians, and psychics, and his analytical psychology, for which he is best known, has an orientation to spirit,
which I thought may provide a framework for understanding the dragon.

After his three evenings of psychic exploration Jung wrote, in a quasi-religious language, that the pleroma was both the beginning and the end of created beings: "It pervadeth them, as the light of the sun everywhere pervadeth the air. Although the pleroma pervadeth altogether, yet hath created being no share thereof, just as a wholly transparent body becometh neither light nor dark through the light which pervadeth it. We are, however, the pleroma itself, for we are a part of the eternal and infinite. But we have no share thereof, as we are from the pleroma infinitely removed; not spiritually or temporally, but essentially, since we are distinguished from the pleroma in our essence as creatura, which is confined within time and space" (Jung 1992, 182). For Jung, the ego requires independence from pleroma—growth requires differentiation, and this leads to *individuation*, the process whereby the undifferentiated becomes individual, and eventually to a state of psychic harmony represented for Jung in the mystic figure of Abraxas, the first archetype of all things. The word *Abraxas* comes from the Greek, and in Gnostic cosmology the seven letters in its name represent the Sun, Moon, Mars, Venus, Mercury, Jupiter, and Saturn. Abraxas appears to be creatura's way of understanding the immensity of pleroma.

Bateson developed Jung's ideas on pleroma, creatura, and Abraxas in his search for an epistemology of living forms in patterns of recursive, nonlinear systems. A scientific rather than a religious thinker, Bateson was interested in the patterns of communication and interaction arising in relationships between phenomena. For Bateson, there is a bridge, or a pathway for messages between pleroma, creatura, and Abraxas. The pleroma can be translated into the language of creatura through metaphor, "the organizing glue" of the world of mental process. Accordingly, Bateson's Abraxas is a transpersonal metaphor for biological unity and mind in nature, rather than what he terms Jung's Gnostic substitute for Jehovah. Either way, Abraxas arises out of the homogeneity of pleroma and the distinctiveness of creatura (Harries-Jones 2002, 3–9, 98–99). The movement of communication between metaphors is a move from the duality of Cartesian mind and matter.

Could Jung's pleroma and creatura represent the two aspects of my initial experiences with the dragon—the one so cold, elemental, outward, and distant in north Wales, and the other seemingly to be my very inward source spiraling through time that I experienced while painting my drum in North Norfolk? Perhaps the concepts of pleroma and creatura could represent different aspects of the dragon, and Abraxas could be a metaphor for the totality of the dragon, a reconnection of mind and nature.

Bateson—in a move from Jung's quasi-religious Gnostic interpretation of Abraxas—invokes varying alternative metaphors of god or goddess. Bateson saw Abraxas as a mythical figure and understood myth as the ability of being able to "wobble ideas around" (Bateson 1991, 237). This "wobbling" makes sense in terms of connecting largely nonverbal experiences of alterity in the language of magical consciousness.

Such communication may be the essence of my relationship with the dragon. Maybe I have been an intermediary in this process of communication. I have argued the case for taking magic seriously as a form of knowledge elsewhere (Greenwood 2009), and space prevents me from developing further this line of inquiry, but working toward a sustained epistemology of imaginal alterity makes sense in terms of communication of different realities, particularly of bringing together mind and nature, and that has been the primary aim of this chapter.

CHAPTER ELEVEN

Historicist Knowledge and Its Conditions of Impossibility

Stephan Palmié

Ño Carlos is in a foul mood. "¡Que cosa de pinga!" he fumes, squarely facing up to the drummers. "¡Que barbaridad! Tocar rumba a mi oricha. Es una falta de respeto." "¿Y quien es el?" he asks pointing toward Tata Francisco who, until a few minutes prior, had been dancing with as much agility as his crippled leg allowed for. The drummers now cease playing and look somewhat annoyed at Carmen, the hostess of the ceremony for which they were hired. Alas, no help is to be expected from Carmen, since it is her at whom Ño Carlos now angrily wags his finger—or rather at her body, which she, for the time being, shares with Tata Francisco who has taken possession of her and is now getting angry himself. "Who told you to stop the music?" he mumbles in the thick ritual register known as "bozal" thought to reflect the mangling of Spanish phonology and grammar by native speakers of African languages.

Tata Francisco, of course, speaks bozal and limps because he is a dead African slave who, in life, was maimed by his master as a punishment for running away. As a "congo," he enjoys a style of liturgical drumming close to the fast and energetic rhythm of Guaguanco. Not so Ño Carlos. Having arrived at a later point in the ceremony, his indignation and surprise become clear once one considers that he is a dead priest of Yemayá, expecting to find himself at a lucumí tambor (I am told he's made that mistake before). Not only does he resent the style of drumming, so inappropriate to the stately presence of the deities he worshipped in life. He might, or so I wonder, also be bothered by the presence of spirits of the dead at what he thinks is a ceremony for the oricha—something practitioners of regla de ocha strenuously try to avoid, since it can portend all kinds of tragic outcomes. But of course, Ño Carlos himself has been dead for about a hundred years!

This awkward situation might not have been thinkable thirty years ago. It is the product of a novel ritual formation known today as "cajon pa' los muertos" (after the characteristic use of a box drum and its focus on spirits of the dead). The "cajon," as some argue, emerged in Havana in the course of Cuba's Special Period—and it has finally broken down what previously were boundaries internal to a heterogeneous formation of ideologically parallel but practically long-intertwined streams of religious tradition.[1] But this is not what I want to address here. Instead, I would like to use the episode recounted just now as a device to illuminate the possibility, or perhaps necessity, to submit Western forms of historicism to the kind of anthropological analysis that our discipline has, for the past forty years or so, successfully trained on non-Western forms of establishing what J. G. A. Pocock (1962) rather felicitously calls "past-relationships."

What I argue is that—much as anthropology cannot afford to rid itself of the nowadays well-established impulse to historicize—we need to recognize that the way we have brought a historical dimension into our work remains beholden, not just methodologically but epistemologically, to the terms of a set of North Atlantic particulars that have paraded as human universals since the second half of the eighteenth century. To this end, I shall enlist the help of spirits like those of Tata Francisco and Ño Carlos.[2] I do so not just because nothing brings out positivism (historical or other) more quickly than talk about ghosts, as Françoise Meltzer (1994) so nicely puts it, but also because Tata Francisco's and Ño Carlos's misunderstandings of their present get me to three issues right at the heart of the matter. These are as follows: first, the constitutive nature of radical temporal alterity or anachronism for any form of historicism; second, a notion of accountability that defines properly individuated human subjects or, to use the more appropriate forensic term, "persons," as authors of their actions; and third, a highly specific regime of evidentiality that underwrites what Reinhard Koselleck (1985) calls the "fiction of facticity" of properly historical data as indexical signs of past eventuation. Once taken together, these three—or so I would argue—operate as key guarantees of the *idea* of what Michel-Rolph Trouillot (1995, 29) calls "historicity 1" and glosses as the "materiality of the socio-historical process."[3]

It is this idea that I intend to submit to what David Bloor (1991) and Bruno Latour (1993b, 2005), albeit in different ways, conceive of as symmetrical forms of scrutiny. In line with Bloor, my goal is thus not to explain or otherwise rationalize the seemingly odd fashion in which the past

is "presentized" when the spirits of the dead interact with the living in
Afro-Cuban possession rituals; rather, I want to bracket this classic anthropological maneuver and instead focus on how properly disciplined
historiography "historicizes" the past. While one certainly could describe
what knowledge is produced on the grounds of *which* assumptions in
the contemporary Cuban cajon pa' los muertos, my concern is a different one—namely, can one come up with similar descriptions in the case
of Western historiography? At the same time, I want to go beyond the
"strong program" in the sociology of knowledge. Taking a page from Latour, I argue for a view of historicism as a form of knowledge that literally produces its own imponderabilia and aporia. These become visible as
such in particular clarity when we confront "historicity 1" and its guarantees with the mumbling and ranting of the likes of Tata Francisco and Ño
Carlos.

                                    *   *   *

That said, what exactly is going on in the ethnographic vignette I just recounted? Clearly, Tata Francisco, Ño Carlos, and I (or for that matter,
the other participants) inhabited an extraordinary moment of temporal
hybridization effected by the copresence of agents belonging to three different positions of a chronological continuum. Setting aside the problem
that the two spirits involved seem to have entertained different notions
about the nature of the event—they understood themselves as acting
within different religious traditions, as it were—we might still say that
their encounter posed a problem akin to those that Pocock calls "problems that produce historians." Only that, far from producing the sense
of discontinuity vital to the emergence of this species of thinker, it did
nothing of the sort. Obviously, no one rose up to say "Wait a minute—you
don't belong here! You're dead. Go back to your finite province of meaning." Yet Pocock's insights into the origins of historical problem awareness
notwithstanding, we still might ask, Why should this event even have engendered such reactions, except on the basis of a highly specific semiotic
ideology that constructs certain segments of the phenomenologically given
world (but not others) as indices of an ultimately absent reality—that of
the past?[4]

    As Marc Bloch (1953, 55) pointed out long ago, historical knowledge
is knowledge from "tracks"—the marks "perceptible to the senses, which
some phenomenon inaccessible to the senses has left behind." Carlo Ginz-

burg (1983) thus speaks of an "evidentiary paradigm" informing modern historiography and sees its origins in hunting, medical diagnostics, divination, and other semiotic endeavors aiming to elucidate current states of affairs by scouring the surface of the present world for signs of transcendence—in this case, past eventuation. To borrow Michael Oakeshott's (1933) terminology, such efforts are contingent upon an organization of the phenomenology of the experienced world "sub specie preteritorum." Viewed thus, symptoms of the past abound, awaiting diagnostic interpretation. In principle, everything can be put under a past-referring description. The tree that grows outside the window was once an acorn. That you are reading this essay may be taken to indicate that someone wrote it. The sheer existence of the University of Chicago's architecture might be held to bespeak the past expenditure of human labor.[5] And so forth. All this is potential evidence for past eventuation.[6] Still, a sign is only a sign if it is recognized as such. As R. G. Collingwood ([1946] 1994, 281) reminds us, "Question and evidence, in history, are correlative." How exactly the surface of the contemporary world is to be carved up in regard to what Arthur Danto (1965) might call candidates for past-referring predicates is far from self-evident.[7] As I will argue, this question points toward what, in semiotic terms, we might call a metapragmatic regimentation of indexicality characteristic of historicist practices of knowledge production. And this is where anachronism and temporal heterogeneity enter the picture with particular force—once, that is, we try to leave the world where ceteris paribus Trouillot's North Atlantic universalisms continue to hold sway.

As Trouillot (1995, 15) points out, "pastness" is a position—and it is the hallmark of historicist forms of consciousness that such positionality becomes premised on perceptions of temporal heterogeneity (i.e., the imaginative imputation of a distance between an objectifiable "then" and and equally objectifiable "now" conceived of as two unambiguously specifyable points in a serial continuum of linear time). "Historical evidence," says Dipesh Chakrabarty (2000, 238), "is produced by our capacity to see something that is contemporaneous with us—ranging from practices, humans, institutions, and stone-inscriptions to documents—as a relic of another time or place." This capacity, however, rests on an epistemology precipitated by, and predicated on, the kind of linear, irreversible time established in the course of the "temporalization of history" (Koselleck 1985) in the aftermath of the French Revolution. As Trouillot (2002, 850) puts it, this moment involved "a fundamental shift in regimes of historicity, most notably the perception of a past radically different from the present, and the perception of a future that becomes both attainable (because secular) and yet indefinitely postponed (because removed from eschatology)."[8] What this shift opened up was a space of experience and horizon of expectations that we continue to inhabit. The effect is akin to what Ernest Gellner (1973) once likened to a "self-writing game": we know that the present constellation reflects a succession of moves; but since we are aware that some moves change the rules of the game itself, we can neither predict future outcomes, nor really reconstruct, with any certainty, how past moves led to the present situation. All we know is that recurrence is highly improbable, stable rules suspect, and linear succession inevitable.

The name of Gellner's self-writing game is history—and to agree to play it is to be a historicist. As Karl Mannheim (1952, 85) wrote in 1924, "Historicism, and historicism alone . . . today provides us with a world view of the same universality as that of the religious world view of the past."[9] As Mannheim clearly saw, this had nothing to do with any advancement, methodological or other, in the discipline of history. On the contrary:

> It is not historiography which brought us historicism, but the historic process through which we lived has turned us into historicists. Historicism, therefore is a *Weltanschauung*, and at the present stage of the development of consciousness it is characteristic of *Weltanschauung* that it should not only dominate our inner reactions and our external responses, but also determine our forms of thought. Thus, at the present stage, science and scientific methodology, logic, epistemology, and ontology are all moulded by the historicist approach. (Ibid., 85–86)

If Mannheim's diagnosis is right—and it certainly held true for the educated Western bourgeoisie at the time—then we have all become historicists by now, swimming in history like fish in water. Ever ready to measure contemporary worlds by reference to the degree to which they differ from the past, as historicists, we conceive of our future in relation to the degree that our present actions are, at least ideally, unencumbered by what we have come to consider—or consign to—the realm of the past (Latour 1993b, 67–72).[10]

As Mannheim makes clear, the temporal regime he analyzed at the moment when it had fully come to saturate not only intellectual debate but ordinary Western common sense was in itself a historical phenomenon. Yet while it may have held for a good two centuries it was—somewhat ironically—thrown into disarray in the waning twentieth century.

Here I am not so much talking about the demise of the secular escha-tology of the world revolution which, alas, never came. Instead, such a state of affairs became apparent piecemeal and in a variety of syndromatic constellations—such as in the emergence of a vast amount of discursive production about "memory" as a metahistorical category, the increasing entanglement of historical and juridical regimes of knowledge produc-tion in the case of Truth and Reconciliation commissions and the North American Reparations Movement, or, if in a different register, the kind of "spectrological" ruminations about the persistence of the past in the present inspired by Jacques Derrida (1994). All this is patently standing historicism on its head—and in the sense that any attempt to analyze why some pasts nowadays appear to resist yielding to anachronism ("that was then, it's over now") and instead linger and haunt the present must imply a critique of historicist conceptions of time, and the metaphysical and on-tological commitments such conceptions implicate us in.[11]

*   *   *

But speaking for a moment in Derridean terms: What exactly is so unset-tling about the idea of time being out of (chronological) joint? Medieval Europe survived on nonlinear forms of temporality for long enough to engender the Renaissance (whose understanding of time wasn't exactly linear, either). Or think of contemporary physicists who might well scoff at the scientifically thoroughly ungrounded, but eminently commonsensical, Newtonianisms that Western historians regularly peddle.[12] Why such in-vestment, on the part of contemporary Western historians, in the notion of an objective (and objectifiable) past irreversably sealed off from the very present off of whose surface the trained diagnostician must nevertheless read symptoms of the absent past in the form of indexically construed "evidence" of temporal otherness? Might not the seemingly strange pro-liferation of temporal hybrids nowadays sailing under rapidly multiplying labels such as "haunting," "unsettled pasts," "historical reckoning," "Ver-gangenheitsbewältigung," or the "devoir de memoire" bespeak a very different "crisis of historicism"? One that paradoxically represents the re-sult of its sucess—that is, the labors of purification in its name expended over the past two centuries or so (Latour 1993b)?[13] For consider this: If historicism depends on the notion that material survivals *from* the past can be construed as indexical signs *of* the past, then might we not run into the somewhat embarrassing snag that such remnants ("Überreste" in the classical German historicist sense) come dangerously close in their semiotic potential to that of "superstitiones" in the original ecclesiastical sense (i.e., equally indexical construed signs of insufficently superceded past pagan beliefs and practices that persist in the Christian present [cf. Keane 2007])? Although we are clearly dealing with two very different projects of purification (or metapragmatic regimentation, if you will), the very notion of "spectral evidence" proffered by the likes of Tata Francisco and Ño Carlos would seem to trouble both.

Which naturally brings me back to my ethnographic vignette. Might Tata Francisco and Ño Carlos help us craft an answer to this quandary? Perhaps not. But they do illustrate some of the issues involved in its making. Clearly, the problem isn't so much that the archival process itself has silenced their history, rendering them undocumented aliens from the foreign country that is the past—*sans papiers*, as it were—and so lost to any attempt to reconstruct their life "like it really was" (von Ranke's famous "wie es eigentlich gewesen"). To be sure, the past is full of such unevidenced dead, and I have previously tried to address the ethical and moral challenges posed by our knowledge that this is so (Palmié 2002). But this is not what I mean here, and it is not really what is at stake in this particular instance. For consider this: I might go and scour the records of the slave trade from western Central Africa, pore over plantation account books and baptismal records in Cuban parish archives, and who knows? I might find a slave shipped to Havana from Luanda, designated as a "congo," and given the baptismal name Francisco. There might be record of his running away and the punishment he received when recaptured. He might appear on the list of incapacitated slaves, and so forth. Would this change a thing?

The problem clearly lies elsewhere: exceedingly well-documented individuals like Ben Franklin, Tom Paine, George Washington, John Quincy Adams, Napoleon, Mark Twain, Sir Arthur Conan Doyle, and Albert Einstein (to name just a few) have not only continued to communicate with the living in Spiritist circles, but have—much to the dismay of professional bibliographers—continued to author copious writings long after the end of their earthly existence.[14] Would the information gleaned from their messages lead historians to enlarge the corpus of evidence for their lives and times, and so, for example, acknowledge that Washington had, in the afterlife, become an ardent opponent of slavery, the very institution he himself had helped write into the US constitution? One doubts it. Or imagine Jefferson dictating his regrets for ever having penned the crucial phrase about a "wall of separation" between church and state to an entranced scribe! Regardless of the fact that (given the 2010 Texas School Board decisions) K–12 school history curricula all over the United States hang in the balance (Shorto 2010; Birnbaum 2010; McKinley 2010), would we not suspect such evidence to be tainted by present issues and concerns? Of course, the historian may well accept all of this as *some* kind of evidence. But not for what it purports to index—namely, Washington's changing his mind about slavery some half century after his death, or Jefferson having second thoughts about a secular state more than two hundred years after its founding.

Neither is the matter settled by arguing that we simply can't be sure of the reality of Tata Francisco's and Ño Carlos's presence—as denizens of the past—in our present. In fact, this is a pseudoproblem quickly dispensed with. I, for one, am not troubled at all by entertaining a healthy dose of skepticism in regard to the notion that Tata Francisco and Ño Carlos were as real that evening in Habana Vieja as, say, the box drum that called them there. Moreover, I take courage in thinking that many of the participants in that ritual occasion would have agreed. Not unlike conscientious Western historians, practitioners of Afro-Cuban religion do not accept on mere face value evidence of the past—in this case, the reality of the presence of dead people. Much in the spirit of the kind of historical criticism that emerged in the seventeenth century from the scrutiny of forensic documents, they, too, probe the reliability and validity of the evidence of the past in front of their eyes. Faked possession, after all, is not at all uncommon. But as in historical criticism, it is the expectable occurrence of forgeries or unreliable witnesses that establishes the value of the "real"—truthfully indexical, rather than merely iconic of the past. Once such criteria are satisfied—and they really are only after what often are lengthy post hoc debates—participants in Afro-Cuban rituals tend to agree that they *were* in the presence of denizens of the past.[15]

Reasonable as such stipulations and procedures may seem on their own terms, we can't really follow them. Why? The simplest reason, in light of the foregoing, is that admitting the spirits of dead people to our present so as to give testimony of and for the past that was their life violates the principle of anachronism. The minute they arrive, they would seem to contaminate the present with the past. In something of an inversion of the historian's cardinal sin of "presentism," (i.e., the unwitting backward projection of present concerns into the past), they throw the semiotics of historicism into disarray. Without temporal distance, the (present) historical sign and its (absent) referent simply collapse into each other. As a result, whatever the spirits of dead people may choose to tell us about their past lives is inadmissible on evidentiary grounds. That Tata Francisco was maimed by his master because he ran away is no historical datum—even though we know very well that slaves *were* maimed in punishment for doing so. From the historian's perspective, his marked limp that evening in Havana was, at best iconic, perhaps symbolic, but certainly not indexical of a past that any concrete (rather than imaginable) human being might have endured.

Like protagonists in historical novels, spirits (however tangibly embodied) may be recast as fictions: ritually enacted thought experiments, if you will. We could look at them as products of some historical imaginary, even a social one, designed to work through essentially ambiguous or troubling past relationships in the form of morally edifying fables or allegories. More charitably but somewhat illogically, Tata Francisco and Ño Carlos might be booked as expressions of "popular memory" that purports to present the past but really only produces the "iconically" retrojected misrecognitions of its own present concerns.[16] In either case, Tata Francisco and Ño Carlos simply cannot be taken at face value for what they purport to be—visitors from, and so immediate sources of information about, the actual past. They violate the first guarantee of the idea of "historicity 1"—the notion that there is an "actual past" *back there, in the past* that historians need to reconstruct as best they can through diagnostic readings of present evidence identified as indexical of conditions and events that are now absent. Put in a nutshell, any endorsement of Tata Francisco and Ño Carlos as irreducible witnesses to their own lives threatens to put historians out of business in an instant.

*   *   *

No less damaging, however, is that they violate a second guarantee of the idea of "historicity 1": namely, the postulate of the temporally coherent, skin-bound, self-possessed, and self-identical human subject as the author of his or her actions—or, in a forensic sense, the individual person capable not only of exercising choice in terms of goal-directed behavior but also of shouldering responsibility for the consequences, intended or not, of his or her own actions. This second guarantee is part and parcel of what Mary Douglas (1979) calls a highly specific "accountability system" hinging on a conception of personhood without which the very notion of "historical agency" becomes tenuous, to say the least. As Dame Mary (1992) notes, one of its earlier clear expressions was given by John Locke in his discussion of "identity."[17] Examining a whole range of fascinating cases to do with other time-transcending entities including plants, animals, and machines, and having concluded that continuity of substance needs to be distinguished from continuity of organization, Locke considers and rejects pegging identity to the soul as separable from material embodiment.[18] He then goes on to famously dismiss the prince's soul transposed into the cobbler's body, as well as the philosophizing cat or parrot and the dull, irrational man.[19] The conclusion he arrives at is that human identity cannot be grounded other than on *personal* terms—that is forensically. It isn't enough that we imagine ourselves the same individual from one day to the next, sleeping or waking, young or old, whole or missing a limb. It is our capacity for reflexive self-identification coupled with, or rather upheld by, our sense of responsibility for our past actions that generates the sense of biographically coherent individual identity.

We might claim that we were temporarily "beside ourselves," "out of our minds." No matter, though. A sternly individualistic accountability system will hold us responsible on the grounds of our continued forensic personhood.[20] Even the thought experiment of alternating consciousness—being Plato by day, Socrates at night with no memory of preceding episodes—won't pass Locke's muster. Why? The answer is clear: agency and accountability must not be ambiguously distributed. No matter what you claim as your identity, then or now, either you are the personal author of your actions or you are not.[21] In the end Locke settles on the same formula that, in a duly secularized fashion, enabled the young Fidel Castro to fling his defiant proposition "history will absolve me" in the face of the court commissioned by Fulgencio Batista. Locke, of course was talking about the Final Judgment "when the secrets of all hearts shall be laid open," and all sublunar juridical conjecture about subjective states of mind would become moot. But that was fast becoming a figure of speech even then.[22]

Let me return here for a moment to my little ethnographic device. Clearly, unlike classic Lockean individuals, held together by a mortal frame of skin, but possessed of a consciousness and memory that renders them not only self-identical over time but juridically responsible for any deeds freely done or obligations freely contracted, Carmen—or Tata Francisco, if we even want to venture that distinction in the case at hand—was neither a unitary self nor temporally coherent. I am sure Carmen only learned in the aftermath that her "muerto" *again* caused trouble, and that further encounters between Tata Francisco and Ño Carlos were to be avoided at all costs. *Just think of the poor drummers*, people will have told her. *How would they ever know what to play if you get possessed right away and can no longer tell them what to do! That's embarrassing, isn't it? Next time Tata Francisco tries to come, go outside and have a smoke. Be responsible.* But how could she—when she's not herself? *I know these idiots are always fighting*, I can imagine her saying. *But how could I keep them from doing so, when I am mounted ["montado"] by Tata Francisco? He enjoys his little rumba, you know?*

This, then brings me back to historicism and another context of its full-blown emergence—namely, the "cultural conventions of political self-legitimation in modern nation states" (Greenhouse 1996, 2), or in Trouillot's (2002, 853) terms, the insertion of a specific form of subjectivity into "a particular regime of historicity and sociopolitical management." Among other things, this entailed, as Henry Maine (1963, 163–65) famously stipulated, a move from status to contract which, not incidentally, became fully enshrined in Anglo-American forensic operationalizations of legal personhood *just as* the abolition of heritable slavery was being accomplished (though of course plenty of "legally entailed" people such as women, children, and the mentally unsound remained in status-bound conditions [cf. Haskell 1998; Stanley 1998]).[23] Such seemingly inconsequential exceptions notwithstanding, at least in the realm of legal fictions, the alienation of one's labor power could henceforth finally and fully proceed on the terms of the socially unencumbered individual's free will, just as the exercise of such will could guarantee one's self-realization in a world of objects, or, in a different inflection yet, the appropriation of the rewards and liabilities arising from one's self-willed and self-embodied agency.

Such a move, of course, was contingent on the kind of linear eventuation in open-ended time constitutive of historicism, and, at the same time, on a specific distribution of agency and accountability in social space. Together, these defined an order which eventually became naturalized to a degree where unstable personhood and nonindividuated agency nowadays reeks of madness, unnatural dependency, or utter cultural incommensurability to most of those who have fully become engulfed by it (vigorous debates about fetal personhood, addiction, codependency, or corporate free speech notwithstanding). Now whether law became modeled after a conception of personhood ultimately arising from the transformation of a political-economic and intellectual order or vice versa is a question too complex and controversial to attempt to address here.[24] What counts for my present purposes is the final ascendance of the contractually capacitated, unambiguously embodied, self-aware, rationally willful, and morally self-regulating individual as the locus of historical agency.

*   *   *

Obviously such a being is of relative recent vintage. Prior to the advent of historicism, Marx's famous dictum that men make their history but not under conditions of their own choosing might not have made much sense to even those devoted to the transformation of the *res gestae* into *historiae rerum gestarum* (and the plural was important!) in the very heart of Europe (Koselleck 1985; Fasolt 2004). Contrary to a prior order in which actors were largely animators rather than authors let alone principals (in Goffman's [1981] sense) of their contributions to the unfolding of a divine plan, the very idea of "making history" presupposes not only an essentially undetermined, open future but a multiply overdetermined (economically, legally, politically, etc.) notion of agency. Such agency is premised on a relation between authentically individual volition and the possibility of choice in the course of action. In other words, it presupposes the idea of a coincidence of principal, author, and animator in the individual subject of historical agency. Western common sense immediately recognizes this as "the way things are, (barring exceptional circumstances)."[25] But such complications introduced by sociolinguistic theory notwithstanding, this says more about the historical and cultural particularity of such "default" assumptions than about their transtemporal, panhuman validity. Joan of Arc may certainly be said to have played a historical *role*. But was she the *subject* of her agency? I am not sure she or her contemporaries would even have understood the question. If for different reasons, to them, "agency" was no more predicable on personally individuated volition than it was for the audiences of Greek tragedy, or, for that matter, the subjects of Marilyn Strathern's (1988) Mount Hagen ethnography.

More importantly, perhaps, and irrespective of where we want to locate its domain of initial cultivation (philosophy, economics, or the law), the "modern" individual (and its conspecifics, rational and reasonable man) has proven an invasive species. Though of "provincial" origin (in Chakrabarty's sense), this being and the "deep collusion between 'history' and the modernizing narrative(s) of citizenship, bourgeois public and private [spheres], and the nation state" (Chakrabarty 2000, 41) on which it thrives has come to extend itself across much of the globe.[26] Chakrabarty, for one, is keenly aware of this problem, and he devotes a whole chapter of *Provincializing Europe* (2000) to why, for example, the idea that the Santal Hool, a nineteenth-century Bengali insurrection, was organized under divine command might point to the limits of historicism. In particular, he takes issue with his colleague Ranajit Guha for concluding his famous interpretation of this case by writing off the fact that the rebels looked "upon their project as predicated on the will other than their own" as a "massive demonstration of self-estrangement" (Guha 1988 quoted in Chakrabarty 2000, 105). "Historians," says Chakrabarty (ibid., 104), "will grant the supernatural a place in somebody's belief system or ritual practices, but to ascribe to it any real agency in historical events will go against the rules of evidence that gives historical discourse procedures to settle disputes about the past."[27] Bracketing Chakrabarty's somewhat disingenuous use of the patently loaded term *supernatural*,[28] and bracketing also the possible recourse to W. I. Thomas's famous postulate that if a situation is defined as real, then it is real in its consequences, we might still recognize the rootedness of Chakrabarty's historians' objections in a specific set of North Atlantic universals. This is so because the rise of the very idea of "historicity 1" was also tied to the emergence of a particular political project, and Guha's invocation of self-estrangement and false consciousness amply bears this out.

To be sure, neither Hobbes's or Locke's conceptions of the nature of the parties constituent to the social contract, Hume's enlightened skepticism about the unitary nature of the self, nor Adam Smith's mercantile theodicy had fully banished transcendental considerations from the purview of the course of human history. Still, the conception of the consciousness of history's agents came to increasingly contract to states of interiority presumably based on a rational hedonic calculus modified by an awareness of forensic responsibility for one's own action. At the same time, the *medium* for the expression of a conception of free will, once released from its Christian moorings in sin and salvation, shifted toward the rationality of what Hegel identified as civil society and the state—that is, the supraindividual union between the objective "idea," and the "personal subject that wills it." This is, of course, Hegel's condition of possibility for the making rather than mere enduring of History. But it is also the foundation of secular liberalism. Democracy, equality before the law, property rights, civic responsibility—all these would seem to flow from it, at least in theory. They are dependent on the notion that human beings are, or at least should be, not just individuals, but autonomous and self-determining forensic persons: authors of their own actions who are unambiguously legible to the state and its institutions, including—we might add—the discipline of history.

But again, might we not take a Latourean perspective on this and say that "we have never been authentically individual, just as our projects have never truly been predicated on a will wholly of our own"?[29] It would be hard, I think, to conclusively wipe such an objection off of the table. One need not attend Afro-Cuban possession rituals to see that "individuals" and their "wills," "agency," and "responsibility" are all highly functional fictions that underwrite a specific and historical, rather than universal and timeless, order. This is an order animated by a particular rather than universal type of agentive subject, and it is rendered intelligible by a regime of indexicality (among many possible ones) in which responsibility for present states of affairs can be assigned to the past actions of such subjects on the basis of proper evidence that they freely chose such courses of action. Little indeed, seems recognizable as "historical agency" unless these conditions are fulfilled. To be sure, Marx never tired of denouncing individuality, free will, and contractual liberty as ideological figments serving materially specifiable class interests and productive of characteristic forms of individual and collective self-estrangement. Still, for a number of reasons Marx is not the best of allies in gaining a purchase on the puzzles posed by Tata Francisco and Ño Carlos, and I doubt if many of us would be inclined to take the above considerations beyond the point of ideological criticism. Of course, anyone can say, "It is perfectly obvious that the 'traditions of dead generations weigh like a nightmare on the brain of the living'—that's precisely what rigorous historicism can liberate us from." But who would dare to turn this around, and say that historicism weighs on our brains like a nightmare?

* * *

This, however, is an argument Constantin Fasolt (2004, 2005) comes close to adumbrating in positing that what Chakrabarty calls "the rules of evidence that gives historical discourse procedures to settle disputes about the past" might themselves not so much offer a solution than indicate the root of the problem. Following a path suggested by Quentin Skinner (1969, 1970), Fasolt poses the ostensibly simple question of what might happen to our view of history if we attended not so much to the propositional content of historiographical utterances than to their pragmatic functions and metapragmatic regimentation (or, in his own, more Austinian/

Skinnerian terms: their illocutionary force and perlocutionary consequences). Like Skinner before him, Fasolt expresses some surprise at the
fact that philosophers of history got bogged down for most of the twentieth century in sheer endless debates about how history "explains" (if at
all), but have rarely attended to the pragmatics of what historical explanations are supposed to "do" in the world.

Skinner largely remained concerned with the implications of speech act
theory and Wittgensteinian linguistic philosophy on the epistemology of
historical interpretation (and did so on much of the same grounds as the
so-called "rationality" debate in anthropology). But Fasolt is after something quite more radical, and his starting point lies in a distinction between
history as a form of knowledge and history as a social practice—one that
continuously shores up the notion of an unbridgeable gap between the
present and the past while at the same time naturalizing the notion of the
autonomous subject of historical agency. "So long as history is viewed as
theory of the past," he writes,

> the distinction between past and present looks like a fact; the past, like an ob-
> ject to be studied; the study of the past, like the proper task of the historian; the
> evidence, like the source from which historians obtain their knowledge; and the
> prohibition on anachronism, like the basic point of method that keeps knowl-
> edge pure. (Fasolt 2004, 14)

What, however, Fasolt asks, if we took into account that the very distinction between past and present is the product of a restless proliferation of
performatives whose locutionary content may well look like knowledge,
but whose illocutionary force is directed toward a project of purification
aiming to put the furniture of the world in a specific—shall we say historicist?—order? What if the discipline of history did not arrive on the scene
après coup to merely rationalize past worlds and their relation to the present but created, or at least reordered, both from the very moment of its inception (including the recursive insertion of a charter of its own rationale,
backdated to Thucydides, or some such mythical ancestor)? "Things look
different," says Fasolt (2004, 14–15), "just as soon as it is recognized that
history is also a form of action." "From that perspective," he continues,

> the distinction between past and present looks like an act of self-determination
> by which the sovereign subject assumes her rightful place in time; the knowl-
> edge historians draw from evidence, like the means by which historians make

the past lie still; and the prohibition on anachronism like marching orders for a mission to make the world safe for autonomy.

Here the very notion of "evidence" devolves toward its matrix of origin: the forensics of modern personhood and the "particular regime of historicity and sociopolitical management," to quote Trouillot once more, within which this form of subjectivity achieved near global normativity. It is in the service of this regime that the so-called critical method, developing from the seventeenth century onward, has come to metapragmatically police the order of indexicality from which historians nowadays stray only at their peril.

There are implications of violence in all of this, and not just on an epistemic level. Like Chakrabarty (2000), who worries about the compulsory historicization of local worlds in the context of a forced globalization of Western normativities,[30] or Stuart Clark (1983) who similarly decries the mistranslation of premodern rural French thought-worlds into the reductive sociological language of the Annales school, Fasolt speaks of historians "invading the foreign country of the past, conquering its inhabitants, subjecting them to their discipline, and annexing their possessions to the possessions of the present as any imperialist who ever sought to impose his power on colonies abroad" (2004, xviii). They do so, armed with a conception of human beings as "free and independent agents with the ability to shape their fate, the obligation to act on that ability, and responsibility for the consequences" (2004, xvi). What they drive from purview of properly rationalized (in the Weberian sense) forms of history are the likes of Tata Francisco and Ño Carlos, particularly if they refuse to stay put in the past and instead act and speak through the bodies of present-day citizens of modern (in this case socialist) nation-states. Historians tend to do so, by a double maneuver that asserts the truth of properly disciplined history by exposing the untenability (within the evidentiary canon of historicism) of other ways of establishing past-relationships. These other ways of figuring forth the past thus turn, in Chakrabarty's (2000, 112) terms, into a Derridean supplement to historicist knowledge production, enabling the ongoing operation of the discipline of history and its search for "proper evidence," while simultaneously (and somewhat ominously) demarcating its limits: the point beyond which historicism loses its purchase on experientially salient social worlds, and the historian his standing within the discipline.

Still, and this is an important caveat, like his colleagues Clark and Chakrabarty, Fasolt is not after some facile relativism. It isn't that the stories Tata Francisco might tell us about his life as a slave are "just as good as," or could serve as an edifying supplement or corrective to, for example, Manuel Moreno Fraginals's (1978) magisterial but near-agentless history of Cuban slavery, as some proponents of ideas of "social memory" might argue.[31] Instead, what they indicate are the limits of historicism—as an "order of things" served by the social institution of the discipline of history and serving, in turn, a historically contingent notion of personhood and distribution of agency in social space on which the (modern) "world as we know it" has come to rest. Neither Chakrabarty nor Fasolt or Clark call for the closing of the history departments where they earn their living, and none of them advocate—in what surely would be a curious reversal of Evans-Pritchard's famous misquote of Maitland—that "by and by history will have the choice of being anthropology or being nothing."[32] But all of them, I would argue, aim to open a space for what one might call an anthropology of historicism as a locally specific, if nowadays near globally diffused, contingent though seemingly inevitable—in short, culturally particular but ostensibly universal—fashion of constructing "past-relationships."

Might there be room in this space for Tata Francisco and Ño Carlos—let alone for the practices that recall them into the bodies of present citizens of the Cuban nation-state (or any other, for that matter)? Might they assist us in "re-provincializing" (in Baumann and Briggs's [2003] terms) the semiotic regime that drove them into a conceptually "remote" (Ardener 1989) corner of a world dominated by historicism?[33] As Fasolt (2005) suggests in a paper that remains unpublished, the answer might be yes. Although he does not frame matters in the language of either the Edinburgh school's "strong program" or Latour,[34] what Fasolt comes close to here is the kind of symmetrical approach that has formed a subtext of my essay all along. Perhaps unsurprisingly, Fasolt (2005) argues that knowledge production about the past is *incidental* rather than essential to the service the discipline renders to the social order that sustains it. "The knowledge is never certain," he writes.

> Far more important is the service historians render to the faith in human liberty on which the modern world was built. For that service does not require their knowledge to be sound. It does not even require that they intend to give it. All it requires that they turn to evidence when they attempt to make their case. For every time they turn to the evidence in order to advance some historical debate, they hold a human being responsible for the evidence on which they base themselves.

This, however, is not just any human being. It is the kind of forensic person that arose in tandem with historicism and is stabilized by its operations, and it is clear where the kind of reductionism Chakrabarty worries about in his attempt to salvage the Santals' concept of selfhood and agency would inevitably find its point of entry—namely, at the moment such attributions of responsibility break down. But Fasolt (2005) goes further down the road toward commensuration.

> From this point of view the study of history can be regarded as the performance of a ritual. The ritual is sacred. Its purpose is to maintain the faith in the proposition that human beings are free and independent agents. That proposition is built into the foundations of the modern world. It cannot be allowed to fall into doubt without threatening social order. It cannot be proved by reason or experience. But it can be protected against the possibility of doubt by the performance of an appropriate ritual. The study of history is such a ritual.

As such, he continues, it shares eminent commonalities not just with the anamnestic functions of the Catholic Eucharist but with its doctrinary logic as well. If the priest's action not just iconially recalls the last supper but *indexes* the real presence of Christ in the host, the historian's actions similarly not just recall the modern person's free will into his or her text but indexically reinstantiate it in the present. Both, it would seem, do so by foisting on semiotically intensely charged parts of their present phenonomenal world (so charged, of course, by their own ritual activities). And both achieve felicity on the basis of socially distributed convictions and their attendant modes of doubt (for needless to say, Catholic theologians have debated the supreme mystery of transubstantiation for centuries). If so, however, what might keep us from analogizing the historian's role to that of the drummers in my (by now seriously overtaxed) ethnographic device? Could we, to spell it out, call them historians? And if the answer were yes, would this tell us anything worth knowing about the respective disciplines to which Afro-Cuban ritual drummers and academic historians subscribe?

*   *   *

The issue, or so it seems at first glance, would hinge on the contextual "conventions" of legibility (in Skinner's terms), or "rules of recognition," that might afford Tata Francisco and Ño Carlos citizenship in the "modern world" and the historicist accountability system that regulates the conditions of its intelligibility. But maybe they do not aspire to such. While perhaps occupying the role of dangerous supplements ("specters" if you will) within the representational economy of disciplined history, they have no intrinsic truck with it, standing outside, looking in, as it were. All historicism can offer them is to banish them to a shady existence—from where they nevertheless continue to haunt it in the form of a past that does not go away because it refuses historical objectification. But that is the historian's problem—not that of Afro-Cuban ritual drummers.

As my ethnographic device announced right from the start, Tata Francisco's and Ño Carlos's presence *in the present* was the product of ritual activity—call it a conjuring with the past, rather than a properly disciplined representation of it, if you will. Nor was the aim of the procedure to attain truthful knowledge about the past. A *cajon* is held and appreciated for all kinds of reasons: for one thing, not unlike academic historians, drummers earn their living that way—though the former do so in authoring representations of the past, while the latter create the conditions for it to present itself. But there are other parties involved. Patrons of *cajones* may sponsor such ceremonies in order to renew or improve personal relationships with spirits of dead people who demand their attention and whose blessings they desire. The mediums in turn cultivate lifelong relations with the dead, periodically lending their bodies to the past that becomes materially *present* when a spirit mounts (*montar*) them, such relationships evolving in a history of mutual recognition and coconstitution.[35] Some of the attendees will expect spirits to offer advice in regard to personal problems or difficult decisions; others will say they attend *cajones pa' los muertos* because they enjoy the music and dancing, much like we might say we enjoy reading a particularly well-written historical monograph. Yet others may have come simply because it is free entertainment, because they live across the street and can't concentrate on the *telenovela* because of the din of the drums, or because they want a taste of the *caldoza* (soup) that is invariably dished out in the aftermath of a *cajon*. In either case, the past that Tata Francisco or Ño Carlos *present* would seem to come unsolicited, if you will. It is the baggage they carry, as they seek recognition from the living and, in turn, recognize the various desires and motivations on account of which the living seek their company.[36] But by and large, picking up a historical monograph from a library shelf may be driven by roughly comparable motivations, and may engender roughly similar outcomes. And if I read Fasolt right, this is exactly what is to be expected. If the production of knowledge about the past is incidental to the services that history renders to the "world as we know it," why should it be different in a world where historiography coexists with spirit possession? For make no mistake here: given the nature of Cuba's educational system, there is no doubt that all of the participants in the ethnographic scenario on which I hung this essay went through a (thoroughly materialistic) education in Cuban and world history.

Of course, we might settle for a solution dividing attendance of spirit possession rituals *qualitatively* from the casual perusal of the latest biography of Abraham Lincoln, or a new scholarly interpretation of the causes of the War of Jenkins' Ear (1739–1748), so as to salvage the rationality of historicism (and its rituals) in contrast to other practices of engaging the past. Yet if so, would we not *still* have to concede that different from purely individual fantasies, dreams, or spontaneous remembrances (right or wrong, by whomever's standard), any ritual form must be premised on collective conditions under which it becomes recognizable, and even more importantly, iterable *as such*, across various instantiations? What *is* at stake in both instances are socially imaginable worlds produced by specific knowledge practices that configure the types of semiotic data that may enter into their canons of verification. Will Tata Francisco demand his cigar and a big swig of rum when he arrives the next time? Will Ño Carlos become upset again when he hears the wrong rhythms played to his oricha? Chances are good. That's what they *do* because of who they *were*. Notions of realism play a role in both instances. But they have their limits. Write a high school textbook representing Abraham Lincoln as a diehard racist who would have happily endorsed slavery if he could have saved the Union, and who busily explored locations in Central America and the Caribbean to which the emancipated might be deported, and you will see what I mean.

Just as the contemporary American secularist might worry over the Texas School Board's revisions when it comes to the faith of the Founding Fathers, so practitioners of Afro-Cuban religion worry about the truth of the utterances of the likes of Tata Francisco and Ño Carlos. In both cases, matters revolve not so much around issues of falsifiability (though they do that, too). They revolve around what can be recognized as "history" or "spirit possession." And they come down to what constitutes a proper instance of a history textbook, and what is a proper instance of a spirit who has taken over a human body (Irvine 1982). In either case, however, the underlying concern is not a socially unencumbered notion of truth or factuality. It is what any answer to such questions might mean for the world "as we know it." The "hardness of facts," Richard Rorty (1991, 80) reminds us, is first and foremost a reflection of a social consensus among those who will, henceforth, live with the truths so produced. No matter, then that in my tired, old ethnographic device the conventional guarantees of Trouillot's "historicity 1" flew out of the window, that chronology melted down into an amalgam of past and present, that personhood disintegrated, that agency became diffuse, that ostensible evidence of the past now seemed to point toward the present, or that, much as in the case of the Santal Hool, improbable principals and authors came to animate people's actions: we still were dealing with socially distributed versions of the past, and ones that were open to no less social dispute and conditional social ratification. All this proves is Trouillot's basic point that although some of us find the idea of historicity 1 good to think with, all we will ever *know* is historicity 2: the past in its inevitably mediated form, for better or for worse.

That said, then do we really need to take this instance of incommensurability between historicism and its multiple and multifarious others as an irrefutable invitation to reductionism? As an anthropologist, I don't think so. And Fasolt's rather sacrilegious intervention—launched from within his discipline rather than mine—would seem to underscore my hunch. Obviously, no less than any historian, the participants in a *cajon pa' los muertos* and the spirits with whom they conjure engage in illocutionary acts the felicity conditions of which are based in the contextual legibility of the performatives they enunciate. But can the perlocutionary effects of the one be brought into any alignment with those of the other? That, it would seem, depends both on how we configure the field of what we might call "the historical" and how we conceive of the historical enterprise itself. If to historicize is to ritualize—no matter what particular set of assumptions about the world is served by doing so—then there is no reason to write off Tata Francisco and Ño Carlos, the Santal Thakur, Joan of Arc's angels, or, indeed, the Franklins, Washingtons, Einsteins, or Jeffersons dictating their posthumous messages to their mediums as irrational delusions awaiting proper "anthropologization" as Chakrabarty might put it.

They all may serve different social mandates and rationalities. That, or so it seems, is the fate of those whose lives are "in the past." As Walter Benjamin might put it, the dead are at the mercy of the living and their struggles over the past. But for precisely that reason the spirits of dead slaves and priests of Afro-Cuban religions are no less constitutive of socially inhabitable and legible present and future worlds than the Texas

School Board's invocations of the faith (or agnosticism) of the framers (authors!) of the Constitution of the United States. Given that a generation of Americans may now be taught to inhabit a world where "made by God" plaques affixed to Kodak spots at the rim of the Grand Canyon are becoming a distinct possibility, I have no problem whatsoever in thinking that I observed a Congolese slave and a dead priest of Yemayá arguing over the style of drumming appropriate to their presence in early twenty-first-century Havana. On the contrary: although I don't know what became of Carmen, the host compromised by the spirits she entertained that evening, she has my full and unqualified sympathy.

Notes

Chapter One

1. Although the video clip for the song does give some hints. The full lyrics of the song can be easily accessed on the Internet.

2. In their discussion of the epistemological and heuristic consequences of a "historical anthropology," John and Jean Comaroff follow Bourdieu's (1986) original critique on the "biographical illusion" and discuss the methodological caveat of using biography as an instrument for ethnographical research, reminding us that it is a projection of a particular (Western, bourgeois) idea of personhood in which anthropologists voluntarily or involuntarily participate in their production of life-histories (Comaroff and Comaroff 1992, 26). Their alert comes as part of the broader effort to "rupture the basic tropes of western historiography—biography and event by situating being and action, comparatively, within their diverse cultural contexts" (1992, 27).

3. http://www.cavyspirit.com/sociallife.htm.

Chapter Two

1. Earlier versions of this chapter have been discussed in seminars at the Department of Anthropology at the University of Oxford, the Department of African History at the University of Basel, and the Department of Anthropology at the University of Heidelberg, as well as in the "Global Encounters" seminar series at the University of Amsterdam. I would like to thank the participants at these seminars for their helpful comments.

2. Fieldwork on African Christianity in Zambia was conducted during a total of seventeen months in 1993, 1995, 1999, and 2001, and was made financially possible by grants from the Free University of Berlin (in 1993), the German Academic Exchange Service (in 1999), and the German Research Foundation (in 2001). This

chapter is mainly based on data from my field research in 1995, 1999, and 2001; my use of the past tense has to be understood accordingly.

3. The ethnographic cases examined in this chapter concern religious communities that resemble what the literature on "African Initiated Churches" (Anderson 2001) calls, for example, "Zionist churches" (Sundkler 1961), "prophet-healing churches" (Turner 1967), or "Spirit-type churches" (Daneel 1971). In using the term "*Pentecostal*-charismatic" in relation to these communities, I am taking into account, first, the historical fact that they "emerged out of the global Pentecostal movement" (Maxwell 1999, 244; see also Maxwell 2006), which originated in Methodist and Baptist sanctification circles. Soon after the so-called "Azuza Street revival" in the United States in 1906, this movement spread to South Africa, from where it diffused to other regions in southern Africa. Secondly, my use of the term "Pentecostal" takes account of the fact that "Pentecostalism is not a denomination or a creed, but a movement, a cluster of religious practices and attitudes that transcends ecclesiastical boundaries" (Cox 1996, 246). This "cluster of religious practices and attitudes" concerns especially the crucial importance ascribed to the working of the Holy Spirit in faith and religious practice. Thirdly, my use of the term "Pentecostal-*charismatic*" is not intended to establish a theological typology (cf. Anderson 2001, 110), nor is it a reference to what, since the 1960s, has been called the "(neo)charismatic movement" (cf. Robbins 2004, 121–22). Instead, I employ this term in order to highlight the fact that, in the churches concerned, inspiration by the Holy Spirit represents an essential basis for religious authority.

4. The Gwembe Valley lies about six to seven hundred meters below the Central African Plateau and extends from the Devil's Gorge on the Zambezi to the confluence of the Zambezi with the Kafue some three hundred kilometers further downriver. The northwest part of the valley belongs to Zambia, the southeast to Zimbabwe. Here I am dealing solely with the Zambian part, which is predominantly inhabited by the Tonga, a Bantu-speaking people with a matrilineal, segmentary, and formerly acephalous form of social organization (Colson 1960; Scudder 1962). In the Gwembe Valley—for a long time one of the most remote regions of sub-Saharan Africa—Christianity was introduced by Western mission societies around the turn of the twentieth century (Luig 1997). Yet it was only after the mid-1950s that it increased its impact in the valley. The construction of the Kariba Dam and mining created a new infrastructure (Colson 1971), which opened up the Gwembe Valley to the Central African Plateau and thus cleared the way for both Western and African indigenous churches to enter the area. In the 1990s, most Tonga of the younger generation in my area of research were associated with a Christian congregation. A considerable number of Western and African-initiated churches coexisted in mutual competition for members. In 1999, for instance, eighteen different churches could be found within an hour's walk from the small rural township of Sinazeze, the main area of my field research. Out of these, eleven were African-

initiated Pentecostal-charismatic churches—that is, churches where the divination and healing of afflictions played a pivotal role. My analysis in this chapter draws on my fieldwork data on these churches.

5. In what follows, due to a lack of space, I will concentrate on *muya usalala* and refrain from discussing the ritual practices associated with non-Christian spiritual entities such as ancestral spirits or *masabe* spirits. At death, the spirit (*muzimu*) of a person is usually inherited by an appropriate member of the matrilineal kin group, who henceforth acquires some of the rights and duties of the deceased. This includes the ritual responsibilities for "appeasing" the ancestors, who are said to induce afflictions if they are not remembered by their descendants or if their demands are not fulfilled (Colson 1955; 1960, 122–61). During the "inheriting" ceremony, the spirit is attached to the heir without entering his or her body and henceforth stays close to the person concerned. On the other hand, *masabe* possession cults deal with the bodily incorporation of spirits that represent "alien humanity" (Colson 1969, 71), foreign cultural practices and technologies, as well as the wild (Colson 1969; Luig 1992, 1993a, 1993b, 1993c, 1994). The incorporation of these spirits manifests itself while dancing *masabe*, which is accompanied by drumming and particular songs. Such temporary incorporations are, among other things, thought to provide some protection against affliction.

6. *Insengo* and *chifunda* are horns or small containers filled with destructive medicine (*musamu*) that are hidden by witches in the thatched roof of their victim's home; *chinaile* are needles with magical powers placed in dust roads, so that the victim dies when stepping on them.

7. Even before the coming of the European missionaries, the Tonga had the concept of a *deus remotus* (*leza*), who was considered to represent the "ultimate reality of power" (Colson 1971, 233) and to have created the world (cf. Hopgood 1950). In precolonial times, however, there was no cult addressed directly to *leza*, contact with whom was thought to be possible only through mediating spirits such as the ancestral spirits (*mizimu*) or the spirits of local rain shrines (*basangu*). The term *leza* was adopted by early Western missionaries when translating the Bible. Nowadays, this term is generally associated with Christianity.

Chapter Three

Acknowledgments: This chapter is the result of research carried out in Mongolia in 2004 with the support of the French Ministry of Foreign Affairs (Egide, Lavoisier Scholarship). It has been presented in several research seminars and has known several versions until it reached its present form. In this process, I have thus accumulated more intellectual debt than I can actually acknowledge here. Nevertheless, I wish to express gratitude to the members of Anthrop-ENS in Paris (2006), of the "Mongolia & Inner Asia Studies Unit" seminar in Cambridge (2008), and of the "Ethnicity and Identity" seminar in Oxford (2009). In particular, I am very grateful to François Berthomé, Julien Bonhomme, Chloe Nahum-Claudel, Giovanni da Col, Emmanuel de Vienne, Anne de Sales, Pierre Déléage, Roberte Hamayon, Caroline Humphrey, Katherine Swancutt, and Sarah Troche, to name only a few. Special thanks go to Tselei, Gansüh, Bümbeejav, Togtuur, and Otgonbaatar for their warm welcome and for their kind patience with my eerie curiosity of ghosts and their manifestation.

1. There has been in the past few years an upsurge of spectral apparitions in the capital city, Ulaanbaatar, and a definite interest on the part of city dwellers in these phenomena (see Delaplace 2010). This certainly goes hand in hand with the great success met by the renewed practice of shamanism in the city over the past decade, something that has not—yet?—reached the remote province of Uvs where Dörvöd herders live. The last shaman in Uvs died in the late 1980s failing to find any successor.

2. While Halh Mongols living in the central regions of the country constitute more than 80 percent of the total population, Dörvöd people are one of the main minorities living in western Mongolia. Although they speak the same language, and although their basic daily life and practices do not seem to differ fundamentally from the rest of the country, Dörvöd people have often been pointed out by ethnographers as having different "customs" (*yos zanshil*) from the rest of the Mongol population.

3. For a more detailed analysis of these narratives, as well as a broader account of Mongolian people's relationship with their dead, see Delaplace 2009a.

4. Bracketed ellipses in fieldwork excerpts indicate ommissions. Unbracketed ellipses in fieldwork excerpts indicate pauses in speech.

5. The anthropological literature counts many discussions on the uncanny character of encounters with ghosts in different societies. For a recent one, located in Malaysia and engaging specifically with Freud's definition of the notion, see Long (2010).

6. This feature is also stressed by witnesses of the experiences gathered in the spiritualist literature. The unfortunate occupants of "haunted houses," for example, describe rapping noises on the wall, as well as repeated steps on the stairs, and the rearrangement of items in an empty room locked from the outside (Flammarion 1924).

7. Once again, this is not specific to Mongolian ghost stories: see Taylor (1993), in particular, for a similar points made about the Achuar of Ecuador.

Chapter Four

Acknowledgments: The ethnographic data presented here are based on my field research among the Toba people of the Argentinean Chaco, financed by CONICET and by Agencia Nacional de Promoción Científica y Tecnológica (SECyT). I would like to thank Oiara Bonilla and Celeste Medrano for the reading of an early version of this text, and Valentín Suárez and Mauricio Maidana for their help in the translation of the Toba stories.

1. The information analyzed here results from the fieldwork carried out from 1999 to 2011, for periods of two to six months, in four Toba communities of the province of Formosa in the Argentinean Chaco: *Namqom*, or Lote 68; *Mala' Lapel*, or San Carlos; *Dañal'ec lachiugue*, or Riacho de Oro; and *Poxoyaxaix Alhua'*, or Santo Domingo.

2. "Guaicurú" is the local denomination of the bird that corresponds to *Herpetotheres cachinnans*. Buckwalter (2001, 30) registered it as "huaqauo': guaicurú, variety of predatory bird." Cf. Martínez-Crovetto (1995, 443). I am thankful to Paola Cuneo for the identification of the bird.

3. Several authors agree that the basic social unit of the indigenous groups of the Chaco was the "band." These bands were constituted through the union of several extended families, whose members were related by alliance or consanguinity (Cordeu and de los Ríos 1982; Miller and Braunstein 1999). The bands moved within a defined territory in relation to the ecological cycles. The tribes were political units, which grouped several bands and also had given names (Karsten 1932, 45; Cordeu and de los Ríos 1982, 163; Braunstein 1983, 24).

4. The concept of owners or masters, as Carlos Fausto explained, "transcends the simple expression of a relationship of property or domain. The category and its reciprocal terms designate a generalized mode of relating that characterizes interactions between humans, between non-humans, between humans and non-humans and between persons and things. It is a key category for understanding Indigenous sociologies and cosmologies" (2008, 366). Among the Toba people, the "owners" are generally conceived as the "mothers" and the "fathers" of animals and plants. At a linguistic level, *-late'e* and *-lta'a* are the terms used to designate the owners, added to the name of the animal and the plant (in kinship terminology these terms designate mother and father, respectively). *Qasoxonaxa* is the nonhuman person that has been represented as a mountain, a boy, and an elephant that, when moving, produces rays, the thunderclaps, and the rain. In the bibliography of the Chaco, we found isolated references to the owners of the species in Métraux (1946, 50–53; 1967, 124), Cordeu (1969–1970, 88), Tomasini (1969–1970, 432–39; 1978–1979), and Tola (2009). In Tola (2010) we find a detailed analysis of the relations that humans entail with these owners.

5. Their classification is the following: (a) places of camping, (b) places of economic and productive activities, (c) preestablished places of encounter between groups, (d) intermediate points or stages of usual itineraries, (e) sites where historical and extraordinary facts happened, and (f) places that work as geographic-territorial limits.

6. See also Salamanca (forthcoming).

7. Bracketed ellipses in fieldwork excerpts indicate ommissions. Unbracketed ellipses in fieldwork excerpts indicate pauses in speech.

8. *Shiỹaxaua* or *shigaxaua*: person. *Shig-* or *shi-*: root of the verb "to go" (*ashic*, first-person singular). *-axaua*: suffix that indicates the idea of an accompaniment (Buckwalter 2001, 370). Through the analysis of other Toba terms we can suppose that this suffix makes reference to a most abstract notion: that of a relation between two terms.

9. The term *Toba* is the official designation of those who denominate themselves as *Qom*. *Toba* does not correspond to a self-designation, but it is a Guarani pejorative term that means "*frentones*." This term made reference to the ancient custom to shave the eyebrow (Balmori 1957, 24–25). Although at present all the *Qom* recognize them as Toba, it is important to mention that, previous to the use of this term, in the Gran Chaco there existed a great sociopolitical diversity, which also exists nowadays. From an external point of view, *Toba* is used to designate one of the indigenous groups of the linguistic family Guaycurú, which is located in the Argentinean Chaco.

10. In contrast to this position, authors such as Françoise Héritier differ. According to Héritier (2004, 260), to maintain—as Strathern did—that complementariness and interchange imply equality between the sexes is fallacious, because the argument of maintaining the complementariness and interchange allows the persistence of inequality. In fact, Héritier (ibid., 261) sustained that complementariness is the base of the hierarchy.

11. For an analysis of the corporal humors, their roll in the definition of the differences between the sexes, and their relation with the kinship systems, cf. Héritier (1994, 1996). For a study of the relation between humors, body, and affection, cf. Héritier and Xanthakou (2004).

12. On the humors as vehicles of emotions, cf. Surrallés (2003).

13. Among the Toba people, two modalities to attack victims by nonvisible means exist: shamanic attacks and witch aggressions. The shamanic practices consist of the sending of objects with power or of pathogenic agents that must be extracted by another shaman (*pi'oxonaq*: from the verb *pi'oxon-* ["to absorb"]; *-aq*: suffix that indicates "the one that is expert in") through a song and suction. These practices are mainly masculine. The witch actions are carried out by old women and involve the contagion technique. The objects that have been in contact with the victim are susceptible to be capture by a sorceress (*conaxanaxae*: from the verb *-cona-* ["to take hold"]). On the subject, cf. Tola (forthcoming).

14. On the possibility that the fetus is affected by nonhumans in Amazonia, cf. McCallum (2001), Fausto (2001), Vilaça (2002), among others.

15. On the notion of *nauoxa*, cf. Karsten (1932, 74), Métraux (1937, 193; 1944, 8–10; 1967, 140–41), Idoyaga Molina (1978–1979, 148), Balducci (1982, 72–74), Wright (1997, 295), and Tola (1999). The same concept appears in societies of other continents (Malinowski [1932] 1976, 166–67; Mead [1930] 1952, 235).

Chapter Five

1. Some of the discussions here were addressed in my dissertation (Cardoso 2004) and further developed in Cardoso (2007).

2. It is impossible to trace here the history of the constitution of this signification, but it is the object of a longer discussion in my dissertation (Cardoso 2004), where a more complete bibliography of the field of studies on Afro-Brazilian religions is also available.

3. Translating names is even more intensely marked by the inescapable tensions involved in the process of ethnographic translation. These *entities* are variously referred to as *almas* (souls), *entidades* (entities), *espírito* (spirit), and *santo* (saint), the latter being a very common reference. I opted not to translate it as saint in order to avoid the commonsense associations it may bring to an English readership. Even if *spirit* may not be a very adequate word, I prefer to retain its apparent inadequacies than any underlying associations.

4. Bracketed ellipses in fieldwork excerpts indicate ommissions. Unbracketed ellipses in fieldwork excerpts indicate pauses in speech.

5. The euphemism also brings up, albeit probably unintentionally, a double play with the notion of falling ill. On one hand, to feel ill is a common way of describing, both in words and gestures, the impeding presence of a spirit upon one's body. On the other hand, health affliction is a common idiom used to refer to the effects of the actions of the spirits upon a person—be it an early sign of mediumship, or of evil workings by a spirit, frequently at the request of a foe but just as commonly as punishment by the spirit himself or herself for some wrongdoing. Most importantly, the euphemism reflects a social etiquette of not attributing mediumship to a stranger, as that might be taken as a serious offense.

6. To some degree this tension is akin to that which Goldman describes as the "intensive multiplicity" (2009, 120) of the individual deities in *candomblé*. Reflecting on the relation of the general categories of *orixás*, deities of *candomblé*, to the individual *orixá* that "belongs" to a particular initiate, Goldman argues that while the general category is limited in its numbers of possibilities (i.e., we can list the different types of *orixás*, such as *Ogun*, *Iemanjá*, and so on), there is an infinite number of possibilities of individual *orixás* (i.e., my *Iemanjá* is individually distinguished from someone else's *Iemanjá*). Or, returning to how I described it earlier, I *work with* an Iemanjá that is uniquely my own, at the same time that she is an *Iemanjá* just like the other unique one someone else works with. Reframing a long-standing theme in the studies on Afro-Brazilian religions (cf. Bastide 2007; Serra, 1995) through the lenses of Deleuzian philosophy, Goldman forcefully argues that initiation in *candomblé* involves an individuation of the *orixás* in a process of composition of person and his or her *orixá*. The nature of the *orixás* is markedly different from that of the spirits of the people of the streets, especially in the sense that the embodied spirits of nowadays are deemed to have lived in times gone by, but there certainly are important resonances here.

7. While I am here addressing stories about the *povo da rua* as creative manifestations that bring the spirits into life, we could say that this narrative engendering of the spirits also affects other "types" of spirits in *macumba* and that it expresses the very possibility of composition of spirits that is at the heart of the religious practice. I do want, however, to stress that the power of the *povo da rua* emanates from their excessiveness, and their own storying, excessive to any singular story, is inextricably woven into the very power attributed to them.

8. This is what Butler calls the efficacy of the performative, a crucial part of the ways "in which subjects are called into social being, inaugurated into sociality" (1996, 44) in the very acts of performance.

9. This relation between performance and its context echoes the notion of "contextualization" (Bauman and Briggs 1990; Briggs 1988) as an effect of performance, in contrast to a notion of context as a social a priori. It is in the acts of performance that what is relevant to their signification is brought into relation to these acts, constituting a frame of signification that is also produced in performance.

Chapter Six

Acknowledgments: This chapter is based on fieldwork undertaken since 1992 and archival work since 2003. I gratefully acknowledge the Economic and Social Research Council, the British Academy, and the Leverhulme Trust for funding this work. Comments from Adam Reed on an earlier version of this chapter were very helpful. And I thank Ruy Blanes and Diana Espírito Santo for their editorial input.

1. The area runs along the main stretch of the Amazon River between Parintins, at the border with the state of Amazonas, and Gurupá to the east, before the mouth of the Amazon at Marajó.

2. There is an excellent biography on Bettendorff by Karl-Heinz Arenz (2010).

3. Nimuendaju (2004, 121) says the term means "creator of the beginning," which makes it sound very Christian.

4. At the initial stage of missionization, the main indigenous leader was a woman, Maria Moaçara, who during the 1660s was married to a Portuguese man (Bettendorff 1990, 172). We learn from Bettendorff that the dead are generally wrapped in cotton (1990, 342), possibly their hammocks, and from another source (Heriarte [1662] 1976) that they are buried, sometimes under the floor of domestic houses, with small figurines made with needles by knitting.

5. The shaman also said that "não é tudo que se vê" (not everything can be seen), echoing similar phrases by others.

6. This discussion of the invisible will be familiar to ethnographers of South American indigenous peoples (e.g., see Campbell 1990; Viveiros de Castro 2007). Yet the familiarity between Amerindian and ribeirinho (or caboclo) constructions of the invisible should not be taken for granted. The superficial similarities can be

useful for comparative purposes but on the whole ribeirinho shamanism should be understood on its own terms and not as a derivative (or an inferior version) of Amerindian forms. The same point goes for the similarity between Portuguese folklore (e.g., Cabral 1987) and other Brazilian regional expressions of spirits and invisible beings (Câmara Cascudo 2002). The same names for spirit beings are widely shared across the Luso-Brazilian world, but this does not necessarily mean they are understood locally to be the same kind of beings. Since this is essentially an ethnographic piece of work, my sensitivity is to the particular local expression, rather than understanding the invisible and encantados as a general phenomenon, disconnected from historical experience.

7. In this section I have been inspired by the lyrical writing of Robert Macfarlane (2007) in *Wild Places*, especially the chapter "River-Mouth."

8. Unusually this encounter seemed to take place during the day and involved a group of people; most contemporary stories occur at night and involve one or two people.

9. For example, no dolphin myths are mentioned by Alfred Métraux (1928) in his exhaustive review of the historical material of the Tupinamba.

10. The other side of Slater's argument is therefore on disenchantment. Building on Weber, she develops an alternative understanding of the process of disenchantment based in the local meaning of *desencantar*: "the voluntary embracing of humanity in all its sorrowful grandeur versus the bitter, often violent loss of possibility" (Slater 1993, 250).

Chapter Seven

Acknowledgements: I am grateful for Diana and Ruy's astute editorial oversight and encouragement, as well as feedback from participants in the 2010 American Anthropological Association meeting session on spirit biographies who heard an early version of this chapter and an anonymous reviewer who read a later draft. I extend my deepest gratitude, as always, to the Cuban religious practitioners who are my ethnographic interlocutors, and most especially to Josefina and her generous spirit(s).

1. For information on these modalities, their practices related to nonmaterial entities, and their interconnections and distinctions, see Barnet (1995), Brown (2003), Espírito Santo (2010), James Figarola (1999), Ochoa (2010b), Schmidt (2005), and Wirtz (2007b).

2. A broken plaster saint statue or threadbare "chicherekú" doll may simply be thrown away, or may, like other kinds of ritual waste, be specifically tossed away in a place thought to spiritually denature it, like the steps of a church or a crossroads. Even when ritual waste is simply tossed into the trash, there remains some notion that it could continue to be spiritually charged and therefore potentially hazardous.

It seems that spirit presence, however evanescent, can leave traces. For a deeper analysis of spiritual contamination of ritual materials, see Wirtz (2009).

3. I thank Diana Espírito Santo for elucidating this point. The same can be said not only of the songs of plegaria used by Spiritist mediums to attract their spirits but of similar songs used by paleros to call their muertos and of Lucumí songs directed to the orichas of Santería.

4. I take inspiration from the empathetic portrayals of marginalized, sometimes mentally ill, people finding solace in spirit possession in Crapanzano and Garrison (1977).

5. In this, Cuban folk religious practitioners are not so very different from some sects of Protestant Christianity in following a logic of materiality in connecting materialism to projects of selfhood (e.g., see Coleman 2006).

6. My actual godfather in Ocha has goodnaturedly tolerated her incursions, especially since she has similarly claimed him as her godchild as well. By now I have, in turn, decided to accept her spiritual guidance as a godmother, for example, in regularly sponsoring spiritual masses and receiving spiritual consultations from her.

7. Under the Cuban Revolution, a socialist program following the Soviet model, distinctions of socioeconomic class were officially abolished, although their vestiges, having been reinscribed by new forces after the 1989 fall of the Soviet bloc, continue to be apparent today in patterns of residence, educational attainment, employment, political access, and even wealth. Nonetheless, Cubans generally refer to class and racial distinctions euphemistically, so a "popular" neighborhood means a poor, predominantly black neighborhood, and people described as "cultos," or educated, refined, have a higher class standing or are whiter than those described as "incultos."

8. These kinds of stereotypical representations are common in related practices elsewhere in the Caribbean and Latin America. Brazilian Umbanda is one example (see Cardoso, this volume; Hale 2009). In some traditions, spirits tend instead to represent stereotypes of historically dominant groups (e.g., the Hauka of Niger [Stoller 1995], the Zaar cult of Sudan [Boddy 1989], and Malagasy spirits [Cole 2001; Lambek 1998; Sharp 1993]).

9. A list of examples would have to start with novelist Alejo Carpentier and folklorist Lydia Cabrera, and the tropes are also evident in Cuban feature films such as *La Vida es Silbar* (1998) and *Miel para Ochún* (2001).

10. The emphasis on vision is especially fitting given that it is, as Espírito Santo (2009) describes, a fundamental trope of Cuban mediumship.

11. Understanding the semiotic and experiential basis of different ontological orientations has (re)emerged as a concern in contemporary anthropology, especially of religion. See, for example, Duranti (2009), Espírito Santo (2009), and Holbraad (2008).

12. Original transcript in Spanish from August 14, 2008, interview: "Y tengo

que recoger y tapar de medio, de medio en toda la casa. Tu viste como está . la casa. Y pido a Diós y los santos, las condiciones, que los espiritus del cabildo me ayuden, para poder lograr lo que (luego tengo que tener?). Y después puedo pintar la casa, poner el cabildo como, como quiero mantener nuestro cabildo."

13. A note on transcription: Bracketed ellipses in fieldwork excerpts indicate ommissions. Unbracketed ellipses in fieldwork excerpts indicate pauses in speech. The number of periods used in an unbracketed ellipsis varies and is meant to convey the length of a pause (e.g., one spaced period indicates a brief pause, and three spaced periods indicate a longer pause).

14. Original transcript in Spanish:

> JOSEFINA: A la hora ya de ponerlo . todo para tener todo para poder decir ok que la gente se pueda empezar a entrar, ya tiene que estar desde, desde la palangana que tu viste . que es el omiero, con todo lo que tiene que contener para encargarse las manos [KRISTINA. Sí.] hasta la otra que debo poner en la esquina allá del altar abajo, que es para la comisión de la curandera de los fundadores del cabildo, que están enterrados allá abajo. Porque tú sabes la historia del cabildo, de que los que fundaron este cabildo fueron esclavos, en el tiempo de la esclavitud, como un palenque de cimarrones, y es una comisión que trabaja aquí . que hay que ponerle su, su recipiente, una cuenca o una palangana y esa con su vela, y dentro de eso hay que ponerle sus cosas que lleva allí, para ellos, con todo [unclear]—
>
> KRISTINA: Como las hierbas.
>
> JOSEFINA: Las hierbas que pertenecen a ellos, y además de las hierbas la cascarilla, y otras cosas que delecta, el alcohól . . .
>
> KRISTINA: ¿Y preparas el omiero entonces?
>
> JOSEFINA: El el omiera también lo preparo.
>
> KRISTINA:¿Y esto es omiero en la jarra allí [*pointing toward jar in front of Elegguá's little house by the door*]
>
> JOSEFINA: Esto allí? Sí. Y tengo una, una palangana blanca alta para [unclear].
>
> KRISTINA: Sí, la he visto sí.
>
> JOSEFINA:¿Qué quiero decir con esto? Esto . es una composición de las dos cosas. De lo espiritual con el santo . porque el muerto . parió al santo. No hay santos sin muertos, estando aquí un diós y un espiritu.
>
> KRISTINA: Ikú lobí ocha. [*laughs*]
>
> JOSEFINA: Así es, así, así.

15. Original transcript in Spanish:

> Ahora, cuando tú dijiste eso, has dicho eso, y yo empecé a sentirme
> en los pies, en las piernas, en todo mi cuerpo, los brazos y todo, y
> la cabeza, estoy erizado con esto, con la corriente, con la práctica
> que cogiste eso solo por decir estas palabras. [*Kristina se rie*] Y
> eso es verdad, y es verdad, sí [*Kristina se rie*] ¡Aaaaa! [*marked
> rising then falling intonation like a siren*] ¡Es la prueba! [Kristina:
> Sí.] La primera que decimos la prueba soy yo, con lo que estabas
> diciendo, con nada más que decir estas palabras, y yo contestarle
> ¿a quién? Y estoy, ya no, pero sentí una corriente que ahora me
> cogió, y eso es la verdad [*Kristina se rie*] en todo mi cuerpo.

Chapter Eight

1. This is the term used in Brazil to designate the space used by various Afro-Brazilian religions and cults, which is normally organized into a complex of rooms with a central space (a *barracão*) for congregation.

Note on translation: In the remainder of the text all italicized terms are native terms: the original Portuguese terms are used in many cases, but in others they have been translated for reasons of textual fluency, in which case the original is given in parentheses or in the footnotes where appropriate.

2. In Portuguese, *uma doutrina de apresentação*. Doctrines are songs that are pronounced during religious ceremonies for calling encantados, healing, and so on. As stated by one Pajé (shaman), "The doctrine is the trademark of an encantado [spirit]. It is what makes him appear, disappear, become angry, or take our side. I do not really like just to sing for no reason, because they will surely come."

3. The native term *linha* refers to specific encantado lineages.

4. In Brazil, *Caboclo* is the term used to identify people of mixed white and Amerindian heritage. In many different Afro-Brazilian religions it refers to a specific genre of entities that participate to varying degrees in each of these religions.

5. Encantados are Tambor de Mina and Pajé entities. This is quite an open and malleable term: depending on the house, their defining categories can include very different entities. They don't possess the same status as *eguns* in Candomblé or Kardecist spirits. They are people who had a carnal life but who disappeared and became *enchanted*.

6. It is important to stress the difference between *festas* (parties) and *curas* (healings): in the former the encantados only enter to play, dance, and talk, but in the latter, as the name suggests, they provide cures and *trabalhos* (works) principally for physical disorders but also for spiritual, amorous, emotional, and financial problems.

7. The noun, *Pajé*, denotes both the practitioners and the religion and provides

these with an ontological dimension that transits between two different universes. The barracões are most often (though not always) wooden structures, commonly found in rural Brazil, where community parties and other collective events normally take place.

8. These terms can be simply translated as the *here* (*cá*) and *there* (*lá*) people, terms also used by the encantados when referring to humans and themselves; for the purpose of textual fluency, in the remainder of the article the English equivalents will be used.

9. The encantados' *linhas* (or *correntes*, currents) are essentially related to their origin as well as their abilities.

10. *Casa* (house) is the name given to the physical space where the religion is practiced and to the kinship relations (consanguineous and above all affective) involved in that space. Each *house* has specific characteristics, such as particular parties and encantados, as well as a certain flexibility in relation to healing practices (which could also be called creativity, according to Hallan and Ingold 2007).

11. As suggested by Gomes (2005) and confirmed in local oral history, it is worth noting that part of Maranhão state is geographically located in the Brazilian Amazon. This ethnography was conducted in an area historically known for alliances between the *maroons* (descendants of slaves who generally live in a rural zone and who are subjects of this ethnography) and different indigenous peoples.

12. I use the terms *Pajé, healer,* and *mineiro* (Tambor de Mina practitioner) indiscriminately, as my native interlocutors defined themselves using all three terms. There is a certain sense in which mina (Tambor de Mina) is considered the practice of spell casting, as opposed to healing and pajelança, though more in ontological terms; pragmatically, all the houses practice and recognize healing as mina.

13. Afro-Brazilians are commonly referred to as *morenos*, primarily in northern states.

14. This region is located on the western border of Maranhão state in the (officially entitled) *Amazônia Legal* territory. Geographically it is an interesting area, consisting of transitory freshwater and saltwater vegetation, as well as numerous islands and bays, which are identified as *lugares de encantaria* (encantaria places), the encantados' dwelling place.

15. The *encantaria* is where the encantados live, a special place where entire encantado families dwell, with kings, queens, and princesses. As one of my informants, Senhor Carmo, said about the Vura settlement, "It is beautiful there! There is a king, a queen, and the commerce belongs to them. There isn't one stall here or there, like here, no, there it all belongs to them!" This and other statements seem to demonstrate that there are well organized places, from a social point of view. The access between "this" world and the encantaria is given in specific spaces, such as water holes, certain tree trunks, and bays; that is, these places act as "portals" between two worlds.

16. In Portuguese, *montando em seus cavalos*. The mediums are called "horses," as the encantados generally "enter" through the *"croa"* (head), which leads to the expression *montar sem eu cavalo*, meaning to "be in a trance."

17. Unlike in candomblé and Brazilian Spiritism (see Goldman 2009; Sansi, 2009), encantado iconography is rare. There are no encantado images; a few encantados are *materialized* in painting or sculpture, because the encantados *are* the place where they live, the animal they incarnate, or the saint who shelters them, such as João da Mata who is São João Batista. On the other hand, the Caboclos are represented with images from the Hollywood imaginary, much like in Cuba, where Amerindian spirits are also represented by what we know to be North American Apache Indians.

18. It is not in the scope of this chapter to enter into a discussion of rupture and continuity in Afro-Brazilian religious tradition. For such a discussion, see Capone (2008), Ferretti (2001), and Sansi (2009).

19. The Pajés refer to the head as the crown (the *coroa* in Portuguese): the encantados' entrance into the body.

20. Vura is a rural community in the Guimarães prefecture, where Senhor Carmo (deceased) had a terreiro for many years. Currently, his son, Preguinho, is the Pajé who is responsible for the house, and his sister, Beatriz, a Pajoa, helps him during healings and festivities in the house. Her guide is João da Mata, and she also claims to receive two of his daughters, the twins Rosilda and Rosenilce.

21. Although in Umbanda the Índios are often synonymous with Caboclos, in the Maranhão Pajés there is a clear difference between the two "lines." The Índios are coarser, less "developed" entities, while the Caboclos are almost always (physically) Afro-descendants, even though they may have some indigenous characteristics.

22. The *encantados de cabeça* (head encantados) are *guides* who accompany the neophyte throughout his earthly voyage, helping him on several different levels: whether by preparing him to become a Pajé or protecting him from natural or supernatural harm (such as sickness or relationship troubles). Depending on their line, the guides may also suggest medicinal recipes for the sick and so forth.

23. The Pajés have an encantado *guide*, a *counterguide*, a *boss*, and one or two *revellers*; each has its role in religious life, whether for healing, socializing (revellers), or doing and undoing spells. If the Pajé has great affinity with his (female) reveller, for example, he will acquire the encantado's characteritics and can even become effeminate, or if the encantado drinks too much, he can become an alcoholic—such is the degree of integration between them.

24. The *fundo* is the same as the *encantaria*, the place where the encantados live.

25. Bracketed ellipses in fieldwork excerpts indicate ommissions. Unbracketed ellipses in fieldwork excerpts indicate pauses in speech.

26. See, for example, Kockelman (2007), Duranti (2004), and Keane (2003a), among others.

27. The fumigations seem to have Catholic origins, wherein incense is placed in censers and used for (spiritual and ambient) cleansing during various ceremonial occasions.

28. It is worth observing, however, that these definitions of *agency* are more linguistic than social, and the extent to which they converge and intersect would be part of a much broader piece of work.

29. In healing rituals and Tambor de Mina (at least in this ethnography's region), the voduns do not appear except on occasion, but here we are dealing with a three-day *despacho* (funerary ritual) following the death of one of the house dancers. There is a strong hierarchy among voduns, nobles, and Caboclos. This region is known for its healing rituals (pajelança), which are seen as the most "syncretic" or least "Africanized" houses by those from the capital.

30. Here agency is ascribed to objects, apparently lifeless "things." A more rigorous discussion about this topic can be found in Henare, Holbraad, and Wastell (2007).

31. One of my interlocutors, the Pajé Hildo from Guimarães, attests to receiving the Amerindian encantados *Urubu* and *Gamela*, a clear reference to the Urubu Kaapor and Kanela indigenous groups: the first speakers of the Urubu Kaapor language, from the Tupi-Guarani linguistic family (Tupi branch), and subsequently speakers of Suya and Timbira, from the Jê linguistic family (Magrco-Jê branch)— Gavião do Maranhão, Canela Ramcokamekra, inhabitants of Maranhão state's southern (Kanela) and Alto Turiaçu regions (in the west). (Cf. Rodrigues 1986.)

Chapter Nine

1. "He's here! He's here! / He's here . . . with God . . . / He's here! He's here! / The Caboclo of the Seven Crossroads!" Invocation chant, see full lyrics: http:// gufec.blogspot.com.br/2006/10/pontos-do-caboclo-das-7-encruzilhadas.html.

2. Note on translation: Henceforth the entity's Portuguese name is used to refer to this figure, or the capitalized term *Caboclo*, to differentiate him from other entities of the same genre, which are referred to with the uncapitalized terms *caboclo* or *caboclos*.

3. Brown's (1986) work continues to be the most important reference on Umbanda history. Many celebrations took place for the "1908 centenary"—and Cumino's (2010) book can be seen as a product of and exponent for the perspective that marks that date. As examples of the consideration of Umbanda as an Afro-Brazilian religion, I highlight the classic works by Bastide (1971), Ortiz (1978), and Queiroz (1989).

4. Among academics, see Concone (1987); among Umbandistas, two examples, from distinct periods, are Pessoa (1960) and Oliveira (2008).

5. On the debates about Umbanda's distant origins, see Bastide (1971), Ortiz (1978), and Giumbelli (2010).

6. On Catholicism, see Mainwaring (1986); on Spiritism, which will be commented on further along, see Lewgoy (2004).

7. The reader may find some proximity with my proposal and Stephan Palmié's contribution to this same volume, especially in what concerns the limits of historicism—even in the mere insistence in the historical terrain and the possible ways to correlate present and past.

8. For general presentations on Umbandista cosmology, see Ortiz (1978), Brumana and Martinez (1991), and Negrão (1996).

9. On Spiritism's Brazilian history, see Aubrée and Laplantine (1990), Giumbelli (1997), and Lewgoy (2004).

10. On Umbandista evolutionism, see Isaia (1999).

11. Alongside pretos-velhos, caboclos, and exus, another genre of entities that occupy a structural place in Umbanda are the crianças (children). Their invocation and recognition can be understood as praising immaturity.

12. These accounts can be found in books such as those by Oliveira (1985) and Cumino (2010), as well as in Umbandista Internet sites. An analysis of Zélio de Moraes's role can be found in Giumbelli (2003).

13. This image, a "psychic painting," can be seen in Cumino (2010, 343), as well as http://povodearuanda.wordpress.com/2007/06/15/historia-da-encarnacao-no-brasil-do-caboclo-das-sete-encruzilhadas/.

14. See http://mafuadohpa.blogspot.com/2007_11_01_archive.html.

15. See Giumbelli (2003). Leal de Souza's newspaper article, which was written in 1924, is transcribed in Cumino (2010, 338–42).

16. This account can be found in various Umbandistas websites; one example is the following: http://povodearuanda.wordpress.com/2007/06/15/historia-da-encarnacao-no-brasil-do-caboclo-das-sete-encruzilhadas/.

17. Ibid.

18. Francisco Cândido Xavier lived between 1910 and 2002. He published more than four hundred psychographic books, consolidating the approximation between Spiritism and Catholicism in Brazil. He became well known for his psychic and philanthropic activities. For further details, see Lewgoy (2004).

19. For Umbandista presentations about Malagrida, see the following Internet sites: http://uumbandaparatodos.blogspot.com/2008/04/quem-foi-o-caboclo-das-sete.html; http://karipuna.blogspot.com/2007/08/malagrida-virou-sete-encruzilhadas-no.html; and http://www.casabrancadeoxala.org/historiadaumbanda/zelio demoraes.html.

20. On the relation between the Jesuits and the diffusion of devotion to the Sacred Heart in Brazil in the eighteenth century, see Mott (1993).

21. I take the opportunity to thank the following people for their help in this respect: Pedro Miranda, president of the União Espiritista de Umbanda do Brasil (Brazilian Umbanda Spiritist Union, heir to the first Umbanda federation and which continues to identify the Caboclo das Sete Encruzilhadas as its *patrono*, or

patron), with whom I spoke in June 2010; Etiene Sales, Umbandista intellectual, to whom I owe certain clues; Glória Said, for her assistance; and José Henrique Motta de Oliveira, Umbandista historian, who provided me with access to certain sources.

22. The Tenda Espírita Nossa Senhora da Piedade moved from São Gonçalo to Rio de Janeiro and, later, to a city in the interior of the state, where Zélio de Moraes had already installed the Cabana de Pai Antônio. The direction of his work passed to his daughters and then to one of his granddaughters. Little is known about Zélio de Moraes's life, perhaps because of this early move to the interior, but while he lived in São Gonçalo and Rio de Janeiro, he was the owner of a pharmacy and a local councillor for two mandates (1924–1929).

23. Cf. account on Umbandista website: http://www.recantodasletras.com.br /biografias/2937302.

24. Cf. account on Umbandista website: http://www.casadopaibenedito.com .br/historia.html.

Chapter Ten

Acknowledgments: The development of my thinking was facilitated by giving two keynote lectures on magical consciousness to the Danish Ethnographic Society/Anthropologist Society annual meeting, University of Copenhagen, Denmark, in November 2007, and to the NORDIC Network for Amerindian Studies "Rethinking Shamanism: Perceptions of Body and Soul in Multidimensional Environments" research seminar, Kastrup, Denmark, on May 27, 2010. I would like to thank Lise Paulsen Galal and Maruska Mosegaard, and Hanne Veber, respectively. Appreciation is also due to Sophia Wellbeloved for the opportunity to present "Threads of the Spiders Web: New Patterns for Exploring Magic and Science" to the the Cambridge Centre for Western Esotericism "Legitimate Forms of Knowledge?" research seminar, Girton College, Cambridge University, on May 14, 2010. I would also like to thank Brian Bates and Liz Archer for invaluable discussions.

1. See also Edith Turner's *The Spirit and the Drum* (1987), *Experiencing Ritual: A New Interpretation of African Healing* (1992), and *Among the Healers: Stories of Ritual and Spiritual Healing around the World* (2005).

2. I started my fieldwork on British practitioners of magic, focusing on issues of identity, gender, and morality, in the 1990s, and my PhD was published as *Magic, Witchcraft and the Otherworld* (2000), later followed by more research on magicians' attitudes to nature published as *The Nature of Magic* (2005).

3. See in particular Schroll and Greenwood (2011, 49–60).

4. The concept of participation has been devalued in much past anthropological writing, being labeled as mystifying and opposed to classificatory thinking. However, more recent work has sought to go beyond opposition and see both

classification and participation as operating like "maps, diagrams or schemas" for social actions and manipulations, both working as "supporting bridges or trampolines for action and creation." See Goldman (2007, 118).

5. See my discussions on Bateson and Ingold in Greenwood (2005, 9–10, 89–97, 136–38, 166, 197, 116).

6. This work was written up in Greenwood (2005).

Chapter Eleven

Acknowledgments: The earliest version of this essay was presented at a session in honor of Michel-Rolph Trouillot at the 2010 American Anthropological Association annual meeting. I would like to thank Ruy Blanes, Jean Comaroff, Paul Johnson, and Kristina Wirtz for their valuable comments and critique.

1. This is not the place to tell the little we know of that story. Let me just say here that while Kardecian Spiritism, the Yoruba-inspired regla de ocha, and the western Central African–influenced reglas de congo have long coexisted in and interacted as part and parcel of a larger Afro-Cuban religious formation in Havana, in dialectical terms, we might say that the "cajon" finally has achieved a synthesis, however ambiguous and unstable it may be. On the other hand, eastern Cuba, where regla de ocha only arrived in the 1930s, has long known such mergers between universes of discourse and practice that, at least in Havana, are still regarded as "finite," if mutually translatable, "provinces of meaning" (cf. Wirtz 2007b, this volume).

2. Different from Todd Ramon Ochoa (2010a) who goes to quite some length in setting me and my past work on such matters up as a Hegelian strawman to his Deleuzian ruminations, I am not at all troubled by a spirit/matter dichotomy when it comes to looking at disciplinary forms of Western knowledge (or even folk-Cartesian common sense) through the lens of an Afro-Cuban ritual complex. Nor are my—and I would venture to guess his—informants as immune to the infiltrations of such metaphysics into their decidedly differently structured practices as he claims them to be. While the notion of "los muertos" certainly can only be reduced to the English phrase "spirits of dead people" on the same (exceedingly problematic) grounds that Evans-Pritchard (1937) used to operationalize the Zande term *mangu* as "witchcraft," contrary to Ochoa's protestations that his informants "never" use the term *espiritú* to refer to "the dead" (in the singular or plural), I wonder if he ever heard the phrase, exceedingly common as it is in my experience, that humans possessed by such beings or entities are "presente solamente en su materia" (present only in their [bodily] matter). But this ethnographic quibble is beside the point here, anyway.

3. A disclaimer: I do not, in the following, aim to dispute Trouillot's important insight into the limits "historicity 1" poses in setting the "stage for" any possible historical narrative (his "historicity 2"). Nor am I concerned in this essay with what he calls the production of "silences" as an inevitable aspect of the complex matrix

of forces and interests operating in the creation, assembly, or narrativization of "historical facts." Given that the "materiality of the sociopolitical process" is only accessible to us in mediated form (i.e., through semiotic operations), what I am interested in are the conditions under which something like "historicity 1" becomes both thinkable and good to think.

4. Here and in the following, my use of the term *semiotic ideology* is indebted to Webb Keane (e.g., 2003b, 2005, 2007) as well as Bauman and Briggs (2003).

5. Though its gothic appearance ought not to be taken as a clue to its erection in the high Middle Ages—that, we might say, is planted evidence.

6. At least on the uniformitarian anthropological grounds of what our own disciplinary forebears established as the "psychic unity" of mankind and the essential and universal, rather than incidental and particular, coevalness of what motivates and shapes instances of human action (i.e., intent and volition as refracted by different and plural cultures). For a classical statement by a historian well-read in the anthropological literature of his day, see Bernheim (1908, 190–97).

7. "History," says Lévi-Strauss (1966, 231), "does not account for the present, but it makes a selection between its elements, according only some of them the privilege of having a past."

8. For perspectives that root some of these developments in a far earlier "historical revolt" unwittingly unleashed by humanist scholarship, see Pocock (1962), Fasolt (2004), or Woolard (2004).

9. Not incidentally Mannheim so argued at the tail end of the so-called "crisis of historicism" in German intellectual life—when the implications of Nietzsche's "genealogical" turning history onto itself had sunk in to a degree where the historicizatiation of "ultimate values" was feared to result in rampant moral relativism. A descent into shocking moral chaos, indeed, was to occur less than a decade after Mannheim's writing. But qualifying Fascism as driven by a historicist ideology is surely to grossly misrepresent both phenomena.

10. After all, ever since Edmund Burke's strictures against the novelties of the French Revolution, it has been a hallmark of Western political conservatism to try and relegate despised "innovation" to a past that true adherents to "tradition" will have to strive to supersede. Like Burke, contemporary conservatives are wedded to historicism—if only because they need to project the past into a future that progressives are always in the process of colonizing for themselves.

11. See Domanska (2006), Cashell (2007), and Bevernage (2008) for statements of these issues.

12. Surely, what goes on in a hadron collider is hardly linear time, nor a clear-cut succession of pasts and presents independent of an observer's situated vantage point. Cf. Adam (1990), Greenhouse (1996), Chakrabarty (2000, 74–75).

13. See Baumann and Briggs (2003) for similar arguments in the constitution of "language" and "languages," and Feierman (1993) for the case of "historical synthesis."

14. Cf. Post (1852) for examples. The secondary literature on their posthumous

exploits is large and rapidly growing. See for example Palfreman (1979), Sollors (1983), Cox (2003), Porter (2005), or Vasconcelos (2008). Sword (1999) and Babb (2005) give vivid accounts of the classificatory travails ensuing when standard bibliographic cataloging practices confront posthumous authorial activities. A particularly apposite case, occasionally cited to this day, occurred in 1923 when the Chancery Division of Britain's High Court of Justice heard *Cummins v. Bond* where a medium sought injunction against a "sitter" (attendant of a séance) aiming to publish an automatically written manuscript authored by a spirit named Cleophas. To the court's dismay, the medium as well as the aspiring publisher expressly denied wanting to be awarded copyright of the text (Lee 1926).

15. "Ver para creer"—seeing is believing—the saying goes. And it is often invoked in ritual contexts. Yet although it doesn't quite work like that (Wirtz 2007b, this volume; Holbraad 2008), one cannot help but notice the parallelism between the realm of hearsay and direct eye-witness testimony in North Atlantic courtrooms (Loftus 1979; Cousins 1989; Philips 1993), or the strange career of photography (as opposed to, for example, painting) as legal evidence (Mnookin 1998).

16. In yet another analytical inflection, Tata Francisco and Ño Carlos might even be written into stories about "embodied memory" that merely repeats the symbolically coded symptomatology of an originary trauma beyond conscious recall and rational resolution.

17. But see Johnson (2011) who, in a brilliant move, traces key components of this ideological configuration to Hobbes's considerations of contractual authorship, "personation," and "Suretyes"—that is, the legal ability to assume debt—in long-distance trade. Though my concern with individuated personhood, will, and agency clearly parallels Johnson's, his analytical goals are rather different from mine.

18. ". . . nobody, could he be sure that the soul of Heliogabalus were in one of his hogs, would yet say that that hog were a man or Heliogabalus" (Locke 1964, 210).

19. Surely, "the same successive body, not shifted all at once must, as well as the same immaterial spirit, go into the making of the same man" (ibid., 211).

20. "Human laws punish both [drunks and sleep-walkers], with a justice suitable to their way of knowledge [i.e., incapable of judging states of interiority], because in these cases, they cannot distinguish certainly what is real, what is counterfeit; and so the ignorance in drunkenness or sleep is not admitted as a plea" (ibid., 217).

21. Perhaps not surprisingly, this is the necessary flipside of Locke's (1963) theory of property in the *Second Treatise of Government*. If proprietorship in one's person is the basis for the rightful creation of further property by applying one's embodied capacities to nature, then the self that appropriates his or her actions in the creation of wealth must equally appropriate—own up to—the liabilities that arise from them.

22. ". . . the apostle tells us that, at the great day, when everyone shall *receive according to his doings, the secrets of all hearts shall be laid open.* The sentence shall be justified by the consciousness all persons shall have that *they themselves*, in

what bodies soever they appear, or what substances soever that consciousness adheres to, are the *same* that committed those actions, and deserve that punishment for them." (Locke 1964, 220, emphasis in the original). Compare Mark Cousins's (1989, 135) elaboration on the notion of "historical judgment": "Routine historical scholarship and the most fantastic philosophies of history can easily slip into a common condition, a privilege accorded to historicity as the one and only proper court for the enactment of a truthful discourse on what has existed. History and truth merge at the point where interrogation and judgment produce a verdict." This, Cousins (ibid.) says is "a fantasy that" much like the idea of the Last Judgment "cancels all other claims so that the concept and referent of history may be joined according to the due processes of law."

23. Writing less than a generation after British emancipation, and on the eve of the American Civil War, Maine (1963, 164), of course, saw these "apparent exceptions" as "exceptions of that stamp which illustrate the rule"—never mind the encumbrances, legal and other, that were placed on the exercise of such will on the part of the freed people in the aftermath of emancipation.

24. See Johnson (2011) for a sophisticated exploration along such lines. Cf. the now-classic statements by Macpherson (1962), Dumont (1971), Sahlins (1976), and Hirschman (1977). Mauss (1985) remains the distinguished predecessor of anthropological theories of personhood—which he, not incidentally, traces from non-Western masking traditions and Greco-Roman theater. In regard to legal history, Haskell (1998) usefully focuses on the nexus between theories of the market, the rise of contractual law since the end of the eighteenth century, and the ambiguities of nineteenth-century theories of the will, while Sayre (1932) remains a good sketch of the transformations of the intimately related concept of the mens rea in criminal law.

25. Legal categories such as duress, undue influence, diminished responsibility, temporary insanity, or possibly even recklessness (volition without intentionality) come to mind here. Barr (2006) provides intriguing insight into the ways in which the rise of the category of legal insanity in late eighteenth-century British law undermined and ultimately destroyed the political potential of "inspired prophecy."

26. Oftentimes with highly paradoxical results: compare Seidman's (1965, 1966) vigorous denunciation of the application of the normative standards of "reasonable man" in British Common Law in African legal systems in the immediate aftermath of decolonization. Seidman, it should be noted, is not concerned with relativizing North Atlantic universals (which he rightly sees as grounded in particular historical experiences but nonetheless views as superior to other possible standards, in this case of juridical nature). What he decries are the glaring contradictions produced by extending the scope of the "reasonability" of the "man on the Clapham Omnibus" to members of African communities. Citing a classic British legal textbook on the notion that "retribution in punishment is an expression of the community's disapproval of crime," he asks, "Which society is expressing its disapproval of crime

when a British judge sentences the male population of a Kenya village to death" for having killed an alleged witch? (Seidman 1965, 48n14).

27. Citing a surprisingly Humean formulation by the protestant theologian Rudolf Bultmann concerning the undecidability, for the historian, of divine intervention in history, Chakrabarty (2000, 105) sees "anthropologizing" ostensibly irrational "belief" as the discipline of history's logical default position. Though he is probably right as far as history is concerned, from the anthropologist's perspective one can only say, "Wish it were that simple!"

28. Surely, the being instigating the revolt in the Santal's view can only be called such from a perspective external to theirs. For a stringent analysis of the problems with such predications in regard to the historiography of "popular belief" in early modern France, see Clark (1983).

29. "When we act," asks Latour (2005, 43), "who else is acting? How many agents are also present? How come I never do what I want? Why are we all held by forces that are not of our making? Such is the oldest and most legitimate intuition of those sciences, that which has fascinated since the time when crowds, masses, statistical means, invisible hands, and unconscious drives began to replace the passions and reasons, not to mention the angels and demons that had pushed and pulled our humble souls up to then." Cf. Buccafusco (2008) on the distinct threat that Spriritism appeared to pose to late nineteenth-century legal theories of "will" (before similar such threats eventually became channeled into psychoanalysis on the one hand and forensic psychiatry on the other). See also the editors' strictures against a critique of "bourgeois individuality," as exemplified by Bourdieu (1986) and Comaroff and Comaroff (1992), that rails against the assumption of the temporally or sociologically coherent self but leaves its (humanistic) core essentially intact (Espírito Santo and Blanes, this volume).

30. "Why is history a compulsory part of education of the modern person in all countries today, including those that did quite comfortably without it until as late as the eighteenth century" (Chakrabarty 2000, 41)—which, of course, would include most European countries as well.

31. See, for example, Shaw (2002), Argenti (2007), or Routon (2008).

32. Though Marshall Sahlins (1985, 2004) has come close to such an argument.

33. This, one might argue with Giumbelli (this volume), is a question that can turn historicism back on its own products by engendering convergences between marginal (but historically documented) Jesuits, fictional (but entirely plausible) Amerindian chiefs, and the biography of their twentieth-century medium upon whose death the entity composed of such heterogeneous "flows" "passed on to" a higher plane of existence. Will Abraham Lincoln pass on to such a "plane of existence" once historians and their (so far) ceaselessly biography-buying American public tire of yet more historiographic output on his life and national significance? A good Durkheimian answer would surely be yes.

34. For the former, see Bloor (1991), and see Latour (1993b) for the latter.

Cf. Bloor (1999) for a polemic differentiating the "strong program" from Latourean "symmetrical anthropology."

35. For a vivid example, see Wirtz (this volume). In line with Ochoa's (2010b) conception of the anomymous "ambient" (rather than "responsive") dead in Palo Monte, we might say mediums and their entities personalize themselves in relation to each other in a manner not all that different from historians who assert their own historical agency by carving out increasingly coherent historical individualities from a sea of phenomenologically given data that are always potentially construable as indices of an otherwise undifferentiated, "ambient" past—the untold "history" in which subscribers to a historicist ontology swim like fish in an ocean constituted by the past agency of both the living and the dead.

36. Much more could be said here about how spirit communications and the interactions between the dead and the living may attain forms of significance that are, in themselves of historical import: such as when people begin to reorient their lives in light of counsel received from the dead; when mediums learn about new aspects of their spirits' past lives and dispositions (which may change) through dreams or oracular means; or when they are belatedly apprised of what their spirits uttered while they were possessed by them. For sophisticated treatments of such issues, see Lambek (2002, 2003) and Price (2008).

References

Adam, Barbara. 1990. *Time and Social Theory*. Philadelphia, PA: Temple University Press.

Ahearn, Laura M. 2001. "Language and Agency." *Annual Review of Anthropology* 30:109–37.

Anderson, Allan. 2001. "Types and Butterflies: African Initiated Churches and European Typologies." *International Bulletin of Missionary Research* 25 (3): 107–13.

———. 2004. *An Introduction to Pentecostalism: Global Charismatic Christianity*. Cambridge: Cambridge University Press.

Antze, Paul, and Michael Lambek, eds. 1996. *Tense Past: Cultural Essays in Trauma and Memory*. London: Routledge.

Appadurai, Arjun, ed. 1986. *The Social Life of Things: Commodities in Cultural Perspective*. Cambridge: Cambridge University Press.

———. 1998. *Modernity at Large: Cultural Dimensions of Globalization*. Princeton, NJ: Princeton University Press.

Ardener, Edwin. 1989. *The Voice of Prophecy*. Oxford: Blackwell.

Arenz, Karl-Heinz. 2010. *De l'Alzette à l'Amazone: Jean-Philippe Bettendorff et les jésuites en Amazonie portugaise, 1661–1693*. Paris: Editions Universitaires Europeennes.

Argenti, Nicholas. 2007. *The Intestines of the State: Youth, Violence, and Belated Histories in the Cameroon Grassfields*. Chicago: University of Chicago Press.

Argüelles Mederos, Anibal, and Ileana Hodge Limonta. 1991. *Los llamados cultos sincreticos y el espiritismo*. Havana, Cuba: Editorial Academia.

Argyrou, Vassos. 2002. *Anthropology and the Will to Meaning: A Postcolonial Critique*. London: Pluto Press.

Århem, Kaj. 1993. "Ecosofía makuna." In *La selva humanizada: Ecología alternativa en el trópico húmedo colombiano*, edited by François Correa, 109–26. Bogotá, Colombia: Instituto Colombiano de Antropología.

Asad, Talal. 1993. *Genealogies of Religion: Discipline and Reasons of Power in Christianity and Islam*. Baltimore, MD: Johns Hopkins University Press.

Aubin, Françoise. 1975. "Le statut de l'Enfant dans la Société Mongole." *Recueils de la Société Jean Bodin* 35:459–599.

Aubrée, Marion, and François Laplantine. 1990. *Le Livre, la table et les esprits: Naissance, évolution et atualité du mouvement social spirite entre France et Brésil.* Paris: J. C. Lattès.

Ayorinde, Christine. 2004. *Afro-Cuban Religiosity, Revolution, and National Identity.* Gainesville: University Press of Florida.

Babb, Nancy M. 2005. "Cataloging Spirits and the Spirit of Cataloging." *Cataloging and Classification Quarterly* 40:89–122.

Baca, George, Aisha Khan, and Stephan Palmié, eds. 2010. *Empirical Futures: Anthropologists and Historians Engage the Work of Sidney W. Mintz.* Chapel Hill: University of North Carolina Press.

Bakhtin, Mikhail. 1981. *The Dialogic Imagination.* Edited by Michael Holquist. Translated by Caryl Emerson and Michael Holquist. Austin: University of Texas Press.

Balducci, María Isabel. 1982. "Códigos de comunicación con el mundo animal entre los Toba-Taksik." PhD diss., Facultad de Filosofía y Letras, Universidad de Buenos Aires, Buenos Aires.

Balmori, Clemente Hernando. 1957. "Notas de un viaje a los tobas." *Revista de la Universidad* 2:23–36.

Barnet, Miguel. 1995. *Cultos Afrocubanos: La Regla de Ocha, La Regla de Palo Monte.* Havana, Cuba: Artex y Ediciones Union.

Barr, Mark L. 2006. "Prophecy, the Law of Insanity, and *The [First] Book of Urizen.*" *Studies in English Literature* 46:739–62.

Barrett, Justin. 2004. *Why Would Anyone Believe in God?* Lanham, MD: AltaMira Press.

Basso, Keith H. 1996. *Wisdom Sits in Places: Landscape and Language among the Western Apache.* Albuquerque: University of New Mexico Press.

Bastide, Roger. 1971. *As Religiões Africanas no Brasil.* São Paulo, Brazil: Livraria Pioneira Editora/EDUSP.

———. 2006 "O Sagrado Selvagem." In *O Sagrado Selvagem e Outros Ensaios,* 250–75. São Paulo, Brazil: Companhia das Letras.

———. 2007. *The African Religions of Brazil: Toward a Sociology of the Interpenetration of Civilization.* Translated by Helen Sebba. Baltimore, MD: Johns Hopkins University Press.

Bataille, Georges. 1987. *O Erotismo.* Porto Alegre, Brazil: L&PM.

Bates, Henry Walter. 1863. *The Naturalist on the River Amazons.* 2 vols. London: Murray.

Bateson, Gregory. 1985. *Mind and Nature: A Necessary Unity.* New York: Bantam.

———. 1991. *A Sacred Unity: Further Steps to an Ecology of Mind.* London: Harper-Collins.

———. 2000. *Steps to an Ecology of Mind.* Chicago: University of Chicago Press.

Bateson, Gregory, and Mary Catherine Bateson. (1987) 2005. *Angels Fear: Towards an Epistemology of the Sacred*. New York: Hampton Press.

Battaglia, Debbora. 1995. *Rhetorics of Self-Making*. Berkeley: University of California Press.

Bauman, Richard. 1977. *Verbal Art as Performance*. Prospect Heights, IL: Waveland.

———. 1986. *Story, Performance, and Event*. Cambridge: Cambridge University Press.

Bauman, Richard, and Charles L. Briggs. 1990. "Poetics and Performance as Critical Perspectives on Language and Social Life." *Annual Review of Anthropology* 19:59–88.

———. 2003. *Voices of Modernity: Language Ideologies and the Politics of Inequality*. Cambridge: Cambridge University Press.

Bawden, C. R. 1968. *The Modern History of Mongolia*. London: Kegan Paul International.

Bear, Laura. 2007. *Lines of the Nation: Indian Railway Workers, Bureaucracy, and the Intimate Historical Self*. New York: Columbia University Press.

Benjamin, Walter. 1968. "The Storyteller." In *Illuminations*, edited by Hannah Arendt, 83–109. New York: Schoken Books.

Bernheim, Ernst. 1908. *Lehrbuch der historischen Methode und der Geschichtsphilosophie*. Leipzig, Ger.: Dunker und Humblot.

Bettendorff, João Felipe. 1990. *Crônica dos Padres da Companhia de Jesus no Estado do Maranhão*. Belém, Brazil: Cejup.

Beverage, Berber. 2008. "Time, Presence, and Historical Injustice." *History and Theory* 47:149–67.

Bhabha, Homi. 1990. "DissemiNation: Time, Narrative and the Margins of the Modern Nation." In *Nation and Narration*, edited by Homi Bhabba, 139–70. New York: Routledge.

Bille, Mikkel, Frida Hastrup, and Tim Flohr Sørensen, eds. 2010. *An Anthropology of Absence: Materializations of Transcendence and Loss*. New York: Springer.

Birnbaum, Michael. 2010. "Historians Speak Out against Proposed Texas Textbook Changes." *Washington Post*, March 18.

Blanes, Ruy L. 2011. "Unstable Biographies: The Ethnography of Memory and Historicity in an Angolan Prophetic Movement." *History and Anthropology* 22 (1): 93–119.

Bloch, Marc. 1953. *The Historian's Craft: Reflections on the Nature and Uses of History and the Techniques and Methods of Those Who Use It*. New York: Vintage Books.

Bloor, David. 1991. *Knowledge and Social Imagery*. London: Routledge.

———. 1999. "Anti-Latour." *Studies in the History and Philosophy of Science* 30:81–112.

Boddy, Janice. 1989. *Wombs and Alien Spirits: Women, Men and the Zār Cult in Northern Sudan*. Madison: University of Wisconsin Press.

———. 1994. "Spirit Possession Revisited: Beyond Instrumentality." *Annual Review of Anthropology* 23:407–34.

Bonilla, Oiara. 2005. "O Bom Patrão e o Inimigo Voraz: Predação e comércio na cosmologia Paumari." *Mana* 11 (1): 41–66.

Bourdieu, Pierre. 1986. "L'illusion biographique." *Actes de la recherche en sciences sociales* 62 (1): 69–72.

Bourguignon, Erika. 1976. *Possession*. Chandler & Sharp Series in Cross-Cultural Themes. San Francisco, CA: Chandler & Sharp Publishers.

Boyer, Pascal. 1994. *The Naturalness of Religious Ideas: A Cognitive Theory of Religion*. Berkeley: University of California Press.

Boyer, Véronique. 1996. "Le don et l'initiation." *L'Homme* 138:7–24.

———. 1999. "O pajé e o caboclo: De homem a entidade." *Mana* 5 (1): 29–56.

Brandon, George. 1993. *Santería from Africa to the New World: The Dead Sell Memories*. Bloomington: Indiana University Press.

Braunstein, José. 1983. "Algunos rasgos de la organización social de los indígenas del Gran Chaco." *Trabajos de Etnología* 2:9–102.

———. 1993. "Territorio e historia de los narradores matacos." *Hacia una nueva carta étnica del Gran Chaco* 5:5–74.

Briggs, Charles. 1988. *Competence in Performance: The Creativity of Tradition in Mexicano Verbal Art*. Philadelphia: University of Pennsylvania Press.

Brown, David H. 2003. *Santería Enthroned: Art, Ritual, and Innovation in an Afro-Cuban Religion*. Chicago: University of Chicago Press.

Brown, Diana DeGroats. 1986. *Umbanda: Religion and Politics in Urban Brazil*. Ann Arbor, MI: UMI Research Press.

Brown, John S., and Paul Duguid. 2002. *The Social Life of Information*. Cambridge, MA: Harvard Business School Publishing.

Brown, Michael F. 1997. *The Channeling Zone: American Spirituality in an Anxious Age*. Cambrige, MA: Harvard University Press.

Brumana, Fernando G., and Elda G. Martinez. 1991. *Marginalia Sagrada*. São Paulo, Brazil: Editora da UNICAMP. English version published 1989. Fernando G. Brumana and Elda G. Martinez, *Spirits from the Margin: A Study in Popular Religion and Social Experience*. Uppsala, Sweden: Acta Universitatis Upsaliensis.

Bubandt, Nils. 2009. "Interview with an Ancestor: Spirits as Informants and the Politics of Possession in North Maluku." *Ethnography* 10 (3): 291–316.

Buccafusco, Christopher. 2008. "Spiritualism and Will(s) in the Age of Contract." University of Illinois College of Law and Economics Working Papers 91. http://law.bepress.com/uiuclwps/papers/art91.

Buckwalter, Alberto. 2001. *Vocabulario Toba*. Formosa: Equipo Menonita.

Butler, Judith. 1996. "Performativity's Social Magic." In *The Social and Political Body*, edited by Theodore R. Schatzki and Wolfgang Natter, 29–47. New York: Guilford Press.

Cabral, João de Pina. 1987. "Paved Roads and Enchanted Mooresses." *Man* 22: 715–35.

————. 2013. "The Two Faces of Mutuality: Contemporary Themes in Anthropology." *Anthropological Quarterly*.

Caillois, Roger, 2004. *El Hombre y lo Sagrado*. México: Fondo de Cultura Económica.

Câmara Cascudo, L. Da. 2002. *Geografia dos Mitos Brasileiros*. São Paulo, Brazil: Global.

Campbell, Alan. 1990. *To Square with Genesis: Causal Statements and Shamanic Ideas in Wayapi*. Edinburgh, UK: Polygon.

Cannell, Fenella. 2006. "Introduction: The Anthropology of Christianity." In *The Anthropology of Christianity*, edited by Fenella Cannell, 1–50. Durham, NC: Duke University Press.

Capone, S. 2010. *Searching for Africa in Brazil: Power and Tradition in Candomblé*. Durham, NC: Duke University Press.

Cardoso, Vânia Z. 2004. "Working with Spirits: Enigmatic Signs of Black Sociality." PhD diss., University of Texas.

————. 2007. "Narrar o mundo: Estórias do 'povo da rua' e a narração do imprevisível." *Mana* 13 (2): 317–46.

Carter, Donald Martin. 2010. *Navigating the African Diaspora: The Anthropology of Invisibility*. Minneapolis: University of Minnesota Press.

Cashell, Kieran. 2007. "Ex Post Facto: Peirce and the Living Signs of the Dead." *Transaction of the Charles S. Peirce Society* 43:345–71.

Castellanos, Isabel. 1990. "Grammatical Structure, Historical Development, and Religious Usage of Afro Cuban Bozal Speech." *Folklore Forum* 23 (1/2): 57–84.

Censabella, Marisa. 2009. "Denominaciones etnonímicas y toponímicas tobas: Introducción a la problemática y análisis lingüístico." *Hacia una nueva carta étnica del Gran Chaco* 8: 213–36.

Chakrabarty, Dipesh. 2000. *Provincializing Europe*. Princeton, NJ: Princeton University Press.

Chaumeil, Jean-Pierre. 1983. *Voir, savoir et pouvoir: Le chamanisme chez les Yagua du Nord-est péruvien*. Paris: Éditions de l'École des Hautes Études en Sciences Sociales.

Clark, Juan. 1986. *Religious Repression in Cuba*. Miami, FL: Institute of Interamerican Studies (University of Miami).

Clark, Stuart. 1983. "French Historians and Early Modern Popular Culture." *Past and Present* 100:62–99.

Cleary, David. 2001. "Towards an Environmental History of the Amazon: From Prehistory to the Nineteenth Century." *Latin American Research Review* 36: 65–96.

Clifford, James. 1994. "Diasporas." *Cultural Anthropology* 9 (3): 302–38.

————. 1997. *Routes: Travel and Translation in the Late Twentieth Century*. Cambridge, MA: Harvard University Press.

Clifford, James, and George Marcus. 1986. *Writing Culture: The Poetics and Politics of Ethnography*. Berkeley: University of California Press.

Cohen, Emma. 2007. *The Mind Possessed: The Cognition of Spirit Possession in an Afro-Brazilian Religious Tradition*. Oxford: Oxford University Press.

Cole, Jennifer. 2001. *Forget Colonialism? Sacrifice and the Art of Memory in Madagascar*. Berkeley: University of California Press.

Coleman, Simon. 2004. "The Charismatic Gift." *Journal of the Royal Anthropological Institute* 10 (2): 421–42.

———. 2006. "Materializing the Self: Words and Gifts in the Construction of Charismatic Protestant Identity." In *The Anthropology of Christianity*, edited by Fenella Cannell, 163–184. Durham, NC: Duke University Press.

Collingwood, R. G. (1946) 1994. *The Idea of History*. Oxford: Oxford University Press.

Colson, Elizabeth. 1955. "Ancestral Spirits and Social Structure among the Plateau Tonga." *International Archives of Ethnography* 47 (1): 21–68.

———. 1960. *The Social Organisation of the Gwembe Tonga*. Manchester, UK: Manchester University Press.

———. 1969. "Spirit Possession among the Tonga of Zambia." In *Spirit Mediumship and Society in Africa*, edited by John Beattie and John Middleton, 69–103. London: Routledge & Kegan Paul.

———. 1971. *The Social Consequences of Resettlement*. Manchester, UK: Manchester University Press.

Comaroff, Jean. 1985. *Body of Power, Spirit of Resistance: The Culture and History of a South African People*. Chicago: University of Chicago Press.

Comaroff, Jean, and John Comaroff. 1992. *Ethnography and the Historical Imagination*. Boulder, CO: Westview Press.

Concone, Maria Helena Vilas Boas. 1987. *Umbanda, uma religião brasileira*. São Paulo, Brazil: USP/CER.

Contins, Márcia. 1983. "O Caso da Pomba-Gira: Reflexões sobre crime, possessão e imagem feminina." Master's thesis, Universidade Federal do Rio de Janeiro.

Contins, Márcia, and Márcio Goldman. 1985. " 'O caso da Pomba-gira': Religião e Violência, uma análise do jogo discursivo entre Umbanda e Sociedade." *Religião e Sociedade* 11 (1): 103–32.

Cordeu, Edgardo. 1969–1970. "Aproximación al horizonte mítico de los Tobas." *Runa* 12 (1–2): 67–176.

Cordeu, Edgardo, and Miguel de los Ríos. 1982. "Un enfoque estructural de las variaciones socioculturales de los Cazadores-Recolectores del Gran Chaco." *Suplemento Antropológico* 17 (1): 131–95.

Corten, André, and Ruth Marshall-Fratani, eds. 2001. *Between Babel and Pentecost: Transnational Pentecostalism in Latin America and Africa*. Bloomington: Indiana University Press.

Cousins, Mark. 1989. "The Practice of Historical Investigation." In *Poststructuralism and the Question of History*, edited by Derek Atteridge, Geoff Bennington, and Robert Young. Cambridge: Cambridge University Press.

Cox, Harvey 1996. *Fire from Heaven: The Rise of Pentecostal Spirituality and the Reshaping of Religion in the Twenty-first Century*. London: Cassell.

Cox, Robert S. 2003. "Vox Populi: Spiritualism and George Washington's Postmortem Career." *Early American Studies* 1:230–72.

Crapanzano, Vincent, and Vivian Garrison. 1977. *Case Studies in Spirit Possession*. New York: John Wiley & Sons.

Cravalho, Mark. 1993. "An Invisible Universe of Evil: Supernatural Malevolence and Personal Experience among Amazonian Peasants." PhD diss., University of California, San Diego.

Csordas, Thomas. 1990. "Embodiment as a Paradigm for Anthropology." *Ethos* 18 (1): 5–47.

———. 1994. *Embodiment and Experience: The Existential Ground of Culture and Self*. Cambridge: Cambridge University Press.

Cumino, Alexandre. 2010. *História da Umbanda: Uma religião brasileira*. São Paulo, Brazil: Madras.

Cunha, Antônio Geraldo da. 1999. *Dicionário Histórico das Palavras Portuguesas de Origem Tupi*. São Paulo, Brazil: Melhoramentos.

Cunha, Euclides da. 2006. *The Amazon: Land without History*. Translated by Ronald Sousa. Oxford: Oxford University Press.

Dalby, Richard. 1988. *The Virago Book of Ghost Stories*. London: Virago Books.

Damásio, António. 2001. "Some Notes on Brain, Imagination and Creativity." In *The Origins of Creativity*, edited by Karl Pfenninger and Valerie Shubik. Oxford: Oxford University Press.

Daneel, M. L. 1971. *Old and New in Southern Shona Independent Churches*. Vol. I. The Hague, Neth.: Mouton Publishers.

Daniel, João. 2003. *O Tesouro Descoberto no Máximo Rio Amazonas*. 2 vols. Rio de Janeiro, Brazil: Editora Contrapunto.

Danto, Arthur. 1964. *Analytical Philosophy of History*. Cambridge: Cambridge University Press.

Daston, Lorraine, ed. 2000. *Biographies of Scientific Objects*. Chicago: University of Chicago Press.

De Graff, M., ed. 1999. *Language Creation and Language Change: Creolization, Diachrony, and Development*. Cambridge, MA: MIT Press.

de la Fuente, Alejandro. 1998. "Raza, desigualdad y prejuicio en Cuba." *América Negra* 15:21–39.

———. 2001. *A Nation for All: Race, Inequality, and Politics in Twentieth-Century Cuba*. Chapel Hill: University of North Carolina Press.

Delaplace, Grégory. 2009a. *L'Invention des morts: Sépultures, fantômes et photographie en Mongolie contemporaine*. Paris: EMSCAT (Nord-Asie 1).

———. 2009b. "A Sheep Herder's Rage: Silence and Grief in Contemporary Mongolia." *Ethnos* 74 (4): 514–34.

———. 2010. "Chinese Ghosts in Mongolia." *Inner Asia* 12 (1): 111–38.

————. 2011. "Le cheval magnétomètre: Dressage et 'choses invisibles' en Mongolie contemporaine." In *Mélanges en l'honneur de Françoise Aubin*, edited by D. Aigle, I. Charleux, V. Gossaert, and R. Hamayon, 121–39. Sankt Augustin, Ger.: Institut Monumenta Serica.

Delaplace, Grégory, and Rebecca Empson. 2007. "The Little Human and the Daughter-in-Law: Invisibles as Seen through the Eyes of Different Kinds of People." *Inner Asia* 9 (2): 197–214.

Déléage, Pierre. 2007. "Trois points de vue sur les revenants Sharanahua." *L'Homme* 183:117–46.

Dempster, Murray, Byron Klaus, and Douglas Peterson. 1999. *The Globalization of Pentecostalism: A Religion Made to Travel.* Oxford: Regnum.

Derrida, Jacques. 1994. *Specters of Marx.* New York: Routledge.

Descola, Philippe. 1986. *La nature domestique: Symbolisme et praxis dans l'écologie des Achuar.* Paris: Maison des Sciences de l'Homme.

————. (1986) 1996. *In the Society of Nature: A Native Ecology in Amazonia.* Cambridge: Cambridge University Press.

————. 1992. "Societies of Nature and the Nature of Society." In *Conceptualizing Society*, edited by Adam Kuper, 107–26. London: Routledge.

————. 2005. *Par-delà nature et culture.* Paris: Gallimard.

de Vienne, Emmanuel. 2010. "Traditions en souffrance: Maladie, chamanisme et rituel chez les Trumai du Haut-Xingu, Mato Grosso." PhD diss., Ecole des Hautes Etudes en Sciences Sociales, Paris.

Devisch, René. 1985. "Perspectives on Divination in Contemporary Sub-Saharan Africa." In *Theoretical Explorations in African Religions*, edited by Wim van Binsbergen and Matthew Schoffeleers, 50–83. London: Routledge and Kegan Paul.

De Visser, Marinus Willem. (1913) 2008. *The Dragon in China and Japan.* New York: Cosimo.

Dixon, R. M. W. 1994. *Ergativity.* New York: Cambridge University Press.

Domanska, Ewa. 2006. "The Material Presence of the Past." *History and Theory* 45:337–48.

Douglas, Mary. 1979. "Passive Voice Theories in Religious Sociology." *Review of Religious Research* 21:51–61.

————. 1980. *Evans-Pritchard.* Glasgow, UK: Fontana Paperbacks.

————. 1992. "The Person in an Enterprise Culture." In *Understanding the Enterprise Culture*, edited by Shaun Hargreaves Heap and Angus Ross, 41–62. Edinburgh, UK: Edinburgh University Press.

Droogers, André. 2001. "Globalization and Pentecostal Success." In *Between Babel and Pentecost: Transnational Pentecostalism in Africa and Latin America*, edited by André Corten and Ruth Marshall-Fratani, 41–61. Bloomington: Indiana University Press.

Du Bois, John. 2007. "The Stance Triangle." In *Stancetaking in Discourse: Subjec-

tivity, Evaluation, Interaction, edited by Robert Englebretson, 139–82. Amsterdam, Neth.: John Benjamins Publishing.

Dumont, Louis. 1971. *From Mandeville to Marx.* Chicago: University of Chicago Press.

Duranti, Alessandro. 2004. "Agency in Language." In *A Companion to Linguistic Anthropology*, 451–73. New York: Blackwell.

———. 2009. "The Relevance of Husserl's Theory to Language Socialization." *Journal of Linguistic Anthropology* 19 (2): 205–26.

Durkheim, Émile. 2000. "Definição do fenômeno religioso e da religião." In *As formas elementares da vida religiosa*, 3–32. São Paulo, Brazil: Martins Fontes.

Edgar, Ian. 2002. "Invisible Elites? Authority and the Dream." *Dreaming* 12 (2): 79–92.

Eisenlohr, Patrick. 2009. "Technologies of the Spirit: Devotional Islam, Sound Reproduction and the Dialectics of Mediation and Immediacy in Mauritius." *Anthropological Theory* 9 (3): 273–96.

Engelke, Matthew, ed. 2009. *The Objects of Evidence: Anthropological Approaches to the Production of Knowledge.* Oxford: Wiley-Blackwell.

Espírito Santo, Diana. 2009. "Making Dreams: Spirits, Vision and the Ontological Effects of Dream Knowledge in Cuban *Espiritismo.*" *Suomen Antropologi* 34 (3): 6–24.

———. 2010. "Spiritist Boundary-Work and the Morality of Materiality in Afro-Cuban Religion." *Journal of Material Culture* 15 (1): 64–82.

———. "Developing the Dead: Cosmology and Personhood in Cuban Spiritism." Unpublished manuscript.

Evans-Pritchard, Edward E. 1937. *Witchcraft, Oracles and Magic among the Azande.* Oxford: Clarendon Press.

Even, M.-D. 1999. "L'au-delà dans les représentations religieuses des Mongols." In *La Mort et l'au-delà: Une rencontre de l'Orient et de l'Occident*, edited by P. Servais, 149–196. Louvain, Belgium: Academia Bruylant.

Ewing, Katherine P. 1990. "The Dream of Spiritual Initiation and the Organization of Self Representations among Pakistani Sufis." *American Ethnologist* 17 (1): 56–74.

Fabian, Johannes. 1983. *Time and the Other: How Anthropology Makes Its Object.* Columbia: New York University Press.

Falzon, Mark-Anthony, ed. 2009. *Multi-Sited Ethnography: Theory, Praxis and Locality in Contemporary Research.* Aldershot, UK: Ashgate.

Fasolt, Constantin. 2004. *The Limits of History.* Chicago: University of Chicago Press.

———. 2005. "History as Ritual." Paper presented to the session of the International Commission on the History and Theory of Historiography at the 20th International Congress of Historical Sciences.

Fausto, Carlos. 2001. *Inimigos fiéis: História, guerra e xamanismo na Amazônia.* São Paulo, Brazil: EDUSP.

————. 2007. "Feasting on People: Eating Animals and Humans in Amazonia." *Current Anthropology* 4 (48): 497–530.

————. 2008. "Donos demais: Maestria e domínio na Amazônia." *Mana* 14 (2): 329–66.

Favret-Saada, Jeanne. 1980. *Deadly Words: Witchcraft in the Bocage.* Cambridge: Cambridge University Press.

Feierman, Steven. 1993. "African History and the Dissolution of World History." In *Africa and the Disciplines,* edited by Robert H. Bates, V. Y. Mudimbe, and Jean O'Barr, 167–212. Chicago: University of Chicago Press.

Fernández, Analía, and José Braunstein. 2001. "Historias de Pampa del Indio." Paper presented at IV Congreso Argentino de Americanistas, Buenos Aires, Argentina.

Ferrándiz, Francisco. 2006. "The Return of Civil War Ghosts: The Ethnography of Exhumations in Contemporary Spain." *Anthropology Today* 22 (3): 7–12.

————. 2010. "The Intimacy of Defeat: Exhumations in Contemporary Spain." In *Unearthing Franco's Legacy: Mass Graves and the Recuperation of Historical Memory in Spain,* edited by Carlos Jerez-Farran and Sam Amago, 304–25. South Bend, IN: University of Notre Dame Press.

Ferretti, Mundicarmo. 1992. "Repensando o Turco no Tambor de Mina." *Afro-Ásia* 15:56–70.

————. 2000. *Desceu na Guma: O caboclo do Tambor de Mina em um Terreiro de São Luís. A Casa Fanti-Ashanti.* 2nd ed. São Luís, Brazil: EDUFMA.

————. 2001. "Pureza Nagê e Nações Africanas no Tambor de Mina do Maranhão." *Revista Ciencias Sociales y Religión/Ciências Sociais e Religião* 3 (3): 75–94.

Flammarion, Camille. 1924. *Haunted Houses.* London: T. F. Unwin.

Flynn Roller, Heather. 2010. "Colonial Routes: Spatial Mobility and Community Formation in the Portuguese Amazon." PhD diss., University of Stanford.

Galvão, Eduardo. 1955. *Santos e Visagens: Um Estudo da Vida Religiosa de Itá.* São Paulo, Brazil: Editora Nacional.

García Hierro, Pedro, and Alexandre Surrallés, eds. 2004. *Tierra Adentro: Territorio indígena y percepción del entorno.* Copenhagen, Denmark: IGWIA.

Geertz, Clifford. 1973. *The Interpretation of Cultures: Selected Essays.* New York: Basic Books.

Gell, Alfred. 1998. *Art and Agency: An Anthropological Theory.* Oxford: Oxford University Press.

Gellner, Ernest. 1973. "Our Current Sense of History." In *The Historian between the Ethnologist and the Futurologist,* edited by Jerôme Dumoulin and Dominique Moisi, 3–24. Paris: Mouton.

Gille, Zsuzsa, and Seán Ó Riain. 2002. "Global Ethnography." *Annual Review of Sociology* 28:271–95.

Ginzburg, Carlo. 1983. "Clues: Morelli, Freud, and Sherlock Holmes." In *The Sign of Three*, edited by Umberto Eco and Thomas Sebeok, 81–118. Bloomington: Indiana University Press.

Giumbelli, Emerson. 1997. *O Cuidado dos Mortos: Uma história da condenação e da legitimação do espiritismo*. Rio de Janeiro, Brazil: Arquivo Nacional.

———. 2003. "Zélio de Moraes e as Origens da Umbanda no Rio de Janeiro." In *Caminhos da Alma: Memória Afro-Brasileira*, edited by Vagner Gonçalves da Silva, 183–217. São Paulo, Brazil: Summus.

———. 2010. "Presença na recusa: A África dos pioneiros umbandistas." *Revista Esboços* 17 (23). http://www.periodicos.ufsc.br/index.php/esbocos/article/view/14757.

Goffman, Erving. 1981. *Forms of Talk*. Philadelphia: University of Pennsylvania Press.

Goldman, Marcio. 1985. "A construcção ritual da pessoa: A possessão no Candomblé.' *Religião e Sociedade* 12 (1): 22–54.

———. 2005. "Formas do Saber e Modos do Ser: Observacões Sobre Multiplicidade e Ontologia no Candomblé." *Religião e Sociedade* 25 (2): 102–20.

———. 2007. "How to Learn in an Afro-Brazilian Spirit Possession Religion: Ontology and Multiplicity in Candomble." In *Learning Religion: Anthropological Approaches*, edited by David Berliner and Ramon Sarró, 103–20. New York: Berghahn Books.

———. 2009. "Histórias, devires e fetiches das religiões afro-brasileiras: Ensaio de simetrização antropológica." *Análise Social* XLIV (190): 105–37.

Gomes, Flávio dos S. 2005. *A Hidra e os Pântanos: Mocambos, Quilombos e Comunidades de Fugitivos no Brasil (séculox XVII a XIX)*. São Paulo: Ed. UNESP/Editora POLIS.

Goodwin, Marjorie H. 1990. *He-Said-She-Said: Talk as Social Organization among Black Children*. Bloomington: Indiana University Press.

Gordon, Avery. 1997. *Ghostly Matters: Haunting and the Sociological Imagination*. Minneapolis: University of Minnesota Press.

Goulet, Jean-Guy A., and Bruce Granville Miller, eds. 2007. *Extraordinary Anthropology: Transformations in the Field*. Lincoln: University of Nebraska Press.

Goulet, Jean-Guy A., and David Young, eds. 1994. *Being Changed by Cross-Cultural Encounters*. Peterborough, Canada: Broadview Press.

Gow, Peter. 1991. *Of Mixed Blood: Kinship and History in Peruvian Amazonia*. Oxford: Clarendon Press.

———. 2001. *An Amazonian Myth and Its History*. Oxford: Oxford University Press.

Greenhouse, Carol J. 1996. *A Moment's Notice: Time Politics across Cultures*. Ithaca, NY: Cornell University Press.

Greenwood, Susan. 2001. *The Encyclopedia of Magic and Witchcraft*. London: Lorenz.

———. 2005. *The Nature of Magic: An Anthropology of Consciousness*. Oxford: Berg.

————. 2009. *The Anthropology of Magic*. Oxford: Berg.

————. Forthcoming. *Magical Consciousness*.

Gumperz, John, and Stephen Levinson, eds. 1996. *Rethinking Linguistic Relativity*. Cambridge: Cambridge University Press.

Gupta, Akhil, and James Ferguson, eds. 1997. *Anthropological Locations: Boundaries and Grounds of a Field Science*. Berkeley: University of California Press.

Guyer, Jane. 2007. "Prophecy and the Near Future: Thoughts on Macroeconomic, Evangelical, and Punctuated Time." *American Ethnologist* 34 (3): 409–21.

Hale, Lindsay. 1997. "Preto Velho: Resistance, Redemption, and Engendered Representations of Slavery in a Brazilian Possession-Trance Religion." *American Ethnologist* 24 (2): 392–414.

————. 2009. *Hearing the Mermaid's Song: The Umbanda Religion in Rio de Janeiro*. Albuquerque: University of New Mexico Press.

Hallan, Elisabeth, and Tim Ingold. eds. 2007. *Creativity and Cultural Improvisation*. Oxford: Berg.

Hallowell, Irving. (1955) 1988. *Culture and Experience*. Long Grove, IL: Waveland Press.

————. 2010. "Culture and Experience." In *Psychological Anthropology: A Reader on the Self in Culture*, edited by Robert A. LeVine, 30–52. Sussex, UK: Wiley-Blackwell.

Hammond-Tooke, W. David. 1986. "The Aetiology of Spirit in Southern Africa." *African Studies* 45 (2): 157–70.

Hannerz, Ulf. 1996. *Transnational Connections: Cultures, People, Places*. London: Routledge.

————. 2003. "Being There . . . and There . . . and There! Reflections on Multi-Site Ethnography." *Ethnography* 4 (2): 201–16.

Hansing, Katrin. 2006. *Rasta, Race, and Revolution: The Emergence and Development of the Rastafari Movement in Socialist Cuba*. Münster, Ger.: Lit Verlag.

Harding, Susan. 1992. "The Afterlife of Stories: Genesis of a Man of God." In *Storied Lives*, edited by George Rosenwald and Richard Ochberg, 60–75. New Haven, CT: Yale University.

————. 2000. *The Book of Jerry Falwell*. Princeton, NJ: Princeton University Press.

Harries-Jones, Peter. 2002. *A Recursive Vision: Ecological Understanding and Gregory Bateson*. Toronto: University of Toronto Press.

Harris, Mark. 1998. The Rhythm of Life on the Amazon Floodplain: Seasonality and Riverine Village. *Journal of the Royal Anthropological Institute* 4:65–82.

————. 2000. *Life on the Amazon: The Anthropology of a Brazilian Peasant Village*. London: British Academy / Oxford University Press.

————. 2010. *Rebellion on the Amazon: The Cabanagem, Race and Popular Culture, 1798–1840*. Cambridge: Cambridge University Press.

Haskell, Thomas L. 1998. *Objectivity Is Not Neutrality: Explanatory Schemes in History*. Baltimore, MD: Johns Hopkins University Press.

Henare, Amiria, Martin Holbraad, and Sari Wastell, eds. 2007. *Thinking Through Things: Theorising Artefacts Ethnographically*. London: Routledge.

Henry, John. 2002. *Knowledge Is Power: How Magic, the Government and an Apocalyptic Vision Inspired Francis Bacon to Create Modern Science*. Cambridge: Icon Books.

Heriarte, Mauricio de. (1662) 1976. "Descripção do Estado do Maranhão, Pará, Corupa e Rio das Amazonas." In *Historia Geral do Brasil*, edited by Francisco Varnhagen, 171–90. São Paulo, Brazil: Editora Nacional.

Héritier, Françoise. 1994. *Les deux sœurs et leur mère: Anthropologie de l'inceste*. Paris: Odile Jacob.

———. 1996. *Masculin/Féminin: La pensée de la différence*. Paris: Odile Jacob.

———. 2004. "Antropologia de corpos y sexos: Entrevista com Françoise Héritier." Interview by Renato Sztutman and Silvana Nascimento. *Revista de Antropología* 47:235–66.

Héritier, Françoise, and Margarita Xanthakou, eds. 2004. *Corps et affects*. Paris: Odile Jacob.

Higbee, E. 1945. "The River Is the Plow." *Scientific Monthly* 60:405–16.

Hirschmann, Albert O. 1977. *The Passions and the Interests: Political Arguments for Capitalism before Its Triumph*. Princeton, NJ: Princeton University Press.

Holbraad, Martin. 2007. "The Power of Powder: Multiplicity and Motion in the Divinatory Cosmology of Cuban Ifá (or *Mana*, Again)." In *Thinking Through Things: Theorising Artefacts Ethnographically*, edited by Amiria Henare, Martin Holbraad, and Sari Wastell, 189–225. London: Routledge.

———. 2008. "Definitive Evidence, from Cuban Gods." *Journal of the Royal Anthropological Institute* 14:S93–S109.

———. 2009. "Definitive Evidence, from Cuban Gods." In *The Objects of Evidence: Anthropological Approaches to the Production of Knowledge*, edited by Matthew Engelke, 89–104. Oxford: Wiley-Blackwell.

———. 2012. *Truth in Motion: The Recursive Anthropology of Cuban Divination*. Chicago: University of Chicago Press.

Hollan, Douglas. 1996. "Cultural and Experiential Aspects of Spirit Beliefs among the Toraja." In *Spirits in Culture, History, and Mind*, edited by Jeanette Marie Mageo and Alan Howard, 213–36. London: Routledge.

Hopgood, Cecil R. 1950. "Conceptions of God amongst the Tonga of Northern Rhodesia." In *African Ideas of God*, edited by Edwin W. Smith, 61–77. London: Edinburgh House Press.

Howard, Philip A. 1998. *Changing History: Afro-Cuban Cabildos and Societies of Color in the Nineteenth Century*. Baton Rouge: Louisiana State University Press.

Howes, David, ed. 2009. *The Sixth Sense Reader*. Oxford: Berg.

Hugh-Jones, Stephen. 1996. "Bonnes raisons ou mauvaise conscience? De l'ambivalence de certains Amazoniens envers la consommation de viande." *Terrain* 26:123–48.

———. 2002. "Nomes secretos e riqueza visível: Nominação no noroeste amazônico." *Mana* 8 (2): 45–68.

Hüwelmeier, Gertrud, and Kristine Krause, eds. 2010. *Traveling Spirits: Migrants, Markets, and Mobilities*. New York: Routledge.

Hymes, Dell. 1996. *Ethnography, Linguistics, Narrative Inequality: Toward an Understanding of Voice*. London: Taylor & Francis.

Idoyaga Molina, Anatilde. 1978–1979. "Contribución al estudio del proceso de gestación, aborto y alumbramiento entre los mataco costaneros." *Scripta Ethnologica* 5 (2): 143–55.

Ingold, Tim. 2000. *The Perception of the Environment: Essays in Livelihood, Dwelling and Skill*. London: Routledge.

———. 2001. "From the Transmission of Representations to the Education of Attention." In *The Debated Mind: Evolutionary Psychology versus Ethnography*, edited by Harvey Whitehouse, 113–54. Oxford: Berg.

———. 2006. "Rethinking the Animate, Re-Animating Thought." *Ethnos* 71 (1): 9–20.

———. 2007. *Lines: A Brief History*. London, New York: Routledge.

———. 2011. *Being Alive: Essays on Movement, Knowledge and Description*. London: Routledge.

Ingold, Tim, and Jo Lee Vergunst, eds. 2008. *Ways of Walking: Ethnography and Practice on Foot*. Aldershot, UK: Ashgate.

Irvine, Judith. 1982. "The Creation of Identity in Spirit Mediumship and Possession." In *Semantic Anthropology*, David Parkin, 241–60. London: Academic Press.

Isaia, Artur Cesar. 1999. "Ordenar progredindo: A obra dos intelectuais de Umbanda no Brasil da primeira metade do século XX." *Anos 90* 11: 97–120.

James, Wendy, ed. 1995. *The Pursuit of Certainty: Religious and Cultural Formulations*. London: Routledge.

James, Wendy, and David Mills, eds. 2005. *The Qualities of Time: Anthropological Approaches*. Oxford: Berg.

James, William. (1902) 1982. *The Varieties of Religious Experiences: A Study in Human Nature*. New York: Penguin Classics.

———. 2000. *Pragmatism and Other Writings*. New York, London: Penguin Books.

James Figarola, Joel. 1999. *Los Sistemas Mágico-religiosos Cubanos: Principios Rectores*. Caracas, Venezuela: UNESCO.

———. 2006. *Cuba La Gran Nganga (Algunas Prácticas de la Brujería)*. Santiago de Cuba: Ediciones Caserón.

Johnson, Paul C. 2011. "An Atlantic Genealogy of 'Spirit Possession.'" *Comparative Studies in Society and History* 53:393–425.

Jones, David E. 2000. *An Instinct for Dragons*. New York: Routledge.

Jung, Carl. 1960. *The Structure and Dynamics of the Psyche*. Vol. 8 of *Collected Works of C. G. Jung*. Princeton, NJ: Princeton University Press.

———. 1992. "Seven Sermons to the Dead." In *The Gnostic Jung*, selected and introduced by Robert A. Segal, 181–93. London: Routledge.

Karsten, Raphael. 1932. "Indian Tribes of the Argentine and Bolivian Chaco: Ethnological Studies." *Societas Scientiarum Fennica* 4 (1): 10–236.

Keane, Webb. 1997. "Religious Language." *Annual Review of Anthropology* 26: 47–71.

———. 2003a. "Self-Interpretation, Agency, and the Objects of Anthropology: Reflections on a Genealogy." *Comparative Studies in Society and History* 45 (2): 222–48.

———. 2003b. "Semiotics and the Social Analysis of Material Things." *Language and Communication* 23:409–25.

———. 2005. "Signs Are Not the Garb of Meaning: On the Social Analysis of Material Things." In *Materiality*, edited by Daniel Miller, 182–205. Durham, NC: Duke University Press.

———. 2007. *Christian Moderns: Freedom and Fetish in the Mission Encounter*. Berkeley: University of California Press.

Kearney, Michael. 1995. "The Local and the Global: The Anthropology of Globalization and Transnationalism." *Annual Review of Anthropology* 24:547–65.

Kendall, Laurel. 2008. "Of Hungry Ghosts and Other Matters of Consumption in the Republic of Korea: The Commodity Becomes a Ritual Prop." *American Ethnologist* 35 (1): 154–70.

Kirby, Peter Wynn, ed. 2009. *Boundless Worlds: An Anthropological Approach to Movement*. Oxford: Berghahn.

Kirsch, Thomas G. 1998. *Lieder der Macht: Religiöse Autorität und Performance in einer afrikanisch-christlichen Kirche Zambias*. Münster, Ger.: Lit-Verlag.

———. 2002. "Performance and the Negotiation of Charismatic Authority in an African Indigenous Church of Zambia." *Paideuma* 48: 57–76.

———. 2007. "Ways of Reading as Religious Power in Print Globalization." *American Ethnologist* 34 (3): 509–20.

———. 2008a. "Religious Logistics: African Christians, Spirituality and Transportation." In *On the Margins of Religion*, edited by João de Pina-Cabral and Frances Pine, 61–80. Oxford: Berghahn.

———. 2008b. *Spirits and Letters: Reading, Writing and Charisma in African Christianity*. Oxford: Berghahn.

———. 2010. "From the Spirit's Point of View: Ethnography, Total Truth and Speakership." In *Beyond Writing Culture: Current Intersections of Epistemologies and Practices of Representation*, edited by Karsten Kumoll and Olaf Zenker, 89–112. Oxford: Berghahn.

———. 2013. "Spirit Idioms and the Politics of Context." In *Spirits in Politics*, edited by Barbara Meier and Arne Steinforth, 91–113. Frankfurt, Ger.: Campus.

Kirshenblatt-Gimblett, Barbara. 1989. "Authoring Lives." *Journal of Folklore Research* 26 (2): 123–50.

Kockelman, Paul. 2007. "Agency: The Relation between Meaning, Power, and Knowledge." *Current Anthropology* 48 (3): 375–401.

Kopytoff, Igor. 1986. "The Cultural Biography of Things: Commiditization as Process." In *The Social Life of Things*, edited by Arjun Appadurai, 64–94. Cambridge: Cambridge University Press.

Koselleck, Reinhard. (1979) 2002. *The Practice of Conceptual History: Timing History, Spacing Concepts*. Stanford, CA: Stanford University Press.

———. 1985. *Futures Past: On the Semantics of Historical Time*. Cambridge, MA: MIT Press.

Koss, Joan. 1977. "Social Process, Healing, and Self-Defeat among Puerto Rican Spiritists." *American Ethnologist* 4 (3): 453–69.

Krause, Franz. 2010. "Thinking Like a River: An Anthropology of Water and Its Uses along the Kemi River, Northern Finland." PhD diss., University of Aberdeen.

Krippner, Stanley. 1989. "A Call to Heal: Entry Patterns in Brazilian Mediumship." In *Altered States of Consciousness and Mental Health: A Cross-Cultural Perspective*, edited by Colleen Ward, 186–206. London: Sage Press.

Krmpotich, Cara, Joost Fontein, and John Harries. 2010. "The Substance of Bones: The Emotive Materiality and Affective Presence of Human Remains." *Journal of Material Culture* 15 (4): 371–84.

Kullmann, R., and D. Tserenpil. 2001. *Mongolian Grammar*. Ulanbaatar: Mongolian Academy of Sciences.

Kwon, Heonik. 2007. "The Dollarization of Vietnamese Ghost Money." *Journal of the Royal Anthropological Institute* 13:73–90.

———. 2008. *Ghosts of War in Vietnam*. Cambridge: Cambridge University Press.

Lambek, Michael. 1980. "Spirits and Spouses: Possession as a System of Communication among the Malagasy Speakers of Mayotte." *American Ethnologist* 7 (2): 318–31.

———. 1981. *Human Spirits: A Cultural Account of Trance in Mayotte*. Cambridge: Cambridge University Press.

———. 1989. "From Disease to Discourse: Remarks on the Conceptualization of Trance and Spirit Possession." In *Altered States of Consciousness and Mental Health: A Cross-Cultural Perspective*, edited by Colleen Ward, 36–61. London: Sage Press.

———. 1990. "Certain Knowledge, Contestable Authority: Power and Practice on the Islamic Periphery." *American Ethnologist* 17 (1): 23–40.

———. 1998. "The Sakalava Poiesis of History: Realizing the Past through Spirit Possession in Madagascar." *American Ethnologist* 25 (2): 106–27.

———. 2002. *The Weight of the Past: Living with History in Mahajanga, Madagascar*. New York: Palgrave-MacMillan.

———. 2003. "Memory in a Maussian Universe." In *Regimes of Memory*, edited by Susannah Radstone and Katharine Hodgkin, 202–16. London: Routledge.

Lambert, Jean-Luc. 2002–2003. "Sortir de la Nuit: Essai sur le chamanisme nganassane (Arctique sibérien)." Special issue, *Etudes Mongoles et Sibériennes* 33–34.

Laplace, Pierre-Simon. 1808. *Exposition du Système du Monde*. Paris: Courcier.

Latour, Bruno. 1987. *Science in Action: How to Follow Scientists and Engineers through Society*. Cambridge, MA: Harvard University Press.

———. 1993a. *The Pasteurization of France*. Cambridge, MA: Harvard University Press.

———. 1993b. *We Have Never Been Modern*. Cambridge, MA: Harvard University Press.

———. 1996. *Aramis, or the Love of Technology*. Cambrige, MA: Harvard University Press.

———. 2005. *Reassembling the Social: An Introduction to Actor-Network Theory*. Oxford: Oxford University Press.

Latour, Bruno, and Steve Woolgar. (1979) 1986. *Laboratory Life*. Princeton, NJ: Princeton University Press.

Leal de Souza, Antônio Eliezer. 1933. *O Espiritismo, a Magia e as Sete Linhas de Umbanda*. Rio de Janeiro, Brazil: s/e.

Lee, Blewett. 1926. "Copyright of Automatic Writing." *Virginia Law Review* 13: 22–26.

Leiris, Michel. 2002. *Espelho da Tauromaquia*. São Paulo, Brazil: Cosac Naif.

Leite, Serafim. 1943. *História da Companhia de Jesus no Brasil*. Vols. 3 and 4. Rio de Janeiro, Brazil: Instituto Nacional do Livro.

Lepri, Isabella. 2005. "Identidade e alteridade entre os Ese Ejja da Bolivia setentrional." *Mana* 11 (2): 449–72.

Lévi-Strauss. Claude. 1968. *La Pénsee Sauvage*. London: Weidenfeld and Nicolson.

Levy, Robert I., Jeannette M. Mageo, and Alan Howard. 1996. "Gods, Spirits, and History: A Theoretical Perspective." In *Spirits in Culture, History, and Mind*, edited by Robert I. Levy and Jeannette M. Mageo, 11–28. New York: Routledge.

Lewgoy, Bernardo. 2004. *O Grande Mediador: Chico Xavier e a cultura brasileira*. Bauru, Brazil: EDUSC.

Lewis, Ioan M. (1971) 2003. *Ecstatic Religion: A Study of Shamanism and Spirit Possession*. 3rd ed. London: Routledge.

Lienhardt, Godfrey. (1961) 1987. *Divinity and Experience: The Religion of the Dinka*. Oxford: Oxford University Press.

Lima-Ayres, Deborah. 1992. "The Social Category Caboclo: History, Social Organisation and Outsiders Social Classification of the Rural Population of an Amazonian Region." PhD diss., University of Cambridge.

Locke, John. 1963. *Two Treatises of Government*. Cambridge: Cambridge University Press.

————. 1964. *An Essay Concerning Human Understanding*. New York: Meridian.

Loftus, Elizabeth F. 1979. *Eyewitness Testimony*. Cambridge, MA: Harvard University Press.

Long, Nicholas J. 2010. "Haunting Malayness: The Multicultural Uncanny in a New Indonesian Province." *Journal of the Royal Anthropological Institute* 16: 874–91.

Luig, Ute. 1992. "Besessenheit als Ausdruck von Frauenkultur." *Peripherie* 47/48: 111–28.

————. 1993a. "The Bacape Movement between Local Identity and Transregional Practices." Paper presented at the "Symbols of Change: Transregional Cultural and Local Practice" conference, Free University Berlin, January 7.

————. 1993b. "Besessenheit als historische Charta." *Paideuma* 39:343–55.

————. 1993c. "Gesellschaftliche Entwicklung und ihre individuelle Verarbeitung in den affliktiven Besessenheitskulten der Tonga." *Tribus* 42:100–120.

————. 1994. "Gender Relations and Comercialization in Tonga Possession Cults." In *Gender and Identity in Africa*, edited by Mechthild Reh and Gudrun Ludwar-Ene, 33–49. Münster, Ger.: Lit-Verlag.

————. 1997. *Conversion as a Social Process: A History of Missionary Christianity among the Valley Tonga, Zambia*. Münster, Ger.: Lit-Verlag.

Macfarlane, Robert. 2007. *Wild Paces*. London: Granta.

MacLellan, Susan. 1991. "Deviant Spirits in West Malaysian Factories." *Anthropologica* 33 (1–2): 145–60.

Macpherson, C. B. 1962. *The Political Theory of Possessive Individualism*. Oxford: Clarendon Press.

Maggie, Yvonne. 1992. *Medo de Feitiço: Relações Entre Magia e Poder no Brasil*. Rio de Janeiro, Brazil: Arquivo Nacional.

Maine, Henry Sumner. 1963. *Ancient Law*. Boston, MA: Beacon Press.

Mainwaring, Scott. 1986. *The Catholic Church and Politics in Brazil, 1916–1985*. Stanford, CA: Stanford University Press.

Malinowski, Bronislaw. (1932) 1976. *La sexualité et sa répression dans les sociétés primitives*. Paris: Payot.

Mannheim, Karl. 1952. *Essays on the Sociology of Knowledge*. London: Routledge and Kegan Paul.

Marcus, George. 1995. "Ethnography in/of the World System: The Emergence of Multi-Sited Ethnography." *Annual Review of Anthropology* 24:95–140.

Martin, David. 2002. *Pentecostalism: The World Their Parish*. Oxford: Blackwell.

Martínez-Crovetto, Raul. 1995. *Zoonimia y etnozoología de los pilagá, toba, mocoví, mataco y vilela*. Buenos Aires, Argentina: Facultad de Filosofía y Letras, Universidad de Buenos Aires.

Matory, J. Lorand. 2009. "The Many Who Dance in Me: Afro-Atlantic Ontology and the Problem with 'Transnationalism.'" In *Transnational Transcendence*, edited by Thomas Csordas, 231–62. Berkeley: University of California Press.

Maués, Raymundo *Heraldo. 1995. Padres, Pajés, Festas e Santos: Catolicismo Popular e Controle Eclesiástico.* Belém, Brazil: Cejup.

———. *Uma Outra "Invenção" da Amazônia: Religiões, histórias, identidades.* Belém, Brazil: CEJUP.

Mauss, Marcel. 1985. "A Category of the Human Mind: The Notion of the Person; the Notion of the Self." In *The Category of the Person: Anthropology, Philosophy, History,* edited by Michael Carrithers, Steven Collins, and Steven Lukes, 1–25. Cambridge: Cambridge University Press.

Maxwell, David. 1999. "Historicizing Christian Independency: The Southern African Pentecostal Movement, c. 1908–60." *Journal of African History* 40 (2): 243–64.

———. 2006. *African Gifts of the Spirit: Pentecostalism and the Rise of a Zimbabwean Transnational Religious Movement.* Oxford: James Currey.

———. 2012. "What Makes a Christian? Perspectives from Studies of Pneumatic Christianity." *Africa* 82 (3): 479–91.

McCallum, Cecilia. 2001. *Gender and Sociality in Amazonia: How Real People Are Made.* Oxford: Berg.

McGilchrist, Iain. 2009. *The Master and His Emissary: The Divided Brain and the Making of the Western World.* New Haven, CT: Yale University Press.

———. 2011. "Paying Attention to the Bipartite Brain." *Lancet* 377 (9771): 1068–69.

McKinley, James C., Jr. 2010. "Texas Conservatives Win Curriculum Change." *New York Times,* March 12.

Mead, Margaret. (1930) 1952. *Educación y Cultura.* Buenos Aires, Argentina: Paidós.

Melo, Rosa Virgínia. 2010. " 'Beber na fonte': Adesão e transformação na União do Vegetal." PhD diss., Universidade de Brasília, Departamento de Antropologia.

Meltzer, Françoise. 1994. "For Your Eyes Only: Ghost Citing." In *Questions of Evidence,* edited by James Chandler, Arnold I. Davidson, and Harry Harootunian, 43–49. Chicago: University of Chicago Press.

Merleau-Ponty, Maurice. (1945) 2002. *Phenomenology of Perception.* London: Routledge Classics.

———. 1968. *The Visible and the Invisible.* Evanston, IL: Northwestern University Press. First published 1964 as *Le Visible et l'Invisible* (Paris: Gallimard).

———. 1974. "The Primacy of Perception." In *Phenomenology, Language and Sociology: Selected Essays of Maurice Merleau-Ponty,* edited by John O'Neill, 196–226. London: Heinemann.

Métraux, Alfred. 1928. *Religion des Tupinamba et Ses Rapports avec celle des Autres Tribus Tupi-Guarani.* Paris: E. Leroux.

———. 1937. "Études d'Ethnographie Toba-Pilagá (Grand Chaco)." *Anthropos, Revue Internationale d'Ethnologie et de Linguistique* 32:171–94, 378–401.

------. 1944. "Nota Etnográfica sobre los Indios Mataco del Gran Chaco Argentino." *Relaciones* 4:7–18.

------. 1946. *Myth of the Toba and Pilagá Indians of the Gran Chaco.* Philadelphia, PA: American Folklore Society.

------. (1946) 1982. *Les indiens de l'Amérique du Sud.* Paris: Gallimard.

------. 1967. *Religions et magies indiennes d'Amérique du sud.* Paris: Gallimard.

Meyer, Birgit. 2004. "Christianity in Africa: From African Independent to Pentecostal-Charismatic Churches." *Annual Review of Anthropology* 33:447–74.

------. 2010. "Pentecostalism and Globalization." In *Studying Global Pentecostalism,* edited by Allan Anderson, Michael Bergunder, André Droogers, and Cornelis van der Laan, 113–30. Berkeley: University of California Press.

Meyer, Marlyse. 1993. *Maria Padilha e toda a sua Quadrilha: De amante de um Rei de Castela à Pomba-Gira de Umbanda.* São Paulo, Brazil: Duas Cidades.

------. 2001. *Caminhos do Imaginário no Brasil.* São Paulo, Brazil: Edusp.

Miller, Daniel, ed. 2005. *Materiality.* Durham, NC: Duke University Press.

Miller, Elmer. 1979. *Los tobas argentinos: Armonía y Disonancia en una sociedad.* Buenos Aires, Argentina: Siglo XXI.

Miller, Elmer, and José Braunstein, eds. 1999. *Peoples of the Gran Chaco.* Westport, CT: Bergin and Garvey.

Millet, José. 1999. "Muerterismo o regla muertera." *Revista de Folklore* 19b (228): 208–16.

Minh-Ha, Trinh T.. 1991. *When the Moon Waxes Red: Representations, Gender, and Cultural Politics.* New York: Routledge.

Mittermaier, Amira. 2011. *Dreams That Matter: Egyptian Landscapes of the Imagination.* Berkeley: University of California Press.

Miyazaki, Hirokazu. 2003. "The Temporalities of the Market." *American Anthropologist* 105 (2): 255–65.

Mnookin, Jennifer L. 1998. "The Image of Truth: Photographic Evidence and the Power of Analogy." *Yale Journal of Law and the Humanities* 10:1–74.

Moreno Fraginals, Manuel. 1978. *El ingenio.* Havana, Cuba: Editorial Ciencias Sociales.

Mott, Luiz. 1993. *Rosa Egipcíaca: Uma santa africana no Brasil.* Rio de Janeiro, Brazil: Bertrand Brasil.

Mueggler, Erik. 2001. *The Age of Wild Ghosts: Memory, Violence, and Place in Southwest China.* Berkeley: University of California Press.

Murphy, Nancey. 2006. *Bodies and Souls, or Spirited Bodies?* Cambridge: Cambridge University Press.

Murphy, Robert. 1958. *Mundurucu Religion.* University of California Publications in American Archaeology and Ethnology, vol. 49, no. 1, 1–154. Berkeley: University of California Press.

Negrão, Lísias Nogueira. 1996. *Entre a Cruz e a Encruzilhada: Formação do campo umbandista em São Paulo.* São Paulo, Brazil: Edusp.

Nimuendaju, Kurt. 2004. *In Pursuit of a Past Amazon: Archaeological Researches in the Brazilian Guyana and in the Amazon Region.* Gothenburg, Sweden: Världskulturmuseet.

Nugent, Stephen. 1990. *Big Mouth: The Amazon Speaks.* London: Fourth Estate.

———. 1993. *Amazonian Caboclo Society: An Essay in Peasant Economy and Invisibility.* Oxford: Berg.

Oakeshott, Michael. 1933. *Experience and Its Modes.* Cambridge: Cambridge University Press.

Ochoa, Todd Ramon. 2007. "Versions of the Dead: *Kalunga*, Cuban-Kongo Materiality, and Ethnography." *Cultural Anthropology* 22 (4): 473–500.

———. 2010a. "Prendas-Ngangas-Eqnquisos: Turbulence and the Influence of the Dead in Cuban-Kongo Material Culture." *Cultural Anthropology* 25:387–420.

———. 2010b. *Society of the Dead: Quita Manaquita and Palo Praise in Cuba.* Berkeley: University of California Press.

Ochs, Elinor. 1994. "Stories That Step into the Future." In *Sociolinguistic Perspectives on Register,* edited by Douglas Biber and Edward Finegan, 106–35. New York: Oxford University Press.

Ochs, Elinor, Carolyn Taylor, Dina Rudolph, and Ruth Smith. 1992. "Story-Telling as a Theory-Building Activity." *Discourse Processes* 15 (1): 37–72.

Oliveira, J. Alves. 1985. *Umbanda cristã e brasileira.* Rio de Janeiro, Brazil: Ediouro.

Oliveira, José Henrique. 2008. *Das Macumbas à Umbanda: Uma análise histórica da construção de uma religião brasileira.* Limeira, Brazil: Editora do Conhecimento.

Ong, Aihwa. 1987. *Spirits of Resistance and Capitalist Discipline: Factory Women in Malaysia.* New York: State University of New York Press.

Orozco, Román, and Natalia Bolívar. 1998. *Cuba Santa: Comunistas, Santeros, y Cristianos en la Isla de Fidel Castro.* Madrid: El País Aguilar.

Ortiz, R. 1978. *A Morte Branca do Feiticeiro Negro: Umbanda e sociedade brasileira.* São Paulo, Brazil: Brasiliense.

Palfreman, Jon. 1979. "Between Scepticism and Credulity: A Study of Victorian Scientific Attitudes to Modern Spiritualism." In *On the Margins of Science: The Social Construction of Rejected Knowledge,* edited by Roy Wallis, 201–36. Keele, UK: University of Keele 1979.

Palmié, Stephan. 2002. *Wizards and Scientists: Explorations in Afro-Cuban Modernity and Tradition.* Durham, NC: Duke University Press.

Palmer, John. 1995. "Wichi Toponymy." *Hacia una nueva carta étnica del Gran Chaco* 6:3–63.

———. 1997. "Wichi Goodwill: Ethnographic Allusions." PhD diss., Oxford University.

———. 2005. *La buena voluntad wichi: Una espiritualidad indígena.* Buenos Aires, Argentina: APCD.

Pels, Peter. 2003. "Spirits of Modernity: Alfred Wallace, Edward Tylor, and the Visual Politics of Fact." In *Magic and Modernity: Interfaces of Revelation and Concealment*, edited by Birgit Meyer and Peter Pels, 241–71. Stanford, CA: Stanford University Press.

Pessoa, José Álvares. 1960. *Umbanda religião do Brasil*. São Paulo, Brazil: Obelisco.

Philips, Susan U. 1993. "Evidentiary Standards for American Trials: Just the Facts." In *Responsibility and Evidence in Oral Discourse*, edited by Jane Hill and Judith Irvine, 248–59. Cambridge: Cambridge University Press.

Pietz, William. 1985. "The problem of the fetish, I." *Res* 9: 5–17.

Pocock, J. G. A. 1962. "The Origins of the Study of the Past: A Comparative Approach." *Comparative Studies in Society and History* 4:209–46.

Pons, Christophe. 2002. *Le Spectre et le Voyant: Les échanges entre morts et vivants en Islande*. Paris: Presses de l'Université de Paris-Sorbonne.

Porter, Jennifer E. 2005. "The Spirit(s) of Science: Paradoxical Positivism as Religious Discourse among Spiritualists." *Science as Culture* 14:1–21.

Post, Isaac. 1852. *Voices from the Spirit World: Being Communications from Many Spirits*. Rochester, NY: Charles H. McDonell.

Prandi, Reginaldo, ed. 2001. *Encantaria Brasileira: O livro dos mestres, caboclos e encantados*. Rio de Janeiro, Brazil: Editora Pallas.

———. 2004. "O Brasil com axé: Candomblé e umbanda no mercado religioso." *Estudos Avançados* 52:223–38.

Price, Richard. 2008. *Travels with Tooy: History, Memory, and the African American Imagination*. Chicago: University of Chicago Press.

Queiroz, Maria Isaura Pereira de. 1989. "Afro-Brazilian Cults and Religious Change in Brazil." In *The Changing Face of Religion*, edited by James A. Beckford and Thomas Luckmann, 88–108. Newbury Park, CA: Sage.

Raffles, Hugh, and Antoinette WinklerPrins. 2003. "Further Reflections on Amazonian Environmental History: Transformations of Rivers and Streams." *Latin American Research Review* 38 (3): 165–87.

Raine, Kathleen. 1991. *Golgonooza: City of Imagination*. Ipswich, UK: Golgonooza Press.

Reddy, Michael. 1979. "The Conduit Metaphor—a Case of Frame Conflict in Our Language about Language." In *Metaphor and Thought*, edited by Andrew Ortony, 284–324. Cambridge: Cambridge University Press.

Riskin, Jessica. 2009. "The Mesmerism Investigation and the Crisis of Sensationist Science." In *The Sixth Sense Reader*, edited by David Howes, 119–50. Oxford: Berg.

Robbins, Joel. 2004. "The Globalization of Pentecostal and Charismatic Christianity." *Annual Review of Anthropology* 33:117–43.

Rodrigues, Aryon D'Alligna. 1986. *Línguas brasileiras—para o conhecimento das línguas indígenas*. São Paulo, Brazil: Edições Loyola.

Rogler, Lloyd H., and August B. Hollingshead. 1961. "The Puerto Rican Spiritualist as a Psychiatrist." *The American Journal of Sociology* 67 (1): 17–21.

Román, Reinaldo. 2007. *Governing Spirits: Religion, Miracles, and Spectacles in Cuba and Puerto Rico, 1898–1956.* Chapel Hill: University of North Carolina Press.

Rorty, Richard. 1991. *Objectivity, Relativism and Truth.* Cambridge: Cambridge University Press.

Rosendahl, Mona. 1997. *Inside the Revolution: Everyday Life in Socialist Cuba.* Ithaca, NY: Cornell University Press.

Routon, Kenneth. 2008. "Conjuring the Past: Slavery and the Historical Imagination in Cuba." *American Ethnologist* 35 (4): 632–49.

Sahlins, Marshall. 1976. *Culture and Practical Reason.* Chicago: University of Chicago Press.

———. 1985. *Islands of History.* Chicago: University of Chicago Press.

———. 2004. *Apologies to Thucydides: Understanding History as Culture and Vice Versa.* Chicago: University of Chicago Press.

Salamanca, Carlos. 2006. "En se glissant dans les fisures de l'utopie: Les Toba aux frontières de l'Etat-Nation." PhD diss., EHESS (Paris).

———. Forthcoming. *La lucha de las familias tobas por poxo axaic alhua: Movilizaciones indígenas, mapas e historias por la propiedad de la tierra en el Chaco argentino.* Copenhagen, Denmark: IGWIA.

Sansi, Roger. 2009. *Fetishes and Monuments: Afro-Brazilian Art and Culture in the 20th Century.* Oxford: Berghahn.

Sansi-Roca, Roger. 2007. "The Fetish in the Lusophone Atlantic." In *Cultures of the Lusophone Black Atlantic,* edited by Nancy Priscilla Naro, Roger Sansi-Roca, and David Treece, 19–39. New York: Palgrave MacMillan.

Santos, Jocélio Teles dos. 1995. *O dono da terra: O caboclo nos candomblés da Bahia.* Salvador, Brazil: SarahLetras.

Saussure, Ferdinand de. 1969. *Curso de lingüística geral.* São Paulo, Brazil: Cultrix, USP.

Sawyer, Mark Q. 2006. *Racial Politics in Post-Revolutionary Cuba.* Cambridge: Cambridge University Press.

Sayre, Francis Bowes. 1932. "Mens Rea." *Harvard Law Review* 45:974–1026.

Sazykin, Aleksej G. 1979. "Hell Imaginations in Non-Canonical Mongolian Literature." *Acta Orientalia* 33 (3): 327–35.

Schlemmer, Grégoire. 2004. "Vues d'esprits: La conception des esprits et ses implications chez les Kulung Rai du Népal." Phd diss., Université Paris 10, Nanterre.

Schmidt, Jalane. 2005. "Cuba's Rival Rituals: 20th Century Festivals for the Virgin of Charity and the Contested Streets of the "Nation." PhD diss., Committee on the Study of Religion, Harvard University.

Schmitt, Jean-Claude. 1994. *Les Revenants: Les vivants et les morts dans la société médiévale.* Paris: Gallimard.

Schoffeleers, Matthew. 1991. "Ritual Healing and Political Acquiescence: The Case of the Zionist Churches in Southern Africa." *Africa* 60 (1): 1–25.

Schroll, Mark A., and Susan Greenwood. 2011. "Worldviews in Collision—Worldviews in Metamorphosis: Toward a Multi-State Paradigm." *Anthropology of Consciousness* 22 (1): 49–60.

Sconce, Jeffrey. 2000. *Haunted Media: Electronic Presence from Telegraphy to Television*. Durham, NC: Duke University Press.

Scudder, Thayer. 1962. *The Ecology of the Gwembe Tonga*. Manchester, UK: Manchester University Press.

Seidman, Robert B. 1965. "Witch Murder and *Mens Rea*: A Problem of Society under Rapid Change." *Modern Law Review* 28:46–61.

———. 1966. "Mens Rea and the Reasonable African: The Pre-Scientific World View and Mistake of Fact." *International and Comparative Law Quarterly* 1: 1135–64.

Seremetakis, Nadia C. 1991. *The Last Word: Women, Death, and Divination in Inner Mani*. Chicago: University of Chicago Press.

———. 1993. "The Memory of the Sense: Historical Perception, Commensal Exchange and Modernity." *Visual Anthropology Review* 9 (2): 2–18.

Serra, Ordep. 1995. *Águas do Rei*. Petrópolis, Brazil: Editora Vozes.

Sharp, Lesley A. 1993. *The Possessed and the Dispossessed: Spirits, Identity, and Power in a Madagascar Migrant Town*. Berkeley: University of California Press.

Sharp, Lynn L. 2006. *Secular Spirituality: Reincarnation and Spiritism in Nineteenth-Century France*. Lanham, MD: Lexington Books.

Shaw, Rosalind. 2002. *Memories of the Slave Trade: Ritual and the Historical Imagination in Sierra Leone*. Chicago: University of Chicago Press.

Shils, Edward. 1958. "The Concentration and Dispersion of Charisma." *World Politics* 11 (1): 1–19.

Shorto, Russell. 2010. "Founding Father?" *New York Times Magazine* February 14.

Silva, Vagner Gonçalves da. 1995. *Orixás da Metrópole*. Petrópolis, Brazil: Vozes.

Simpson, Jacqueline. 2001. *British Dragons*. Ware, UK: Wordsworth.

Skinner, Quentin. 1969. "Meaning and Understanding in the History of Ideas." *History and Theory* 8:3–53.

———. 1970. "Conventions and the Understanding of Speech Acts." *Philosophical Quarterly* 20:118–38.

Slater, Candace. 1993. *Dance of the Dolphin: Transformation and Disenchantment in the Amazonian Imagination*. Chicago, Chicago University Press.

Smith, N. J. H., E. A. S. Serrão, P. T. Alvim, and I. C. Falesi. 1995. *Amazonia: Resiliency and Dynamism of the Land and Its People*. Tokyo: United Nations University Press.

Sneath, David, Martin Holbraad, and Morten Pedersen. 2009. "Technologies of the Imagination: An Introduction." *Ethnos* 74 (1): 5–30.

Sollors, Werner. 1983. "Dr. Benjamin Franklin's Celestial Telegraph, or Indian Blessings to Gas-Lit American Drawing Rooms." *Social Science Information* 22:983–1004.

Spix, Johann Baptist von, and Karl Martius. 1981. *Viagem Pelo Brasil, 1817–1820.* Belo Horizonte, Brazil: Editora Itatiaia.

Spyer, Patricia, ed. 1998. *Border Fetishisms: Material Objects in Unstable Places.* London: Routledge.

Stanley, Amy Dru. 1998. *From Bondage to Contract: Wage Labor, Marriage, and the Market in the Age of Slave Emancipation.* Cambridge: Cambridge University Press.

Steedly, Mary. 1993. *Hanging without a Rope: Narrative Experience in Colonial and Postcolonial Karoland.* Princeton, NJ: Princeton University Press.

Stengers, Isabelle. 2000. *The Invention of Modern Science.* Minneapolis: University of Minnesota Press.

Stépanoff, Charles. 2007. "Les corps conducteurs: Enquête sur les représentations et le statut de l'action rituelle des chamanes chez les Turcs de Sibérie méridionale à partir de l'exemple Tuva." PhD diss., Ecole Pratique des Hautes Etudes, Paris.

Sternberg, Hilgard O'Reilly. 1998. *A Agua e o Homem na Várzea do Careiro.* Belém, Brazil: Museu Paraense do Emilio Goeldi.

Stewart, Donald W., and David Koulack. 1993. "The Function of Dreams in Adaptation to Stress over Time." *Dreaming* 3 (4): 259–68.

Stewart, Kathleen. 1991. "On the Politics of Cultural Theory: A Case for 'Contaminated' Cultural Critique." *Social Research* 58 (2): 395–412.

———. 1996. *A Space on the Side of the Road: Cultural Poetics in an "Other" America.* Princeton, NJ: Princeton University Press.

Stoller, Paul. 1989. *Fusion of the Worlds: An Ethnography of Possession among the Songhay of Niger.* Chicago: University of Chicago Press.

———. 1995. *Embodying Colonial Memories: Spirit Possession, Power, and the Hauka in West Africa.* New York: Routledge.

Stoller, Paul, and Cheryl Olkes. 1987. *In Sorcery's Shadow.* Chicago: Chicago University Press.

Strathern, Marylin. 1988. *The Gender of the Gift.* Oxford: Oxford University Press.

———. 2004. *Partial Connections.* Walnut Creek, CA: Altamira Press.

Sundkler, Bengt. 1961. *Bantu Prophets in South Africa.* London: Oxford University Press.

Surallés, Alexandre. 2003. *Au cœur du sens: Perception, affectivité, action chez les Candoshi.* Paris: CNRS / Maison des Sciences de l'Homme.

Swancutt, Katherine. 2008. "The Undead Genealogy: Omnipresence, Spirit, Perspectives, and a Case of Mongolian Vampirism." *Journal of the Royal Anthropological Institute* 14: 843–64.

Sword, Helen. 1999. "Necrobibliography: Books in the Spirit World." *Modern Language Quarterly* 60:85–112.

Tambiah, Stanley. 1991. *Magic, Science, Religion and the Scope of Rationality.* Cambridge: Cambridge University Press.

Taussig, Michael. 2009. *What Color Is the Sacred?* Chicago: University of Chicago Press.

Taylor, Anne-Christine. 1993. "Des fantômes stupéfiants: Langage et croyance dans la pensée achuar." *L'Homme* 126–128: 429–47.

———. 1996. "The Soul's Body and Its States: An Amazonian Perspective on the Nature of Being Human." *Journal of the Royal Anthropological Institute* 2 (2): 201–15.

———. 2006. "Un corps fait de regards." In *Qu'est-ce qu'un corps*, edited by Stéphan Breton, 148–99. Paris: Musée du Quai Branly.

Tedlock, Barbara. 1987. "Working with Dreams in Pastoral Counseling." *Pastoral Psychology* 36 (2): 123–30.

Thomaz, Omar Ribeiro. 1992. "Xeto, Marromba, Xeto! A representação do índio nas religiões afro-brasileiras." In *Índios no Brasil*, edited by Grupioni Luiz, 205–16. São Paulo, Brazil: Secretaria Municipal de Cultura.

Thurschwell, Pamela. 2009. "Refusing to Give up the Ghost: Some Thoughts on the Afterlife from Spirit Photography to Phantom Films." In *The Sixth Sense Reader*, edited by David Howes, 223–46. Oxford: Berg.

Tola, Florencia. 1999. "Fluidos corporales y roles paternos en el proceso de gestación entre los Tobas orientales de Formosa." *Papeles de Trabajo* 8:197–221.

———. 2002. "Ser madre en un cuerpo nuevo: Procesos de cambio en las representaciones tobas de la gestación." *Relaciones* 26:57–71.

———. 2005. "Socialidad en el mito: Hombres, mujeres y animales desde la perspectiva toba." *Latin American Indian Literatures Journal* 21 (1): 59–79.

———. 2006. " 'Después de muerto hay que disfrutar, en la tierra o en el mundo celestial': Concepciones de la muerte entre los tobas (*qom*) del Chaco argentino." *Alteridades Antropología de las creencias* 16 (32): 153–64.

———2007. " 'Eu nao estou só(mente) em meu corpo': A pessoa e o corpo entre os toba (*qom*) do Chaco argentino." *Mana* 13 (2): 499–519.

———. 2009. *Conceptions du corps et de la personne dans un contexte amerindien: Les toba du Gran Chaco.* Paris: L'Harmattan.

———. 2010. "Maîtres, chamanes et amants." *Ateliers du LESC (Société d'Ethnologie de Nanterre)*, edited by Valentina Vapnarsky and Aurore Monod Becquelin, 34. http://ateliers.revues.org/8538.

———. Forthcoming. "Chamanisme et sorcellerie chez les Toba (Qom) du Gran Chaco sud-américain: Quelques remarques sur une conception non individuelle du corps." In *Epistémologie du Corps, Quelles pratiques corporelles?*, edited by Bernard Andrieu.

Tomasini. Alfredo. 1969–1970. "Señores de los animales, constelaciones y espíritus de los bosques en el cosmos mataco mataguayo." *Runa* 12 (1–2): 427–43.

―――. 1978–1979. "La narrativa animalística entre los tobas de occidente." *Scripta Ethnologica* 5 (1): 52–81.

Toren, Christina. 1999. *Mind, Materiality and History: Essays in Fijian Ethnography*. London: Routledge.

Trevelyan, Marie. 1909. *Folk-Lore and Folk Stories of Wales*. London: Elliot Stock.

Trouillot, Michel-Rolph. 1995. *Silencing the Past: Power and the Production of History*. Boston, MA: Beacon.

―――. 2002. "North Atlantic Universals: Analytical Fictions, 1492–1945." *South Atlantic Quarterly* 101:838–58.

Tsing, Anna L. 1993. *In the Realm of the Diamond Queen: Marginality in an Out-of-the-Way Place*. Princeton, NJ: Princeton University Press.

Turner, Edith. 1987. *The Spirit and the Drum*. Tucson: University of Arizona Press.

―――. 1992. *Experiencing Ritual: A New Interpretation of African Healing*. Philadelphia: University of Pennsylvania Press.

―――. 2005. *Among the Healers: Stories of Ritual and Spiritual Healing around the World*. Westport, CT: Praeger.

―――. 2006. *Heart of Lightness: The Life Story of an Anthropologist*. Oxford: Berghahn Books.

Turner, Harold W. 1967. "A Typology for African Religious Movements." *Journal of Religion in Africa* 1:1–34.

Turner, Terence. 1993. "De cosmologia a história: Residência, adaptação econsciência social entre os Kayapó." In *Amazônia: Etnologia e História Indígena*, edited by Eduardo Viveiros de Castro and Manuela Carneiro da Cunha, 46–66. São Paulo, Brazil: Núcleo de História Indígena e do Indigenismo da USP/FAPESP.

Vainfas, Ronaldo. 2005. "From Indian Millenarianism to a Tropical Witches' Sabbath: Brazilian Sanctities in Jesuit Writings and Inquisitorial Sources." *Bulletin of Latin American Research* 24 (2): 215–31.

Van de Port, Matthijs. 2005. "Circling Around the *Really Real*: Spirit Possession Ceremonies and the Search for Authenticity in Bahian Candomblé." *Ethnos* 33 (2): 149–79.

―――. 2011. "(Not) Made by the Human Hand: Media Consciousness and Immediacy in the Cultural Production of the Real." *Social Anthropology* 19 (1): 74–89.

Vasconcelos, João. 2008. "Homeless Spirits: Modern Spiritualism, Psychical Research and the Anthropology of Religion in the Late Nineteenth and Early Twentieth Centuries." In *On the Margins of Religion*, edited by João Pina-Cabral and Frances Pine, 13–38. Oxford: Berghahn Books.

Vásquez, Manuel A. 2009. "The Global Portability of Pneumatic Christianity: Comparing African and Latin American Pentecostalisms." *African Studies* 68 (2): 273–86.

Vertovec, Steven. 1999. "Conceiving and Researching Transnationalism." *Ethnic and Racial Studies* 22 (2): 447–62.

———. 2009. *Transnationalism.* London: Taylor & Francis.

Vilaça, Aparecida. 2002. "Making Kin out of Others." *Journal of the Royal Anthropological Institute* 8:347–65.

———. 2005. "Chronically Instable Bodies: Reflections on Amazonian Corporality." *Journal of the Royal Anthropological Institute* 11:445–64.

Vitebsky, Piers. 1993. *Dialogues with the Dead: The Discussion of Mortality among the Sora of Eastern India.* Cambridge: Cambridge University Press.

Viveiros de Castro, Eduardo. (1977) 2002. *Individuo e sociedade no Alto Xingu: Os Yawalapíti.* Master's thesis, Museu Nacional, Rio de Janeiro, Brazil.

———. 1992. *From the Enemy's Point of View: Humanity and Divinity in an Amazonian Society.* Chicago: University of Chicago Press.

———. 1996. "Os pronomes cosmológicos e o perspectivismo ameríndio." *Mana* 2 (2): 115–44.

———. (1996) 2002. "Perspectivismo e multinaturalismo na América indígena." In *A inconstancia da alma selvagem*, by Eduardo Viveiros de Castro, 345–400. São Paulo, Brazil: Cosac and Naify.

———. 1998. "Cosmological Deixis and Amerindian Perspectivism." *Journal of the Royal Anthropological Institute* 4 (3): 469–88.

———. 2003. *And.* Manchester Papers in Social Anthropology 7. Manchester, UK: University of Manchester.

———. 2007. "The Crystal Forest: On the Ontology of Amazonian Spirits." In *Inner Asian Perspectivism*, edited by Rebecca Empson, Caroline Humphrey and Morten A. Pedersen, special issue, *Inner Asia* 9 (2): 153–72.

Voss, Ehler. 2011. "The Struggle for Sovereignty: The Interpretation of Bodily Experiences in Anthropology and among Mediumistic Healers in Germany." In *Encounters of Body and Soul in Contemporary Religious Practices: Anthropological Reflections*, edited by Anna Fedele and Ruy Blanes, 168–78. Oxford: Berghahn.

Wallace, Alfred R. (1875) 2009. *On Miracles and Modern Spiritualism: Three Essays.* Cambridge: Cambridge University Press.

Ward. Colleen, ed. 1989. *Altered States of Consciousness and Mental Health: A Cross-Cultural Perspective.* London: Sage Press.

Weinreb, Amelia Rosenberg. 2009. *Cuba in the Shadow of Change: Daily Life in the Twilight of the Revolution.* Gainesville: University Press of Florida.

West, Harry. 2005. *Kupilikula: Governance and the Invisible Realm in Mozambique.* Chicago: University of Chicago Press.

Wilde, Oscar. (1887) 1984. "The Canterville Ghost." In *The Penguin Book of Ghost Stories.* London: Penguin.

Willerslev, Rane. 2007. *Soul Hunters: Hunting, Animism, and Personhood among the Siberian Yukaghirs.* Berkeley: University of California Press.

———. 2009. "'To Have the World at a Distance': Reconsidering the Significance of Vision for Social Anthropology." In *Skilled Visions: Between Apprenticeship and Standards*, edited by Cristina Grasseni, 23–46. Oxford: Berghahn Books.

Wimmer, Andreas, and Nina Glick-Schiller. 2002. "Methodological Nationalism and Beyond: Nation-State Building, Migration and the Social Sciences." *Global Networks* 2 (4): 301–34.

Wirtz, Kristina. 2007a. "Enregistered Memory and Afro-Cuban Historicity in Santería's Ritual Speech." *Language and Communication* 27:245–57.

———. 2007b. *Ritual, Discourse, and Community in Cuban Santería: Speaking a Sacred World*. Gainesville: University Press of Florida.

———. 2009. "Hazardous Waste: The Semiotics of Ritual Hygiene in Cuban Popular Religion." *Journal of the Royal Anthropological Institute* 15:476–501.

———. 2011. "Cuban Performances of Blackness as the Timeless Past Still among Us." *Journal of Linguistic Anthropology* 21 (1S): E11–E34.

Woolard, Kathryn A. 2004. "Is the Past a Foreign Country? Time, Language Origins, and the Nation in Early Modern Spain." *Journal of Linguistic Anthropology* 14:57–80.

Wortham, Stanton. 2001. *Narratives in Action: A Strategy for Research and Analysis*. New York: Teachers College Press.

———. 2005. *Learning Identity: The Joint Emergence of Social Identification and Academic Learning*. Cambridge: Cambridge University Press.

Wortham, Stanton, Elaine Allard, Kathy Lee, and Katherine Mortimer. 2011. "Racialization in Payday Mugging Narratives." *Journal of Linguistic Anthropology* 21 (S1): E56–E75.

Wright, Pablo. 1997. "Being-in-the-Dream: Postcolonial Explorations in Toba Ontology." PhD diss., Temple University.

———. 2002. "L''Evangelio': Pentecôtisme indigène dans le Chaco argentin." *Social Compass* 49 (1): 43–66.

———. 2008. *Ser-en-el-sueño: Crónicas de historia y vida toba*. Buenos Aires, Argentina: Biblos/Culturalia.

Contributors

RUY BLANES (PhD, University of Lisbon, 2007) is currently postdoctoral researcher at the Institute of Social Sciences of the University of Lisbon (ICS-UL) and visiting fellow at the Department of Anthropology of the London School of Economics and Political Science. His current research site is Angola, where he is working on the topics religion, mobility (diasporas, transnationalism, the Atlantic), politics (leadership, charisma, repression, resistance), temporalities (historicity, memory, heritage, expectations), and knowledge. He has authored a monograph on his PhD research among Pentecostal Gypsies in the Iberian Peninsula (2007) and is forthcoming on a monograph on prophetic trajectories in Angola. He has also coordinated a volume titled *Encounters of Body and Soul in Contemporary Religious Practices* (2011, with Anna Fedele). He is also currently vice president of the APA (Portuguese Anthropological Association) and coeditor of the journal *Advances in Research: Religion and Society* (Berghahn).

VÂNIA ZIKÁN CARDOSO (PhD, University of Texas at Austin, 2004) is adjunct professor of Anthropology at the Federal University of Santa Catarina, Brazil. Her research centers on Afro-Brazilian religious practices, and she is particularly concerned with questions of performance, narrative, cultural poetics, and sociality. She is the organizer of *Caroço de Dênde* (2002) and *Diálogos Transversais em Antropologia* (2008), and is co-organizer of *Etnobiografia: Subjetivação e Etnografia* (2012) and the forthcoming collection *A Terra do Não Lugar: Diálogos entre Antropologia e Performance* (2013). She is coeditor of the journal *Ilha: Revista de Antropologia*.

ANA STELA DE ALMEIDA CUNHA (PhD, University of São Paulo, 2003) is postdoctoral researcher at CRIA (Centro em Rede de Investigação em Antropologia—FCT//Portugal), and her principal academic research interests lie in the field of ethnolinguistics, anthropology of religions in the African Diaspora, and visual anthropology. She is also interested in educational processes—especially in the Amazonian area, in Brazil—and acting as creator and coordinator of social projects. Currently, she conducts field research in Congo (DRC), Brazil, and Cuba, consolidating an academic career focused on relations between the Iberian world and the African presence in the Americas.

GRÉGORY DELAPLACE (PhD, École Pratique des Hautes Études, 2007) is a lecturer in anthropology at the University of Paris Ouest Nanterre La Défense and a member of the Laboratoire d'Ethnologie et de Sociologie Comparative. His research interests revolve around the invisible and the ways in which Mongolian people have come to grips with it through shamanic rituals, encounters with ghosts, crafted images, and the like. He is the author of *L'invention des morts: Sépultures, fantômes et photographie en Mongolie contemporaine* (Paris: EMSCAT).

DIANA ESPÍRITO SANTO (PhD, University College London, 2009) is currently postdoctoral fellow at the Centre for Research in Anthropology (CRIA), based at Lisbon's Universidade Nova. She wrote her PhD dissertation on popular forms of Cuban Spiritism and on concepts of personhood and knowledge. In her recent research she has focused on questions of learning, materiality, and ontological fluidity in the Brazilian spirit mediumship tradition of Umbanda. She has published several articles in anthropology journals, is coeditor of a forthcoming volume on the role of materiality in generating cosmology, and is currently completing her monograph on Cuban spirit mediumship.

EMERSON GIUMBELLI (PhD, Federal University of Rio de Janeiro, 2000) is professor of Anthropology in the Federal University of Rio Grande do Sul (UFRGS, Brazil), where he coordinates the Center for Religious Studies (NER). He is the author of *O Cuidado dos Mortos: Uma história da condenação e legitimação do espiritismo* (1997) and *O Fim da Religião: Dilemas da liberdade religiosa no Brasil e na França* (2002). His topics of research include anthropology of religion, anthropology of modernity, secularism, and the presence of religions in public spaces.

SUSAN GREENWOOD (PhD, London, 1997) has lectured courses on shamanic and altered states of consciousness at the University of Sussex, where she is a past visiting senior research fellow, and on the anthropology of religion at Goldsmiths College, University of London. Her publications include *Magic, Witchcraft and the Otherworld* (Berg, 2000); *The Nature of Magic: An Anthropology of Consciousness* (Berg, 2005); *The Anthropology of Magic* (Berg, 2009); *Magical Consciousness: An Anthropological and Neuropsychological Approach* (forthcoming); "World Views in Collision—World Views in Metamorphosis: Toward a Multi-state Paradigm" (with Mark A. Schroll), *Anthropology of Consciousness* 22, no. 1 (2011): 49–60; "Magical Consciousness: A Legitimate Form of knowledge," in *Defining Magic: A Reader*, edited by Bernd-Christian Otto and Michael Stausberg, for the Critical Categories in the Study of Religion series (Equinox, 2012); and "Magical Consciousness: Relationships with the Natural World, Animals and Ancestors," in *Religion and the Subtle Body in Asia and* *the West: Between Mind and Body*, edited by Geoffrey Samuel and Jay Johnston (Routledge, 2013).

MARK HARRIS (PhD, London School of Economics, 1996) is reader in social anthropology and currently head of department at the University of St. Andrews. He has carried out fieldwork with people who live on the banks of the River Amazon in Brazil since 1992. From 2003 he has also conducted archival research on the history of the region. His books include *Life on the Amazon: The Anthropology of a Brazilian Peasant Village* (Oxford, 2000) and *Rebellion on the Amazon: Popular Culture, Race, and the Cabanagem in the North of Brazil, 1798–1840* (Cambridge, 2010), which received the Honorable Mention for the Warren Dean Prize, 2011. He has edited *Ways of Knowing: New Approaches in the Anthropology of Experience and Learning* (Berghahn, 2007) and *The Child in the City* (with Anna Grimhaw, Prickly Pear Pamphlets, 2000). He was awarded a British Academy Postdoctoral Fellowship in 1996 and the Philip Leverhulme Prize in 2004. He is currently writing a history of the politics of religious experience in the Brazilian Amazon from prehistory to the present.

THOMAS G. KIRSCH (PhD, European University Viadrina, Frankfurt [Oder], 2002) is professor of social and cultural anthropology at the University of Konstanz. He taught at the Department of Anthropology in Halle and then at the Department of Anthropology at Goldsmiths College, University of London, before coming to Konstanz in 2009. Between 1993 and 2001, he conducted fieldwork in Zambia. He is the author of *Lieder der Macht: Religiöse Autorität und Performance in einer afrikanisch-christlichen Kirche Zambias* (1998) and *Spirits and Letters: Reading, Writing and Charisma in African Christianity* (2008), and coeditor of *Permutations of Order: Religion and Law as Contested Sovereignties* (2009) and *Domesticating Vigilantism in Africa* (2010). He has published articles in some of the major refereed journals for anthropology and sociology in Germany. Other articles were published in the journals *American Anthropologist* (2004), *Visual Anthropology* (2006), and *American Ethnologist* (2007). Since 2003, he has also conducted ethnographic fieldwork on issues of human safety, security, and crime prevention in South Africa.

STEPHAN PALMIÉ (PhD, University of Munich, 1989; habilitation, University of Munich, 1999) is professor of anthropology at the University of Chicago. His research centers on Afro-Cuban religious formations and their relations to a wider Atlantic world, conceptions of embodiment and moral personhood, practices of historical representation and knowledge production, biotechnology, and constructions of race. He is the author of *Das Exil der Götter: Geschichte und Vorstellungswelt einer afrokubanischen Religion* (1991), *Wizards and Scientists: Explorations in Afro-Cuban Modernity and Tradition* (2002), and *The Cooking of History: How Not to Study Afro-Cuban Religion* (2013), and editor of *Slave Cultures and the Cultures of Slavery* (1995) and *Africas of the Americas: Beyond the Search for Origins in the Study of Afro-Atlantic Religions* (2008). He is coeditor of *Empirical Futures: Anthropologists and Historians Engage the Work of Sidney W. Mintz* (2009) and *The Caribbean: A History of the Region and Its People* (2011), as well as a five-volume critical edition of C. G. A. Oldendorp's late eighteenth-century manuscript on the history of the mission of the Moravian Brethren in the Danish Virgin Islands (2000–2010).

FLORENCIA C. TOLA (PhD, École des Hautes Études en Sciences Sociales de Paris, 2004) is researcher at the National Council of Scientific and Technologic Research of Argentina (CONICET), professor of anthropology at the University of Buenos Aires, and associated member at the Centre Enseignement et Recherche en Ethnologie Amérindienne du Laboratoire d'Ethnologie et de Sociologie Comparative (University of Paris West Nanterre La Défense and Centre National de la Recherche Scientifique). Her research centers on indigenous people of the Gran Chaco, especially on Toba (Qom) notions of personhood, conceptions of body, and kinship. She is the author of *Les conceptions du corps et de la personne dans un contexte amerindien* (2009), *Reflexiones dislocadas: Pensamientos politicos y filosóficos qom* (2011), written in collaboration with Toba philosopher Timoteo Francia, and *Yo no estoy solo en mi cuerpo: Cuerpos-personas múltiples entre los qom del Chaco argentino* (2012), and coeditor of *Léxico, clasificación nominal y categorización etnobiológica en el Gran Chaco* (2010) and *Naturaleza, Poder y Emociones en el Gran Chaco* (in press).

KRISTINA WIRTZ (PhD, University of Pennsylvania, 2003), a linguistic and cultural anthropologist, is associate professor of anthropology at Western Michigan University. Her ethnographic research on folk religion, ritual and folklore performance, racialization, and the meaning of "blackness" in Cuba has been published in journals such as *American Ethnologist, Journal of the Royal Anthropological Institute, Journal of Linguistic Anthropology, Text and Talk*, and *Religion in Africa*; in the monograph *Ritual, Discourse, and Community in Cuban Santería* (2007); and in a forthcoming monograph entitled *Performing Afro-Cuba*.

Index